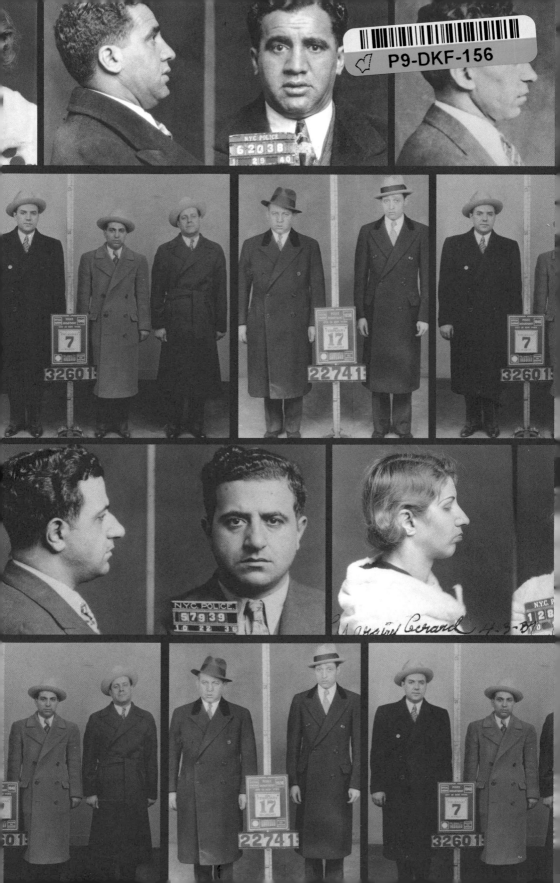

A BROTHERHOOD
BETRAYED

ALSO BY MICHAEL CANNELL

*Incendiary: The Psychiatrist, the Mad Bomber,
and the Invention of Criminal Profiling*

The Limit: Life and Death on the 1961 Grand Prix Circuit

I. M. Pei: Mandarin of Modernism

A BROTHERHOOD
BETRAYED

THE MAN BEHIND
THE RISE AND FALL OF MURDER, INC.

MICHAEL CANNELL

MINOTAUR BOOKS
NEW YORK

First published in the United States by Minotaur Books, an imprint of St. Martin's Publishing Group

A BROTHERHOOD BETRAYED. Copyright © 2020 by Michael Cannell. All rights reserved. Printed in the United States of America. For information, address St. Martin's Publishing Group, 120 Broadway, New York, NY 10271.

www.minotaurbooks.com

Designed by Devan Norman

Library of Congress Cataloging-in-Publication Data

Names: Cannell, Michael, author.
Title: A brotherhood betrayed : the man behind the rise and
    fall of Murder, Inc. / Michael Cannell.
Description: First edition. | New York : Minotaur Books, [2020] |
    Includes bibliographical references and index. |
Identifiers: LCCN 2020017246 | ISBN 9781250204387
    (hardcover) | ISBN 9781250204400 (ebook)
Subjects: LCSH: Reles, Abe, 1906–1941. | Mafiosi—New York
    (State)—New York—Biography. | Assassins—New York (State)—
    New York—Biography. | Mafia—New York (State)—New York—
    History—20th century. | Organized crime—New York
    (State)—New York—History—20th century. | Murder—New York
    (State)—New York—History—20th century.
Classification: LCC HV6452.N72 M34225 2020 | DDC 364.1092
    [B]—dc23
LC record available at https://lccn.loc.gov/2020017246

Our books may be purchased in bulk for promotional, educational, or business use. Please contact your local bookseller or the Macmillan Corporate and Premium Sales Department at 1-800-221-7945, extension 5442, or by email at MacmillanSpecialMarkets@macmillan.com.

First Edition: 2020

10 9 8 7 6 5 4 3 2 1

For Cricket and Evie

CONTENTS

Betrayal is the only truth that sticks.

—ARTHUR MILLER

The squealer must die.

—ABE RELES

PROLOGUE: "SOMETHING HAS HAPPENED"

November 12, 1941

The sun rose at 6:39 a.m. that morning over a sea the color of dishwater. The first light of a cold fall day shone on the Coney Island pier, stilted above a scouring shore break. It shone on the rickety wood latticework upholding the Cyclone roller coaster and on the round immensity of the Wonder Wheel with its crisscrossed spokes. Seagulls barked. A few fishermen casting for bluefish may have left a trail of footprints on the beach, but Coney Island was otherwise a ghost-town version of its summer self. A stiffening onshore wind kicked up whitecaps and whistled among shuttered penny arcades and souvenir shops. In mid-November, gaiety was on off-season hiatus.

Two full years had passed since the Nazis blitzed Poland. Afterward the poet W. H. Auden sat in a Fifty-second Street dive bar, in Manhattan, and wrote these lines:

Waves of anger and fear
Circulate over the bright
And darkened lands of the earth

Anger and fear were in full supply in the fall of 1941. America was not yet mobilized for war, but the nation braced for the inevitable. Banner newspaper headlines reported torpedoed British destroyers sinking

into the cold North Atlantic and Wehrmacht tanks rolling to the out-
skirts of Moscow. President Franklin Roosevelt had initiated the first
peacetime draft in order to begin military training. The preparation
for war reached even here, on this bleak barrier beach where New York
City faced the Atlantic Ocean.

At 7:15 a.m. William Nicholson, chief clerk of the Coney Island
draft board, entered his office in room 123 of the Half Moon Hotel,
a sixteen-story buff-brick building fronting the boardwalk ten blocks
west of the arcades and amusement rides. Military doctors had recently
screened a batch of draftees for gonorrhea and nearsightedness. The
recruits had pressed their inked thumbs to paper and affirmed their attraction to girls. Nicholson arrived shortly after dawn that Wednesday
morning to see the men off to boot camp. They would muster at 8 a.m.
or so beneath murals of Spanish ports in the hotel's Galleon Grill, then
leave for Grand Central Terminal.

Nicholson's window overlooked the gravel roof of the hotel kitchen
annex. After settling down at his desk he noticed an unmoving figure
lying on the gravel. He called the hotel operator and asked her to con-
nect him to the eleventh-floor office of Alexander Lysberg, the night
hotel manager. "Something has happened," Nicholson told him.

"What is it?" Lysberg said.

"I can't tell you over the phone," Nicholson said.

Lysberg rode an elevator downstairs. When he entered the draft-
board office Nicholson gestured to the window. Sprawled like a rag
doll on the kitchen roof lay the body of a hairy, thickset man. His
rubbery lips were agape, revealing a lolling bovine tongue. His beefy
left cheek was imprinted with roof deck gravel. The impact of the fall
from his sixth-floor room, number 632, had split the crotch of his dark
suit pants. His white button-down shirt lay open to the waist. His eyes
stared unblinking into a clouded Brooklyn sky. Two knotted strips of
white bed sheet fluttered at his side.

Even from a distance the two men recognized the body. Thirty-five-
year-old Abe Reles, kinky-haired and jut-jawed, had served for a decade
as the assassin-in-chief for an underworld death squad loosely known
as Murder, Inc. When the principals of a coast-to-coast organized
crime network identified an informant in their ranks, or a foot soldier
who breached their loyalty code, they passed a murder contract down
to Reles, who either took up his weapon—gun, garrote, ice pick—or,

more often, delegated the job to lieutenants. A veteran detective called them "probably the worst ring of killers in American history." Their victims died horrible deaths, gangster deaths. They dumped bodies like garbage in shallow lime pits or left them doubled-up and decomposed in the trunks of cars abandoned on lonely streets.

Dead men could not testify: such was Reles's lurid strategy. The tactic worked for a decade. Then, in February 1940, Reles abruptly turned against his lifelong friends and closest compatriots in crime. He abandoned his career as an underworld assassin to become an informant—the most talkative and damning in mob history. In a series of marathon meetings conducted over coffee and sandwiches in the district attorney's offices on the fourth floor of the Brooklyn Municipal Building, he disclosed to prosecutors the vast and intricate workings—the grudges and revenge, alliances and betrayals—of an elaborate criminal underground, a country-within-the-country, that law enforcement had previously only glimpsed in isolated pieces. Reles revealed another America hidden in shadow with its own banks and penal system, its own tax code and law enforcement.

The history of organized crime had been written over the decades in increments based on court appearances and police logs. Now, for the first time, heroes and villains, potentates and snitches, were revealed in a single dark opera told with flourish by a key player.

Speaking like a streetwise stand-up comic, Reles confessed to eleven murders. He resolved several dozen more, including deaths unknown to the police. He brought all the dirty work out into the light with the relish of a natural storyteller. He recalled with cinematic detail victims hatcheted, cudgeled, set on fire, trussed and dumped in peaceful upstate lakes, macerated by bullets, and, in at least one case, buried alive. His accounts were almost too gruesome to be real.

Reles made vivid for prosecutors the whole sweeping epic of life and death in the mob, mostly in Brooklyn, but as far afield as Miami and Los Angeles. After two decades of dodging and defying the law, he lifted the lid for the first time on an entire underworld, with all its thuggery and casual cruelty.

Reles was the keystone, the Jenga piece, in a government push to end once and for all the mob's long-reaching free hand in murder, racketeering, extortion, loan-sharking, drug smuggling, prostitution, and gambling. District attorneys waged their campaign to restore law and order, but also to advance themselves professionally. Whoever busted the mob would earn a path to higher office. The mobster's loss was the prosecutor's gain.

In the months before he tumbled from that hotel window, Reles helped send four to the electric chair, including his two best friends. Now, in November 1941, the proceedings were poised to enter a weightier phase as prosecutors prepared to try the mob lords, men who would qualify for the Mount Rushmore of crime.

As the authorities battled to bring down the big bosses, the danger to Reles and other informants correspondingly intensified. It was known that the defendants or their allies still at large would try to arrange for Reles to die before he testified against them, before he could send them to the Sing Sing death house. Newspaper readers held their collective breath, waiting to see if layers of police protection could hold against the gathering forces of underworld revenge. Reles himself had told prosecutors that mob law decreed that "the squealer must die."

The Brooklyn district attorney rented a ten-room wing of the Half Moon Hotel, known as the Rat Suite, where he sequestered and safeguarded Reles and five other mobsters-turned-informants behind a steel door manned by a twenty-four-hour police guard. Lawyers in the D.A.'s office called them informants; their old street corner friends called them stool pigeons, canaries, and snitches.

Reles fell to his death hours before testifying in his biggest role, as the marquee witness in the trial of mob overlord Louis "Lepke" Buchalter. The police took up a saying: the canary sang, but could not fly. Like many expressions coined on New York streets, it was part wisecrack, part truth.

Police concluded that Reles died while escaping their custody, and newspapers initially reported it as such, but the ink had barely dried on afternoon papers before speculation began that Reles may not have gone out the window voluntarily. Did he fall, or was he pushed? And who might have pushed him? As the months passed, clues implicating both police and city officials accrued. As the question heated up, the mayor himself came under suspicion.

The riddle of who might have murdered Abe Reles, and on whose order, remains one of the great unanswered questions in the history of organized crime. The puzzle would lie at the heart of grand juries and a Senate inquiry, to no conclusive end. It would reverberate through police stations, party clubhouses, a mayoral mansion, all the way to the doors of the White House.

A prosecutor later wrote that when Reles went out the window he "left behind so peculiar, astonishing, remarkable, weird and mystifying a set of circumstances, that they haven't been unraveled yet—and they probably never will be."

PART ONE

THE RISE

1

SCHLAMMERS

Abe Reles had nothing to do but skulk on the corner with other fifteen-year-old dropouts. In Brooklyn of the 1920s, the street corner was a tutorial, a tribal gathering, a stage for posturing, a bully pulpit, a marketplace, and a Darwinian proving ground. Boys cadged cigarettes, ate knishes smeared with spicy mustard, drank egg creams, and rolled dice for nickel bets. They filched apples from pushcart vendors, threw rocks at laundry wagons pulled by swaybacked horses, and traded punches with boys from neighboring corners. The street rang with Yiddish insults. *Pisher! Schlemiel! Momzer! Chozzer!*

Even at age fifteen, Reles ruled his own street corner like an underage general. He stood only five foot two, but he had thickset-man strength, with Popeye arms that dangled unnaturally almost to his knees and fists that a prosecutor later called "a set of hammers." He stared down all comers with the fat face of a Pixar villain. His rubbery lips rested in a sneer. He spoke with a baritone rasp, already roughened by daily packs of Lucky Strikes, and deformed by a lisp.

Add to his unhandsome appearance the grating "dese" and "dems" of a Brooklyn patois so thick and constant that he sounded like a parody of the New York street punk. "He spoke," *The Brooklyn Daily Eagle* wrote years later, "with an impediment suggesting a mouthful of marbles."

However witless he might seem, Reles had a gift for mean manipulation and bully tactics. He had an eye for weakness and the muscle to exploit it. The term "street smart" might have been coined with him in mind. He scared even his friends.

As a teen Reles could already see criminal possibilities beyond the street corner. He gravitated to a *pasticceria* in the East New York neighborhood where grizzled Italian men with bad teeth, Brooklyn padrones, read neatly folded racing forms and the Italian-language newspaper *Il Progresso* with solemn concentration. They drank cup after cup of tar-thick espresso and fattened up on *riccios,* buttery Italian croissants.

The proprietor, Louis Capone (no relation to Al Capone), was a well-groomed Neapolitan with a gentle manner and watery blue eyes. His broken nose lent his swarthy face a cockeyed aspect as he hovered about the café tables, formally shaking hands and patting forearms. He spoke of the old country and neighborhood gossip.

The padrones understood that Capone's real job was racketeering: The pasticceria was only a front and recruiting tool. He lured useful young toughs like Reles with free coffee and pastries. He engaged them with his avuncular singsong accent and riccios warm from the oven, then asked if they wanted to earn pocket money running a few hoodlum errands in their spare time. He could offer them more work, he said, if things went well.

Things did go well for Reles—so well that he became Capone's full-time enforcer, bagman, and lookout. He spent his days shaking down whorehouses and collecting extortion payments from defenseless bakers and grocers. Reles was Brooklyn's toughest teenage runt, an undersized street punk with a hair-trigger temper. He stopped to commiserate with butchers and tobacconists after a brick thrown from the street shattered their shop window, and a second brick broke it again after a pricey repair. How unfortunate, Reles said, that a good-for-nothing kid was breaking their window and they could do nothing about it. What you need, he suggested, is a watchman to protect your shop. Reles could arrange it for thirty dollars up front and five dollars a week thereafter.

If they failed to pay promptly Reles barged in, all bulging arms and menace. He ripped goods from shelves and threw his oversized fists. He put his face close and, through sprays of spittle, issued threats in his odd baritone lisp. *I give you a nice deal and this is how you repay me, you schmuck? If you want to be my fucking friend, you'll have the fucking money ready next time.* He might throw them to the floor and press his foot to their neck. His anger was real and dialed to a piercing pitch.

Reles commanded his own small gang made up of his childhood friends: Harry Strauss, a linebacker-sized heavy who took sadistic joy in violence, and Martin Goldstein, a mean little wiseass with wide-set frog eyes and an oily, sneering presence. Together they were *schlammers,* the Yiddish term for intimidator.

As the schlammers made their rounds, Reles sometimes encountered his father, Sam, a stooped figure in a shapeless old hat, kibitzing in Yiddish with customers as he sold pants and shirts from a wooden pushcart parked among the fruit and pickle vendors on Pitkin Avenue, Brownsville's commercial thoroughfare. Sam and his wife, Rose, had arrived in 1900 from the Jewish slums of Galicia, an Austro-Hungarian province. They settled in the Brooklyn neighborhood of Brownsville instead of the noisome Jewish ghetto of Manhattan's Lower East Side because it was roomier, cheaper, and newly linked to the city by elevated subway and, in 1903, the opening of the Williamsburg Bridge.

Brownsville was grimy beyond today's imagining. It was a district of tenements and factories rising from the swampy flats of northeast Brooklyn, an outpost where newcomers could, with luck, hustle up a living doing manual labor and usher their children along the paths of advancement.

For Jewish immigrants like Sam and Rose, survival was success. They undertook a wrenching break from everything and everyone they knew in their shtetl to embark on a monthlong ocean passage in steerage while subsisting on herring and potatoes. Landing in Brownsville was triumph enough. Brooklyn was their Plymouth Rock, a hopeful new start.

Reles saw no heroics in his parents' plight. He was unmindful of the ways in which they valiantly assumed hardship so that he and his brother, Max, and sisters, Bessie and Esther, could grow up American. He found the crude comforts of the tenement life pitifully inadequate and a source of shame. He looked down on his father, Sam, with his foreign manners and low station edging on penury. He pitied his weary mother, constantly washing clothes and cooking kreplach and krupnik soup, herring and blintzes over the sad little potbelly coal stove in their flat. Their Old World ways were alien to him, and embarrassing. He was tired of kugel. He wanted steak.

Reles grew up in a neighborhood that was, if anything, tougher than the Lower East Side. "More guys carried guns," wrote Sammy Aaronson, who operated a gym where amateur boxers pounded punching bags, "and instead of six beatings a day there were six an hour." It was probably the toughest neighborhood in America, maybe the toughest ever.

Reles was shrewd enough to observe that the wealthiest, most powerful men in Brooklyn were the racketeers Louis Capone reported to— big shots with fist-thick rolls of cash and long-hooded cars. Their money and political weight was a source of wonder to street-corner kids. Reles could see that the men moved in a secret world, a brotherhood ruled by its own code of honor.

The racketeers set an example for boys like Abe Reles: Americans need not labor for their luxuries, as his foolish father did. They simply grabbed their wealth. If Reles had to seize the golden calf with a Smith & Wesson shoved in his overcoat pocket, then so be it.

Prohibition uplifted gangsters like Meyer Lansky, Legs Diamond, and Lucky Luciano, and glamorized them. Before the Volstead Act shut the taps in 1920, small-time neighborhood crooks held up passersby and burgled homes. Prohibition was their deus ex machina, a gift bestowed from gangster heaven. Almost overnight local thugs were collaborating with larger networks to supply New York's five thousand speakeasies. They smuggled cases of Scotch whiskey on freighters and rented speedboats and caravans of midnight trucks. The hootch earned them undreamed of profits. The money piles grew higher and higher. So much money flowed into their wallets that they could easily pay police and politicians look-the-other-way money on a massive scale.

Men who had scrabbled for a lowly mugger's stipend now swaggered about town in the new gangster uniform of cashmere Chesterfield coats with velvet collars, magnificently tailored pinstripe suits, silk shirts, and zooty snap-brimmed fedoras. They smelled of cigars and hair oil. They drank champagne and highballs with blinged-out chorus girls at the Hotsy Totsy Club on Broadway and jigged to Louis Armstrong uptown at the Cotton Club, where flappers, some still in their teens, shimmied on tables in perilously short dresses. They handed out prizefight tickets to police and politicians and flew to Miami to bet on Thoroughbreds. People around them laughed louder than normal, in the ingratiating way of flunkies and flatterers. Lucky Luciano would hand girls a hundred dollars just for smiling at him.

Prohibition enriched gangsters, but it also popularized them. Instead of preying on their neighbors, they now fulfilled a public need. Men were intent on drinking away memories of the Great War and flappers sought illicit pleasures. Americans spent as much on illegal booze as on meat. "The gangster discovered, overnight, that he was no longer a tolerated neighborhood thug, but a big business man," wrote Hickman Powell, a reporter for the *New York Post*. "No longer despised by all except his own kind, he found himself regarded as a public benefactor."

Reles viewed the top mobsters as a junior associate regards the company president stepping from a private jet: with envy and aspiration. In imitation, Reles and his sidekicks wore the gangster uniform of double-breasted suits with ample lapels, silk ties, and rakish fedoras. They drove Ford speedsters and Nash coupes with sculptural hood ornaments and leather upholstery as plush as a nightclub banquette, most of them stolen. They also adopted the gangster manner of speaking in quick, clipped slangy phrases delivered out the side of their mouths, an affectation later mimicked by the actor James Cagney. They spoke in coldly casual terms of sugar (money), packages (dead bodies), ice (bribes), and the hot squat (electric chair). They might have only fifty dollars or so, but they kept the bills in small denominations to make an impression when they pulled the wad from their pockets.

Every rightful gangster assumed a street name as part of their induction into a brotherhood. The roll call included Cockeyed Louie, Dopy Danny, Little Lefty, Charlie Spinach, and Benny Eggs. In keeping with tradition, Reles's friend Harry Strauss became Pittsburgh Phil, even though he had never been to Pittsburgh. Martin Goldstein went by Buggsy. Reles took his nickname from Max "Kid Twist" Zweiback, one of the first prominent Jewish gangsters, who was gunned down in a fight over a music-hall singer outside a Coney Island saloon by a jealous rival named Louie "The Lump" Pioggi. From now on Reles was Kid Twist, Brooklyn's toughest teenage thug, punching his way up the hoodlum ranks.

In addition to the strong-arm duties Reles discharged for Louis Capone, he and his sidekicks, Pittsburgh Phil Strauss and Buggsy Goldstein, now shouldered assignments from the Shapiros, three brothers asserting control of the Brownsville rackets and a dozen whorehouses. They also ran floating poker games throughout the borough, including a women-only game in Coney Island, known as Caravan, which played until dawn in a series of apartments rented for thirty dollars a night. These were not lightweight contests. Losses drove two women to suicide. Many more collapsed into the predatory arms of loan sharks, also controlled by the Shapiros. If women defaulted they paid off debt by working in a Shapiro brothel, without telling their husbands.

The Shapiros were a few years older than Reles, and better off. Their immigrant parents, Joseph and Anna, named their sons Irving, Meyer, and William, solid American names, and accompanied them weekly to the Synagogue of the Glory of Israel. Joseph and Anna expected that their sons would attend school, learn a trade, become professionals, and lead respectable lives.

The Shapiros were good boys, solid and respectful, at least their parents thought so until they began gambling and fighting in the concrete yard outside Public School 84, an unpopular penitentiary-like high school. When their teenage sons failed to come home at night, the parents embarked on night tours of the Brownsville speakeasies and pool halls, squinting through cumulus clouds of cigarette smoke in search of their errant sons. They returned home crestfallen after midnight, Anna crying. They had lost their sons to another world, a dark side of America they didn't grasp. No dinnertime admonishments could restore their sons.

Meyer, the handsome, tousle-haired middle son, ran the Shapiro rackets. He was Brooklyn's smoothest, smuggest junior mob boss, and seemingly invulnerable. He had carried a gun even as a teenager hawking newspapers on a street corner. By his early twenties he had survived four shootings. Scars from fourteen stabbings cross-hatched his husky body. As result, he was said to have a deathly fear of knives. He had been arrested dozens of times and was implicated in the kidnapping and rape of a fourteen-year-old girl named Catherine Sherman. According to Catherine's mother, Meyer offered to buy the girl a new roadster if she agreed to "forget it."

Meyer worked all the rackets. He operated a dozen brothels staffed with girls as young as fifteen gathered from farms and factories, collected tribute from every floating craps game in Brownsville, and rented Reles and his schlammers out as fists-for-hire in labor disputes. He also lent money on a six-for-five basis, meaning the borrower paid a weekly premium of one dollar for every five dollars lent, or slightly more than 1,000 percent annually.

The largest income of all came from the cast-iron slot machines installed in every pharmacy, pool hall, and candy store. They were illegal, but ubiquitous. Customers slipped a nickel into a slot and, by pulling a lever hinged to the machine's right side, spun three dials displayed under a glass panel. The dials spun and spun until they came up watermelon, orange, lemon. Or cherry, plum, apple—or some other mismatch. On those rare cases, roughly one in four hundred spins, when the three reels settled on the same fruit, a satisfying gush of nickels showered forth.

The slots seemed an innocuous diversion, wholesome even, but the daily yield of nickels buttered the mob's bread. Each machine made fifty dollars a week or more. Mobsters who placed two hundred in their territory, as the Shapiros did, made $5,000 a week.

Meyer's older brother, Irving, was a failed prizefighter, an under-card flailer and flop who acted as a glorified bodyguard, protecting his younger brother from the beatings and bullets of rival gangs. Irving was known as "the Little Shot." The *Daily News* called him "punch-drunk Irving Shapiro, former palooka of the prize ring." The young-est brother, Willie, was a hanger-on, another failed prizefighter, who lacked toughness and smarts.

Meyer knew enough to pay tribute to the big bosses upstream of them, but he ran his own operation with punishing precision. "I'm the boss of Brownsville," Meyer confidently told those around him.

The patrolmen of Brownsville's 73rd Precinct walked past cloth-ing stores on Livonia Avenue where Manhattan women came for bar-gains, past ragged urchins playing stoopball, past butcher shops with the kosher symbol displayed in their windows, past haughty whores in slippers and flowery kimonos shouting with laughter and gesturing at passing men, past fat housewives with canvas bags of fruit and meat haggling with bearded pushcart vendors, past wagons pulled by weary fly-bitten horses, past howling beggars. The streets smelled of garlic, burnt kerosene, horse dung, and sweat.

The patrolmen greeted Reles by name when they saw him on their rounds. They hauled him in cussing, over and over, for assault, rob-bery, and disorderly conduct, with handcuffs clamped over his thick, hairy wrists. They locked him up in a holding cell in the back of the precinct house to await his court appearance. Sometimes they arrested him on bogus vagrancy charges just to get him off the streets. No hint of remorse showed on Reles's face. Only defiance. He made a show of yawning, as if the pointless legal proceedings bored him.

Reliably, after every arrest, a heavyset woman named Lena Frosch wearily trudged up the courthouse steps. She looked like Gertrude Stein's Brooklyn sister, a heavy woman with a heroic bosom and round metal-framed glasses set across her wide beefy face. She parted her dark hair on the side, as a man would.

She was known for her uniformly black wardrobe, accessorized with shawl and handbag, and for her ability to nod off in straight-backed courthouse chairs. She found an empty seat by a clerk's desk and dozed until bailiffs led Reles in to plead before a judge.

Mrs. Frosch was a bail-bond agent. The Shapiros hired her to pay Reles's bail and handle the associated paperwork. She ran the business with her wispy, silent husband, Israel, and their son, Abraham, a failed pharmacist who mostly mooched cigarettes from court clerks.

As much as anything, Mrs. Frosch was an adroit fixer. After bailing Reles out she bribed or threatened witnesses to prevent them from testifying against him. At least once she moved a witness out of state and therefore outside the court's jurisdiction. She handled Reles as she would a child, advising him on the chances of conviction or a suspended sentence. When a follow-up court date came up, she made sure he appeared.

Mrs. Frosch did her job so well that Reles began to act as if he were untouchable. "Some detective will put a bullet in you," a frustrated judge told Reles as yet another charge unraveled.

"All cops are yellow," Reles answered, "and I'll fight any single one with guns, knives, or broken glass." He walked from the courthouse laughing.

Reles was a savage man leading a charmed life, but the charm would not last forever. Reles did the Shapiros' dirty work for them, collecting payments and schlamming defiant merchants, but the handsome, well-dressed Meyer expressed only contempt for the short, ungainly Reles with his rubbery lips and lopsided mop of Brillo hair. He treated Reles as another expendable thug.

After a felony assault charge in 1925, Officer Ruditsky of the 44th Precinct thrust Reles into the holding cell in back of a station house, with its sagging wood floors and ancient woodwork varnished a hundred times over.

As usual, a guard led him handcuffed into the courtroom. It was a familiar routine, except this time the reassuring figure of Mrs. Frosch, with her handbag and shawl, wasn't there to arrange a lawyer, lean on witnesses, and bail him out. The Shapiros had failed to send her, either by mistake or by design.

As a result, the judge sent Reles, now nineteen, to Elmira Reformatory, an upstate juvenile penitentiary devoted to the improving powers of discipline and regimentation. No more pool hall nights, no more stolen cars, no more whores borrowed from the Shapiros' brothels. Instead, Reles took an assigned inmate number, a khaki uniform, and a routine of toil in its workshops. For two years he slept in a cellblock alongside burglars, forgers, and car thieves, marched in military formation, and performed manual labor beneath the reformatory's Victorian turrets and towers—all the while contemplating his vengeance.

2

BABYLON BROOKLYN

At 10:45 p.m. on Sunday, November 4, 1928, Arnold Rothstein rose from his regular booth at Lindy's, a Times Square restaurant, where he was drinking after-dinner coffee with friends, and walked six blocks to the Park Central Hotel, on Seventh Avenue, to haggle over a gambling debt. He made his way past boxy streetcars and yellow taxis, neon signs, and the lightbulb-bright marquee for a new Oscar Hammerstein musical. He was a tall figure, silky smooth, with the cultivated pallor of a vampire. He gambled all night and slept all day.

Rothstein's friend Damon Runyon called him "The Brain." He was a gambling savant and underworld mastermind. With his uncanny facility for probabilities, he could see profit where others could not. He bankrolled casinos, racetracks, and an inventive series of swindles engineered by an up-and-coming generation of gangsters. He held life insurance policies on those he partnered with, so that his investment returned even if they did not. It was widely believed that he fixed the 1919 World Series, though he never faced charges. He conducted himself as an underworld aristocrat with fine manners and well-cut suits. According to mob lore, Rothstein served as the model for the corrupt gambler Meyer Wolfsheim in *The Great Gatsby* and Broadway craps-game king Nathan Detroit in *Guys and Dolls*.

In October, Rothstein had lost more than $322,000 during a three-day stud poker game held in the West Fifty-fourth Street apartment of Jimmy Meehan, an ex-convict and jewelry thief. He had suffered an uncharacteristic cold streak at the racetracks the preceding summer, and he left Meehan's table that night unwilling, or unable, to settle up. "I'm Rothstein," he told the seven card players facing him across the table. "That name ought to be good for the money."

Rothstein's name, formidable and feared, was indeed good for the money, but not forever. Two weeks later the creditors sent word that he had exhausted their patience. An intermediary phoned Abe Scher, the Lindy's cashier, and asked him to relay a message to Rothstein's regular booth: he was wanted immediately in room 349 at the Park Central. Rothstein told his friends to expect him back in half an hour. Before he left he placed a bet, his last, that Herbert Hoover would be elected president two days later.

He walked over to find four creditors drinking whiskey and water. At 11 p.m., after some preliminary talk, Rothstein suggested that he might not pay up after all, because his opponents had cheated. One of them—it's not clear who—shot Rothstein six times in the crotch with a .38-caliber pistol, a short-barreled variety known to gangsters as a "shake hands rod" because it can be palmed and fired while extending one's hand. Rothstein limped down two flights of stairs. He collapsed while trying to hobble out the hotel's Fifty-sixth Street service entrance to hail a cab. An elevator operator found him. "I was shot," Rothstein told him. "Get me an ambulance."

When detectives asked who shot him, Rothstein, prostrate and bleeding, only shook his head. "You stick to your trade," he said, "and I'll stick to mine." He died two days later, on Election Day, at Polyclinic Hospital, in Hell's Kitchen. Had Rothstein lived, he would have collected $500,000 on Hoover's victory.

Abe Reles followed the story of Rothstein's demise from Elmira Reformatory, where the gangster grapevine passed along news of the underworld. He took careful note when word came that Meyer Lansky, Bugsy Siegel, and other former Rothstein associates immediately took over his operations. The underworld hates a vacuum.

Rothstein's downfall held lessons pertinent to Reles's own future: A king who wavers can be deposed, should be deposed, and his riches divided. No man stands above gangland law, no ruler is sovereign.

If Rothstein could fall, so too could the smooth, arrogant Shapiro brothers with their shiny silk suits and luxe girlfriends. They had left their dirty work to him, then abandoned him to face a judge without a fixer. Maybe Meyer Shapiro was too careless and entitled to send Mrs. Frosch to bail Reles out. Or maybe Meyer sensed that the menacing and motivated Reles threatened his dominance of the Brownsville streets. Either way, Reles would not forgive them.

By the time he put on his civilian clothes and walked out of Elmira Reformatory for good on April Fool's Day, 1930, he was no longer content to be a lowly schlammer, a glorified gofer. He would be his own boss, and that meant stealing Meyer Shapiro's throne.

"You start stealing, and you see how it reaches around, and you try to advance yourself," he said of this shift in his life. "You see the next man in the rackets go higher and higher, and you want to go higher, too. Everybody wants to get ahead in the world. [But] if you want to get ahead, you've got to fight your way up. There's nobody to help you get ahead. Nobody approaches you and says, 'Come along with me.' No, you've got to be smart enough to dope the situation out for yourself. You have got to advance yourself, and how you make your bed, that's how you lay in it."

Regime change would require permission from Albert Anastasia, the mob's top man in Brooklyn and overlord of the borough's rough waterfront. To overthrow the Shapiros without his blessing invited execution.

Petitioning for a meeting with Anastasia was like requesting an audience with a prince. Reles waited weeks before Anastasia sent word through intermediaries that he would see Reles down by his home in the Erie Basin, a strip of land at the butt end of Red Hook, Brooklyn, built from discarded ballast and building parts dumped into the harborfront.

Reles must have known that Anastasia could tip off the Shapiros, in which case Reles would walk into an ambush. But no ambush closed on him as he made his way through Red Hook. Reles sat down across from Anastasia, a short, powerfully built man with a dark complexion and wavy black hair, heavy-lidded dark eyes and a round fleshy chin. He spoke sparingly in a hoarse, low-pitched Italian accent.

Albert was an assumed name. He was christened Umberto Anastasio in a tiny church in Tropea, a fishing village near the toe of the Italian boot. In 1919 he came to New York as a barefoot fifteen-year-old deckhand on the tramp steamer SS *Sardegna* and jumped ship to work on the docks of Italian south Brooklyn, where longshoremen swung crates of cargo from open holds in net slings and loaded them on waiting trucks. Three of his brothers joined him on the docks; the fourth became a parish priest in Brooklyn.

The docks boomed with business in those years after World War I. Anastasia insinuated his way into the leadership of the powerful longshoremen's union, which pocketed part of every paycheck and demanded tribute for the right to work. Every dockworker came to fear Anastasia. He was illiterate and barely spoke English, but his dark eyes smoldered with threat.

At least one man was not intimidated. A dockworker named George Turello got tired of kicking a portion of his daily wages back to Anastasia. He told Anastasia that he was done paying the mafia tax, and he threatened to organize a rival union that operated on honest terms. On the night of March 7, 1921, Turello was found lying in a Union Street gutter with a bullet hole just behind his ear. Prosecutors found enough witnesses to convict Anastasia. For eighteen months he sat on death row, but he never made the final walk to the death chamber. His lawyer won a retrial on a technicality. By the time the new trial convened, four prosecution witnesses had mysteriously died. The others abruptly changed their minds: maybe they hadn't seen Anastasia that night after all. The court dismissed his case.

In the course of the legal proceedings a court clerk mistakenly changed the *o* in Anastasio to an *a*. He permanently adopted his altered last name, along with a new first name, Albert, in order to spare his family shame.

The man who cheated the death house returned to the Brooklyn docks with a new name and an aura of invincibility. He came back from Sing Sing to reclaim control of a dark, marginal precinct where men settled scores with bailing hooks and iron bars. "America . . . ended at Columbia Street," wrote the playwright Arthur Miller, who worked at the Brooklyn Navy Yard for two years. The *New York Sun* reporter Malcolm Johnson, whose articles gave rise to the movie *On the Waterfront,* called the docks "an outlaw frontier."

Anastasia ruled that frontier with total authority. Nothing was transacted without dollars going up the chain to him. No ship was loaded without a payoff. No truck rolled before its owner paid tribute. No longshoremen worked without kicking back part of their pay. When the dice rolled in waterfront taverns and when whores led johns upstairs, Anastasia claimed his cut. "Albert is the head guy on the docks,"

Reles said. "He is the law." Those who broke Anastasia's law faced harsh consequences. "With him it was always kill, kill, kill," a mob informant later testified. In the waterfront precincts Anastasia was known as the Lord High Executioner. Everyone respected him, but nobody liked him. "Anastasia's middle name was death," the *New York Post* once wrote. "He walked with death, he traded in death, he seemed to have a pact with death. He lived in the shadow of the electric chair, but he was never disturbed by it."

Anastasia had viewed the Shapiros with distrust even before Reles came calling. The brothers were reckless and arrogant and guilty of trespassing on other gangsters' rackets. The Shapiros had broken the rules, and the Lord High Executioner would not tolerate transgressions. When Reles asked permission to overthrow the Shapiros, Anastasia consented. Murder was a solution Anastasia had lived by for more than a decade, and he endorsed it now. Yes, Anastasia said, he would back Reles as the new chief of Brownsville, as long as he received part of the profits.

In the months when Reles languished in Elmira Reformatory, his friend Buggsy Goldstein opened a pool hall beneath the elevated subway. It was a dark, dilapidated den, half-shadowed even at midday by overhead subway girders. For Reles, it was a meeting place and refuge, a long room full of men's voices and the click of pool balls and the smell of chalk.

Reles spent an entire afternoon in Buggsy's pool hall trying to hustle a stranger named George DeFeo. Reles lost a hundred dollars that day, but gained a crucial contact. Before the last ball sank Reles had learned that DeFeo's older brother, William, worked with Meyer Lansky and Bugsy Siegel, two of the biggest Jewish gangsters. Through the DeFeo brothers Reles arranged for Lansky and Siegel to supply him with illegal slot machines in return for a percentage of the profits.

Reles had relied until now on his friends Buggsy Goldstein and Pittsburgh Phil Strauss, but he would need to recruit more muscle to take on the Shapiros. In the spring of 1939, he drove out to Sally's Bar and Grill in Ocean Hill, an Italian neighborhood just north of Brownsville, to meet with a gang he had occasionally tangled with led by Harry "Happy" Maione and his deputy, Frank "Dasher" Abbandando.

His overture to the Italians broke with custom. Gangsters of all ethnicities had by rule of habit stayed within their own parochial fence lines. Reles was cunning enough to see that new working friendships outside his tribal stronghold could lead to greater criminal possibilities. He was at the forefront of a new underworld movement to subordinate ethnic differences for the sake of power and profit, but would it work?

Maione was a short, sadistic twenty-two-year-old who lived with his mother in a twenty-seven-dollar-a-month apartment. He made a runtish impression, with little black marble eyes set in a moon face and skin so sallow it looked almost blue. He began pimping for a runaway girl at age sixteen and diversified into a dark portfolio of rackets. When a policeman nabbed him for assault and robbery, he tried to deck the patrolmen and steal his gun. The patrolmen laid him out on the pavement with a single blow. That was just the start: he would earn thirty-five arrests by age thirty-one. Friends called him Happy as a joke: he perpetually scowled. Abbandando, his lieutenant, was a strapping oaf with Vitalis-slicked hair nicknamed Dasher because he burned up the basepaths of Elmira Reformitory's baseball diamond. Maione was all menace, Abbandando all muscle.

Abbandando's mother said of him: "All the time he talk about money. He says everybody make money, so he make money too. But he never make money, he only get into trouble—much trouble. I take him to the priest in the Church of Our Lady of Loretta. I make him confess. It does no good. That Maione boy, he is a bad boy, but my son think he is great man. . . . I try to make him go to school, but Frank say what he need school for, schools don't teach how to make money. [Happy Maione], he teach to make money."

Maione insisted on meeting Reles at Sally's Bar, his home turf. Both sides came armed in case talks led to offense. Reles made his pitch over beer and sandwiches: join us and we'll split the profits fifty-fifty after we kill the Shapiros. It was likely a more generous division of profits than Maione expected. They shook hands all around. Thus was born one of the first Jewish-Italian collaborations in the underworld. Reles dubbed it the Combination.

Over the following week Reles, backed by Goldstein, Strauss, Defeo, and their new Italian partners, marched into a series of restaurants and speakeasies, candy stores and pharmacies, to replace the Shapiro slot machines with their own. The proprietors naturally complied. To object was to invite a smack in the face or lurid threats directed at a wife or daughter.

The Shapiros considered the Brownsville slots their exclusive domain. By replacing them Reles committed not just a provocation but a war declaration. His rebellion would last more than a year. Everyone in Brownsville knew how it would end: either Abe Reles or Meyer Shapiro would die on the street. The other would command the neighborhood.

Reles's defection left the Shapiros shorthanded. They made up the muscle by hiring Joey Silver, a boxer who spent days and nights working out with Willie Beecher, a retired flyweight who ran a gym behind a second-floor pool hall. Bettors called Silver "the six-minute wonder" because he wilted after two rounds.

The Shapiros were unaware that Silver was a mole: Reles bribed him to tell where to ambush the Shapiros and when. Wherever the Shapiros went, Reles and his men seemed to anticipate. They moved among apartments. They altered daily routines. No matter what, Reles was there.

The coup began on June 4, 1930. At 2:30 that morning Meyer Shapiro and two of his schlammers were standing outside the all-night Globe Cafeteria, a block from Goldstein's pool hall. Two cars slowed to deliver a fusillade. Bullets whistled over their heads, bullets whizzed around them. A twenty-seven-year-old bystander, a taxi driver, was grazed on the right side of his head while entering the cafeteria. A Shapiro underling crumpled to the pavement with a shattered right ankle, then crawled into the cafeteria for shelter. Meyer went down with a hit to the right side of his stomach. The bullet struck him on a scar from a gunshot wound inflicted a year earlier. "Don't butt in," he told detectives when they arrived in the quiet interlude that follows shootings. Hours later the *Daily News* printed its headline, "Gang Feud Feared As Bullets Fell 3."

Four miles east, at Brooklyn's fortress-like police headquarters on Bergen Street, a report of the shooting landed on the desk of Brooklyn Chief of Detectives Vincent J. Sweeney, an up-from-the-streets Irishman with the slicked-back graying hair and hard-set jaw of a movie detective. Sweeney had been a policeman for twenty-seven years. He had walked Brooklyn streets long enough to know what was coming: an escalating gang war, accompanied by public hysteria. He labeled the report "not for the press."

Tabloids reported that Meyer Shapiro would soon die from his wound, but a Brownsville hospital released him to plan his revenge.

Gossips seated on their Brownstone stoops tracked the ambushes and counter-ambushes as they followed the back and forth of the Brooklyn Dodgers season. They disagreed on who shot Meyer Shapiro, but they knew the shooter, whoever it was, would not live long.

Meyer shrewdly inflicted the one wound more painful than a direct attack on Reles. On a Saturday evening Reles's eighteen-year-old fiancée, Rosie Kirsch, was walking down Pitkin Avenue after seeing an early show with Reles at the Loew's Pitkin movie palace. Afterward Reles had gone to meet his crew, leaving her to window-shop.

Rosie and Reles made an unlikely couple. He was squat and hairy with a bulldog gait; she was petite with dark good looks. Her attraction to him is a mystery of the heart. She may have gravitated to him, knowingly or not, for his power. He was powerful enough at any rate to cut the line at the movie theater and receive deferential treatment in stores and restaurants. His power, in turn, endowed her with neighborhood stature.

On that evening, as Rosie walked among the shops, Meyer Shapiro drove a Packard up behind her. He grabbed her and threw her in the car. He managed to pin her down, kicking and yelling, while driving to a deserted street where he beat her, raped her, and beat her again. He left her in an open field. Meyer sent word to Reles: you're welcome to what's left of her. If Reles wasn't a motivated killer before, he was now.

Reles was deranged with rage, but he plotted his reprisal with cool calculation. An hour past midnight on the morning of June 11, 1930, Reles, DeFeo, and Goldstein drove west past darkened two-story homes on Glenmore Avenue in the Italian neighborhood of East New York. Their mole, Joey Silver, had called earlier in the evening to say that Reles could find the Shapiros in this area. Tonight Reles intended to be the cat, not the mouse.

They parked on Linwood Street to collect a sackful of nickels from a newly installed slot machine tucked among the shelves of cured salami and cheese in an all-night corner grocery. Back outside they found a slit in their rear left tire. If the slit triggered suspicion, they didn't show it. They took off coats, rolled up sleeves, and muscled the spare tire in place.

While their heads were bowed to the task, a car nosed out of a parking space fifty yards away and rolled slowly up Glenmore Avenue. Three .45-caliber Thompson submachine guns, the signature weapon of Prohibition gangsters, emerged from the rear window. A spray of bullets hit the grocer's plate-glass window, sending it shattering to the ground. A bullet neatly took off part of Goldstein's nose as he scurried for cover. Sheets of blood ran down his mouth and chin and splattered the sidewalk. Reles lay spread eagle, bleeding from two bullets to the back. Only DeFeo stood fully exposed during the fusillade. A spurt of bullets struck him in the head and torso. He was dead by the time the shooters accelerated out of sight down Glenmore. The Reles group had unknowingly entered into an ambush. How did the Shapiros know their location? Reles would later learn that Joey Silver, their mole, had betrayed them.

In the hours after DeFeo's death, Chief Sweeney dispatched his men in force to quell the accelerating gang war. The courts had proven too ineffectual and corrupt to do the job. Sweeney would revert to the NYPD's old rough-handed enforcement methods to drive both factions from the borough. He subscribed to the old police saying: There is plenty of law at the end of a nightstick.

Bands of detectives armed with billy clubs raided every Brooklyn gang refuge the police knew of—a string of speakeasies and backroom gambling dens stretching from Canarsie to Cobble Hill. "Gangland is due for the lesson that it can never hope to gain even a fraction of the foothold in Brooklyn that it has obtained in Chicago," Sweeney told reporters, referring to the lawlessness inflicted by Al Capone's reign in that city.

While DeFeo rode a gurney to the morgue, Reles and Goldstein marched, bandaged and handcuffed, into holding cells. They would stay there, Chief Sweeney insisted, until Reles identified the shooters. He refused. He was still silent when a judge dismissed them five days later. The Brownsville stoop-sitters knew the Shapiros had staged the attack, and they knew what would happen next.

Over the following weeks the Reles gang stalked the three square miles of Brownsville in stolen Buicks and Pontiacs, up Livonia and down Dumont, over on Linwood and back on Essex, past the outdoor market with its jam of pushcarts and the glowing marquee of the Loew's Pitkin Theatre. They cruised past kids playing punchball and women in housedresses leaning from windows to call the kids upstairs for dinner. They looked for Meyer the way hunters look for a trophy kill.

Meyer remained safe as long as he was in Label's pool hall on Sutter Avenue, a stronghold of thugs loyal to him.

Sammy Aaronson, the boxing trainer, wrote: "If you wanted someone to help you break a head, beat up a guy, break a strike, buy dope, set a fire, plan a robbery, or muscle a peddler, you could find him at Label's. The place was alive with junkies and firebugs and shylocks and killers and pimps and rag-pickers and bookies and pickpockets. . . . I've seen guys dragged out of Label's screaming while a cop stood on the corner of Sutter and Rockaway and looked the other way."

However, Meyer couldn't stay in the smoky, sweaty confines of Label's forever. On July 23, 1930, Reles and his men approached Label's in a car when they spotted Meyer standing outside. They slowed to fire, but missed as Meyer ducked for cover behind a row of parked cars.

The skirmishes went back and forth through the warmth and humidity of the Brooklyn summer, with the two sides trading attacks and counterattacks while the stoop-sitters kept score. Joey Silver, the double-crosser who had helped the Shapiros ambush Reles on the night DeFeo died, was not surprisingly singled out for assassination. On August 26 he was driving through the intersection of Essex Street and Blake Avenue when Happy Maione jumped on his sedan's running board. He held on with his left hand while reaching his right arm through the window to press a pistol to Silver's chest. Silver died before the sedan rolled to a stop.

For a year the Reles crew shadowed the Shapiros, exchanging fire in seventeen ambushes while Reles by increments appropriated the Shapiro's operations. Then, as summer passed, the year-old slot-machine war fell silent. A long, unspoken truce took hold as both sides retrenched and recruited new foot soldiers. The Brownsville streets quieted.

The following summer Reles came back for the kill. On July 11, 1931, Irving, the oldest Shapiro brother, was in Monticello, New York, a Jewish resort area three hours north of the city, where an associate was on trial for installing stolen slot machines in casinos. A bodyguard named Jacob "Smoky" Epstein drove him home in a maroon sedan, arriving past midnight at the Century Democratic Club, a political clubhouse where they joined Meyer for drinks and a few rounds of cards. At 3 a.m. or so, Meyer proposed that they retire to an all-night Turkish bathhouse over on Cleveland Street for a *schvitz* and some vodka. Irving agreed, but he wanted to change clothes first. Epstein drove Irving to Blake Avenue and parked across the street from the building where the

Shapiro family shared an apartment. Irving told Epstein that he would return in a few minutes. His parents, two sisters, and his brother Willie were asleep upstairs.

Irving opened the front door to his apartment building. Someone had unscrewed the overhead lightbulb, leaving the vestibule in near total darkness. Irving stepped through the blackness to a locked inner door and reached into his pocket for his keys. Before Irving could retrieve them, Reles and another gunman stepped from the gloom. Reles had expected Meyer and Irving. The brothers were almost always together. But he was prepared to execute whichever Shapiro entered. They raised their pistols and shot Irving twice in the face. "The impact jerked his head back, like the end of a bullwhip, and spun him around," a district attorney later wrote. "Sixteen more bullets hemstitched his spine before he hit the floor." Epstein could hear the crack-crack of gunfire from across the street. Before the tenth shot fired, he had thrown his car into gear and pulled away.

Irving's funeral procession filled Blake Avenue and spilled onto side streets as the cortège of thirty-five cars set off for Mt. Lebanon Cemetery in Queens, accompanied by sixty uniformed policemen and forty detectives. The procession paused at the Glory of Israel Synagogue for the customary prayer for the dead, but the rabbi locked them out. Irving's parents wept and consoled each other in Yiddish.

Meyer knew the bullets were meant for him. It was incumbent on him to reply in kind. He and two aides answered a week later by firing from a passing car into the window of Buggsy Goldstein's pool hall ten minutes after spotting him and Reles standing in its doorway. The lurch and swerve of the car may have thrown the shooters off, or they may simply have been poor shots. Either way they missed the pool hall altogether, riddling instead an adjacent lingerie shop. More than a dozen women in various stages of undress ducked into a back room as the bullets shattered a showcase and imbedded themselves in walls.

At 3 a.m. on the morning of July 19 Meyer Shapiro and three of his men left a card game in an East New York clubhouse and headed by car to a diner for an early breakfast. They were driving on Church Avenue when Reles, Strauss, and Abbandando pulled alongside and discharged a 12-gauge sawed-off shotgun and a .38-caliber revolver from the back of a Buick sedan stolen from an ironworks. All shots missed.

The Buick, by chance, drove toward an oncoming police car. Patrolman Harold Schreck drew his pistol and called for the men to halt, but the Buick sped by. Schreck recognized Reles as the car whizzed past. He made a U-turn and followed, firing with his left hand and steering with his right. The two cars exchanged more than thirty shots, but none landed. A second patrol car joined the chase as Reles skidded on trolley tracks and raced through stop signs and zigzagged from Utica Avenue, over to Livonia and Howard, and into Brownsville. Schreck could see one gun, and then another, thrown from the car window. After three miles the Buick stopped abruptly at the intersection of Livonia and Howard Avenues. The three men got out and ran, but not fast enough. The patrolmen chased them to the ground and pistol-whipped them. Near the abandoned car they found the weapons, both still warm from use. The police watched Brooklyn hospitals that morning to see if Meyer showed up with bullet wounds, but he did not. Nine months later a jury acquitted Reles, Strauss, and Abbandando of grand larceny. "Gentlemen," the judge told the jury, "you have let three killers go."

On August 30 Meyer tried yet another drive-by assault. Once again he missed. That was enough for Chief Sweeney. With the back-and-forth gang war in its second year he now took measures to sweep the streets clean of combatants and enforce a cooling-off period. On September 4, his detectives arrested Reles along with Buggsy Goldstein, Happy Maione, and Pittsburgh Phil Strauss at a Turkish bath and questioned them all night about the deaths of George DeFeo, Joey Silver, and Irving Shapiro. Reles's police record was now a catch-and-release saga—twenty-two arrests, including three homicide charges, followed by twenty-two dismissals.

This time Reles and his trio were charged with robbery and vagrancy, trumped-up allegations designed to confine them. A judge agreed to postpone their hearing in order to keep them locked up without bail a few extra days, but he released them for lack of evidence on September 9. They were free for no more than a minute. Reles and his men walked down the steps of the Brooklyn courthouse to find detectives waiting to arrest them for possessing unregistered firearms.

When police apprehended the four men in the bathhouse, five days earlier, they had confiscated a key ring found in Goldstein's pocket. One of the keys opened locker 90 in the bathhouse changing room. Inside police found two suitcases. One contained three .38-caliber revolvers, three .32-caliber revolvers, and a sawed-off double-barreled shotgun—all cleaned and loaded. The second suitcase contained a thousand revolver cartridges and 150 shotgun shells.

When news of the arsenal reached Meyer Shapiro, he concluded that he could not match Reles's firepower. He was the hunted, no longer the hunter. The time had come for him to find a hideaway outside Brooklyn. "The White Lights of Broadway and the dimly lighted night clubs have beckoned to him," wrote *The Standard Union*, a Brooklyn newspaper, referring to Times Square. "Shapiro is said to be safe so long as he keeps away from Brooklyn."

Broadway was not far enough. At 7:30 a.m. on the morning of September 17, four days after a judge released Reles and his friends on bail, a newsboy found a body dumped inside the unlocked basement door of a dingy tenement just north of Houston Street, near the East River, in Manhattan. The victim had died from a single shot behind the left ear. Police found a coat and vest in the street gutter, indicating that the killers had shot their victim on the street, then dragged the body to the basement. Fingerprints identified him as Meyer Shapiro. His death came sixty-six days after his older brother Irving died. Meyer was twenty-two years old.

Later that day seventeen-year-old Willie Shapiro, the last of the three Shapiro brothers, walked into the Bellevue morgue to identify the body lying on a slab. *The New York Times* reported that he "glanced insolently around the place."

"How did you know about the shooting?" an attendant asked.

"A copper walked into the house and told me," Willie answered. With that he lifted the white sheet and identified his brother, then abruptly walked out.

Like Irving, Willie was a failed prizefighter, a washout who took a pounding to head and gut in early undercards fought in half-empty arenas. All the while he watched and learned as his older brothers assembled a business based on slot machines, extortion, and brothels. After Meyer's death, Willie assembled his own gang. From his new perch he loudly declared his intention to avenge his brothers' deaths, but his boast rang hollow. Of the three Shapiro brothers, Willie was the dimmest and softest. Reles didn't pay him much attention. Willie was easy to ignore, until he set up a floating craps game held on street corners and in vacant lots. That was a move that encroached on established games controlled by Reles. It would not be tolerated.

At 10:30 p.m. on July 18, 1934, a twenty-two-year-old mechanic named Sidney Weiss went for a walk near his home in Canarsie. It was a balmy, clear night lit by a quarter moon, a lovely night for a stroll. On the far side of a fence, where Flatlands Avenue ended at a tidal creek that drained into Jamaica Bay, Weiss spotted three men digging in a low sand dune while a fourth stood watch. One of the diggers paused when he spotted Weiss and walked over to the fence to exchange a word. Weiss noticed the man wore a double-breasted suit and silk tie—a strangely formal wardrobe for late-night ditchdigging.

"Hot night isn't it?" the man said. Weiss agreed. Minutes later Weiss noticed the man and his companions throw shovels in the trunk of a car and drive off down Flatlands Avenue.

Weiss slept poorly that night. The memory of the four men working in darkness troubled his mind. Who were they, and why were they digging at that hour? Weiss suspected the worst. He returned to the sandpit the next morning to investigate, accompanied by a gaggle of curious boys who had been fishing in a nearby creek. Weiss sunk his own shovel into the loosened sand. After a few spadefuls it hit hard against a buried object: a human foot. Before digging any further, he called to a patrolman in a nearby police cruiser who helped him finished the ghastly job.

Detective Harry Beck of the Brooklyn homicide squad drove out for a look. Beck had chased the Shapiros for years, and he immediately identified the body laid out in the sand as Willie Shapiro. He had been strangled with a cord and savagely beaten in the back of Sally's Bar and Grill. A single mighty blow cratered a portion of his skull. An autopsy found sand in his lungs, indicating that he was still alive when stuffed in a laundry bag and dropped in his grave.

The Shapiros had fallen like dominos. Reles played a role in all three murders. With Willie's death, he could now claim undisputed control of Brownsville. "It stinks," he said, "but I own it."

Word passed in the pool halls and the stoops that Kid Twist was the new boss. The rackets, bookmaking, slot machines, shylocking, craps games, and brothels—all the profits flooded in to Reles and trickled down to his friends Goldstein, Strauss, Maione, and Abbandando.

Their collective income brought them closer to the mob lords that they had admired as teenagers. Reles and his crew jumped up in income, but also in stature. Now in their early twenties, they had graduated from small-time schlammers to masters of America's most murderous neighborhood. More important, they had impressed the big New York bosses with their murderous instinct and audacity. They stood on the verge of the big time.

A gift for the vicious allowed Reles to unseat the Shapiros, but surviving on top would require something else—a shrewdness, an adroitness. In the weeks after Irving and Meyer died, an aspirant to their throne named Israel "Jake the Painter" Goldberg began boasting loudly in bars and pool halls that he could take Reles down. He swore he would kill Reles on sight. The stoop-sitters gave him an even chance.

Brownsville was small enough that everyone eventually crossed paths. Reles ran into Goldberg at the intersection of Sackman Street and Livonia Avenue on a September night. Goldberg was carrying a pistol; Reles had only his wits. But he had a gift for talking, and he cajoled Goldberg to join him at a nearby bar to discuss their situation. Over a series of drinks, and more drinks, Reles persuaded Goldberg that they should surprise everyone by doing business together. If they became partners—why not?—both would benefit. Golberg's hostility ebbed as he listened and drank. By the time they left the bar Reles had swayed him. They were future partners now and new best friends. A drunken sentiment of goodwill had prevailed. Reles paused as they parted, as if a thought had just come to him.

"Hey Jake, you've got a pistol," he later recalled saying.

"So?"

"So you know what will happen if they catch you with [the pistol]."

"And what do you know?" Reles later said. "He gimmee the piece."

There may have been a moment when Goldberg realized that in the thrall of all that boozy talk he had committed a grave mistake, an error of trust. Within seconds Reles turned Goldberg's gun on him and shot him six times. He dropped the gun and ran until he saw a patrolman. He then kicked in the window of a bakery and waited for the handcuffs. A report of murder came over the police teletype while Reles was in the precinct house.

"There's one rap you can't hang on me," Reles told the policeman taking his mug shot. "I was here when it happened."

Reles and his confederates were no longer teenage hirelings. Photographs from the time show hardened young men. The war with the Shapiros had forged them into a lethal team. They had what prosecutor's called "killer's eyes." They were professionals now, endowed with rigid resolve.

3

THE COMMISSION

On the first warm April day of 1931, Lucky Luciano, a serpent-eyed mob lieutenant, invited his boss, Giuseppe "Joe the Boss" Masseria, to lunch at Nuova Villa Tammaro, a little seafood trattoria in a two-story Coney Island building plastered like a cake with fake balconies, balustrades, and other Italianate flourishes. Its green awning evoked the Italian flag. The restaurant was on a drab cul-de-sac two blocks north of the tourist strip, near the creek that divides Coney Island from the rest of Brooklyn.

Masseria was a round-shaped man with a pig face who for three years had served as the *capo di tutti capi,* the boss of bosses. His childhood friends in Sicily had called him Cork because of his stout, shapeless body. His table manners matched his girth: he slurped spaghetti, splattering tomato sauce over his vests and wide ties.

Masseria was fat, but tough. He ran his operation with mean intent. When a grocer groused that his extortion payments had doubled, Masseria ordered the store burned to the ground, killing the grocer's wife and daughter as they slept in a second-floor apartment.

Masseria was what the younger generation of mobsters scornfully called a Mustache Pete, an Italian-born mafioso. America had no extradition laws, so it served as a sanctuary for killers and thieves escaping *la polizia.*

Like most Mustache Petes, Masseria had no interest in adapting to American life. He never drank beer or watched baseball. Nor did he care to learn proper English. He was forever Sicilian, a living link to the customs of the Cosa Nostra, with all its ruthless tactics and parochial suspicions of those outside its self-protective tribe. He lived in a Sicilian stronghold embedded within New York. The Mustache Petes stuck to the old ways. They stuck to their clan.

The old bosses like Masseria talked of honor and loyalty, but they distrusted everyone. Their Sicilian ancestors suffered millennia of successive invaders—Carthaginians, Greeks, Phoenicians, Romans, Vandals, Normans, Spaniards, Bourbons. All used Sicily as their granary and enslaved its sons. Generations of Sicilians thus grew up with an inbred distrust of outsiders. Suspicion was baked into the Sicilian soul.

Masseria carried that ancient wariness with him when a murder charge chased him to New York at age sixteen. He scorned Jewish and Irish mobsters. Neapolitans were only marginally more tolerable. Even after decades in New York, he stayed stubbornly faithful to the parochial Old World code of loyalties and blood feuds. In the Little Italy neighborhood of Manhattan, the Sicilians lived east of Mulberry Street; the Neopolitans and other southern Italians lived to the west. Each tribe stayed in its place.

Like the other Mustache Petes, Masseria refused to modernize his criminal methods, even when it became clear that the easy bootlegging money would not last. His intransigence and petty prejudices frustrated a younger cohort of fully Americanized gangsters, particularly Luciano, who grew up among Jews on East Thirteenth Street on the Lower East Side. His first employer, a hat manufacturer named Max Goodman, treated Luciano as a son. His closest childhood friends included the Jewish gangsters Meyer Lansky and Bugsy Siegel.

Masseria, king of the Cosa Nostra, warned Luciano to stay away from his friends in the so-called Kosher Nostra. Why brood over ancient wrongs? Luciano answered. The dollar was what mattered in America, and the dollar didn't distinguish between Sicilians and Jews. Luciano and his friends had decided that the Mustache Petes stood in the way of a more profitable future.

Both men knew that the rift would hang over their lunch. At 12:30 p.m. Masseria parked his steel-armored sedan, a massive car with inch-thick bulletproof glass, in a Coney Island garage. Leaving two bodyguards at the restaurant door, he worked his way through a feast of antipasto, lobster, and spaghetti with clam sauce washed down with a bottle of Chianti. He ate as if devouring his last meal, as he always did. Luciano ate sparingly.

The restaurant was empty by the time Masseria laid down his fork. He and Luciano lingered at their corner table playing pinochle, as they often did after meals. They had played one hand and were about to deal another when, at exactly 3:30 p.m., Luciano excused himself to use the bathroom. While he was gone four gunmen calmly entered the restaurant with pistols raised and delivered five shots to Masseria's back. The last shot passed through his brain and exited an eye socket. His bodyguards had slipped away by prior arrangement.

Detectives arrived to find Anna Tammaro, the proprietor's mother-in-law and cook, leaning over the body. Masseria lay on his back, his arms outstretched, with playing cards scattered about an enlarging pool of congealing blood. A press photographer captured Masseria's body laid out on the floor with arms flung wide like a snow angel. His lifeless right hand held the ace of spades, the death card. A shooter may have placed the card to send a macabre message, or, more likely, the photographer staged the shot. The gunmen dropped two pistols in an alley beside the restaurant and fled in a blue sedan. Four hours later the car was found abandoned with three more pistols on the backseat.

Having removed himself to the bathroom, Luciano could truthfully tell detectives that he saw nothing. The waiters could not, or would not, identify the shooters from a book of mug shots kept in police headquarters. Nobody was charged, except for Mrs. Tammaro, who sold wine in violation of the Volstead Act.

With Masseria's assassination, the title of *capo di tutti capi* passed to his great rival, another Mustache Pete named Salvatore Maranzano. Both bosses were short and fat, but they differed in every other way. While Masseria was a thundering intimidator, Maranzano was a contemplative leader who motivated and manipulated with soft-spoken charm. He never raised his voice, but his silence held menace.

As a boy growing up in Sicily, Maranzano had planned to study for the priesthood, and his bookish bent persisted even as he smuggled booze for a living. In his pedantic fashion he made sure people knew that he spoke Latin and collected books about his hero, Julius Caesar. He aspired to rule the underground as Caesar had ruled ancient Rome, with a formal hierarchy of bosses, lieutenants, and soldiers.

Maranzano tried to ennoble his operation—prostitution, bootlegging, and drug smuggling concealed within a legitimate real-estate brokerage—by moving his headquarters from drab quarters in Little Italy to the New York Central Building, a marble and bronze tower (later named the Helmsley Building) straddling Park Avenue. On the afternoon of September 30, 1931, Maranzo was there, in his ninth-floor office, waiting for Lucky Luciano. Their meeting was ostensibly to discuss ways of working together now that Maranzano was *capo di tutti capi*, but he knew that Luciano came with intent to kill, just as Luciano had arranged to kill Masseria five months earlier.

Maranzano understood that he must kill or be killed. It was a posture that Caesar, his hero, would have endorsed. For his counterstrike Maranzano hired a twenty-two-year-old Irish psychopath named Vincent "Mad Dog" Coll, who dressed in blue serge suits and striped club ties, to murder Luciano, but he came hours too late. At 2 p.m. that afternoon four men impersonating IRS agents stormed Maranzano's office. Waving revolvers and counterfeit badges, they disarmed seven men in the outer office, then allowed them, along with a secretary, to flee to the elevator bank and down the fire stairs. They then charged Maranzano's inner office, pinning him against a wall and stabbing him six times. They sank knives into his chest and stomach, then sliced the corners of his mouth open to form a sickening grin as he lay on the floor bleeding to death. Like Caesar, he was stabbed to death by conspirators. They finished him off with shots fired to the face. The killers made off just as Mad Dog Coll arrived.

In a grisly bit of poetic justice, Luciano had selected an all-Jewish assassin team headed by Samuel "Red" Levine, an Orthodox hit man who wore a yarmulke under his fedora and refrained from killing on the Sabbath. It was Levine who stabbed Maranzano in the heart.

Three months after Maranzano died, Luciano convened leaders of more than twenty regional gangs in the Blackstone Hotel in Chicago to plan their collective future without the blood-feuding Mustache Petes. Delegates gathered under the crystal chandeliers and intricate white molding of the hotel's Crystal Ballroom—Izzy Bernstein of Detroit, Bugsy Siegel of Los Angeles, Harry Rosen of Philadelphia, Spunky Weiss of Pittsburgh, and Al Capone, who, as hometown boss, played host.

Luciano presided. When Americans deplored the influx of Italians as a taint on national purity, as many did, they imagined somebody like Luciano, the menacing product of Old World vice and violence. He had dark Sicilian good looks, with black wavy hair and cold, appraising slit eyes. A scar on his cheek gave his right eye a sinister sag. The *New York Times* columnist Meyer Berger called him "droop-eyed and unwholesomely dark." He was the perfect smooth Italian gangster—elegant and forbidding.

Decades later Ian Fleming, author of the James Bond books, described Luciano as "a neat, quiet man with a tired, good-looking face. Whether he deserves the notoriety attached to his name or not, he has certain physical characteristics which one associates with men of power and decision—unsmiling, rather still eyes, a strong decisive jawline, and a remarkable economy of movement and expression." Fleming's description could as easily have applied to James Bond.

Luciano said little, but he did not need to. He had pulled off the underworld equivalent of a hostile takeover. He rose to a dictatorial pinnacle by eliminating the Mustache Petes above him. The assembled bosses assumed he would declare himself the new *capo di tutti capi*. While monarchs might pass, the crown, by custom, lived on in succession.

Luciano flouted the convention. He renounced the title, proposing instead a radical reimagining of the American underworld. Standing before the delegates in a hotel ballroom swirling with cigar smoke, he suggested that they now replace the pointless, wasteful vendettas and blood feuds of the Mustache Pete era with a cooperative, democratic, and multi-ethnic alliance. To grow efficiently—and assume an aspect of legitimacy—they must, he said, adopt a more open, businesslike structure. A new organization, the racketeering version of the United Nations, would extend from coast to coast and include gangs of all races. His plan was simple: less blood meant more money for everyone.

As he later said, "I explained to them that we were in a business that had to keep moving without explosions every two minutes—knocking guys off just because they come from a different part of Sicily, that kind of crap was giving us a bad name, and we couldn't operate until it stopped. Masseria and Maranzano had been our real enemies, not the law; we could handle the law."

Prohibition would linger, unpopular and universally flouted, for another two years, but repeal was now a fait accompli. For gangsters, flush times would end. To thrive without the effortless wealth of bootlegging, the mob should, Luciano said, adopt a more businesslike structure with a national board of directors to establish general policies and resolve territorial squabbles. A kangaroo court would adjudicate punishment for those members, or their underlings, who violated rules or informed on their brethren. With delegates in agreement, organized crime would finally be organized, the mafia would be modernized. If the old crime operations operated as families with absolute loyalty to the patriarch, the new model would run like General Motors or Pan American.

The new confederacy, Luciano said, would be called "The Commission." The men stood up and shook hands. (Sixty-seven years later *Time* magazine included Luciano on its list of the "100 most influential business geniuses of the century" for his "dark vision of Big Business.") That night Al Capone, the Chicago boss, threw a banquet in Luciano's honor. The two men sat on the dais like princelings as waiters poured drinks and a jazz band played. Over the course of the meal, guests presented Luciano with envelopes thick with cash, the customary tribute of the Mustache Pete days. Luciano waved them away. "I don't need the money," he said. "I got plenty, and besides, why should you be paying anything to me when we're all equals?"

The celebrants in the ballroom that night included the short, squat figure of Abe Reles. He knew almost nothing of the world beyond Brooklyn, and he had never before circulated among national crime figures. He was like a minor league player called up to the majors for his first game.

Reles had earned his invitation by disposing of the Shapiros and establishing himself as the chief of an up-and-coming Brooklyn gang composed of Jews and Italians in the new multi-ethnic model Luciano envisioned. As much as anything, it was the *way* Reles disposed of the Shapiros that impressed the higher-ups: with a viciousness verging on sadism. Reles did not know it yet, but the Commission had him in mind for a critical role.

4

MURDER FOR MONEY

On March 3, 1933, Abe Reles rode into Manhattan to meet with Louis "Lepke" Buchalter, the highest-ranking Jewish mobster in New York, at his Fifth Avenue office overlooking Madison Square Park. His rooms resembled a moderately prosperous law office, with understated furnishings and views over the tree canopy to the Flatiron Building and the Met Life tower, landmarks of wealth and respectability.

Buchalter and his partner, Jacob "Gurrah" Shapiro, were known as the Octopus Boys. Their tentacles reached into some two hundred fifty criminal enterprises, though they were best known as rulers of the garment industries clustered around Seventh Avenue, where hundreds of business owners, large and small, either paid tribute or faced the consequences: sabotage, arson, union strikes, and worse. Buchalter's men descended on the delinquent and averse like Visigoths, destroying goods and threatening wives and daughters with violation. Workers were forced to the street and beaten.

With his control of the garment industries consolidated, Buchalter methodically expanded his hegemony from one industry to the next—taxis, movie theaters, window wipers, bakers, fur truckers, milliners—always threatening, always extorting. In most cases he controlled both industry and labor: businesses paid him for protection, workers paid a portion of their union dues. Slipups were not forgiven, not ever.

Buchalter was known to all by his childhood nickname, Lepke, a Yiddishism for "Little Louis." He was one of eleven children raised in a dark, overcrowded tenement flat above his father's hardware store on Henry Street, on the Lower East Side of Manhattan. His father died when Buchalter was fourteen. Soon afterward, his mother moved to Colorado to live with Buchalter's older brother, leaving Buchalter to fend for himself. As a teenager he survived on his wits in the maze of crowded, filthy streets. He met his future partner, Gurrah Shapiro (no relation to the Shapiro brothers of Brownsville) while both were trying to rob the same pushcart.

A series of rough stays in reformatories hardened Buchalter's soul, but outwardly he appeared soft, almost meek. New York's *Daily Mirror* called him "a quiet-spoken little man who padded softly through the underworld labyrinths like a cat; a boss gangster who never raised his voice, even in anger, but whose mellow-toned orders packed a terrific wallop—and death, if they were disobeyed."

By the time Reles met him, in 1933, Buchalter had acquired the satisfied look of a prosperous bond trader. He was a dark, small-framed man, no more than five foot seven, with big ears, dimples, and doleful hound-dog eyes. New Yorkers rarely saw his name in print. He abstained from the flamboyant gangster life, choosing instead to live quietly with his English wife, Betty, a former nightclub hostess, and a stepson, Harold, whom he adopted. He carried Harold's photograph inside the back cover of his platinum pocket watch. The three lived in an expensively furnished apartment in a doorman building on Central Park West, two blocks north of Columbus Circle. In the evenings he read magazines or played pinochle. He rarely had more than one drink.

Buchalter was a brooding, self-contained presence in the underworld. He kept his own counsel. When he spoke, he spoke softly. A probation report called him "a quiet fellow with an almost apologetic manner."

Behind Buchalter's mild demeanor, though, lurked a dark power. "There was sinister magic in the name Lepke among his shivering victims," wrote the columnist Meyer Berger, "and among the disloyal in his cabinet."

Reles was surely aware of the dark power when he came to Buchalter's office to discuss a job offer of sorts. Buchalter had helped Luciano realize his plan for a cooperative alliance of gangs supervised by a board of directors. They also formed a makeshift court to hear cases and dole out punishments for those who informed on them or otherwise broke the mob's code of behavior. Now the Commission needed an agency to carry out those punishments.

The Commission, Buchalter explained, had chosen Reles to form an assassination team, a kill squad. They must never kill out of jealousy or love, Buchalter said, only for business. Their job was to kill potential informants and other betrayers. The premise was simple: dead men can't talk, dead men can't testify.

Reles qualified because of his neutrality: he did not affiliate himself with any specific mob boss, and his gang was Jewish-Italian, so it could not be accused of siding with one ethnicity. Most important, he had shown that nothing scared him, nothing shook him. Brownsville was the deadliest neighborhood in the country, and Reles was Brownsville's deadliest man. He showed an unflinching efficiency in his war with the Shapiros and in his lockdown grip on the Brownsville rackets. He impressed Buchalter with the number of murders he committed, but also with the manner in which he and his men enacted them—ice-pick stabbings, drive-by shootings, adversaries thrown from speeding cars, bodies crushed under car wheels, and a victim buried alive. They were not just tough, they were savage. And their savagery conveyed a certain perverse pleasure in their work. In the popular conception of gangsterism, Italians were the tough guys. Reles was so tough that the Italians would now delegate murder to him.

On most days for the next decade, Reles and his men slept through the morning. In the early afternoon they met at a run-down candy store that served as their headquarters, dispatch bureau, and situation room. Rose's Candy stood between a hat shop and a hosiery store on the corner of Livonia and Saratoga Avenues. Just above the candy store a Chinese restaurant called Hollywood Royal dished out chow mein. Every five minutes or so the licorice and Necco Wafers on the glass candy-store shelves rattled in their jars as the elevated IRT bound to or from Canarsie shook the steel scaffolding almost directly overhead.

Reles sat in his booth like a potentate as a host of petitioners and supplicants came and went: protectorates bearing tribute, low car thieves seeking assignment, intermediaries negotiating police payoffs.

The bird-like, white-haired proprietor, Rose Gold, was a tough-talking sixtysomething, a grandmother in housecoat and apron, who sold Tootsie Pops and Heath Bars to schoolchildren through a little street-facing window while Reles and the boys played cards and drank egg creams in a back booth beside a pay phone. Rose served as den mother, guardian, and banker. Reles called her Midnight Rose because the candy store stayed open all night. When the men needed bail for disorderly conduct or gambling, she showed up with the cash. If patrolmen snooped, she brushed them away. On the side she ran a loan-sharking business with her son.

Reles had originally called his squad the Combination, because it consisted of Jews and Italians, but it became universally known as Murder, Inc., after a pudgy Irish reporter named Harry Feeney coined the phrase in the *New York World-Telegram*. The United Press later wrote, in one of the many breathless accounts of the murder-for-money team: "Murder, Inc deals out death-on-the-dotted-line. A verbal contract—a few dollars passed—body encased in cement and tossed in the river—another thrown from a speeding auto . . . That was death-de-luxe—a service for the underworld to rid itself of those of its own who had become too dangerous, too demanding or irritant in one way or another."

As the assignments came in, Murder, Inc. enlisted aimless and idle apprentices off the street for low-level tasks. They often entrapped young recruits by encouraging them to borrow money from loan sharks to impress girls or gamble. Once in arrears, these boys had no choice but to do as told: holdups, shakedowns, car theft, and murder. "The punk is subject to call," Reles later said. "He is under orders 24-hours a day. He asks no questions. He does what he is told to do—to break a head, to kill a man or do any other kind of work."

The recruits were like freshmen in Murder University. They were responsible for stealing cars, driving during murder runs, and abandoning the cars with a body, or "package," left in the trunk. A lower caste of gofers and supplicants loafed outside the candy store, hoping Reles would hire them for errands or chores. The spot was known throughout Brownsville as the Corner.

Reles turned the keys of stolen cars used in a crime over to a long-haired, stubble-faced man named Oscar "The Poet" Friedman, who, in the mob's arcane division of labor, worked as an "evaporator." He specialized in breaking cars down with a blowtorch and selling the parts to junk dealers. When Reles said, "Give it to Oscar," it meant the job was done. When he wasn't stripping cars, Friedman sat in a park and read worn copies of ancient texts, usually the quatrains of Nostradamus or poems by the Persian mathematician and astronomer Omar Khayyam.

The murders followed an established routine. A mob boss in Miami, Detroit, or a dozen other cities could request the assassination of one of his own men if he suspected him of leaking information to detectives, stealing funds, insubordination, or some other betrayal. An assignment could also come from the Commission's big bosses—Luciano, Buchalter, and the rest. Their kangaroo court drank wine or whiskey in a restaurant's back room as they weighed arguments for and against an execution.

When the pay phone rang in Midnight Rose's, the back booth fell silent. The Reles lieutenants Buggsy Goldstein and Pittsburgh Phil Strauss volunteered for every murder they could, often for the thrill of the kill. Buggsy liked to truss his prey with a length of rope running up their back from ankle to throat in such a way that every kick tightened the noose. The more they struggled, the more they strangled.

Goldstein had macabre techniques, but Strauss had volume. He may qualify as the most prolific killer in mob history, with a body count exceeding a hundred. He was known as "the flying gangster" because Reles relied on him for out-of-town jobs. Strauss headed to the airport as groomed and well-dressed as any middle manager so as not to arouse suspicion. He boarded planes with a suitcase containing a clean change of clothes, a toilet kit, a loaded pistol, a meat cleaver, and a length of rope. Strauss rarely knew his target personally; he often didn't know their name or the nature of their offense. A local associate, known as a "finger man," was responsible for studying the victim's habits and routines. He picked Strauss up at the airport and drove him to a reconnaissance spot, a parked car or barstool, where Strauss could see his victim. In the meantime, a local crew stole two cars—one to transport Strauss to and from the murder and one to block the police from the crime scene. They also stole separate sets of license plates to make identification more difficult.

The boss who ordered the kill was careful to establish an alibi. He might schedule the murder during an event where he would be publicly seen, or he might embark on a cruise so that the passenger list would clear him in court. One boss scheduled a murder during his daughter's dance recital.

The kill could be accomplished with a garrote looped around a neck, a meat cleaver to a forehead, or a burst of gunfire. Afterward, the local gang methodically burned all evidence—weapons, cars, and sometimes bodies. Strauss left town before police could round up suspects. He rarely knew the victim's name until he read about the murder the next day.

The big hits earned Reles gangland glory, but he never lost sight of the need to fortify his authority within Brownsville. Every boss, no matter his level, had to watch his backyard.

In November 1933, Alex "Red" Alpert, a nineteen-year-old petty thief with a spongy mop of black hair and a stringy mustache, got into a shouting match with Strauss over the value of stolen jewelry that Alpert invited him to fence. Alpert offered the goods to Strauss for $3,000. Pittsburgh Phil said he would pay no more than $700. Alpert cursed him out and walked away. By the Brownsville street code, Alpert had committed an unforgivable act of defiance.

Strauss was still fuming over Alpert's impudence hours later when he joined Reles in the back booth at Midnight Rose's. Reles and Buggsy found Alpert and repeated Strauss's offer one last time: he would take the jewels for $700. Alpert laughed.

Reles would have to address the insolence quickly and harshly. He accordingly summoned a close companion of Alpert's named Walter Sage, a low-level gambler who loitered on the Corner with the other hangers-on hoping for handout work. Reles told Sage to arrange a bogus middle-of-the-night rendezvous with Alpert on Van Siclen Avenue in East New York. Sage did as told—he wouldn't dare resist—though he knew what it meant for his friend. At dawn the next morning a patrolman found Alpert's body on the lawn of a two-story house a block from Alpert's home on a quiet residential block in East New York. A .38-caliber slug had entered his back just below the right shoulder blade and lodged in his neck. There was no blood on the ground. Police took that to mean his killers threw him from a passing car.

Later that day detectives picked up Reles, Strauss, Goldstein, and their hireling, Dukey Maffetore, and charged them with murder. Alpert's mother, a small, wan woman, told police that she knew Reles killed her son. Six days later a judge released the four suspects for lack of evidence. The next day Alpert's mother walked from her home to the local precinct house and demanded to know if detectives had caught the men who murdered her son. She made the walk almost daily for seven years, every day walking home disappointed. Eight years would pass before her son's death made headlines, eight years before authorities gave her a proper hearing.

In those Prohibition years Reles and his men operated with near impunity while the cash flowed in from extortion, loan-sharking, and other rackets. They were flush, and they flaunted their wealth with new wardrobes of chalk-striped and herringbone double-breasted wool suits with padded shoulders and high, pointed lapels. They wore broad-brimmed fedoras with wide bands and silk ties. They dressed as if expensive clothes could dignify their occupation.

Reles in particular enjoyed a new prosperity. He bought a Chrysler, then a LaSalle, and rented a summer house in White Lake in the Catskill Mountains upstate. He drove the Brooklyn streets like he owned the borough. Pedestrians recognized him as Kid Twist, and they paid him deference, as they would a young prince. In restaurants proprietors came forward to shake his hand and waved him into the best banquette.

In this season of fresh prosperity, Reles married his slim, dark-complexioned girlfriend, Rosie Kirsch. If she blamed her entanglement with Reles for the rape inflicted on her by the late Meyer Shapiro, she had apparently forgiven him. Not surprisingly, Rosie's hardworking immigrant parents did not approve. "You are married to a crook," her mother told her in Yiddish. "Who knows what he does?"

An outsider might call the couple a mismatch. In the calculus of courtship, Rosie appeared too pretty for the lisping, low-browed Reles. In additional to his simian physical presence, he burdened her with a sense of entrapment: gangster wives were usually lonely. Reles never included her when he conducted business at bars, restaurants, and racetracks. Like all gangster wives, she spent solitary days wondering when her husband would die, and how she would greet that eventuality. Would she return home from the cemetery with a sense of dread or liberation?

On the other hand, gangsterism had its compensations. Reles's crooked money bought Rosie a fur coat and other comforts. He made it possible for her parents to open their own small business, a lunch counter. He also conferred on her a certain standing, a local respect, as she circulated about the neighborhood. For good or bad, she had made a Faustian bargain.

Reles was short and ungainly, but his friend Pittsburgh Phil Strauss was tall and handsome in a gangsterish way, with dark eyes and bull neck. He was the kind of big athletic man that women noticed, and he knew it. He reportedly spent an hour each day at the barbershop and manicurist. The *Daily News* called him "the Beau Brummel of Death." He was a vicious charmer.

When detectives brought Strauss into the Manhattan police headquarters on a murder charge, Police Commissioner Lewis Valentine, a man of dour rectitude, came down from his second-floor office to examine the killer alongside detectives and other police officials so that they might take his measure and recognize him when they next saw him. Only criminals of a certain prominence warranted a "lineup," as they called it. Strauss stood against a wall in a well-tailored overcoat with velvet collar, a pearl-gray fedora, and a matching blue shirt and tie worn with a blue striped suit. "Look at him," Valentine said. "He's the best dressed man in the room and he's never worked a day in his life. . . . When you meet men like Strauss, don't be afraid to muss them up. Blood should be smeared all over his velvet collar."

While Reles led a conventional domestic life, Strauss pursued women with an animal appetite. A veteran detective later said of Strauss: "The best dresser in Murder, Inc. often boasted that he was too smart to marry, and he had a parade of girlfriends that looked high class if you didn't see them in the sunshine. This fellow was the most cruel of the ring, and would stab a victim fifty times when three would do the trick, and he beat up and drove away one woman after another. He was oiled and creased and massaged like a fashion plate."

The one woman Strauss did not drive away was Evelyn Mittleman, a willowy blonde turned brunette. Even as a teenager she was a siren of the Brooklyn underworld, a fixture in the Surf Avenue Boys Club and other low Coney Island nightspots for gambling and jazz. In nightclubs she leaned forward to have cigarettes lit for her. She crossed her legs like a movie star.

Thirty-one-year-old Hymie Miller picked Mittleman up in a Coney Island club when she was seventeen. He took her to Los Angeles, where he played bit parts in movies and owned a café favored by gamblers and the small-time racketeers who had moved west to squeeze payments from the movie industry. He must have run afoul of them. After locking up the café one evening in November 1937 and walking a few blocks to his apartment, he was shot four times in the face. The bullets blew his nose off and pierced his neck. He died the next day.

Back in New York, Mittleman moved on with Robert Feurer, another mid-level gangster. Feurer took her to a dance in Brooklyn where she met Sol Goldstein, a handsome, well-assembled man who worked the rackets in the Fulton Fish Market. Feurer disapproved of her flirting with Goldstein, and Goldstein disapproved of Feurer scolding her for it. In keeping with gangland chivalry, Goldstein later killed Feurer. Mittleman naturally shifted her affections to Goldstein, who made the mistake of parading his prize all over Brooklyn. When Strauss saw the couple outside a Brooklyn pool hall, he stopped to talk to her. Now it was Goldstein's turn for jealousy. When Goldstein mouthed off, Strauss beat him into submission with a pool cue. He did not kill Goldstein. That would come later.

A prosecutor would later call Mittleman "the Kiss of Death Girl." Three boyfriends, three deaths. Now she was with Strauss. "His pictures had been in all the papers as way up on the public enemy list and all the girls were wild to go with him," Mittleman told a detective. "So I just picked him for myself. If he ever killed anyone I never saw him do it, so to me he's a spender and a pretty good guy who's not too smart."

The detective later noted that she "continually nagged [Strauss] about his uncouthness. He'd never been treated like that before, and as a result he was anxious to rise in the girl's esteem, and she kept on him. 'I've got to have three hundred dollars next week,' she'd say, 'or I'm taking up with a guy in Philadelphia who will give me turtle soup where you give gravy.'"

If the Murder, Inc. men could not win over a woman with bluster, they simply took her. Happy Maione and Dasher Abbandando propositioned a seventeen-year-old nightclub singer after her debut at a Brooklyn club. She refused to even look their way. They waited outside until the club closed, then forced her into a car. They drove her to a remote parking lot where they took turns raping her. They were reluctant to release her afterward for fear that she might go to the police. She listened as they debated whether to bury her or buy her off. They settled on the latter. That night they drove to her mother's house and handed her a roll of cash totaling $500. Keep quiet, Abbandando told her, or they would kill both mother and daughter.

All the men of Murder, Inc. acted as if nothing could touch them, Reles most of all. On January 13, 1934, a Saturday night, he was driving with a friend who spotted two girls window-shopping on Stone Avenue. He honked his horn and waved. He swerved over to the curb and offered a crude come-on. When the girls brushed him off, his temper took over. "Suddenly, he drove his car right onto the sidewalk, trying to run them over," said Detective James Boyle, who responded when he heard Reles honking. "They parted and fled and he almost ran down other pedestrians before his car swerved to the road again. The noise he made blowing his horn had attracted a radio car, and I jumped on the running board and we chased him. He drove like mad. He had reached Thatford Avenue before traffic cleared enough so I could fire two shots. He gave up."

"You ain't got nothing on me," Reles told Boyle as the handcuffs went on. Boyle arrested him for reckless driving and disorderly conduct. At the Monday hearing Reles's lawyer asked for leniency. He said with a straight face that his client was the poor son of hardworking immigrants. The judge suspended the charges, saying, preposterously, that Reles's substantial court record did not reflect criminal intent.

A month later Reles pulled into a garage on East Ninety-eighth Street, in Canarsie, where a gate blocked his entrance. He expected things done for him immediately. He registered impatience by pushing on the horn. He honked and honked until the garage attendant, a black man named Charles Battle, emerged from the recesses of the garage. While swinging the gate open Battle grumbled a few curses of irritation. Reles jumped out and, after a tussle, fractured Battle's skull with a whiskey bottle.

That night an intruder entered the garage and stabbed the attendant, Alvyn Sydnor, to death in the darkness. Police suspected Reles had returned to the garage for Battle, but killed Sydnor by mistake. Both attendants were black, and about the same age.

After the attack Reles called Rosie, then nine months pregnant with their first child, to say that he would hide for a while at Louis Capone's house. He wouldn't say why, only that it involved an incident in a garage. About two weeks later, during a drunken card game, Reles went to an upstairs bedroom and shimmied down a bedsheet that he tied to a radiator. He slipped away into the dark Brownsville streets, leaving Capone waiting downstairs with a handful of cards.

A few minutes later Reles banged on the door of the house Reles and Rosie shared with her parents. Rosie said: "My mother came out and asked him in Jewish, 'What are you doing here?' He didn't answer and I jumped up out of bed and I said, 'What's the matter? What brings you here?' He was in a white undershirt and pants. He smiled at me but he didn't answer, and he looked so foggy and he smelled from liquor. He just looked and mumbled, 'I thought you had the baby.' . . . He just sat in the kitchen and just stared and he put his head on the kitchen table and nobody slept anymore."

Reles did not elude the police for long. At Reles's arraignment for the Sydnor murder, Magistrate Judge Thomas F. Casey, a heavy-jowled man with hair parted down the middle, eyed his record of thirty-two arrests. He joked that patrolmen seemed to enjoy bringing Reles in. "The only way I can escape arrest," Reles said, "is to join the Foreign Legion, I suppose."

"Remember, it will be Friday the thirteenth," Judge Casey said, referring to Reles's hearing. "Looks like an unlucky day."

"Thirteen is my lucky number," Reles said.

As it turned out, he was lucky. Prosecutors had established a motive, but they lacked the corroboration required to bring a case: nobody saw Reles stab Sydnor. "Abe Reles is Public Enemy Number One," Judge George Martin said, in discharging Reles. "He is one of the most vicious characters we have in Brooklyn. He has been arrested thirty-two times, but has borne a charmed life. However, if he does not stop now, I am certain that his career will be ended by prison sentence for life, or some detective will put a bullet in him."

Reles leaned over from the defense table and spoke to Assistant District Attorney William Kleinman, who then rose to address the judge. "Your honor, the defendant has just told me to tell you that he would take a chance with any cop with a pistol or anything else."

Judge Martin said: "There are eighteen thousand policemen in our department, and I am certain that 17,999 would at any time take Reles into a locked room without weapons of any kind, and I will bet Reles would come out in sections. He could stab anybody in the back with his gang by his side to protect him, but would never take part in a stand up hand-to-hand fight. He hasn't that kind of courage, he's just a coward."

Prosecutors could not bring Reles to trial for killing Sydnor, but they did try him for assaulting Battle. During jury selection Judge Martin received a tip that a gunman planned to enter the courtroom and shoot Reles. He banged his gavel and asked spectators to file out to the corridor where bailiffs searched them. No spectators would be admitted for the rest of the proceedings. The trial continued with Reles's swarthy, menacing presence at the defense table.

On May 8 the jury let Reles off easy, convicting him of third-degree assault, a mere misdemeanor. Judge Martin reacted with visible anger. He had expected to sentence Reles to ten years, but the conviction limited him to no more than three. "This man is as bad as [John] Dillinger," Judge Martin told the jury. "He is probably the worst character in Greater New York and I'm sorry you let him get through your fingers."

Reles told his mother that he was going on an extended business trip. In reality he walked through the steel gates of the Welfare Island Penitentiary, a long, low prison with a crenellated castle-like roofline standing on a thin two-mile strip of island in the East River. (Welfare Island was later renamed Roosevelt Island.) Inmates were close enough to see the windows of the fashionable apartments of Sutton Place in Manhattan, and boats of every description passing upstream and down—all close but maddeningly beyond reach.

The penitentiary was once called Damnation Island. Reles found much of its wretchedness still intact. Inmates worked on chain gangs. The sick languished untreated in cold cells, some near death. Addicts shots themselves up with heroin from syringes acquired on the prison's prodigious black market. Troublemakers went to the cooler, a cell with no light or toilet. If that failed to subdue them, guards blasted them with high-powered hoses. A month after Reles arrived, eight hundred inmates protested the miserly, half-rotten meals by staging a food strike. They banged iron spoons and tin plates against iron tabletops.

Reles faced no such hardship. The Commission made sure that he bunked in special quarters, where privileged inmates lived in comfort, apart from the squalor and deprivation of the main wards. They ate meals in a private dining room furnished with fresh vegetables, milk, and cream stored in an icebox.

Mickey Sycoff, who ran Reles's loan-sharking operations, regularly brought him cash to buy liquor and other black-market supplies, and he kept Reles's wife Rosie comfortable and secure. Buggsy Goldstein brought weekly news and relayed Reles's orders back to Murder, Inc.

Reles was like a prime minister in exile, a shadow leader. He maintained a measure of control from afar, but his authority was inevitably challenged. Spider Murtha, a tall, hook-nosed former featherweight boxer, had cultivated a reputation as one of Brooklyn's toughest for his rough manner of extorting money from whorehouses and speakeasies. He boasted that he was a "cop beater." Instead of guns he favored close-quarters fighting with broken bottles and razors, striking and parrying with nimble boxer footwork.

Murtha bragged in saloons and pool halls of his intention to usurp Reles's operations. It was an act of foolhardy defiance given that Reles had the backing of Buchalter and Anastasia.

In the early hours of March 3, 1935, Reles's troopers Dasher Abbandando, and Max "The Jerk" Golub followed Murtha and his dark-eyed girlfriend, a twenty-three-year-old widow named Flo Nestfield, to the Palace Hotel in Brooklyn after a night out. The two men waited on the street until the couple left the hotel at 10:30 a.m. the next morning and followed them a block down Atlantic Avenue. They walked up behind, shoved Nestfield to the side, and shot Murtha five times—twice in the head, three times in the chest. Patrolmen found Murtha slumped on his side, as if sleeping, beside a girder supporting the elevated subway. His head rested in a puddle of penny-colored blood roughly the dimensions of a bathroom rug. His fedora lay slightly askew, almost undisturbed by his fall. A bullet had abraded the back of one hand as he threw his arm up in defense.

Nestfield, who stood feet from her boyfriend when he fell, haughtily denied seeing anything. She didn't recognize the shooters, she said, and could not imagine their motive.

The police did, however, locate a witness, a policeman's widow named Minnie Jones who happened to drive by the crime scene. In her statement she described a rare moment when the layers of bluster and boasting parted, and she glimpsed an unguarded emotion in one of the two shooters. "His whole body was shaking but still holding the smoking gun," she told the police, "and his face had a look of complete terror on it, as if he were scared to death of what he had done."

Even with Reles confined, the killings continued. Murder, Inc. was fulfilling its mandate to safeguard mobsters by eliminating all those who could testify against them. The mob was policing its own by devouring its own.

On December 3, 1935, detectives arrested Buggsy Goldstein and Pittsburgh Phil Strauss for the September 30 murder of rival gangsters Joseph Amberg and Morris Kessler. The victims were lined up against a wall in a Blake Avenue garage and perforated with bullets. Witnesses said they saw Goldstein and Strauss run from the garage. As the two men were led into a police lineup, a procedure that allowed patrolmen and detectives to study the suspects' appearance, Goldstein leaned over to speak with a police captain. "The papers list me as Public Enemy No. 6," he said. "That's a lousy rating. I've worked hard and I hope to get a better rating than that." Goldstein and Strauss were released for lack of evidence.

In the summer of 1936 district attorneys closed in on Joseph "Socks" Lanza, a 250-pound bulldog-faced Sicilian who controlled the Fulton Fish Market in lower Manhattan with the usual racketeering bully tactics—roughing up buyers, sabotaging trucks, throwing sulfuric acid in dealers' faces. Lanza's real name was Joseph, but mafiosi called him Socks because he threw a quick punch. Lanza knew that he faced certain conviction if any of his close associates talked.

The pool of potential talkers included Sol Goldstein, one of Evelyn Mittleman's former boyfriends. His face was scarred from the beating Pittsburg Phil Strauss had delivered with a pool cue. Goldstein had acquired an exhaustive knowledge of Lanza's dirty tricks during his years at the Fulton Fish Market. But that was behind him now. Goldstein was newly married to the pretty red-haired daughter of a successful car salesman. He intended to lead a conventional, honest life. He hoped to be among the few to escape gangdom. "Sol is away from the tough boys at last," his mother told his sister.

On a humid August evening Goldstein was dressing for a night out with his wife during their honeymoon in the Catskills, a mountainous upstate resort area popular among middle-class Jews. Goldstein was knotting his silk tie when the phone rang in his honeymoon bungalow. He answered and exchanged a few words. He told his wife Helen that he had to conduct a little business before dinner. A car pulled into the driveway. "I'll be back in a few minutes," he told Helen. He took a seat in the back between the Murder, Inc. foot soldiers Anthony "Dukey" Maffetore and Abraham "Pretty" Levine, an ominous arrangement. As the car headed down Glen Wild Road, Maffetore squeezed Goldstein's neck in his biceps while Levine knocked Goldstein out with a single blow of a hammer. They could easily have killed Goldstein, but Strauss had ordered them to deliver Goldstein to him at Loch Sheldrake, a Catskill hotel favored by gangsters. "Just snatch the bum and bring him here," he said. "Don't knock him off." Later that night Strauss bound Goldstein's inert body with rocks and rowed it to the middle of Lake Sheldrake, the deepest lake in the region and a favorite summer spot for swimming and canoeing. Strauss heaved the body overboard and rowed to shore alone. In keeping with the Murder, Inc. mandate, Strauss killed Goldstein to prevent him from talking to prosecutors about Socks Lanza's rackets. Jealousy was not supposed to motivate Murder, Inc. but in this case it did. With Goldstein's death, Evelyn Mittleman's three previous boyfriends had all died.

The details of Goldstein's death would not be known until 1940. "For four long years, mystery and silence surrounded the disappearance of the son who had made his mother so happy when he stopped running with the tough boys, and took up with a 'nice girl,'" a prosecutor wrote when Goldstein's death was finally resolved.

Two months after Goldstein's body sank into the murk of Lake Sheldrake, Reles walked out of Rikers Island, a new jail where he served the last eight months of his sentence. The Commission gave him $1,600 in cash, a reward for toughing out his months of incarceration with his mouth shut. He had resisted the temptation to shorten his sentence by telling district attorneys the details of specific murders and murderers. Reles, the good soldier, returned to Brooklyn as a gangland stalwart and resumed his role as field general for Murder, Inc.

Ten days later, on the night of October 26, detectives found Reles in a parked car on Livonia Avenue. Chief Sweeney had ordered them to bring in anyone with an arrest record and no legitimate income on a vagrancy charge, a directive specifically designed to harass and detain Reles. It was his thirty-third arrest since 1920. At the bail hearing Reles peeled two hundred-dollar bills from a fat roll and walked free. He slipped back into his old seat in the back booth at Midnight Rose's as if nothing had happened.

With Reles back from prison, Murder, Inc. continued to extend its authority across the country. In the summer of 1937, the Detroit chapter of the Commission, known as the Purple Gang, condemned its former associate Harry Millman, a handsome, hard-drinking labor racketeer. Millman, who was Jewish, could not control his hatred for the city's Italian operatives. He went rogue, shaking down mafia brothels and provoking Italian racketeers into fistfights in cafés and restaurants.

"I happened to be in a club one night when [Joseph] Bommarito [an Italian mobster] and some other Italians were there," a witness recalled. "Millman walks over to Bommarito's table and says 'Something stinks here real bad, like a polecat.' Bommarito jumps up, grabs Millman, and they have a go at each other. They tore the place up and both of them were a mess. They took Bommarito to the hospital. Millman's clothes were torn and he was covered in blood. But he cleaned himself up and stayed for a drink."

In August, Purple Gang agents tried to rid themselves of the Millman problem by placing ten sticks of dynamite under the hood of his three-month-old LaSalle coupe while he was drinking and dancing inside the Club Ten Forty, a downtown cabaret, with an attractive woman named Hattie Fleisher, wife of Purple Gang lieutenant Harry Fleisher, who was serving time in Alcatraz for tax evasion. The assassins rigged the explosives so that a spark plug would ignite the dynamite when Millman turned the ignition. They had not anticipated that Millman would valet park. Willie Holmes, a black doorman, fetched the car from a nearby parking lot a few minutes after 3 a.m. The blast nearly severed his legs. It flung his torso partly through the rear window. The car hood spun high like a Frisbee, landing on the roof of a five-story building. Engine parts pockmarked the walls. The shock wave blew out nearby windows.

The next afternoon Millman arranged through a third party to meet two homicide detectives on a street corner, then accompanied them to Detroit police headquarters. Millman sat in the homicide office nervously twisting and tearing up scraps of paper as he answered questions. Detectives were trying to determine if Harry Fleisher's friends had planted the bomb to punish Millman for pursuing Hattie while her husband languished in jail. Millman claimed to be perplexed by the attack.

"I can't understand this," he told an assistant district attorney. "I haven't any enemies left over from the old days and I'm not doing anything now that would make anybody want to get me. If they wanted me they could find me easily enough."

Millman told the truth about one thing: he would not be hard to find. All September and October he walked the downtown Detroit streets unguarded and, by his account, weaponless. At night he roistered in the predictable bars and nightclubs. It was so widely assumed that Millman would be killed that many hotels and restaurants turned him away for fear that he might die on their premises. "His number is up and it's only a question of time," said a Detroit detective. "He has kept himself on the street with his gun and his fists. He is going to die one of these days and die violently."

However susceptible Millman might seem, the Purple Gang delegated the job to Murder, Inc. On Reles's orders, Pittsburgh Phil Strauss and Happy Maione went to the train station with suitcases packed neatly with pistols and a change of clothes. On the night of November 24, Millman was sitting at a crowded cocktail bar in a corner kosher delicatessen in a nice neighborhood when Strauss and Maione entered and shot him nine times. They walked off down a dark street, leaving behind a single clue: a green felt hat. Nobody was ever charged.

On the evening of July 8, 1939, twelve hundred sturdy men with broad shoulders and rough hands, all of them longshoremen, converged on a Brooklyn union hall for a meeting. They had sweated through an uncomfortably hot Saturday. Dusk offered only a modest respite as the men of the International Longshoremen's Association local 929 packed a sticky, sweaty auditorium.

The gathering was the latest in a series of urgent meetings held over the summer to discuss the union's future. Each gathering drew bigger, rowdier, foot-stomping crowds as an insurrection gathered force in the grimy cobbled streets of Brooklyn Heights and Red Hook, where rows of piers extended like fingers into New York harbor. The men had come in swelling numbers to hear one of their own, a lean, handsome twenty-eight-year-old named Peter Panto speak out against waterfront corruption and the suffocating mob tax that every dockworker paid.

At 5 a.m. each morning an army of overall-clad men who spoke no English walked down to the piers carrying rusty iron bailing hooks on belts, the dockworker's basic tool. They smoked the day's first cigarettes and warmed their hands by trash can fires while waiting for the ritual known as "the shape-up," a hiring process brought with them from the Sicilian countryside. At dawn they formed ragged semicircles around

each pier's hiring boss. No man could work unless he agreed to conditions dictated by Albert Anastasia. First, they had to pay the hiring boss
as much as 10 percent of their wage. They had to accept "gang-cutting,"
which meant that fifteen men would do the work of twenty. The extra pay
went to the hiring boss and up the chain of command. They had to pay
three dollars a month to have their hair cut at a barbershop designated by
the union, even those men who were entirely bald. In the fall they bought
grapes at marked-up prices from an appointed dealer, whether they intended to make homemade wine or not. And they bought tickets to
the City Democratic Club's Columbus Day Ball held at the St. George
Hotel in Brooklyn Heights on the understanding that they would not
attend.

Panto, who had worked his way up to hiring boss despite his oppo-
sition to the mob tax, now threatened to depose Albert Anastasia and
the other mob lords who suppressed and robbed the workers, most of
them immigrants who struggled to feed their families in a daily state
of anxiety. They had no fallback: jobs for immigrants were scarce in
Depression-era New York. If they ran out of money they were forced
to borrow from mob shylocks who charged 10 to 20 percent interest a
week. "The idea," an investigator later said, "is to keep the men poor.
Then they can be controlled more easily, controlled through fear—fear
of not working, fear of being unable to pay the shylocks."

Panto stood before his rough congregation that evening with his
fedora pushed back on his head. He had soft brown eyes and a fetching
gap-toothed smile. He was small for a dockworker—just five foot nine
and 163 pounds—but he commanded the room. *Fratelli,* he said by way
of greeting. Brothers. Speaking to the longshoremen in their native Italian, he called for an open and honest election to oust the mob proxies
running the union, and an end to the kickbacks that drained worker
pay. *Siamo forti,* he said. We are strong. "All we have to do," he added,
"is stand up and fight." The men got to their feet and roared their assent,
long and hard. Anastasia's infiltrators stood among them, listening and
observing. (The throng also included twenty-four-year-old playwright
Arthur Miller, a recent college graduate living nearby. He would base a
play called *The Bottom of the River* on Panto. It would not be produced
for seventy-six years.)

New York was by far America's biggest port; half the goods that
entered or left the country flowed through its docks. If Panto's South

Brooklyn rebellion, informed by his communist sympathies, spread to the city's nine hundred piers, the mob would lose critical income. And if the uprising took hold among the other unions under its control the mob would suffer more severe losses.

So it surprised nobody when Albert Anastasia hit back. Almost every day his schlammers roughed up men standing on Brooklyn street corners passing out copies of "Shape Up," the mimeographed newsletter published by Panto supporters. In early July union head Emil Camarda summoned Panto to his President Street office to warn him that the "the boys" disapproved of his speeches. Camarda spoke in code, but the threat was clear: Anastasia would not tolerate resistance. Panto ignored him.

The summer sun hung over the Manhattan skyline on the far side of the East River when Panto left work at the Moore-McCormack pier, just south of the Gowanus Canal, at 5 p.m. on the afternoon of July 14, 1939. He headed to his boardinghouse on North Elliott Place, near the Navy Yard, where he loitered with his fiancée, dark-haired twenty-year-old Alice Maffia, and her younger brother, Mike. She was a sweet, unassuming girl who worked in a factory fabricating moth-proof bags. Panto and Alice were to marry two months later. They talked about going to the beach the next day.

At 10 p.m. two men knocked. Panto stepped outside for a word. He came back to kiss Alice goodbye. "I'm going to meet a couple of guys I don't trust," he said. He promised to return within an hour to help make sandwiches for their Saturday beach trip. If he failed to return by 10 a.m. the next morning, he said, Alice should call the police.

He was never seen again.

Dové Panto? Dové Panto? Where is Panto? In the days after his disappearance the words appeared scrawled in chalk on the stone side of the Montague Street ramp leading down to the docks. They appeared in paint on warehouse walls, loading trucks, and inside ship holds. Anastasia's men wiped them away, but they always came back. *Dové Panto? Dové Panto? Dové Panto?* The question spread outward from the docks to tiled subway walls and office buildings. They appeared on leaflets scattered and blowing along the dockside streets—Columbia, Sackett, President, Van Brunt, Court. *Dové Panto? Dové Panto? Dové Panto?* The question was repeated like an urgent incantation—like a demand, a plea, a cry.

The Brooklyn stoop-sitters assumed the worst. Panto lay crumpled lifeless in the basement of an abandoned building, perhaps, or he drifted along the muddy harbor bottom.

Abe Reles knew where Panto lay. Just as he knew the resting place of Sol Goldstein. But he didn't care to discuss it. Not yet, anyway.

A few days after Panto disappeared, a car pulled up on a waterfront street beside a group of longshoremen who supported Panto's campaign. Dukey Maffetore leaned out the car window and drew his hand across his throat. He smiled as he made the cut-your-throat death signal and said, *"Benedetto,"* a friendly Italian greeting. Sugarcoating threats with niceties was part of the mob's etiquette.

On August 16 Alice Maffia wrote the editors of *The Brooklyn Daily Eagle* a letter appealing for help. A month had passed since she kissed him good-bye, and she clung to a last filament of hope before accepting the worst. "I am a poor girl," she wrote. "I don't know how to go about doing the things that will find Pete. Tell the police you know about Pete and that his girl is pleading for your help. . . . Please, I beg you to do everything you can."

Murder, Inc. managed to quell the waterfront uprising, at least temporarily, by removing its charismatic leader. Now Reles took other measures to protect Anastasia's hold on the docks. In early September Reles ran into Pittsburgh Phil Strauss at a late-night craps game held behind a wall in a vacant lot. Strauss had eaten dinner with Anastasia earlier that night. They had discussed the need to eliminate a sad-sack minor bookie named Irving "Puggy" Feinstein, who had incurred deep debts at the racetrack. In his desperation to pay off his arrears, Feinstein encroached on gambling operations run by the venerable Mangano crime family, Anastasia's allies in the waterfront rackets. Anastasia could easily have sent one of his own men to kill Feinstein, but the murder would be harder to trace back to him if assigned it to Murder, Inc. Now Reles and Pittsburgh Phil had to find Feinstein. Even as veterans of the interconnected, incestuous circles of Brooklyn gangsters, they had never met Feinstein—until he ran into them by chance.

At about 8 p.m. on Labor Day night, September 4, Reles, Pittsburgh Phil Strauss, and Buggsy Goldstein were standing on the Corner, the gathering spot outside Midnight Rose's, when a man walked up Livonia Avenue. They noticed that his nose was flattened, the by-product of a wretchedly failed boxing career. The stranger walked over to them in an oddly familiar way to announce that he was looking for Louis "Tiny" Benson, a 420-pound money collector for loan sharks. He owed Benson fifty dollars, he said.

Haven't seen Tiny, they said.

If you do see him, the man said, mention that Puggy from Borough Park came by. As the man walked off down Livonia Avenue Strauss nudged Reles. That's him, he said. That's Puggy Feinstein.

Minutes later Goldstein picked Feinstein up in a maroon sedan driven by Dukey Maffetore and said he would help him find Tiny. They drove around talking about baseball and horse racing while pretending to look for Tiny. Then Maffetore drove them to Reles's house on East Ninety-first Street with the false notion that Tiny might be there.

Meanwhile, Reles and Strauss had gone to Reles's home to prepare. Reles sent his wife, Rosie, and Goldstein's wife, Betty, to see a movie, and he woke his mother-in-law, Rose Kirsch, who was sleeping in the next room, to ask where she kept the ice pick (the pantry) and the clothesline they used at the rented lake house (a suitcase in the basement).

Reles and Strauss drank milk while they waited. Strauss positioned himself in a chair beside the front door so that Feinstein would not see him when he entered. Reles sat facing the door to command Feinstein's attention. They turned the radio on to disguise the sound of the tussle. When Feinstein walked in, accompanied by Goldstein and Maffetore, Strauss jumped from his chair and choked Feinstein's neck between forearm and chest. "This guy Puggy kept on fighting and kicking," Reles later said, "so I turned the radio on louder and got the rope." Strauss threw Feinstein to the floor, where Goldstein bound his neck to his legs in his signature method so that the noose gradually tightened around Feinstein's neck as he kicked and struggled. Reles slid newspaper under Feinstein's head so that the blood trickling from the corner of his mouth would not stain the living room rug. "I was going to move out of there anyhow," Reles later said.

When the death throes ended and the body lay still, Reles and Strauss carried it out a side door and heaved it into the trunk of Maffetore's car and drove to an empty lot in a remote stretch near Sheepshead Bay. Reles ordered the body burned to eliminate fingerprints and other means of identification. Goldstein and Maffetore stopped at a gas station on Eastern Parkway to pick up a two-gallon can of gas. They told the attendant that they had run out of gas a mile away.

Buggsy poured the gasoline and applied a match. As their sedan drove off, a neighbor, alarmed by the blaze, went to investigate. He poured a bucket of water on the fire. Through the smoke he could make out a charred head. He managed to extinguish the rest of the flames, revealing the scorched remains of Puggy Feinstein lying in a fetal position, still bound head to foot. The clothing was burned off his body, except for his shoes and socks. His skin was the color of charcoal. His wristwatch had stopped at 12:15.

The Murder, Inc. men had worked up an appetite. They headed to Joe's, a Sheepshead Bay seafood restaurant and ordered shore dinners. On the drive over, Strauss and Goldstein squabbled over their respective failings. "Strauss told Buggsy that he was useless because he couldn't handle rope," Reles later said, "and Goldstein told Strauss that he couldn't even mug a guy right." When the clams and lobster landed on the table, they put quarrels aside and ate and drank like deserving men who had done a decent day's work.

PART TWO

THE DOWNFALL

5

TWENTY AGAINST THE UNDERWORLD

On the late afternoon of February 16, 1934, Fiorello La Guardia, the fiery new mayor of New York City, strode with intent up the steps of a police station on West 100th Street wearing a black felt hat and black overcoat. He "threw open the door," wrote *The New York Times*, "and strode angrily inside."

La Guardia, egg-shaped and red-faced, was in a perpetual rush to clean up the corrupt, crime-weary city he had inherited six weeks earlier from Mayor John P. O'Brien, a Tammany Hall instrument. "The flaming torch of reform, held aloft in the grip of Fiorello La Guardia, threw its cleansing light over the sin-drenched metropolis," wrote Paul Sann, a veteran reporter for the *New York Post*.

La Guardia's motto, invoked in nearly every speech, was "patience and fortitude." He showed a lot more fortitude than patience in these early days as mayor.

From the moment he took the oath of office, wearing a tuxedo in City Hall, La Guardia moved seemingly without stop. He looked like Humpty Dumpty with his jiggling double chin and his tubby belly bulging through baggy double-breasted suits, but he nonetheless possessed a restless, pugnacious energy to tackle the next problem . . . and the next . . . and the next. He was a firebrand, a fighter. Opponents tarred him as a communist, but in truth he disavowed party ideologies—right or left. La Guardia was an independent force for reform prepared to take on all comers. He had driven Tammany from City Hall and pushed it to the margins of city politics. Now he would take on the Commission, starting with their slot machines.

Of all the mob's offenses in the years after Prohibition, slot machines were the most pervasive and profitable. If La Guardia could end the slots, he figured, he could end the killing, or at least diminish it. He told reporters who accompanied him uptown that day that slots were "mechanical pickpockets," a small-scale vice, but so seductive that twenty-five thousand had taken up residence in New York grocery stores, bars, and restaurants, whether the proprietors wanted them or not. They were commonplace, but not harmless—at least not to Mayor La Guardia. He warned that slots served as a gateway vice for city kids. Hordes would become habituated to gambling, resorting to theft in order finance their addiction. As the son of Italian immigrants, La Guardia was also uncomfortably aware that slot machines fed the public perception of Italians as gamblers and criminals.

No politician had a keener sense of public symbolism than La Guardia. He recognized that slot machines were not the gravest threat the mob presented, but they were the most ubiquitous. Their presence in every corner bodega and candy store broadcast that Reles and his confederates, not the police, ruled the city.

His anti-slot campaign began with the trip to West 100th Street. "As you were," he told the policemen who jumped to their feet inside the police station.

"He threw aside his black felt hat and black overcoat with determined gestures," the *Times* wrote. "His unruly black hair tumbling down over his forehead and his black eyes flashing fire, he crossed the room quickly and seated himself behind the big oaken desk where the lieutenant usually presides."

The on-duty officers stood side by side against a wall looking like chagrined schoolboys. They knew the mayor had come to their station house to address their failures—publicly and with the fanfare he was known for.

La Guardia had called into use an obscure provision of the city charter that allowed him to temporarily serve as a magistrate judge. He sat in a makeshift court in the station house, a high-ceilinged room with yellow-painted walls, in order to confront a woman arrested earlier in the day for possessing a slot machine in the candy store and luncheonette she operated with her husband eleven blocks away, at Amsterdam

Avenue and 111th Street. The wife was a tiny, frightened, pregnant woman named Anna Jurovaty. She was too timid to say a word when La Guardia asked if she wanted a lawyer. Her husband, Ludwig, explained that a man who identified himself only as Mr. Cohen had installed the slot machine against their will, saying "that everything will be all right."

La Guardia asked a police lieutenant if he had gone to the 116th Street address associated with the phone number printed on the slot machine.

"No, sir," the lieutenant said.

"Don't you think you should have gone there?" the mayor asked.

"Well, you can't find Mr. Cohen there," the lieutenant said with a knowing smile.

"Well, see who you do find there," the mayor said, his squeaky high-pitched voice now rising in anger. "Place an officer there until you find somebody."

La Guardia released Jurovaty on five dollars bail, the smallest sum permissible under the law, but scolded the police standing by for not pursuing the gangsters who owned the machine and installed it in her store. "Get busy and arrest these racketeers," he told them. A sidewalk crowd cheered the mayor as he walked down the station house steps and into a waiting car. Then he sped off to confront the next iniquity.

Eleven months later, in January 1935, Mayor La Guardia stood hatless on a city barge floating in Long Island Sound, fifty miles east of Manhattan, just off Eaton's Neck, a location chosen for its depth. A few loose strands of his slicked-down hair fluttered in the wind. With an amused glance at a newsreel camera, he lifted a sledgehammer and swung it down hard on a few of the 1,155 confiscated slot machines piled around him on the barge. He then helped policemen heave the first of the machines into 108 feet of cold water.

Dumping slot machines overboard was the kind of flamboyant gesture La Guardia relished. He shrewdly used the press to publicize the city's newly declared war against the Commission and its kind. In his colorful manner, the mayor made known that the rule of law would prevail and the forces of mayhem and violence unleashed by Prohibition would abate.

Most New Yorkers were not so sure that the city would prevail. Newspaper editorials suggested in their shrill way that municipal officials were overmatched. A murderous spirit was loose in the streets. La Guardia might never restrain it.

During the cash-fat years of Prohibition, gangsters amassed so much easy money that they routinely paid off patrolmen, police captains, judges, and so on up the municipal ranks. To make known the extent of the corruption, Mayor La Guardia released a report showing that 91 percent of gambling arrests recorded over an eight-month period never came to trial. Of the 9 percent that reached court, a third resulted in fines of less than fifty dollars. In New York the Commission's personnel, high and low, could run card games and craps without consequence.

This disclosure and others shamed the Manhattan district attorney, William C. Dodge, a mousy-looking Tammany designate with spectacles and a weak hairline, into impanelling a grand jury to investigate gambling and racketeering. Dodge spoke assuredly of indictments and convictions, but as he held forth, the jury foreman, a prominent real-estate broker named Lee Thompson Smith, and his fellow jurors began to suspect, and then conclude, that Dodge never intended to produce more than a few minor indictments for appearance's sake. The proceedings were a sham.

Led by Smith, the grand jury loudly declared its intention to mutiny, to jettison Dodge as so much deadweight, and carry on without him. The district attorney, Smith said, was "useless."

Smith must have known that resistance could risk his life. Murder, Inc. had shown that it would go to any length to protect its associates. Sure enough, he and another juror received threatening postcards at their homes. "Thanks to the papers for publishing your name and address," the postcards read. "It will be in the interest of your physical and mental welfare and that of your family to vote the right way on indictments."

Smith persevered, nonetheless. On May 9 he and his fellow jurors locked Dodge and his assistants out of their chambers. They continued for two months without them, calling witnesses on their own. The press called them "the runaway jury."

Operating in place of the prosecutors, the runaway jury began to make connections between organized crime and politics. "We have heard rumors," Smith told General Sessions Judge Morris Koenig, "which lead us to believe that several politicians are [corrupt], and one in particular."

Smith was referring to James Hines, a hard-bitten Tammany district leader and District Attorney Dodge's primary political backer. Hines mostly operated in Harlem, where he worked in concert with the Jewish mobster Arthur Flagenheimer, who went by the name Dutch Schultz.

Since the first days of Prohibition, gang leaders, Jewish and Italian, routinely paid bribes—or "contributions"—to Tammany Hall to ensure that the district attorneys under Tammany's sway stayed out of their way. In keeping with that practice, Schultz pressured Hines to make sure that District Attorney Dodge defanged the grand jury. In other words, Schultz leaned on Hines, his Tammany contact, and Hines leaned on Dodge, his handpicked district attorney. By this chain of influence the Commission called the shots, even in the grand jury room.

On June 10, 1935, the runaway jury disbanded, calling on New York Governor Herbert Lehman, a round-faced scion of the Lehman Brothers banking family, to start afresh by appointing a special prosecutor—a man immaculately removed from the city's dirty influence machine, if such a man could be found.

"It has become evident to us," Foreman Smith said, "that the uncovering of organized crime is not a mere police routine, but a major undertaking, requiring a prosecutor of unusual vigor and ability, free to devote his entire energies and skill to combating the apparently well-organized and richly financed criminal forces."

Twelve days later Lehman came down from Albany to consider the appointment, as Smith urged. He conferred with Mayor La Guardia and Police Commissioner Valentine and studied the grand jury minutes.

Lehman was a reform Democrat. To avoid the appearance of corruption or cover-up, he appointed a respected old Republican jurist, Supreme Court Justice Philip McCook, to preside over a twenty-three-person grand jury, and he recruited four distinguished Republicans as candidates for special prosecutor. Lehman invited them, one by one, to his Park Avenue apartment in hopes of persuading each to accept the assignment. All four declined. Instead, they unanimously and publicly recommended thirty-four-year-old Thomas Dewey, a straight-arrow Republican lawyer and former federal prosecutor who would later become governor of New York and twice a failed presidential candidate.

Lehman considered Dewey too young, but he eventually acceded. He announced Dewey's appointment on the afternoon of June 29, 1935.

He was so rushed that he told the press about it before finalizing the arrangement with Dewey, who was in Boston that day giving his cousin Elizabeth away at her wedding. "The news of Lehman's announcement did not reach me," Dewey later wrote, "until I bought a newspaper when my train reached New York City that evening." When Governor Lehman called the next morning, Dewey accepted the post on the condition that he have a free hand and cooperation from every city agency.

Dewey was earning $50,000 as a Wall Street lawyer. He would now take a pay cut of $33,000 on the presumption that prosecuting the Commission would pay off in a more valuable currency: political capital. His parents had raised him with the impossibly precocious expectation that he would rise to the presidency, or at least the Senate. Here was his chance to take an important step toward that objective. There could be no better way to earn national eminence than as the special prosecutor who busted the mob. "If he makes good," a political columnist wrote, "the road ahead of him is the road to the heights."

The assignment offered career-making rewards, to be sure, but could as likely lead to humiliating public failure. The underworld had reached like a parasite into hundreds of professions and pastimes of everyday American life. Its various corruptions were so entrenched that prosecutors might never weed it out. "The Young David," one newspaper wrote in a headline, "Is Sent In Against the Gang Goliath."

Abe Reles presented a particular obstacle. To prosecute the mob, Dewey would have to convince insiders and outsiders and those on the margins to inform and testify in spite of the history Murder, Inc. already had of intimidating or killing anyone who might talk. The battle for the hearts and minds of witnesses amounted to a personal power struggle between Dewey and Reles.

With his wide, handsome Midwestern face and well-tended dark mustache, Dewey could be mistaken for a young Ernest Hemingway, though he had none of the author's brash charisma. On the contrary, Dewey was stiff to the point of paralysis, even with family and friends. An aide remembered him as "cold, cold as a February icicle." Alice Roosevelt Longworth, Teddy Roosevelt's daughter, said Dewey was as rigid as the "little man on a wedding cake." Nobody ever questioned his honesty, though, nor his effectiveness.

Worldly Easterners like Mrs. Longworth might call Dewey rigid, but townsfolk in solidly middle-class Owosso, Michigan, population eight thousand, felt sure that their young prodigy was born for greatness. In 1902 his father, a staunchly conservative publisher and editor of *The Owosso Times*, announced his only child's birth by printing a notice that a "10-pound Republican voter was born last evening to Mr. and Mrs. George M. Dewey."

From the beginning, Dewey was Owosso's boy wonder. He went to school for twelve straight years without logging a single absence or tardiness, as his mother proudly told reporters. In the evenings, after choir practice, he sat in the parlor of the family's comfortable Victorian home on Oliver Street and listened to his father read *Congressional Quarterly* aloud. He was that kind of kid.

Whatever greatness young Thomas achieved would doubtless occur under the auspices of the Republican Party. Like most of his Owosso neighbors, Dewey's puritan New England ancestors transplanted their right-thinking values to the upper Midwest. Their brand of high-minded conservatism looked with suspicion on Tammany Hall as the symbol of East Coast big-city corruption and vice cooked up by unwholesome immigrants. Thomas was groomed to be a voice of moral indignation from the heartland, to demand the restoration of decency and order.

Young Dewey would make this his mission. He conducted himself with a determination that felt like a form of ruthlessness. He joined the other sharp-witted Owosso boys at the University of Michigan, where he sang basso cantante in a church quartet and glee club, and entered Columbia Law School at age twenty-one. "To tackle the big city he was equipped with a musical scholarship, a fine baritone voice, and a tenor's ego," wrote Hickman Powell of the *New York Post*.

Dewey became a chief assistant U.S. attorney in 1931. When his boss resigned in November 1933, Dewey became, at the impossibly precocious age of thirty-one, the youngest United States Attorney in the history of the Southern District of New York by fifteen years. He was only eight years out of law school. Tabloids called him the "baby prosecutor." In courtrooms he looked like the wholesome student-council president wearing a mustache for a school play.

The same qualities that would later make Dewey a clumsy candidate— a prim rectitude and bloodless efficiency—made him a lethal prosecutor. In November 1933, as an assistant district attorney, he earned notice by convicting Waxey Gordon, a heavyset former pickpocket and Arnold

Rothstein protegé who earned millions as a bootlegging baron, for tax evasion and, in quick succession, indicted the even more notorious Dutch Schultz, another Rothstein protegé, for the same offense.

Dewey prosecuted Gordon with machine-like thoroughness, calling one hundred fifty witnesses. In his summation Dewey presented Gordon as the first conquest in a larger, grander crusade to extinguish corruption and restore a sense of law and order to America. He told a reporter that "the heart of this nation is the rural small town." The subtext was clear: a Galahad from the heartland, the proud and pure son of Episcopalian ancestors who landed in Massachusetts in 1634, would return a wayward city to order, a city led astray by immigrants spreading crime and chaos like a contagion brought from Europe.

"As you retire to your room, gentlemen," he told the jury in his full-throated baritone, "I ask you to bear in mind that the people of this country look to you twelve men as to the course of justice in this country. Are we to have justice in the courts? Is justice to be effective in this country in the courts, or is it not?"

The jury reached a guilty verdict within fifty-one minutes. Moments later the judge sentenced Gordon to ten years. (His nineteen-year-old son Theodore, a medical student, died in a dawn car accident after driving all night from North Carolina to beg the court to reduce his father's sentence. Gordon attended the funeral in chains, weeping and broken, before proceeding to North Eastern Penitentiary in Lewisburg, Pennsylvania.)

The verdict cast Dewey as a rising star, a figure of national promise. "It is my firm conviction," the judge said, "that never in this court nor in any other court has there been such fine work done, either on behalf of the government or on behalf of any private client. . . . The spectacle of such a young leader presenting this complicated case in a manner that could not be surpassed by the most experienced or the most famous trial lawyer, has left with the court a sense of admiration."

Despite his triumph, Dewey resigned weeks after the verdict. Franklin D. Roosevelt would by custom systematically replace Republican district attorneys when he became president in March. Dewey returned to private practice with an office in the Equitable Building a block from Wall Street and a roster of well-paying clients.

Less than two years later, in July 1935, Dewey gave up private practice to resume his crusade as a governor-appointed special prosecutor in a time of crisis. Judge McCook convened a grand jury on July 29. In an address broadcast over three local radio stations a day later, Dewey made clear that he would not target specific crimes, such as gambling or commercial racketeering or prostitution. He would pursue them all, the entire ugly, sprawling landscape of organized crime, as well as the crooked lawyers, judges, and politicians who enabled them. His goal was "to destroy organized crime and racketeering of all kinds."

The radio address was a call to arms and an entreaty. He invited disaffected mob associates and businesses extorted by them to his office for a confidential talk. Not one potential witness came forward. Those inclined to talk kept silent for fear of retaliation. Reles had won this round. "The business people feared the crooks more than they trusted the law," Dewey said. "They felt it safer to pay taxes to the criminals than to invite their revenge."

The gangsters laughed at Dewey, calling him "boy scout."

If it was not abundantly clear before, it was now: Abe Reles stood directly in Dewey's path. The race was on to see if Dewey could squeeze witnesses and informants into saying what they knew, in Dewey's office and in the courtroom, before Reles could ensure that they never spoke again.

Every war needs a war room. Dewey set up his on the fourteenth floor of the Woolworth Building, a Gothic spire a block south of Mayor La Guardia's City Hall office and a short walk from the Supreme Court Building where he would argue before the grand jury.

With the mayor's financial support, Dewey's staff included ten accountants, twenty stenographers, and seventy-five police officers, known as the X-Men, just out of the police academy and therefore unknown to the racketeers and free of corrupting entanglements. A dozen trustworthy detectives came in to direct them. Dewey personally selected twenty young assistant district attorneys. Applications arrived at a rate of a hundred a day. "In less than an hour he raked me fore and aft with questions, held me up to the light, put me under a microscope and turned me inside out," one hireling said of the interview. "He rooted out facts deeply buried in my subconscious mind and put together an inventory of my physical, mental, and spiritual condition and its possible development. Not only did he put it together, he never forgot it."

Dewey housed his assistant district attorneys in a warren of sound-proof offices partitioned by frosted glass walls. He called them "twenty against the underworld."

Dewey understood that witnesses and informants would only come to him if they felt safe. In the Woolworth Building lobby he posted detectives familiar with the underworld players, and he personally designed the fourteenth floor so that informants could come and go securely, without fear of Murder, Inc. surveilling them. "Any man who comes to see us can enter the building lobby through any of four entrances and can ascend by any of half a dozen elevators that serve the fourteenth floor," Dewey said. "He emerges into a public corridor, in use by many other tenants beside ourselves, which will be under constant surveillance by a police officer. There will be no loitering in these corridors and we have boarded up all the passageways. There is also a private means of reaching our offices. We have arranged things so that no one will wait more than five minutes in our reception room." Desks and filing cabinets were sealed at night with impregnable locks, the kind banks used, to prevent theft of evidence. He installed venetian blinds to thwart snooping from neighboring buildings.

In the weeks after Dewey's appointment, he showed himself to be fast and formidable. His team rounded up twenty-two loan sharks and charged them with two hundred fifty-two separate crimes. His detectives raided union offices and garment workplaces, seizing cartons of business records and studying the ledgers line by line. He tapped phones and brought hundreds of witnesses in for questioning. He held many of them in jail as material witnesses and threatened them with indictment unless they talked.

Like all good prosecutors, he built a case from the bottom up. He did not yet grasp the nationwide reach of the Commission and its elaborate, layered structure, but he knew that in the new criminal world the bosses floated above the fray while directing foot soldiers to do the incriminating work. Dewey would start with the foot soldiers and work his way up. To kill a plant, he said, you must pull out the roots.

On April 27, 1935, Dutch Schultz paced the marble halls of the federal courthouse in Syracuse, New York, waiting for the jury to return a verdict on tax evasion charges. Shortly before 3 p.m. he entered a dark-paneled courtroom filled with sunlight and seated himself at the mahogany defense table. He had, as always, a sickly appearance. He wore the ill-fitting thirty-five-dollar suit of a failing salesman and had a face the gray-white color of spackle. "To me he always appeared slightly haggard," an investigator wrote, "as if pressed with the details of his intricate violence-ridden empire."

The molls in Schultz's orbit liked to say that he looked like Bing Crosby, but with a flattened nose. They flattered him. In reality he "had eyes like peeled grapes," a columnist wrote, and "his brown hair looked as if it had been held under a running faucet."

Schultz was perpetually twitchy with anxiety, but especially now. His nervous hands fluttered about as he waited for the jurors to file in after more than twenty-seven hours spent deliberating his fate.

Two years earlier, during Dewey's tenure as a federal prosecutor, he charged Schultz with failing to pay taxes on $2 million of income from selling oceans of adulterated beer cooked up in a secret Bronx brewery, and from an illegal lottery known as the numbers racket he operated in Harlem.

Numbers players bet a penny, dime, or quarter on a combination of three numbers up to 999. Winners received six hundred times their investment: a dime bet could therefore win sixty dollars. An elegant French Caribbean woman named Stephanie St. Clair, known on the streets as Madam Queen, operated Harlem's so-called policy rackets for years, employing hundreds of bookmakers and runners who delivered the money and betting slips to headquarters. The numbers was Harlem's only homegrown business until Schultz and his men intruded. She tried to fight him off by personally entering stores that ran his betting operations. She smashed glass cases, tore up betting slips, and tipped off the police. But Schultz prevailed, as usual, with bullying and strong-arm tactics.

Schultz might prevail over Madam Queen, but federal prosecutors were a different matter. He now faced sixteen years on Alcatraz Island and a $40,000 fine. He shrewdly waited in hiding until Dewey returned to private practice before he surrendered in Albany. His conviction was by no means assured after key witnesses mysteriously disappeared. The stabbed body of one witness was found rope-bound and wrapped in blankets near Troy, New York.

The jury filed into the courtroom at 3 p.m. The giant, ruddy faced foreman rose to report that after twenty-seven hours of deliberation "there are no indications that we will agree." The jury was deadlocked. Schultz whooped when Judge Frederick H. Bryant declared a mistrial. The foreman and his fellow jurors bowed to the court and filed out. Judge Bryant ordered a new trial to be held in Malone, New York, a farming hamlet almost within sight of the Canadian border.

Schultz was an easy man to hate. The entirety of the New York underworld knew him to be a miserly, mean-spirited, petty tyrant seized by episodic rages of psychotic violence, but he ingratiated himself to the modest farming folk of Malone. Schultz, a notorious penny-pincher, took up residence in a Malone hotel and devoted himself to acts of magnanimous local charity, as if to prove that he was nothing like the villain they had read about in newspapers. Through the spring and summer of 1935 he attended church services, played in bingo games, dropped hundred-dollar tips, bought rounds of beer in taverns, donated new uniforms to the local semipro baseball team, gave toys and candy to sick kids, and sent flowers to widows. He walked up Main Street and down Elm greeting the elderly and patting small children on the head. He won the farmers over with kindness and cash. They came to think of Schultz as Robin Hood in a double-breasted suit.

The Malone trial concluded on August 2. Judge Bryant returned from dinner at 8 p.m. that evening and took his place on the bench. "Gentleman, have you agreed upon a verdict?" he asked the jury, which had deliberated for twenty-eight and a half hours.

"We have," replied the foreman. "We find the defendant not guilty."

Judge Bryant sat bolt upright, as if prodded by an electric shock. His judicial reserve gave way to fury. A gray strand of hair fell over one eye. He banged his gavel to quiet the cheers. "Your verdict is such that it shakes the confidence of law-abiding citizens in integrity and truth," he told the jurors, who mostly avoided his gaze. "It will be apparent to all who followed the evidence in this case that you have reached a verdict not on the evidence but on some other reason." With that the judge announced the defendant discharged, wrapped his robe about his tall frame, and disappeared into his chambers.

Schultz himself looked stunned. He had entered the courtroom that day white as a bedsheet. In his agitation he crushed a gray fedora in his hands during the formalities leading up to the verdict. When the jury foreman announced the acquittal, Schultz shot his lawyers a bewildered look, then turned and smiled—a smile of vindication—at newspaper reporters seated in the gallery behind him. A spectator dashed from the courtroom to spread the word. As Schultz walked out with hat in hand a crowd of men and women standing on the courthouse steps and lawn applauded, as if saluting a hometown hero. They cheered a man they recognized as an underdog who stood up to everything they disliked about the big downstate city. "If New York thinks he's so dangerous," a man asked a reporter, "why don't they get rid of him down there?"

The Schultz acquittal met with immediate condemnation outside Malone. The country's top justice official, U.S. Attorney General Homer Cummings, called his release "a terrible miscarriage of justice."

Mayor La Guardia declared Schultz unwelcome. Every New York City patrolman was ordered to arrest Schultz on sight. "He won't be a resident of New York City," La Guardia said. "There is no place for him here."

Schultz was riffling through a sheaf of congratulatory telegrams in his Malone hotel when a reporter told him that La Guardia had declared him persona non grata. "So there isn't room for me in New York," he said with a shrug. "Well, I'm going there."

He had to. The two trials had kept him away for more than nine months. Schultz had to return to the city or forfeit his racketeering operations. He employed a hundred or so men—schlammers, bookies, and bodyguards—who had stuck with him during his upstate hiatus, but their loyalty had limits.

Schultz had another reason to go home: he had not told anyone, at least not publicly, but his twenty-one-year-old wife, Frances, had given birth to a boy on July 25, the third day of his Malone trial. They named him John David Flagenheimer. "It's a boy, and it's mine, alright," he told reporters. But he would say no more.

Asked if he would allow Schultz back in order to see his baby, La Guardia said no. "I'm thinking now about all our other little babies, who are more important."

If La Guardia had a specific plan for barring Schultz from the city he would not share it. Nor would his police commissioner, Lewis Valentine, provide any details. They were most likely relying on Dewey to put Schultz out of business.

It was widely assumed that Dewey would place Schultz at the top of his target list, if only to finish what he had started when he indicted Schultz two years earlier for conspiracy to evade paying $92,103 in federal income tax and to correct the embarrassing miscarriage in Malone.

Dewey would not directly acknowledge as much, but through intermediaries he did leak to the press that he considered it a matter of pressing importance to convict Schultz, and that he felt tax evasion was not the best course. Dewey intended to take Schultz down with straight-ahead racketeering charges—a more ambitious route than tax evasion charges, but one that, if successful, would more effectively break the mob's back. His plan would, however, require witnesses, lots of them. "The success of our investigations," he said, "will depend in large measure on the willingness of racket victims to tell their story."

Schultz was uncomfortably aware that Dewey could ruin him. A conviction would send him away for ten years or more. While he was gone younger gangsters would take over his operations. He would leave prison in his mid-forties, a middle-aged man with nothing to fall back on. And he would miss a decade of his son's childhood.

At about this time Dewey's wife, Frances, who was pregnant with their second son, received a series of threatening phone calls at home, one of which instructed her to come down to the morgue to identify her husband's body. Dewey was fine, but the call traumatized their household.

Schultz faced his own trauma. When he heard that Dewey was targeting him, he called an emergency meeting of Commission delegates, a group that included Lucky Luciano, Meyer Lansky, Bugsy Siegel, and Lepke Buchalter. Schultz might be the first boss Dewey indicted in his new offensive against the underworld, he told them, but Dewey would eventually jail them all, or electrocute them, if they did not take bold action. The only solution, he said, was to assassinate Dewey. The men looked at Schultz with varying degrees of alarm and skepticism.

The Commission was a crime nation, but it was in some ways deeply risk averse. Luciano and Buchalter liked to know that events would unfold according to a carefully worked-out plan. Schultz's volcanic moods and impulsive temperament threatened them all. They nonetheless agreed, reluctantly, to explore the feasibility of an assassination. They assigned the reconnaissance to Albert Anastasia, who would coordinate with Reles and Murder, Inc.

To disguise himself while he studied Dewey's daily habits, Anastasia borrowed a baby from a friend. For four consecutive mornings he walked the baby in a pram back and forth outside Dewey's apartment building at 214 Fifth Avenue, near the northwest corner of Madison

Square Park. He found that Dewey, rigidly punctilious, left home every morning at exactly 8 a.m. and walked to a pharmacy around the corner, where he drank coffee at a lunch counter while his guards stood sentry out front. He sometimes placed sensitive calls from the pharmacy pay phone because he suspected his work phone could be tapped.

Anastasia reported his findings to the Commission the following week. If he sat in wait at the lunch counter, Anastasia said, he could shoot Dewey and the pharmacist with a revolver fitted with a silencer, then slip past the bodyguards waiting on the sidewalk. Or Reles and his men could take out the guards from a passing car.

Schultz was asked to leave the room while the delegates deliberated. They agreed that the hit could succeed, but all but one voted against it. (The sole dissenting vote was cast by Gurrah Shapiro, Buchalter's partner.) Buchalter, in particular, argued that murdering Dewey would invite too much heat. "We'll have the whole world around our ears," he said. "That's no good." Besides, they had no need to kill Dewey as long as Reles continued to eliminate witnesses. "No witnesses," Buchalter said, "no indictments."

When Schultz reentered the room and heard the verdict, he erupted. Every man in attendance knew of Schultz's barbaric temper; every one of them considered him a hothead and a liability. The Commission's new rational order of crime required that killing be done for a practical reason, but Schultz had a reputation for killing in anger. He once ended a drunken money squabble with an aide by drawing a pistol from beneath his vest. "One jerk at his vest and he had it in his hand," his lawyer, J. Richard "Dixie" Davis, later wrote. "All in the same quick motion he swung it up, stuck it in Jules Martin's mouth, and pulled the trigger. It was as simple and undramatic as that—just one quick motion of the hand. The Dutchman did that murder just as casually as if he were picking his teeth. No one had time to move. Julie Martin didn't even have time to look surprised. . . . Martin was right in the middle of a sentence as the gun blasted like a howitzer in the flimsy little hotel room."

Now Schultz stood and shouted at the delegates with the same eye-bulging fury. He berated the most powerful men in the underworld. Dewey *must* go, he told them. He *would* go. He would send his own men to kill the prosecutor, whether the Commission approved or not. Then he walked out.

The delegates were not pleased that Schultz had rejected their ruling.

Nor did they appreciate him flouting their authority. If Schultz went rogue and killed Dewey the pressure would come down on all of them. Worse, if detectives arrested Schultz for murdering Dewey he might flip and testify against them in exchange for lenience. In Luciano's cold calculation, it was Schultz who must die, not Dewey. The room agreed.

At 10:15 p.m. on the night of October 23, 1935, a driver named Piggy Schecter parked a stolen black sedan outside the Palace Chophouse, a second-rate Newark tavern and former speakeasy that had served as Schultz's clubhouse since he checked into the Robert Treat Hotel around the corner several weeks earlier. Schultz was avoiding New York because he still owed $36,937 in state taxes. (Piggy was not a regular Murder, Inc. wheelman. He was recruited because, as a truck driver, he knew Newark's back roads. He got his nickname by delivering farm goods to market.)

Anybody doing business with Schultz could find him in the chophouse's back room any afternoon or evening. Two Murder, Inc. agents, Charles "Bug" Workman and Emanuel "Mendy" Weiss, stepped from the car with their coat collars turned up and fedoras pulled low, just like movie gangsters. They pushed open the tavern door. A bartender, Jacob Friedman, glanced up from drying glasses. When he saw Weiss's sawed-off 12-gauge shotgun and Workman's .38- and .48-caliber pistols he ducked behind the bar. Keep quiet, they told him.

The dining room was empty, with napkins folded and cutlery set primly for the next day's meals. The gunmen could hear men's voices coming from a private dining room at the end of a narrow sixty-foot hallway. Schultz had neglected to post a lookout, an uncharacteristic oversight. Workman and Weiss burst into the private room. Schultz's three lieutenants—his fat, slobby driver, Lou "Lulu" Rosenkrantz; his bookkeeper, Otto "Abbadabba" Berman; and a bodyguard, Abe "Abie the Killer" Landau—looked up from a white tablecloth cluttered with glasses. They had finished their T-bone steaks and french fries more than two hours earlier. They had lingered at the round table in the far right corner to tally weekly profits from policy rackets and gambling operations. A seven-column balance sheet added up to a cash surplus of $148,369 for the previous seven weeks.

For a small moment the room stood still, suspended before the men looked up from their balance sheet. Then Workman and Weiss raised their weapons and fired away, hitting walls and windows and riddling the three seated men. Bullets tore into Landau's shoulder, upper left arm, and wrist as he grabbed for his .45. Rosenkrantz's broad belly made an easy target; he was hit in the chest, stomach, and right foot as he rose and came at the shooters. All three bullets went clear through his body. Berman was struck in the neck, shoulder, elbow, and wrist. He flopped from his chair onto the tile floor.

Schultz made it a rule to sit facing the entrance in every room, but his place at the table was empty. Workman kicked open the bathroom door where he found Schultz standing at one of two urinals. He was wearing a topcoat and gray fedora. Schultz ducked the first .45 slug. The second hit him on the left side, just below his chest.

Friedman, the bartender, raised his head from behind the bar in time to see Weiss retreat through the dining room to the front door and out onto East Park Place. Landau and Rosenkrantz followed. Blood ran from their wounds as they blasted back at Weiss with .45s. Their errant shots shattered glassware, wine bottles, and a cigarette machine. Rosenkrantz collapsed before he could reach the front door. He lay on the floor bleeding from six bullet wounds. Landau staggered outside after Weiss, shooting wildly. Stray shots hit the window of a building across the street and the rear of a bus lumbering into a depot. A bullet brushed the temple of an elderly man stepping down from a streetcar. He did not realize he had been grazed until he reached up and found blood on his hand. When Landau's Smith & Wesson ran out of bullets he dropped it to the sidewalk and fell onto a garbage can.

Meanwhile Schultz lurched from the bathroom holding his side. "He was reeling like he was intoxicated," said Friedman, the bartender. "He didn't say a cockeyed thing. He just went over to the table and put his left hand on it, so to steady himself. Then he plopped on the chair, just like a drunk would."

Schultz laid his head on the table. Blood seeped down the side of the white tablecloth. A mirror above his head bore spider cracks from two bullets. "Get a doctor," Schultz said. "Quick."

Rosenkrantz managed to raise himself from the floor and, holding the bar for support, asked Friedman for change. He dropped a nickel into a pay phone and dialed 0. "I want the police," he told the operator. "Hurry up." The police officer who came on the line heard a faint request—"Send me an ambulance. I'm dying"—then silence.

Callers had already alerted the police. "You been shot?" a police lieutenant asked Schultz when he found him doubled over in the back dining room.

"Yeah," Schultz said. "The pain is awful."

"Why don't you lie down," the lieutenant said.

"I can't," Schulz said. "It hurts too much."

The policeman who rode with Schultz in an ambulance asked him to name the shooters, but, in keeping with gangland code, he refused. The *Daily News* reported that Schultz opened his wallet and handed $725 to the ambulance attendant pressing an absorbent bandage to his wound. "Here," he reportedly said, "I'd rather you have this than the State. See that I get the best of care." Just before reaching the hospital he pulled a $300 roll from another pocket and gave the attendant that as well.

In the operating room doctors found that the .45-caliber bullet had penetrated Schultz's stomach, large intestine, gallbladder, and nicked a corner of his liver. He was in shock and hemorrhaging. Doctors dosed him with morphine and transfused him. "His chance of recovery," a doctor told reporters, "is about zero."

Murder, Inc. was not done for the night. As Schultz lay in his Newark hospital room, his lieutenant in charge of policy operations in Harlem, Martin "Little Marty" Krompier, lay swathed in hot towels in the underground Hollywood Barbershop, just off an entrance to the BMT subway at Forty-ninth Street and Seventh Avenue. Upstairs on the street newsboys were selling editions of the *Daily News* and the *Mirror* with the first reports from Newark. At midnight a man entered the barbershop and fired a .38 into the ceiling, scattering customers. He then shot Krompier four times—three slugs entered his stomach, the fourth hit his chest—but not fatally. He was writhing on the floor when police arrived and administered treatment, followed by a band of reporters. He told them he couldn't be killed that easily.

Schultz's mother, Mrs. Emma Neu Flagenheimer, walked into Newark City Hospital at 5:30 a.m. to begin the deathwatch. "I don't know why anyone would do this to him," she said.

By morning Schultz's wound festered with infection. His temperature rose to 106 degrees with what doctors called "a dying fever." With time likely running out, a Newark detective interrogated Schultz in his hospital bed while a police stenographer took dictation. In his delirium Schultz babbled nonsense threats to his enemies and incoherent entreaties to friends:

Q: Who shot you?

A: The boss himself. . . . Yes, I don't know. I am sore and I am going up and I am going to give you honey if I can. Mother is the best bet and don't let Satan draw you too fast.

Q: What did the big fellow shoot you for?

A: Him? John? Over a million, five million dollars. . . . Come on, open the soap buckets. The chimney sweeps. Talk to the sword. Shut up, you big mouth. Please help me up. . . . French-Canadian bean soup. I want to pay. Let them leave me alone.

Q: Was it the boss who shot you?

A: Who shot me? No one.

Q: We will help you.

A: Will you help me up? O.K. I won't be such a big creep. Oh, Mama. I can't go through with it, please. Oh, and then he clips me. Come on. Cut that out. We don't owe a nickel. Hold it. Instead, hold it against him. I am a pretty good pretzler . . . Winifred . . . Department of Justice. I even got it from the department. Sir, please stop it. Say listen the last night!

The police hoped that Schultz's answers, however incoherent, might reveal who shot him, or offer other insights. The transcript was of no use to police, but it did earn a footnote in literary history. The Beat writer William Burroughs saw a poetic quality in Schultz's blathering. He used the dialogue as the basis for a screenplay about the gangster's life titled *The Last Words of Dutch Schultz.*

Police said that they had never seen a criminal so frightened as Schultz in his last hours. "As we have often noted," the columnist Walter Winchell wrote of Schultz in his memoir, "gangsters, like dictators, always look good until the last ten minutes."

In a final moment of clarity, Schultz sent for the Rev. Father Cornelius J. McInerney, a pastor of St. Philomena's church, in Livingston,

New Jersey. Schultz was the son of German Jews who settled in the Bronx, but he asked to die Catholic. His conversion may have been a parting favor to his twenty-one-year-old redheaded wife, Frances, a former hatcheck girl at the Maison Royal nightclub, who sat at his bedside fingering her rosary beads. She had eaten with him that night at the chophouse, then went to the movie house around the corner while he conducted business. She returned to find a crowd of police outside the chophouse. She figured they were conducting a raid, so she went home, where she heard the news on the radio. She then went directly to the hospital.

While nurses prepared Schultz for a transfusion Father McInerney baptized him, heard his confession, and administered last rites. Hours before Schultz died he received a telegram from Stephanie St. Clair, the Harlem numbers queen Schultz had roughly pushed aside. "As ye sow," the telegram said, "so shall ye reap."

A final transfusion failed to revive him. He sank into a coma and died at 8:35 p.m. In Harlem, where Schultz had taken over the illegal numbers lotteries, players took his time of death as an omen. Hundreds, possibly thousands, put their money down on the number they hoped or believed would win that day: 835. It did not.

Schultz lived as a miser, but his wealth was legendary. He kept thousand-dollar bills and diamonds stolen from a Broadway jewelry store in a waterproof iron chest so stuffed with loot it was hard to close. He is believed to have buried the chest in the Catskills, in upstate New York, in order to hide his wealth should he be prosecuted for tax evasion. The chest has never been found.

On the night of the Schultz shooting, Bug Workman fled the chophouse to find that his accomplices, Mendy and Piggy, had left without him in the getaway car. While police and curious neighbors converged on the chophouse Workman ran through a small park, where he abandoned his overcoat, in spite of the thrashing rain, to make identification harder. He slept briefly in a garbage dump, then walked until he found a train station and rode back to Manhattan.

Workman's friend, a retired light heavyweight named Danny Fields, hid him in an apartment, at Eighth Avenue and Twenty-first Street, that he kept for his girlfriend, an upstate divorcée. Workman was rumpled and shell shocked. He looked, the girlfriend later said, "as if he had slept in his clothes for a couple of nights." Fields threw Workman's suit in the incinerator and lent him one of his own.

Workman, wrote the *Daily News,* "was as complex a man as ever worked for the mob, a sharp-shooting, ruthless, no-questions-asked exterminator when he was not serving as a loving, devoted family man." When a Buchalter underling named Izzy Teitelbaum instructed Workman to leave town, he at first refused to abandon his pregnant wife, Katherine. He could be oddly softhearted for a triggerman. Fields warned that he had no choice. Detectives had staked out his apartment on Avenue A. They would spot Workman if he came home, and they would follow Katherine if she tried to join him.

While the morning papers wallowed in assassination coverage, Workman boarded a train for Miami, where he stayed in a beach bungalow. Then, when Katherine did join him, they moved to the Beach Park Hotel, a white-stucco Art Deco confection across Ocean Drive from the beach. Albert "Tick Tock" Tannenbaum, a tall, thin Murder, Inc. gunman, and his wife were also guests. Workman secretly fumed. While he laid low, Mendy Weiss was back in New York taking credit for killing Schultz. On New Year's Eve, Workman drank too much and unburdened himself. He told Tannenbaum how he, not Weiss, had shot Schultz, and how Weiss and Piggy had abandoned him. Even worse, he said, Weiss had told associates that he and Piggy left the crime scene without Workman because he was lingering to rifle the victim's pockets, a serious breach of etiquette. It was an indiscretion he would later regret.

The twenty handpicked assistant district attorneys in Dewey's offices on the fourteenth floor of the Woolworth Building arrived with nearly identical white-shoe pedigrees—Ivy League diplomas followed by law degrees from Harvard, Yale, or Columbia. They were like indistinguishable white male worker bees in Dewey's hive. All but one.

Eunice Hunton Carter was raised in Harlem and schooled at Smith College, where she received both bachelor's and master's degrees in four years—only the second woman to do so. She went on to become the first black woman to graduate from Fordham Law School. After graduation she worked as a legal assistant in Women's Court on Sixth Avenue, in Greenwich Village, which mostly heard prostitution cases. In 1935 Dewey hired her from a pool of six thousand applicants after an exacting screening process Dewey personally conducted.

Shortly after joining Dewey, Carter met with him in his office, a high-ceilinged room partitioned by a frosted-glass wall. His desk was rigidly ordered with a notepad, cigarette box, two symmetrical ash trays, a tablet calendar, and a neat pile of scratch pads. The surroundings were rigid and austere, but Dewey was often strikingly relaxed in his office. He leaned back in his desk chair, fingers folded behind his head, then sprang to his feet and paced. His habit was contagious: colleagues found themselves pacing with him while they talked.

It is not known if Carter paced, but she did share with Dewey an observation: while working in Women's Court she noticed that prostitutes were almost always represented by a man named Abe Karp, a lawyer the women could not afford on their own. Without exception they posted bail provided by the same bail bondsman, and they offered the same familiar alibi, as if rehearsed: I was just visiting a cousin, your honor. I had no idea it was that kind of place. Carter sensed the workings of a shadowy centralized organization, a racket, controlling the prostitution business.

Dewey at first expressed reluctance to pursue prostitution. Suppressing vice normally fell to patrolmen and magistrates. Enforcing morality was not his job. He was after the big bosses of crime. But he came to agree with Carter that a large-scale criminal operation was at play after she traced the lawyer and bondsman back to Lucky Luciano, the architect of the Commission and one of the mob bosses overseeing Abe Reles and Murder, Inc. Luciano didn't personally operate the brothels, but he controlled them. In exchange for bail and legal muscle the women kicked back half their earnings to him. They were practically his slaves. If Dewey wanted to indict Luciano on charges other than tax evasion, Carter said, this might be a way.

About the time that Carter conferred with Dewey, a young graduate of Columbia Law School named Frank Hogan ran into an elderly judge who sat on the Circuit Court of Appeals. Hogan told the judge that he hoped to join Dewey's staff. "Oh, that's a waste of time," the judge said. "[His investigation] won't amount to anything. In six months it will be dead."

The mob had such an iron grip on the unions and businesses in its sphere, and the fear of Murder, Inc. was so severe, that jurists assumed Dewey would fail to find witnesses willing to testify. Thanks to Reles, it was nearly impossible to get anyone to take the risk of speaking out against the mob.

Dewey had a possible solution. His plan was to find witnesses that he held evidence against and force them to choose between cooperation or jail. He started with the prostitutes. He would threaten them, coddle them, and care for them until they talked.

The intelligence-gathering began in secret. A hundred and sixty-four plainclothes detectives gathered in pairs on assigned street corners on the night of February 1, 1936. Dewey switched them up so they were not with their normal partners. As temperatures slid to thirteen degrees they stamped their feet and exhaled wreaths of condensation, awaiting final instructions. They were to conduct lightning raids synchronized at exactly 9 p.m. on forty-one brothels—or "disorderly houses," as newspapers primly called them—but they would not know the addresses until they opened sealed brown manila envelopes at precisely 8:55 p.m. Dewey suspected, and with good reason, that detectives bribed by Luciano and his men would alert the brothels if they knew their assignments beforehand.

At the designated time the police teams knocked on the doors of seven brothels in Brooklyn and thirty-four in Manhattan housed in town houses and tenement back rooms. At most addresses an assertive knock sufficed. If not, detectives busted open the door. Inside, naked women shrieked, and men in stages of undress, including a handful of prominent lawyers and Wall Street bankers, tried to flee out windows or dodge and weave their way past the police and out the front door. One woman ran down a fire escape in her negligee and into the custody of a patrolman waiting on the sidewalk.

The men in underwear and half-buttoned shirts were allowed to slink off into the cold, punished only by embarrassment. This was not a vice sting. Dewy had dispatched the teams of detectives for one reason: to collect women capable of testifying against Luciano.

Detectives handcuffed 110 prostitutes and brassy-voiced madams, including some of the city's most famous and flamboyant—Jennie the Factory, Frisco Jean, Gashouse Lil, Polack Frances, Silver-tongued Elsie, Fat Rae, and Cold Potato Annie. Police booked the prisoners at a Greenwich Street precinct house, then transported them downtown in groups of three and four by taxi, instead of police wagon, to avoid notice. The women entered the Woolworth Building through the Broadway entrance and walked through the cathedral-like lobby with its barrel-vaulted ceilings and veined marble walls to the night elevator. Dewey had rented the thirteenth floor, the floor below his own, in order to process and interrogate the women, with a team of twenty stenographers taking down their accounts.

At first the women offered the usual alibis: they claimed to be blameless art students, switchboard operators, seamstresses, or tourists caught by happenstance. They were tawdry and sullen as they smoked cigarettes and waited on the thirteenth floor smelling of liquor and perfume. They expected to be bailed out shortly, as they always were. Most still wore their brothel outfits—bright silky low-cut dresses with no underwear and high heels.

The women were portioned out to assistant district attorneys who questioned them, one by one. Dewey's staff was still working its way through the group when dawn light filled the rooms and the bells of Trinity Church chimed from seven blocks away. Nobody slept for thirty-six hours. From the interviews Eunice Carter assembled a lurid sketch of the operations: as many as two thousand women, most recruited from small towns, rotated weekly among some two hundred brothels so customers found fresh attractions. Women worked twelve-hour shifts, six days a week, earning $150 to $300 a week, keeping only $50 or less. The rest went for bookers, doctors, room and board, and to Luciano's fund to pay bail if arrested. "They worked us like dogs for a couple of years," one woman said, "and then they kicked us out."

After a vice sting police would normally book the women, then release them, but Dewey prevailed on Judge McCook to come to the Woolworth Building on Sunday afternoon to hold seventy women as material witnesses on $10,000 bail each, far beyond their means, so that Dewey's staff could try to persuade them to turn state's evidence. The women, bleary-eyed and blowsy, formed a line down the corridor outside Dewey's private office. "Not guilty," they told McCook, and with that they departed for the Women's House of Detention.

Now, as guests of the state, they were given the choice of testifying before the grand jury in exchange for immunity, or going to Women's Court to face sentences as long as ten years. Persuading the women to cooperate was "a backbreaking job because the fear the witnesses displayed was so great," said Hogan, who had by now succeeded in joining Dewey's staff. "Witnesses would have done anything to avoid testifying against Luciano."

Hogan was engaged to be married, but for five months he spent almost all his time with the prostitutes. He spent so much time with the women, and he was so solicitous, that the women called their row of cells "Hogan's Alley." They called him "Father Hogan" for his solemn manner.

Hogan knew enough about addiction to visit the women fifty-six or so hours after their arrest, the worst stage of withdrawal. Just as the women's shaking and nausea reached a high point Hogan appeared at their cell. If they agreed to testify Hogan would send them to a convalescent ward where nurses alleviated their pain.

The decision to cooperate could cost the women their lives if Dewey failed to jail their overseers. "If I talked, they'd slit my throat," one told Dewey. "God, how I hope you get them. If you don't, it's curtains for me. They'll grab me the minute I'm out of here."

Dewey was careful to be solicitous. He offered the women sandwiches and coffee during the long interrogations. He bought them clothes. Doctors treated their venereal diseases—half of them had both syphilis and gonorrhea—and helped wean them off heroin. Dewey and his surrogates made clear that he would drop charges against those willing to share what they knew about Luciano's connection to their work. He circulated the same message within the Women's House of Detention behind the Jefferson Market Courthouse: inmates could win their freedom with useful testimony. Those who agreed to talk would be treated to comfortable hotels, he promised, with plenty of room service and cigarettes and trips to the movies included.

Most women kept their lips sealed. They knew how Abe Reles and Murder, Inc. punished informants. "Plenty of girls who talked had their feet and stomach burned with cigarettes and their tongues cut up," one said after being asked repeatedly to testify. A madam said a schlammer had slugged her with a lead pipe when the mob suspected her of talking.

The most important witness for Dewey to win over was Nancy Presser, a head-turning, heavy-breasted blonde with the creamy complexion of a sorority sister. Al Capone sent for her when in New York. Luciano himself called her to his suite at the Waldorf Astoria.

Presser had worked as a high-end prostitute for eight years with a hotel clientele of stockbrokers, bootleggers, and other sugar daddies, all the while sending money home to her family in upstate New York. But now, at age twenty-six, her glow had dimmed with dissipation. She had given up opium for morphine, taking a quarter of a cube three times a day. It helped with the hangovers. She was working around the clock in a two-dollar-a-trick whorehouse when the police caught her in their raid. Prosecutors tried for days to get a coherent response from her while she suffered from heroin withdrawal and lingering pain from a pimp's angry blow to the side of her head. When asked if she would testify, Presser walked Dewey to the window of their meeting room in the Women's House of Detention, an Art Deco prison in Greenwich Village. "Look out there," she said, pointing to the elevated Sixth Avenue subway. "Some of the mob guys stand out there at night and shake their fists up at us. They even know what floor we're on."

Dewey reassured the women that Reles's killers could not reach them. Besides, they would soon go to jail if the women cooperated. He asked for their trust. The entire criminal apparatus, he promised, was coming down. In the end, Presser and a handful of others agreed.

In the midst of the interrogations, Dewey summoned to his office twenty-one-year-old Gay Orlova, a White Russian showgirl and gossip-column fixture. She looked like an older, sexed-up version of Shirley Temple, complete with dimples and curls. Her manner might have been ditzy, but there was nothing hapless about her: She spoke three languages and, at age fifteen, navigated her way from Petrograd to Broadway on cleavage and cunning. When her visa expired, she avoided deportation by eloping with a nineteen-year-old second-balcony usher from the Majestic Theatre, where she danced barely dressed in the chorus line of a musical called *Murder at the Vanities*. On hearing news of her marriage, songwriter Earl Carroll telegrammed her from California: "Congrats but why didn't you at least marry a first balcony usher instead of a second?"

The marriage lasted only a few days. The usher obtained an annulment, claiming the marriage had been "kissless."

Orlova met Luciano at Palm Island, a private Miami enclave where he and other flush gangsters spent winter weeks betting at racetracks. Luciano had a power over women. "He had a flashing white smile, and a debonair manner, with a steely showing of harsh cruelty underneath," wrote Hickman Powell of the *New York Post*."

She attached herself to him. In the course of long evenings in Miami, and back in New York, she overheard a great deal about the inner workings of his operations. It is impossible to know how much, if any, she revealed to Dewey.

With or without Orlova's help, Dewey had now amassed enough

evidence to earn a warrant for Luciano's arrest, though bringing him in would be tricky. Detectives could not simply collar him on a street corner the way Brooklyn cops snatched Reles for vagrancy. Luciano sequestered himself in a world of wealth and security. He presided over a profitable nationwide organization, and his pockets accordingly swelled with earnings. He occupied a private box at the Saratoga Race Course and lived as "Mr. Charles Ross" in a two-room suite on the thirty-ninth floor of the Waldorf Astoria Hotel on Park Avenue where bodyguards and lieutenants stood sentry. His spacious closets were filled with tailor-made suits, lots of them. He had a particular fondness for black cutaways, which, combined with his grim countenance and combed-back black hair, made him look like an Italian Dracula.

Luciano was alone in his suite at the Waldorf Astoria when a friendly contact in the hotel manager's office called to say that men who looked like detectives were riding the elevator up. "I figured it was a good time to take a vacation," Luciano later said. "Right then I didn't know what they was after me for but I wasn't going to stay around and see. I just decided to go somewhere out of New York until things could cool down. I didn't even pack my clothes. I don't remember taking nothing with me, not even a toothbrush. I left with only the clothes I was wearing, went down the freight elevator, got in my car, and took off."

Luciano called for his private Lockheed and flew to Miami, where he received a cold reception. His arrival contributed to growing local concern that gangsters were taking control of the city's twenty or so seasonal nightclubs then preparing for the winter season.

Luciano did not like his sullen, swarthy face photographed, particularly by newspapers. He stayed mostly hidden in Miami, but detectives surveilled him as he came and went from his Miami Beach hotel. They contacted New York Police Commissioner Lewis Valentine to ask if he would like Luciano detained for questioning in connection with the Schultz murder. Valentine had no legal grounds to order Luciano's return, he said, but he would welcome a chance speak to him.

When news of this exchange with Valentine leaked to the press, Luciano boarded his Lockheed and took off again. He was now like an exiled head-of-state searching for a sanctuary in which to alight with his illegal millions. He spent the winter in Hot Springs, Arkansas, a gangster-friendly town that condoned gambling and prostitution. He hid himself only halfheartedly. Gay Orlova accompanied him for afternoons at the Oaklawn Park Racetrack and nights at the Majestic Hotel.

If Orlova told Dewey anything of value when he questioned her, she presumably kept her disclosures a secret from Luciano. Though every shrewd gangster knew that a girlfriend eventually presented security risks.

On April Fool's Day, 1936, Luciano, deeply tanned and relaxed, was walking with a Hot Springs sheriff on a redbrick promenade known as Bath House Row that connected eight ornate spa buildings where he took daily soaks in thermal waters and mud baths. He was dressed for the racetrack, but before he could reach his car, a New York detective named Stephen P. DiRosa stepped in his way. He spoke to Luciano in Italian and thrust a warrant at him. "Anger flooded [Luciano's] face a deeper shade," wrote Meyer Berger in *The New York Times*. "For a moment he was speechless, then he found his tongue. 'You,' he blurted through thick lips. 'You're a hell of an Italian.'"

DiRosa smiled. He clapped handcuffs on Luciano's wrists and led him to the Garland County Jail. It was reported that Orlova had betrayed his location to Dewey, though that was never confirmed.

Luciano prided himself on his skill at eluding the authorities, and he had succeeded for five months. Now he was in a basement holding cell. "To have the hated prosecutor reach across state lines for him was bad enough," Berger wrote. "He thought he had covered his tracks completely . . . and here, to add insult to injury, not only was he taken by a Dewey man but by one of his own people."

Dewey sent a young assistant district attorney, Edward McLean, to Hot Springs by train and plane with orders to bring Luciano home to stand trial. Luciano did not yield. He fought extradition with every trick and loophole at his disposal. He hired the county's best lawyers, demanded writs of habeas corpus, and appealed to a higher court. He offered a $50,000 bribe to the Arkansas attorney general for release. It required the intervention of the governor and a squad of state rangers with rifles raised to pry him loose from Hot Springs and transport him fifty miles over mountain roads to the Pulaski County jail in Little Rock.

Finally, after two weeks of legal wrangling, Dewey's detectives seized Luciano when a stay expired at 12:01 a.m. on the morning of April 17. The train departing Little Rock waited ten minutes beyond departure time for Luciano to board. He entered a private stateroom guarded by three detectives and accompanied by McLean. At St. Louis, twenty policemen surrounded the group as they switched to the South-western Limited.

The trip was otherwise uneventful as Luciano sped east toward a reckoning with Dewey. He stared at the passing landscape without expression. "Luciano was uncommunicative and there wasn't much conversation," said McLean, who sat next to Luciano for much of the trip. "We didn't talk about his case at all. He ate well and slept soundly."

Three more detectives boarded the train when it stopped briefly in Albany, and an entire squad stood guard against Murder, Inc. when the train pulled into Grand Central Terminal at 8 a.m. on the morning of April 18. Detectives waited until passengers had cleared the platform, then led Luciano out handcuffed to two guards. A crowd of three hundred rush-hour commuters paused to catch a glimpse of him, as they would a movie star. He wore a pearl-gray fedora and a tailored suit unwrinkled despite two days on the train. A porter had shined his shoes to perfection. "He was watched through the day," the *Daily News* wrote, "like a priceless jewel."

Luciano rode in an unmarked car full of detectives and accompanied front and back by squad cars to the copper-domed downtown Manhattan police headquarters. He was led down an external staircase to a basement for booking, where he admitted to eleven arrests and identified his profession as racetrack bookmaker. He unsmilingly told a police captain that he "didn't know anything about" the charges against him.

At 5:30 p.m. police marched Luciano up the broad granite steps of the New York County Courthouse and through the rotunda to stand before Justice McCook for arraignment. He faced twenty-four counts of prostitution on four indictments. Justice McCook set bail at $350,000 (the equivalent of $6.5 million in today's currency), a sum beyond even Luciano's reach.

Days later Luciano's girlfriend, Gay Orlova, held a press conference at Dave's Blue Room, an all-night Seventh Avenue restaurant popular with performers and songwriters, to protest Dewey's treatment of her boyfriend. Luciano, she said, "was just like any other fellow. He's nice." Not coincidentally she was looking for work on Broadway at the time. She spoke to reporters wearing a Paris gown and a $4,000 coat of silver fox.

Orlova might not live long enough to find a job. Luciano would not hesitate to have Reles kill a witness that could harm him, even his girlfriend. In fact, she noticed a swarthy figure following her during late nights out. One of her regular dates was so concerned that he avoided her. Orlova's friends convinced her to leave town, a precaution which may have saved her life.

The trial convened on Centre Street on May 11, 1936, amid concern that Reles might try to rescue Luciano. Policemen armed with machine guns and tear-gas canisters guarded the hallways of the Centre Street courthouse. Snipers watched from rooftops. Luciano and his nine co-defendants marched into the courtroom like an underground army, accompanied by more than a dozen defense lawyers, and occupied the first three rows of seats.

Dewey had sixty-eight witnesses lined up. He knew that Luciano's lawyers would try to discredit their testimony by calling them lowlifes. He preempted them by acknowledging in his opening that his case would rest on "prostitutes, madams, heels, pimps, and ex-convicts."

He added, "We can't get bishops to testify."

Dewey began by calling a trio of Waldorf Astoria staff—a chambermaid, a waiter, and a manager—to testify that the ten men at the defense table used a two-room suite on the thirty-ninth floor to run their prostitution empire, or, as the *Daily News* called it, "counterfeit love." Dewey asked each witness to step down from the stand and identify the men by laying a hand on a defendant's shoulder as he called their names: Lucky Luciano, David Betillo, Jimmy Federico, Abe Wahrman, Meyer Berman, Jesse Jacobs, Ralph Liguori, Jack Ellenstein, Thomas Pennochio, and Benny Spiller. During a recess Luciano and his co-defendants switched ties and exchanged positions on the theory that Dewey had coached the witnesses to identify the defendants by wardrobe and seat.

As the chambermaid walked by Luciano on her way from the stand, she smiled at him and said, "You naughty boy to be in here." Luciano smiled back.

Through the first week of testimony Dewey scored points, but failed to land a death blow. In Luciano he was contending with a new kind of mob boss who stood two or three degrees of separation from the implementation of crimes. Dewey badly needed a way to directly link Luciano to the brothels. At the end of the second week he called his star witness, Florence Brown, known in the underworld as Cokey Flo, a scrawny, white-faced twenty-eight-year-old heroin addict with short, wavy brown hair and a lower lip so comically pouty that a cartoonist might have drawn it.

Cokey Flo was a girlfriend of sorts to one of the married defendants, Jimmy Frederico, a short, grouper-faced man with longshoreman shoulders and slicked-down middle-parted hair who supervised the day-to-day management of the brothel syndicate. Dewey read into testimony a letter Cokey Flo wrote to Frederico in Raymon Street Jail after his arrest on February 1: "When a week goes by and still no word from you, I get terribly frantic. . . . You still mean a lot to me, as much as always. This trouble makes no difference to me. I still think as much of you as ever. . . . Everything that is good and fine and sweet in the world will be embodied in your image for me. Some of the happiest moments in my life were spent in your company. Perhaps some unhappy ones too, but thoughts of them fade away when the image of your smiling face comes to my mind."

Thirteen weeks after writing the letter, Cokey Flo herself was arrested for soliciting an undercover detective. At the time she was working as a live-in typist and assistant to Dorothy Russell Calvit, an aspiring writer and daughter of the famous stage actress Lillian Russell. Cokey Flo would occasionally slip out of Calvit's two-bedroom suite at the Hotel Alamac, on Seventy-first Street and Broadway, to pick up johns at a bar. The twenty-five dollars a week Mrs. Calvit paid her was not enough to pay for her fix.

While awaiting sentencing in the Women's House of Detention, Cokey Flo wrote another letter, this one to Dewey, offering to recount under oath what she knew about Luciano's prostitution ring in return for a reduced sentence. "I got disgusted," she later testified, "and I told Mr. Dewey I wanted to go straight and get out of this business."

When Cokey Flo entered the courtroom on May 21 heads turned to see a ragamuffin in a ratty blue dress and scarlet lipstick. She took the stand five days after completing a heroin-withdrawal program in the House of Detention, and she looked it. Justice McCook took an avuncular interest in the prostitute's well-being throughout the trial. He granted her sips of brandy during breaks in her testimony.

Cokey Flo might have been frail, but she warmed to the telling with hauteur and defiance. Her voice rose in confidence as she described in detail five meetings in which Luciano discussed operations of the

$12-million prostitution ring with her boyfriend Jimmy Frederico. She recalled Luciano expressing frustration with his underlings and fear of Dewey. She quoted him as saying "we ought to fold up for a while. There are too many investigations going on." And she described a dinner held in a smoke-filled uptown Chinese restaurant in which Luciano contemplated an elaborate plan to franchise whorehouses on a large scale, "the same as the A & P," he said, referring to the supermarket chain.

Until now Luciano had sat through the proceedings expressionless and "cobra-eyed," as the *Daily News* described him. But as Cokey Flo testified he wrote notes with great agitation.

In cross-examination, Luciano's lawyer, David P. Siegel, made a point of calling her a whore, not a prostitute. He tried to impeach her credibility by forcing her to acknowledge her seven years of addiction. "A quarter of a grain of morphine before breakfast every day," she said. "Another shot before dinner and a third one just before I went to bed."

Siegel asked if she spoke slowly because she had dosed herself during a recess. "I'm just talking slow so I can get everything right," she said. Siegel asked the judge to order physicians to examine her in the judge's chambers to determine if she was under the influence. The physicians reported that she was not. Cokey Flo walked back to the stand while glaring at Siegel.

Finally, having lost his tussle with Cokey Flo, Siegel suggested she was fabricating her entire testimony in order to reduce her sentence. Had she even met Luciano? When asked, she identified him at the crowded defense table as "the man with the yellow pencil." Luciano threw down the pencil and glared at her.

"Do you still love Frederico?" she was asked. Her eyes rested lightly on him sitting with his co-defendants. "I don't know," she said so quietly that the courtroom strained to hear her. "I'm not sure."

Cokey Flo was Dewey's coup de grâce, but she was only one in a series of prostitutes to testify. Nancy Presser told the court that one of Luciano's men, a man she once considered her boyfriend, forced her into a brothel by threatening to "cut me up so my own mother wouldn't know me." She told of hearing Luciano order an underling to "wreck the joint," referring to a brothel run by a madam who refused his orders.

For the first time Luciano looked ruffled. He smoothed his hair and whispered to his lawyers during Presser's testimony.

Presser had not wanted to talk. She knew that Murder, Inc. burned women's feet and stomachs with cigar butts and cut out their tongues in revenge for damaging statements. But Dewey convinced her that she would be safe. "For two hours," he told the jury, "I sat with Nancy Presser trying to persuade her to testify and that she would not be murdered. If you want to know what responsibility is, try to persuade a witness trembling with terror to go on the stand." After her testimony Presser was moved to a secret location to safeguard her until she returned for cross-examination.

A third prostitute, twenty-six-year-old Thelma Jordan, who came from a respectable Kansas family, said in a husky, spent voice that one of the defendants threatened her with death if she cooperated with Dewey. She wore a black silk dress and a black hat which drooped over her eyes. "I knew what happened to people who talked." She said that she overheard a Luciano lieutenant telling Presser that if any women testified "their pictures would be sent to their home-town papers with stories of what they were doing for a living."

Jordan had grown up in a small prairie town where her father worked as street cleaning commissioner. After two years at a local college she got pregnant. She joined a traveling carnival to save her family from disgrace. She burst into tears when a defense lawyer demanded her true name and hometown. "I won't tell you," she screamed. Justice McCook ordered her to answer, but after conferring with her at the bench he changed his mind. "I have talked to the witness," he said, "and have concluded that nothing can be served by bringing innocent people into this matter. The witness will not be required to answer."

Mildred Balitzer, a hard-boiled bleach-blonde, and a drinker and former addict who ran a brothel with her husband, testified that one of Luciano's men threatened to kill her while Dewey held her as a material witness. Police were transporting her from one guarded apartment to another, she said, when she saw an old friend named Gus Franco. She furtively asked the police to step away so that Franco would not know she was in custody as a material witness. "The officer stayed across the street," she said. "Gus told me if I testified against these defendants I would be killed—not only me, but also my youngster." Balitzer and her husband had a fifteen-year-old daughter.

After calling sixty witnesses, Dewey rested his case at 6:40 p.m. on May 29. Speaking to reporters in the hallway afterward, Luciano professed confidence. "I certainly expect to be acquitted," he said. In reality he feared that Dewey had established enough evidence for conviction. His defense lawyer wanted to counter by calling his girlfriend, Gay Orlova, as a witness, but Luciano objected. "I don't want her mixed up in this case," he told reporters.

Instead Luciano insisted on testifying in his own defense in defiance of his lawyer's advice. He took the stand at 2:05 p.m. on June 3 neatly dressed, as always, in a gray flannel double-breasted suit and natty black necktie. His wavy black hair was slicked in place. His voice was low pitched. He sat back in his chair, occasionally shrugging in response to questions. "Cool as a cucumber," wrote a court reporter.

In response to his lawyer's friendly questioning, he stated blandly that he had never received a single dollar from the proceeds of prostitution. "I gave to them," he said, "I never took." Turning to the jury, he said that a prosecutor with political ambitions was cramming an unfair case down their throats. He flatly denied the charges against him, adding that he had seen only one of his co-defendants, his lieutenant, a short, almond-eyed man named John "Little Davie" Betillo, before the trial opened.

By testifying, Luciano exposed himself to cross-examination. The courtroom spectators hushed as the moment arrived. After months of manhunts and maneuvers, the young special prosecutor confronted a sovereign leader of the underworld, face-to-face, in the packed courtroom. Dewey rose from his seat and stood, saying nothing. He let anticipation build.

"I looked over and watched that little bastard Dewey get out of his chair and walk towards me," Luciano later said. "At that second I was more scared than I ever had been in my whole life. He walked over real slow, and he had a look on his face like I was a piece of raw meat and he'd been going hungry for a month."

If the courtroom was a theater, Dewey was its most skillful actor. He stood only five foot eight, but he commanded the room. His voice was his strength, a sonorous baritone refined by operatic training and years of choral singing. He used it to set a mood in the courtroom the way a musical score brings a movie to woeful lows or thrilling heights. "His hoarse whisper of scorn carries across the room like a note from a plucked bull-fiddle," *Life* magazine wrote. "His accusations crack like nightsticks on rioter's skulls. And when, with repressed indignation, he sums up the sins of the accused, few jurors can resist the plain testimony of their senses that the throaty voice of Dewey is the authentic voice of an outraged community."

Dewey turned his voice on Luciano over the course of a battering four-hour cross-examination, attacking Luciano again and again over details of his criminal career, cornering him into admitting in haltering, slowly voiced confessions that he had lied repeatedly to the police and, at least once, lied under oath. He admitted that he "may have lied a little," but insisted that he was "telling the truth now."

Dewey forced Luciano to admit to a Florida conviction for carrying concealed weapons. He admitted lying to obtain a pistol permit and admitted that he was once caught with two revolvers, a shotgun, and forty-five rounds of ammunition in his car as he drove down Fifth Avenue. "I was hunting pheasants," he said. Dewey shouted his disbelief.

Luciano also conceded that he had sold drugs at the age of eighteen, worked as a gunman, and cheated on taxes. "With rapier-like verbal thrusts, the prosecutor threw lies back into Lucky's teeth until he sat miserably silent, lost for an answer," wrote the *Daily News*. "He virtually cowered in the witness chair. Sweat beaded his swarthy brow. He cringed at each new edged question and hid behind half-audible 'I don't knows' and 'I can't recalls.'"

Dewey's year-by-year research showed that Luciano had not held a legitimate job since 1920. At one point he interrupted Dewey to state that he had owned "a piece of a restaurant" at Broadway and Fifty-second Street eight years earlier. "Oh, the only legitimate business you've had in eighteen years, you forgot?" Dewey said. Luciano nodded.

Dewey's research was so complete, so detailed, that more than once Luciano broke from his sullen resistance to say, "I wonder where you ever got that?"

Dewey mocked Luciano's six years of flagrantly bogus tax returns, which showed that he never earned more than $22,500 a year, despite his luxurious lifestyle.

"You just picked those figures on your income out of the sky, didn't you?" Dewey asked.

"I just thought it was the proper amount I should give the government," Luciano responded.

Dewey suggested that Luciano chose to pay federal income tax, but not state tax, because the federal government was more likely to prosecute gangsters for nonpayment. Luciano denied it.

Luciano's most uncomfortable moment came when Dewey picked up from the prosecution table a sheaf of telephone records from the Waldorf Astoria and the Barbizon Plaza, his previous residence, listing repeated calls, some made as late as 3 a.m., to Celano's restaurant on Kenmare Street, on the Lower East Side, which, Dewey told the jury, was the prostitution ring's headquarters. Luciano's swarthy face shone with perspiration as he responded. He went to Celano's two or three times a month, he said, but only for spaghetti. He had never met his co-defendants there, he added.

The icy poise for which Luciano was famous had melted by the time he stepped down at the end of the day. "I felt like I'd been through a washing machine," he told an interviewer years later, "and I really looked like it. I went to the washroom, and my shirt was all wrinkled and I seemed to be perspiring from head to foot . . . I never felt so tired, like I could sleep for a week. I couldn't wait to get out of the courthouse. I practically ran."

By the end of the day, Dewey had established a clear picture of Luciano as a gunman, a drug smuggler, a perjurer, and a tax cheat. But he failed to deliver the finishing blow—a clear and indisputable connection between Luciano and the prostitution rings.

Dewey had the final say. In his five-hour summation he acknowledged that Cokey Flo and other witnesses were prostitutes, and that the jury might find them untrustworthy. Nonetheless, he said, "you must give her story the same weight as you would do that of a respectable person. If you believe what she says, then the story stands, and the fact that she is a prostitute is of no moment."

He paused and gave the jury a dead-on look. "We did not offer a witness we didn't believe."

Then he turned from the jury to gaze directly at Luciano, as if inviting them to do the same. Intentionally or not, a flicker of emotion showed on Dewey's face. He reached his hand out and pointed at Luciano. That man, he said, had committed "a shocking, disgusting display of sanctimonious perjury—at the end of which I am sure not one of you had a doubt that before you stood not a gambler, not a bookmaker, but the greatest gangster in America."

The jury ate dinner, then retired for deliberations at 10:53 p.m. on the evening of June 6, 1936. Despite the drama of Dewey's summation, a straw poll of newsmen covering the trial predicted acquittal by thirteen to one, but nobody knew if the jury would agree.

The jury weighed the accumulated month's worth of testimony of mobsters and prostitutes for six and a half hours—straight through a Saturday night—while the judge dozed in his chambers with a full percolator of coffee and a toilet kit. Dewey walked alone to a small private room on the top floor of the courthouse and went to sleep on a sofa. The defendant's wives and other family slept in the hallway. Just outside the courtroom, in Foley Square, hundreds of Italian-Americans waited with their eyes on the courtroom. They asked anyone who exited the building for news.

At 5:05 a.m. a bailiff knocked on the judge's door; the jury had reached a verdict. At 5:30 a.m. Luciano stood before the bar, scowling. The herd of manacled co-defendants shuffled into the courtroom behind him, "their quivering, shifty faces registering various degrees of apprehension," wrote the *Daily News*.

The jury's dour expressions foretold the verdict: they found all ten defendants guilty of all charges against them. Only one juror had wavered during the long night. Martin Moses, a grizzled language teacher who, by coincidence, lived in an apartment building raided by Dewey's detectives, had held out until dawn. On the third round of balloting he relented. He wept quietly during the verdict and the long singsong roll call recitation of jury polling. "Guilty . . . guilty . . . guilty . . . guilty." Each man was found guilty on sixty-two counts. The word "guilty" was pronounced 558 times in all over a period of forty minutes. Luciano stood expressionless at the rail. He hardly blinked. A police captain, armed and alert, stood at Luciano's side with his right hand resting on a holstered gun.

Frank Hnida, Dewey's bodyguard, noticed a man at the back of the courtroom straining forward from his chair with his right hand inside his coat. Hnida motioned to another detective and together they ushered the man out with his arms restrained. When they forced his hand from his coat they found that he held a silver crucifix.

After Justice McCook thanked the jury for their service, the ten convicted men marched into an anteroom, ankle manacles dragging on the marble floor, and into a van, which delivered them back to the Tombs, where they would await sentencing. "The top Mafia leader in

New York and his whole mob had been convicted in a single case," Dewey later wrote, "and I felt the majesty of the law had in truth been vindicated."

Eleven days later Justice McCook sentenced Luciano to thirty to fifty years in state prison. His criminal reign was over, for now anyway. He traveled in shackles to the Clinton Correctional Facility in Dannemora, New York, a Siberian stretch hard against the Canadian border, where his influence bought him a private cell with curtains and an electric stove.

"When I get out," he said, "I'll follow the horses from Saratoga to Belmont to Florida to California. I'll sleep with my windows open so I can reach out and hold the air in my hands. I'll never lock a door again . . . When night comes I'll go outdoors. I'll talk to everybody I see. Wherever I hear noise, I'm going to go in and look at people and watch them. I'll watch women laughing and dancing. I'll laugh and dance too."

Dewey jailed Luciano, and ten years later he would grant him early release. There could be no way of knowing in advance, though, the strange and terrible world events that would lead to his exoneration. As he settled into his new cell, Luciano could take only the smallest comfort, if any at all, in Gay Orlova's pledge to wait for him. She would wait all fifty years if she had to, she promised, just before she left for Paris.

Ten months after Luciano went to Dannemora, an early morning crowd filed into the Strand Theatre, a high baroque movie palace on the northwest corner of Broadway and Forty-seventh Street, for a preview of *Marked Woman*. The marquee bore the names of its two stars, Humphrey Bogart and Bette Davis.

The Strand's eight grand chandeliers dimmed at 9:30 a.m., hushing the sold-out crowd to silence. Before the movie started, a disclaimer declared the characters fictitious, but the audience knew better. *Marked Woman* was the story of a prostitute, sanitized by scriptwriters as a "nightclub hostess," loosely based on Cokey Flo. In the Hollywood version she turns against the despotic Lucky Luciano character and falls in love with the earnest, dedicated Thomas Dewey character, played by Humphrey Bogart. The real Cokey Flo enjoyed no such happy ending. She avoided whatever revenge might come to her on the streets of New York by traveling to London, Cincinnati, Hot Springs, Phoenix, and

California. Her passage was paid with proceeds from a series of articles she wrote with Mildred Balitzer for *Liberty*, a general-interest magazine.

In November 1937, she sent Barent Ten Eyck, one of Dewey's assistant district attorneys, a postcard from Ciudad Juarez, Mexico, where brothels and drugs were plentiful. She was never heard from again.

A few years earlier, in the outlandish Prohibition days, gangsters were objects of glamour and envy. Not anymore. Public sentiment had turned against them. In *Marked Woman,* the judge calls the Luciano stand-in "a low and brutal character, an unprincipled and aggressive egotist."

If Hollywood was a barometer of cultural shifts, then the prosecutor was now the leading man. Dewey fit the part. He had now won fifty-two straight convictions, a perfect record. In his biggest case he engineered the most significant court action ever accomplished against organized crime. At age thirty-four he became the first prosecutor to convict a top mob figure for his primary criminal pursuit instead of employing the loophole of income tax evasion. Because much of the court drama surrounding Luciano involved sex, the public closely followed the developments. (They paid far closer attention, in any case, than to Al Capone's tax evasion trial ten years earlier.)

The public's preoccupation with the Luciano case boosted Dewey's stock. He went from promising young prosecutor to an overnight American hero with a public profile that put him in the company of the great figures of the day—Lou Gehrig, Errol Flynn, Charles Lindbergh. A movie studio offered Dewey $150,000 to play the hero in a gangster movie. He declined.

In order to convict Luciano, Dewey had to convince witnesses and informants, most of them women, that he could protect them from retaliation and threats, largely by shutting down the Commission. In that sense he was contending with Reles as much as Luciano. The Luciano campaign was over, but the struggle with Reles was just starting as Dewey shifted his focus. The dark and dubious mantle of Public Enemy No. 1 now shifted to Lepke Buchalter.

6

LEPKE

On Saturday, September 5, 1936, a young milkman named Dave Margolin made his 6 a.m. deliveries outside the sleepy Catskill village of Hurleyville, New York. The first autumn colors touched the leaves overhanging the dirt road as he followed his route, stopping among cottages and boardinghouses. Racks of cold bottles rattled gently in back.

At the Paramount Manor Hotel he found a black taxi, a Lincoln sedan, blocking the long uphill driveway. The sun would not rise for another fifteen minutes or so, but in the twilight Margolin could see that the taxi's driver-side door hung open. He stepped from his truck and walked up to find a man in a white shirt and dark blazer lying face up in the driveway. His left ankle was crossed over his right with both feet resting on the running board of his Lincoln, as if he were napping with his feet propped up. Beneath his head a dark reddish-brown halo of drying blood soaked the gravel. His unmoving eyes looked to the brightening morning sky. Blood and bits of brain painted the taxi interior and gravel. Directly overhead, the hotel sign spanned the driveway: "Paramount Manor: Hotel of Happiness."

Margolin ran a hundred yards up the driveway to the hotel office and called the constable in the town of Fallsburg, New York, who, in turn, called a state police sergeant and a county sheriff. Within the hour sheriffs working with the Sullivan County coroner identified the man as thirty-four-year-old Irving Ashkenas, a Lithuanian-American cab driver who split time between Brooklyn and the Catskills. During the summer he lived in a lakeside cottage with his wife and two children.

The coroner pulled five bullets from Ashkenas's body, including one from his brain, or what was left of it. A local newspaper, *The Liberty Register,* reported that "authorities believed the taxi operator had driven one man, or possibly two, in his car to the gate of the Paramount Manor hotel, and this man, or these men, accomplished the killing."

Sheriffs collecting evidence at the roped-off crime scene assumed for now that Ashkenas was a taxi driver, and no more. They were not aware of his second livelihood as a Buchalter bodyguard, driver, and garment-district enforcer. He was on parole after serving almost five years in Sing Sing and Attica prisons for killing a dress manufacturer named Jacob Rothenberg at the corner of Broadway and Thirty-ninth Street six years earlier. Ashkenas's then girlfriend called Rothenberg that day with a saucy invitation to meet across the street from his workplace—a classic ploy. When Rothenberg arrived, Ashkenas hit him with a roundhouse punch. Rothenberg died when his head hit the curb.

The terms of Ashkenas's parole obliged him to share information about Buchalter's involvements. When Buchalter learned that Ashkenas was talking, he called Reles, who in turn dispatched a Murder, Inc. crew to find Ashkenas in Sullivan County. These details would not be known for four years.

Ashkenas was the first victim in an intensifying campaign by Reles and Murder, Inc. in the wake of Luciano's conviction. Until his incarceration in Dannemora the Commission's leadership had seemed safely beyond reach—impregnable and untouchable. Luciano's detention showed that killing potential informants might not be a fail-safe deterrent after all, given the unrelenting prosecutor now amassing evidence on the fourteenth floor of the Woolworth Building. Dewey had demonstrated that he could win over witnesses, lots of them, in spite of the terror Reles brought. Potential informants were still afraid, but now they had a proven prosecutor to confide in. Dewey promised to protect them, and they were beginning to believe him.

Reles now redoubled his push, starting with Ashkenas, to eliminate all lower-tier associates—wheelmen, gofers, hit men, and union associates—before they could testify to any activities and decisions that would damn Buchalter and other higher-ups. The race was on to see who could get to the informants first—Reles or Dewey.

Eight days after the milkman stumbled on Ashkenas's body, four gunmen waited at 6:30 on a Sunday morning outside an apartment building on Wyona Street, in the East New York neighborhood of Brooklyn. They sat in a stolen black Chevrolet sedan watching for a man named Joe Rosen to emerge from his home in a two-story brick building with generous bay windows.

Rosen once owned a small independent trucking company that for twenty-four years earned a handsome profit, $50,000 a year, hauling unfinished clothes from garment-district sweatshops to New Jersey tailors who stitched the finish work. As Buchalter solidified his control of the garment district, he decreed that manufacturers employ only trucking firms that he invested in, thereby driving Rosen out of business.

Rosen was reduced to running a small corner candy store down the block from his home, but selling licorice and baseball cards for small change would not pay his expenses. Buchalter sent Rosen two hundred dollars through an intermediary on the condition that he leave town. Rosen went to his son's home in Reading, Pennsylvania, but only for three days. Embittered and broke, he talked openly of restarting his trucking business, Buchalter be damned. And he spoke loudly, and recklessly, of his desire to unburden himself of his frustrations in Dewey's office.

"That bastard Rosen is going around Brownsville shooting his mouth off that he's going downtown," Buchalter said, referring to Dewey's office. "He and nobody else are going down any place or do any more talking—or any talking at all."

And so, on the early morning of September 13, 1936, Sol Bernstein, Mendy Weiss, Pittsburgh Phil Strauss, and a junior associate named Jimmy Feraca waited in a car outside Rosen's home. When he walked to his candy store, they followed at a surreptitious distance and parked out front. Bernstein was driving. He left the motor running.

Moments after Rosen unlocked the front door and sorted through the wads of Sunday newspapers deposited on the stoop, Feraca took up a position outside, gun in hand. Weiss and Strauss entered and pumped Rosen with twenty-eight sawed-off shotgun slugs. He collapsed backward on the two-toned tile floor with his arms spread wide like a child making an angel imprint in the snow. His head rested at the foot of a Coca-Cola icebox. The newspapers scattered.

Louis Stamler heard the shots from his home across the street. He had risen at 6:45 that morning to get his son up for his job in a neighborhood deli. He looked out a second-floor bedroom window. He managed to write down the license plate number as the sedan pulled away and followed a well-practiced getaway route—across Sutter and down Van Sinderen. A sidewalk newsstand operator thirteen blocks from the shooting took note as the sedan peeled around the corner of Livonia and Van Sinderen Avenues and abruptly stopped. The men got out and crossed a bridge over subway tracks and got into a pair of waiting cars.

Rosen's wife identified his body at the morgue. "I know why they killed him," she said when the attendant pulled back the sheet, revealing his ten bullet wounds. "He was going to Dewey."

Mrs. Rosen seemed to know who did it, and so did Brooklyn homicide detectives. The next day they arrested Pittsburgh Phil Strauss and Happy Maione at the Oriental Danceland, a Coney Island nightclub and restaurant. The police waited until the outlandish ceremonies of Coney Island's Mardi Gras celebration subsided, then waded into the nightclub as an elaborate dinner got under way. Police took Strauss and Maione to the Coney Island precinct and charged them with vagrancy, the standard allegation used to detain gangsters. "A man was murdered by gangsters Sunday," Police Commissioner Lewis Valentine told reporters. "It's better to have them locked up."

But Valentine could not keep them locked up without evidence. Knowing who murdered Joe Rosen and producing the corroboration required in court were not the same. Within a day Strauss and Maione returned to the streets. They could not know it now, but the Joe Rosen execution would turn out to be among the most consequential of all their killings.

Murder, Inc. killed Joe Rosen to protect Lepke Buchalter from whatever damning testimony Rosen might give, but no amount of killing could keep Dewey off Buchalter's back. His life had by now deteriorated into the miserable plight of the prey. When he left his apartment a uniformed doorman still held the door for him, and he still walked out onto the magnificence of Central Park West, but every morning he could see detectives parked in an unmarked police cruiser. He could see them through his rear window following him to his office on Madison Square Park, weaving through the lanes of Broadway traffic to stay in his slipstream. They were there when he left his office for lunch and when he rode uptown at day's end. In the evenings he could look from his living room window and see them parked below. They were always there, always waiting for him.

Buchalter felt renewed urgency to eliminate potential informants, but he was unable to order hits by calling Reles because he suspected that Dewey had tapped his phone. Instead the two men met in hotel bathrooms and subway platforms. "I sneak away from the cops," he told an associate. "I lose them . . . mostly in the subway."

In November 1936 Buchalter and Shapiro were convicted in federal court in Manhattan and sentenced to two years and fined $10,000 each for violating antitrust laws by attempting to control the $75 million fur industry in New York. The judge called the sentence "a mere slap on the wrist," given Buchalter's violent methods. Furriers who resisted his demands were beaten on the street in broad daylight. Buchalter didn't care that they were also Jewish. Their faces were splashed with vials of sulfuric acid. At least one died when his car blew up. Another was thrown from a tenth-floor window. Buchalter's army of 250 men sabotaged elevator cables and torched warehouses.

The sentence was lenient considering Buchalter's butchery, but he and Shapiro would still face whatever murder and extortion charges Dewey brought—if Buchalter showed up. Dewey suspected that Buchalter might try to disappear before entering another courtroom.

In November 1936 Dewey met with Martin T. Manton, a white-haired judge with a pince-nez perched on his nose who had sat for twenty-one years on the prestigious U.S Second Circuit Court of Appeals in New York. The court was scheduled to hear Buchalter and Gurrah's appeal on the federal antitrust conviction early the next year. Dewey asked Manton, as the court's senior judge, to deny Buchalter bail, or at least set bail beyond Buchalter's reach. He urged Manton to keep Buchalter safely locked up so he could not disappear.

Judge Manton consented. However, in clear violation of their agreement, Manton the next day freed Buchalter and Shapiro on $10,000 bail. As if that weren't devious enough, Manton's court then overturned the conviction altogether, claiming the case lacked evidence.

Dewey was livid. He launched a yearlong investigation that showed that Judge Manton had accepted a total of $439,481 in bribes, mostly in cash, in return for lenient court rulings. Dewey outlined his findings in a letter to the House Judiciary Committee. Manton promptly resigned. A month later a federal grand jury charged him with bribery and conspiracy to obstruct justice. Prosecutors called it cash-for-carry justice. He was convicted and spent nineteen months in the federal penitentiary in Lewisburg, Pennsylvania.

Judge Manton's conviction heightened Dewey's reputation as an unstoppable force—a judicial juggernaut. Seated in his customary spot in the back of Midnight Rose's candy store, Reles must have asked himself: If Dewey could bring down a respected federal judge, a man once considered for the Supreme Court, what might he do to Murder, Inc.? Dewey, the champion of justice who could not be influenced, threatened them all.

Conditions were toughening up, and not just because Dewey applied heat. In the prosperous Prohibition days mobsters had earned friends throughout the judicial system, with payoffs steadily making their way as needed to officials at all municipal levels—patrolman on the beat, prosecutors, statehouse politicians, and judges. When Prohibition ended in 1933, the underworld's flow of easy income dried up, forcing leaders and legmen to branch out into drug trafficking, prostitution, numbers rackets, and other risky ventures.

Reles and his men were thus in a heightened state of guardedness when, in mid-May 1937, Pittsburgh Phil Strauss by chance spotted a low-level loan shark and heroin addict named George "Whitey" Rudnick exiting a police car. At six feet and 140 pounds Rudnick looked scrawny and undernourished in the way that addicts do. His heroin habit made him receptive to an easy deal.

Reles and Rudnick were boyhood friends at Elmira Reformatory, where they played baseball together in the yard. Now Rudnick was what mobsters called a floater, a loose associate who ran odd errands. He had been part of the squad that helped Reles chase down and kill the Shapiro brothers. In fact, Rudnick had contracted tuberculosis after Meyer Shapiro stabbed him during a scuffle.

Reles would not let friendship interfere with the chance to send a blunt message to potential informants in Dewey's orbit: talking to the law would earn them a clear-cut death sentence. He and Pittsburgh Phil Strauss made three trips out to Sally's Bar and Grill to choreograph the kill with Happy Maione and Dasher Abbandando. They stood and drank beer at one end of the bar, away from the other patrons.

Their first step was to ask a gofer to steal a typewriter and deliver it to the two-story brick house that Reles shared with his wife and

in-laws. Seated together in the living room, Strauss and Reles composed a bogus note to be placed on Rudnick's body as a warning to
potential informants. "We didn't know how to adjust the ribbon so I
held the ribbon while Strauss typed the note," Reles later said. "There
were three notes written because we had an argument on how to spell
the word 'friend.'" Strauss spelled it f-r-e-i-n-d. Reles insisted it was
f-r-i-e-n-d. They tore up two notes before settling on Strauss's version.

Reles and Abbandando spent three nights, from midnight to 5 a.m.,
cruising for Rudnick among Brownsville pool halls and saloons in a little tan Ford that Abbandando borrowed from an acquiantance on the
pretense of taking a girl on a date. Abbandando was close friends with
Rudnick, and therefore useful in the pursuit. Rudnick was more likely
to get in the car with Abbandando along.

Meanwhile Strauss and Maione watched for Rudnick at Sally's Bar
and Grill, a few steps from the Sunrise Garage, where they intended
to kill him. "We knew we would catch him at either spot when he was
making his rounds," Reles said.

On the third night Reles found Rudnick walking at 4 a.m. or so
near Midnight Rose's. "I spotted Rudnick coming along Saratoga Ave.,
right in close to the building," Reles said. "I said to Dasher, 'Here he
comes.' The Dasher looked and said, 'you're crazy.' Then he looked
closer again and said, 'you're right.'"

Abbandando got in the tan Ford and pulled alongside Rudnick as
he walked north to Dumont Avenue. From the corner Reles could see
Rudnick walk over and exchange a few words with Abbandando through
the car window, then he got in. On some pretext Abbandando drove Rudnick to the garage where Strauss and Maione waited. Rudnick may have
suspected what awaited him. The late-night invitation to ride, even with a
friend, had ominous implications in their circles. But he had no way out.

Rudnick would not be the only one to die that night. By coincidence
Happy Maione's ailing seventy-year-old grandmother, Anna Selenga,
lived in a three-room apartment almost directly across the street from
the Sunrise Garage. Her passing at 1:45 a.m. that night provided a con-
venient alibi.

Maione's extended family held a vigil at her death bed—weeping,
preparing food, kneeling in prayer. *May all the saints and the Father
and the Son and the Holy Ghost watch over her.* Maione walked back

and forth through the night, shuttling from his dying grandmother's side to the murder scene in the garage.

Reles arrived in his own car at 4:30 a.m. "I knocked on the garage door after waiting a while," he later said. "Maione came to the door and said the job was done." Reles entered to see that Strauss had stabbed Rudnick with an ice pick—thirteen times in the neck, fifty times in the chest—and strangled him with clothesline.

"I went in and Strauss had an ice pick in his hand," Reles said. "Maione had a meat chopper in his hand. Rudnick's body was on the floor. . . . Abbandando was holding Rudnick by the shoulders and Strauss was putting a rope around his neck."

Abbandando went outside and called for a wheelman named Angelo "Julie" Catalano, a slight and sallow former taxi driver who was killing time playing cards with Joe "The Baker" Liberto, the garage night attendant, in an adjacent Sinclair gas station. At Abbandando's bidding, Catalano dropped his cards and put on gloves so that he would leave no fingerprints. At 3:30 a.m. he pulled into the garage in a black Buick sedan stolen from another garage, on Liberty Avenue, while its attendant was asleep. Abbandando grabbed Rudnick's feet and dragged him to the car's rear door. Strauss and Maione hoisted Rudnick up by his head and struggled to fold his six-foot frame so that he would lie hidden from view behind the front seat. They assumed Rudnick was dead until they heard a wet gurgling cough.

"This fucking bum ain't dead yet," Strauss said.

Maione reared back and delivered the meat cleaver to Rudnick's forehead just below the hairline. "That will finish him now," he said.

They bundled the body in back while Maione threw a bucket of water on the garage floor and Abbandando swept the blood down a drain. Reles told Catalano to drive the Buick over to Jefferson Avenue with its cargo in back. As instructed, he abandoned the car by a curb as the sun rose.

At 7:40 a.m. two patrolmen found the stolen car with Rudnick's body crammed in the backseat. By then his face had turned a deep cyanotic blue, and his tongue lolled like that of a dead deer strapped to a hunter's car. A glint of white bone showed where the meat cleaver had been carved into his forehead.

Detectives retrieved the typewritten note addressed to Rudnick planted in his back pocket: "Thanks for the information you gave me. Come over and see me soon again." Reles had forged the name of an assistant district attorney on Dewey's staff. The note was an obvious fake, written as a warning to those who might be tempted to violate the criminal code: if you talk, you die.

As far as Reles was concerned the pathetic case of Whitey Rudnick was now closed, or nearly so. He still had to worry about Catalano and Liberto, who had seen and heard enough to betray Murder, Inc. if they chose to.

On July 6, 1937, Buchalter faced a critical test. Eight months earlier a federal court had convicted him and Shapiro of violating federal anti-trust laws. The corrupt judge Martin Manton presided over an appeals court that reversed that ruling. Now that Manton had resigned in disgrace his court agreed to retry the two men on the original charges.

When the court convened, the judges in their dark robes took their assigned places and the prosecutors stood in a line at their table. All the principals were there, arranged in their places like actors on a stage set, except for Buchalter and Shapiro. As Dewey feared, they had forfeited bail and vanished. "Things are getting too hot here," Buchalter had told a friend. "I'll have to lam."

A federal judge ordered their immediate arrest. With Buchalter and Shapiro now officially fugitives, an urgent international manhunt geared up. On November 9, 1937, the State of New York offered a $5,000 reward for Buchalter's capture, a bounty later increased to $50,000, with half donated by the federal government. An unspoken competition arose between the FBI and Dewey's investigators to see who would catch Buchalter. FBI director J. Edgar Hoover called him "probably the most dangerous criminal in the U.S." Dewey circulated a million "Wanted: Dead or Alive" circulars with a police photograph of Buchalter wearing a light gray double-breasted jacket, both suit coat and vest unbuttoned, and a light gray fedora. He looked like a gentleman strolling through Central Park on a Sunday afternoon. The image was published in newspapers and shown in movie theaters before the feature.

Buchalter sightings came in from around the world—California, Palestine, Cuba, England, Canada, France, Puerto Rico, and Germany. In actuality Buchalter was hiding in Brooklyn the entire time, disguised by a thick Groucho Marx mustache and an extra fifteen pounds or so on his small, well-padded frame. When he went out he wore dark glasses and a fedora pulled low.

Reles acted as Buchalter's consigliere of concealment, arranging a series of hideouts—a room above the Oriental Danceland in Coney Island and a furnished room daringly close to the big gray granite Brooklyn police headquarters on Bergen Street. He also lived for a while in the Flatbush apartment of Dorothy Walker, the widow of gangster Simon "Fatty" Walker who died in a shootout in the Hotsy Totsy Club on Broadway. Buchalter shared a bedroom furnished with twin beds with Walker's son Milton, who trimmed Buchalter's hair and mustache and supplied him with reading material. "He read magazines, hundreds of magazines," Milton said. "That's all he reads. I would buy him three or four a day." As far as Milton was concerned, Buchalter was hiding because of an income tax difficulty.

Buchalter surfaced sporadically for a restaurant lunch, or to visit his wife, Betty. But a fugitive could never linger. He lived a lonely, anxious life but did not yet consider surrender. "Let them find me first," he told Reles.

Of all the gangsters in hiding, Buchalter was the hardest to locate because he was by nature discreet and averse to flashy cars and nightlife. "Give him some books and magazines," said Major Garland Williams of the Federal Narcotics Bureau, "and he's content to hold up in one room for six months."

If friends or associates wanted to see Buchalter they had to meet Reles on whatever Brooklyn street corner he specified. Reles would vet the petitioner. If they passed muster, he would escort them to the hiding place. Reles was Buchalter's guardian, his liaison, and his intermediary to the outside world—the world of family and friends that Lepke had relinquished in order to avoid incarceration, or worse, the electric chair. He had given up most of what he valued in life in order to stay alive.

Reles brought Buchalter newspapers, magazines, and meals. He delivered pressing news from the Commission and idle gossip. He would on occasion take Buchalter out for late-night drives for the pleasure of seeing the world he had relinquished—young couples walking to dinner hand in hand, movie palaces with blinking marquees, gaggles of stoop-sitters laughing over gossip, chords minor and major jumping from jazz bars.

The two men, the guardian and guarded, not surprisingly grew close. Reles often slept on a sofa or spare bed in Buchalter's hideout, returning bleary-eyed in the morning to his wife, Rosie who, as usual, had only the sketchiest motion of where he had been.

Reles balanced his new responsibilities as Buchalter's keeper and confidante with his ongoing duties as the Commission's enforcer-in-chief. Under his management the pace of killings quickened in the summer of 1937.

In July, Reles learned that Walter Sage, the underling who four years earlier had helped ambush Red Alpert, was skimming profits from the gang's slot machines installed in a dozen or so Catskill resort hotels, a hundred miles northwest of the city. The Commission had sent Sage to manage the slots. Now he would have to pay for his greed. "What does the bum think?" Reles said. "He's a trolley conductor?"

Reles had an insidious knack for orchestrating killings. He often sent the target's most intimate friends to do the job because their reassuring presence tended to dispel suspicions. The target was more likely to get into a car, for example, if his best friend was driving. The tactic had the added benefit of testing the friend's loyalty.

In this case Reles sent Sage's best friend and former roommate Irving "Gangi" Cohen, a hulking man with close-set dark eyes and the frame of a heavyweight boxer. On the evening of July 27, the sort of warm summer night best enjoyed with windows thrown wide open, Cohen and a local associate named Jack Drucker picked Sage up at the expansive tile-roofed Hotel Ambassador, in Fallsburg, New York where Sage lived during the summer resort season. Sage was known as a dresser. He met Cohen and Drucker in the lobby wearing a gray striped suit and a purple striped shirt with matching handkerchief protruding like a bouquet from his suit pocket.

They set off in a stolen green Packard sedan for drinks and dinner at the Hotel Evans, a popular nightspot for gangsters in the small resort town of Loch Sheldrake. Sage was unaware that Pretty Levine, Pittsburgh Phil Strauss, and Tick Tock Tannenbaum followed at a discreet distance in a second car—a common Murder, Inc. maneuver. Sage sat in the passenger seat. Cohen and Drucker sat in the rear. (It's not known who was driving.)

Cohen periodically leaned forward to talk with Sage as they wound their way past fields and farms on Old Monticello Road. After four miles or so Drucker quietly unsheathed an ice pick in back. Cohen wrapped his arms around his best friend's neck from behind, pinning him to the seat while Drucker stabbed Sage thirty-two times in the chest and neck. He missed once, sinking the ice pick into Cohen's left forearm. Meanwhile, Sage fought back, pivoting his shoulders left and right, trying to release himself from his best friend's grip. In desperation Sage yanked the steering wheel, sending the Packard veering off the road. By the time the car stopped hard in a ditch Sage had ceased to struggle. He was dead, or close to it.

Drucker was wiping blood off the ice pick when the chase car pulled up. Strauss stepped out and told Cohen to fetch a length of rope from the rumble seat. Cohen's mind may have been disarranged by his participation in his best friend's murder moments earlier. He was seized by a suspicion, more like a conviction, that he was set up to be the next victim. It occurred to him that the ice pick sunk into to his left arm was no accident, and the rope he retrieved from the rumble seat might soon be around his own neck. If Reles could get him to murder his best friend, then what was to prevent him from being next in line?

Cohen was speaking to Drucker when he broke from the group mid-sentence. He bolted for the woods, his 240-pound bulk ducking branches and sprinting over felled tree trunks. The men called Cohen's name a few times, then gave up. Maybe the killing had affected his bowels, one said. They shrugged and returned to the messy matter at hand.

The next morning a Loch Sheldrake resident named Orville Miller found Cohen hiding in his garage. Cohen pulled a gun and forced Miller to drive him to a bus station in Monticello while he slumped from view in the backseat. From there Cohen disappeared into the heartland.

Sage's body lay in the car trunk for eighteen hours. The next night Strauss hog-tied it and lashed it to the stripped-down frame of a slot machine before dumping it from a rowboat into Swan Lake, a popular summer gathering spot four miles south of the hamlet of Liberty, New York. Strauss assumed the body would eventually be found. When it was, the slot machine tethered to the putrefied body would serve as a macabre warning to those who might consider mishandling profits, but he did not expect the body to be found soon. He assumed that the thirty-two stab wounds would allow the gas to escape from the decomposing body, and it would therefore sink to the bottom. But because the heart was still pumping blood when Drucker stabbed Sage, the holes closed up and the body inflated like a balloon.

Four days later, on a nearly perfect July day, the bloated body, carrying the slot machine frame with it, bobbed to the surface, horrifying vacationers swimming and rowing nearby. "Think of that," Strauss later said. "With this bum you gotta be a doctor, or he floats."

Police identified the body by matching its fingerprints with those in New York police files, and from the initials "WJS" tattooed on a biceps, alongside a bird of paradise and a peacock. Sage's family never claimed the body. He was buried in a potter's field not far from the quiet stretch of road where he died.

Nobody saw Cohen back in Brooklyn after he made his panicked dash into the woods. Nobody knew where he went or what happened to him until, more than two years later, the best friends Pretty Levine and Dukey Maffetore went to the Loew's Theatre in Brownsville to see *Golden Boy*, a black-and-white movie about a gifted violinist named Joe Bonaparte, played by William Holden, who takes up boxing to earn a quick fortune. The two men sat in the dark as Joe prepared for a climactic fight in Madison Square Garden against an opponent named Chocolate Drop. A trainer rubbed Joe down in the locker room before leading him to the ring in the cavernous arena. The bell clanged, and the boxers closed and engaged—uppercuts, jabs, hooks. A few punches into the round the film cut to reaction shots from the ringside crowd. The camera lingered for a beat on the unmistakable bulk of Gangi Cohen standing among dark-suited onlookers. Levine and Maffetore sat through the rest of the movie in shock. They went directly to Midnight Rose's to report what they'd seen. No, they said, the actor did not look like Gangi Cohen. It *was* Gangi Cohen, right there in a Hollywood movie. They placed bets. Nobody believed Levine and Maffetore until they all went over to the movie house for the late show. If this career in crime doesn't work out, they joked, we can always go to Hollywood.

At almost exactly the same time a policeman in upstate Sullivan County spotted Cohen in the ringside scene during a double feature and reported his finding to the local district attorney. Cohen's confidential life in the California sunshine was no longer a secret. "It was an apparition," a prosecutor later wrote. "Sullivan County law enforcement had been hunting that figure for three years to answer questions about murder."

In the days after sprinting into the woods Cohen had traveled as far from Brooklyn as he could—beyond Ohio, beyond Kansas, beyond Nevada. He landed in Los Angeles, where a light heavyweight prizefighter turned movie actor named Max "Slapsie Maxie" Rosenbloom helped him get small studio parts under the name Jack Gordon. He easily won gangster roles, because of course he looked the part. Cohen went from hood to Hollywood, where he hid within plain sight of the whole world.

As the murders mounted, Lepke Buchalter stayed hidden under Reles's safekeeping. He expected his closest associates to follow him into hiding, as his partner Gurrah Shapiro had done. He instructed Max Rubin, a silver-haired schoolteacher turned textile cutter who collected union dues for him in the garment district, to leave the city altogether, to disappear until the Dewey investigation cooled. Rubin had been Buchalter's go-between in his negotiations with Joe Rosen before he ordered Rosen killed. "Things are very, very hot around here," Buchalter told Rubin. "You cannot stay around."

Buchalter was motivated by self-preservation more than concern for Rubin's well-being. The farther Rubin traveled from home, the less likely he would be to speak to Dewey. Rubin went to Saratoga, but hated it. He had nothing to do but watch movies. Nor did he like his month's stay at the Carlton Hotel in downtown Salt Lake City, where he received four fifty-dollar money orders through Western Union. He also lived for a week in New Orleans where he helped Frank Costello operate slot machines. It didn't matter where he went. He missed his wife and two children, and he eventually returned to New York without telling Buchalter.

Rubin was walking up Amsterdam Avenue late one night in a driving rain when a car stopped. A door swung open. A gruff voice ordered him in. He could guess where they were going. Buchalter was waiting for him under the protection of the dripping awning of a dark, closed-up store near 150th Street, in Washington Heights. He asked Rubin why he had defied orders. "Lepke, I want to come home," he said. "I'm lonesome. I don't like running around the country. I want to see my family. You can trust me."

"How old are you?" Buchalter asked.

"Forty-eight."

"You've reached a ripe old age," Buchalter said. He turned and walked off into the rain.

Rubin knew that his homecoming was a form of betrayal. His peril compounded when, after a discussion with Frank Hogan, an assistant district attorney on Dewey's staff, he agreed to share what he knew of Buchalter's extortion rackets before a grand jury in late September. Rubin must have known that Reles would come for him, but he unaccountably rejected Dewey's offer of protection.

A week after leaving the grand jury room Rubin emerged from a subway station in the Bronx and walked down Gun Hill Road toward his apartment in a new six-story building a few blocks away. His family waited for him there, the wife and children that he had missed so much during his months in exile. He was passing a barbershop across from Montefiore Hospital when a gunman ran up behind him and fired one shot into the back of his head. The bullet went through his skull and out his neck, embedding itself in a wooden barber pole.

Rubin survived after a touch-and-go month in Fordham Hospital. Because the bullet severed neck muscles, his head would tilt to one side for the rest of his life. He otherwise fully recovered.

The Rubin shooting helped Dewey in one respect: it conveyed a sense of urgency to the public. Rubin still lay in intensive care with a fifty-fifty chance of survival when Dewey sat alongside FBI director J. Edgar Hoover at a forum held at the Waldorf Astoria Hotel and broadcast on WJZ radio. Dewey spoke in his capacity as special prosecutor, but also as a candidate for Manhattan district attorney. He sought a more permanent office from which to wage his fight and begin his political climb.

Dewey observed that a new era of "streamlined and modern" crime called for a new kind of prosecutor, one who, like him, was not picked for political considerations. Dewey's immediate prospects depended on the success or failure of his war on the Commission, which he said verged on triumph. "The shot which struck down Max Rubin was the frightened act of a desperate criminal underworld," he said. "The racketeers have flung down their challenge. I accept that challenge."

Dewey's work translated into political success, as he knew it would. Shortly after 10 p.m. on the night of November 2, 1937, Dewey and his wife, Frances, met reporters at his campaign headquarters after receiving confirmation of his landslide election as Manhattan district attorney. Dewey was so popular that polling places in Brooklyn posted placards explaining that he wasn't running in that borough. For the first time in twenty years, Tammany had lost control of the Manhattan district attorney's office.

His election, on a reform ticket shared with Mayor La Guardia, was a form of vindication, a signal that voters had faith in his anti-racketeering drive. He had made good by jailing Lucky Luciano. Now they endorsed his intentions to continue the push from his new post. "The fight against crime is begun," he said. "We shall meet the challenge of the underworld." It was a pledge to New Yorkers and a warning to Buchalter, Reles, and the rest: the endgame was coming.

So great was Dewey's momentum, so lauded was he for his crime fight, that within a year the New York Republican Party chose him, at age thirty-six, to run for governor against Herbert Lehman, the incumbent who had appointed Dewey special prosecutor.

On October 31 Dewey traveled by train on a final push of his gubernatorial campaign through the heart of New York State. He was met at nineteen station stops by local dignitaries, marching bands, and heaving crowds in the thousands. At every stop he blamed the Democrats, including his opponent, the incumbent governor, for allowing Murder, Inc. and other gangs to thrive without fear of prosecution.

The waiting throng in Syracuse was so massive that Dewey had to stay aboard the train for twenty minutes while police cleared a path for him. That night voters heard on the radio the same hoarse whisper of scorn rising to a full-throated baritone that had swayed juries. Dewey's voice spoke for an indignant populace demanding order and justice. On the radio, as on the stump, Dewey claimed that Lehman was a well-heeled frontman for corrupt machine politics. "Murder is safe in Brooklyn," he said. "Two out of every three murders remain unsolved. Two out of every three murderers are never indicted. [They] walk the street as free men." Criminals "operated with immunity in Brooklyn, and the reasons lie deep in a corrupt and contented political system."

The speech played well in New York's rural upstate regions, where farm families tended to share Dewey's Midwestern suspicions of immigrant enclaves in New York and other cities, but upstate resentment was not enough to propel Dewey to the governor's mansion. He lost by just 70,000 votes. It was the most closely contested New York State election in a decade. At 12:45 a.m. on election night Dewey sent a telegram from his campaign office on East Forty-fourth Street to Lehman's office two blocks away congratulating him on winning a fourth term. "I wish you every success and happiness," he wrote.

Dewey lost, but only by 1.4 percent, a margin so slim against a popular incumbent that he could still claim a victory of sorts. For the first time people spoke of Dewey as a national figure, a potential candidate for the White House, at either end of the ticket, in 1940. A Gallup poll released in May 1939 gave him a slight lead over President Franklin D. Roosevelt in the next year's presidential election. He could be the new leadership the Republican Party needed to challenge President Roosevelt—if he could finish his dirty job in New York.

Five months earlier, on June 14, 1937, Harry Anslinger, director of the federal narcotics bureau and originator of America's war on drugs, disembarked in New York after a transatlantic voyage on the luxury liner SS *Washington*. As he reached the bottom of the gangway a blond woman handed him an envelope. She disappeared into the crowd before he could speak to her. Inside the envelope Anslinger found an unsigned letter that read as follows:

"I can furnish you with valuable information about the smuggling of large quantities of heroin by a certain gang. I must deal with you directly, otherwise a leak might upset everything. Please answer in the *New York Times* personal column, saying, "X-2 telephone me.""

The tip sounded far-fetched, but Anslinger felt that he could not responsibly ignore it. So he placed the classified ad, as instructed. The next morning the woman called to say that she was willing to share what she knew, but only if Anslinger met her in person. "And come alone, buster," she said. "I may have to trust you, but I don't want no roundtable conference."

Anslinger was a bald, bull-necked man with a passing resemblance to Benito Mussolini. He walked over from the bureau's Washington office to meet the mystery woman at the lobby bar in the Mayflower Hotel, four blocks north of the White House. Her boyfriend, she explained over a drink, had cheated on her. She wanted to punish him by giving the narcotics bureau details of the drug ring he helped run with Buchalter's backing.

Three men from the Bronx, she explained, shipped bundles of heroin from Shanghai to Marseilles hidden in a series of handsome steamer trunks. The trunks were then loaded aboard luxurious transatlantic liners—the RMS *Queen Mary*, RMS *Majestic,* and RMS *Aquitania*—as the property of a handful of stylish young women, often traveling first class. When the couriers disembarked on the West Side piers of Manhattan, customs inspectors, bribed $1,000 each, provided color-coded "clearance stamps," indicating the trunks had already cleared customs. Porters carried the trunks to waiting cars, which ferried the heroin to a laboratory in the Bronx for processing.

Buchalter had worked it all out like intricate machinery, and it succeeded. Each round-the-world trip delivered $100,000 worth of pure heroin, which in its diluted form sold on the New York streets for $5 million or so. As the primary backer, Buchalter at first demanded 60 percent of the profit, but settled for half. Over fourteen months the ring smuggled 1,463 pounds of heroin.

Anslinger had suspected that Buchalter might be running drugs, but he lacked evidence until now. Prosecutors protected Madame X-2's identity, but other insiders spoke to the grand jury in exchange for immunity.

Buchalter, still a fugitive, already faced felony racketeering charges, and Dewey was amassing murder charges against him. Now Buchalter faced a legal peril on a third front. On December 1, 1937, federal prosecutors indicted Buchalter, in absentia, for financing the drug smuggling operation. He was one of thirty charged with a conspiracy to violate federal narcotics laws and bribing customs officials.

Buchalter normally operated in a discreet, methodical manner, but now, as the pressure mounted, he relied on Reles and Murder, Inc. to eliminate witnesses at a faster pace. "Day after day men would disappear," Anslinger later wrote, "or the child of an individual who had information would be found dead."

As the investigations and indictments piled up, Reles continued to shuttle Buchalter among Brooklyn hideouts. Buchalter intended to play the long game, to lie low until Reles and his squad had killed enough witnesses, or sufficiently intimidated them, that prosecutors ran out of people to put on the stand. He expected the eight associates who had followed him into hiding to do the same. But after more than a year spent underground they began to tire of isolated days and nights in basements and back rooms, of sporadic contact with wives and children, of worrying that they might have to go on like this forever. It did not go unnoticed that Max Rubin had come out of hiding and survived, though just barely.

Hyman Yuran, a dress manufacturer who doubled as a money

collector and extortionist, was among the first to betray Buchalter by giving himself up. He had been arrested with Buchalter and twelve others back in August and disappeared just before speaking before the grand jury. He hid for year, then, in December 1937, gave up and agreed to testify.

Seven months later Yuran was vacationing at the Ambassador Hotel in the Catskills. His phone rang. After a brief exchange, he told his wife, Lena, that he had an unexpected appointment. A blond woman waited behind the wheel of Yuran's car. They drove off together. His wife never saw him again.

The next defector was Benjamin Levine, third in command behind Buchalter and Shapiro in the garment racket and the primary conduit through which millions of dollars flowed. On February 11, 1938, just as detectives closed in on his hiding place, Levine walked into Dewey's office in the Woolworth Building and identified himself to Murray I. Gurfein, an assistant district attorney. He had been a fugitive for sixteen months, moving almost constantly from one hiding spot to another.

Of the sixteen originally arrested with Buchalter, Levine brought to nine the number of men now in custody. Buchalter's fortifications were beginning to crumble, though he and Shapiro showed no signs of surrender. They were out there somewhere, but where? Five days after Levine turned himself in, Dewey received word that Buchalter and Shapiro were in Warsaw. Polish newspapers reported that the pair had written a letter to Jeanette Suchestow, fiancée of Prince Michael Radziwill, threatening to kidnap her unless they received payment. *The Jewish Morning Journal*, a newspaper published in New York, claimed that Warsaw police had arrested the two fugitives.

When the *Journal* article came out, Dewey and his staff telegrammed Polish authorities. Late in the day they received a report that Buchalter might actually be in Mexico City instead. Federal agents were looking for a man who had entered Mexico using a fake passport with a photo that looked suspiciously like Buchalter—dark eyes, long nose, swarthy countenance. In the end, it was another false alarm.

The manhunt turned up nothing, but it made life more anxious for the hunted. So anxious that Gurrah Shapiro concluded that his self-imposed detention was as bad, or worse than jail. "I'm tired of the government being so close to me all the time," he said. "I decided to surrender."

At 3:30 p.m. on April 14, 1938, the squat, heavy-jawed figure of

Shapiro walked down West Eleventh Street, in lower Manhattan, and entered a hulking jail known as the Federal Detention House. "I'm Jake Shapiro," he told a guard. "I want to surrender." He was immediately locked up in a cell. He was convicted two months later and sent to a penitentiary in Pennsylvania. "In court the big ox bawled like a baby," wrote the *Daily News,* "and went off to the federal pen." He never saw the outside world again.

Dewey's crackdown, combined with Buchalter's war of extermination, left the underground in a heightened state of fear and paranoia. Buchalter trusted no one but Reles, and nobody trusted Buchalter. Everyone looked over his shoulder, everyone looked out for himself.

It was in this atmosphere of mistrust that Buchalter received a letter from a former strong-arm lieutenant named Harry "Big Greenie" Greenberg, who supplied Murder, Inc. with blackjacks, lead pipes, and guns. The U.S. had deported Greenberg to his native Poland in 1935, after his long record of grand larceny and burglary made him unwelcome. But he and his wife, Ida, jumped ship before landing in Poland and relocated to Canada, where Greenberg figured that he could profit from Buchalter's predicament. Greenberg wrote Buchalter a letter reminding his old boss of the wealth of incriminating details he knew. He asked for $5,000 to keep his mouth shut. Greenberg did not use the word blackmail in his letter. He didn't need to. Instead of money, Buchalter sent a gunman to Canada. But Greenberg, sensing trouble, quietly stole back into the U.S. with Ida, using his dead father-in-law's passport. They arrived in Hollywood in June 1939. No one knew the couple's location, least of all Buchalter, until a freakish billion-to-one encounter brought the couple out of hiding.

Month by month, through the 1938 calendar and into 1939, Dewey supervised the global manhunt in hopes of returning Buchalter, handcuffed and broken, to a New York courtroom. A conviction would add further weight to Dewey's reputation as a force for law and rectitude and help propel him, comet-like, to the political career his parents had imagined for him—a career as a moral crusader against the corruption and vice of Eastern melting pots.

The manhunt now escalated in urgency, if only to halt the steady one-by-one murder and disappearance of Buchalter associates. As bloody as it was, the purge would only intensify over the coming months while Buchalter remained in hiding. The targets included Leon Scharf, a garment industry boss crucial to Buchalter's racketeering operations. Dewey had arrested Scharf on August 23, 1937, along with Buchalter and Shapiro, but released him on $10,000 bail when he agreed to testify against his former associates. In September 1938 Scharf married Rae Katz, a platinum blonde with gleaming almond eyes who had recently divorced a convicted forger. Two months after they married, Scharf and Rae left their apartment on West End Avenue, on the Upper West Side of Manhattan, to pick up a wedding gift in New Jersey. They never returned. "I verily believe both are dead, having been unlawfully made away with by those who did not desire to have Leon appear as a witness in behalf of the prosecution," Rae's father said in an affidavit. In December 1938 Leon Scharf and Hyman Yuran missed a court appointment and forfeited bail. They were now officially fugitives, though everyone knew they might just as likely be dead.

Those Buchalter associates who were not already dead or disappeared now scrambled for safety. In December 1938 a thirty-four-year-old assassin and convicted jewel thief named Albert "Plug" Schuman asked a police inspector to help him find an honest job. Schuman had coined a saying popular among gangsters: "Shoot them twice in the back of the neck, and they won't wiggle." Now, he said, he had decided to "cut out all that other stuff and go straight."

There was no such thing as a neutral stance. If Schuman went straight, if he dropped from Buchalter's ranks, he was essentially defecting. Buchalter asked Reles to make sure it didn't happen.

Schuman made a tricky target because he was perpetually suspicious. In keeping with his longstanding practice, Reles recruited Schuman's close friend Irving "Knadles" Nitzberg to help entrap him. The job followed a classic Murder, Inc. script. On January 9, 1939, Nitzberg and Tick Tock Tannenbaum arranged to drive Schuman to an early morning card game in a stolen car. Schuman rode through Canarsie in the passenger seat with Nitzberg seated directly behind him. Tannenbaum drove. Reles followed in a second car.

Nitzberg waited for the prearranged signal. When Tannenbaum asked for a cigarette, Nitzberg pulled out a .38 behind Schuman's seat and shot him twice in the neck—Schuman's own signature move. Tannenbaum then pulled over next to an empty lot. The two men jumped out and fled in Reles's car. When the police arrived they found Schuman in a black coat and hat slumped against the car door like a sleeping passenger on a long drive. Meanwhile, Reles drove Nitzberg and Tannenbaum to his house, where they wiped blood off their coats.

Three weeks later Isadore Friedman and Louis Cohen, longstanding Buchalter agents who performed years of hits and dirty work, were shot on a Lower East Side street. Cohen had returned fire three times before falling dead in a vacant lot on Lewis Street, his .38 lying at his feet. Friedman was found fifty feet away. He was shot in the back and neck as he tried to run.

Reles continued to work his way down the list of targets. Joseph Miller was a wealthy fifty-year-old coat manufacturer who gave Buchalter entrée to the garment district. He cooperated with Dewey. At 8 p.m. on March 23, 1939, he parked his car outside his home on West Tremont Avenue in the Bronx and walked to his front door. Two men stepped forward with revolvers raised and shot him four times in one arm, twice in the other. Miller wrestled the gun from one and began to hit him in the head with it. Miller almost had his attacker subdued when the second man shot him in the hip, dropping him to the sidewalk. Miller was left for dead, but he survived.

Abraham "Whitey" Friedman was one of the thirteen men Dewey indicted for racketeering in the garment industry. After six months languishing in jail as a material witness, he agreed to cooperate. Dewey rewarded him by cutting his bail from $35,000 to $15,000. Friedman paid it, and walked free. His friends urged him to lie low, but lying low was not his way. He was known as the toughest of the tough. He went right back to making book in the garment district. He walked home, in Brownsville, on the night of April 26, 1939. He was about to turn to enter his redbrick apartment, at 22 East Ninety-sixth Street, where his wife, Tillie, was cooking dinner, when a sedan pulled up. A man carrying a double-barreled shotgun got out. He shot Friedman twice in the left shoulder and in the back of the head. He died before an ambulance arrived.

While Reles closed on the informants, the authorities closed on Reles. On May 4, 1939, Reles's den mother, Rose Gold, the candy-store proprietor, was charged with racketeering and perjury in connection with fraudulent bail bond transactions. The candy store's bank records showed deposits and withdrawals of as much as $10,000 a day, an indication that Mrs. Gold was serving as a covert banker for Murder, Inc.

Mrs. Gold stood in State Supreme Court, a tiny, bird-like sixty-seven-year-old woman, less than five feet tall, with wisps of white hair. She responded to the judge's questions with a weak whisper. When her son, Sam Siegel, saw her leaving court escorted by detectives, he fainted and collapsed to the ground in a courthouse hallway. Either shock or theatrics drove him to the floor, though it's hard to know which.

Mrs. Gold awaited trial in the Women's House of Detention, having failed to provide the $50,000 bail. Her attorney, a lanky defense lawyer named Burton B. Turkus, failed to get her bail reduced to an affordable sum, although he warned that she might die in jail from a heart ailment. The judge concluded that she stood a greater risk of dying on the street, where Reles could get to her. "There are persons to whose interest it would be," the prosecutor told the judge, "if this woman should not be available at trial."

In the days after her arrest, sightseers gathered at the corner of Livonia and Saratoga Avenues to gape at what the newspaper coverage of her arrest called the headquarters of Murder, Inc. A year later, on the eve of her trial, Gold pled guilty to seven counts of perjury.

Morris "Moise" Diamond, a fifty-three-year-old business manager for the Teamsters Union, had steadfastly, and bravely, resisted Buchalter's extortions in the garment district. He willingly told Dewey what he knew about the murder of a union president. Diamond must have known that he would eventually pay for sharing information with prosecutors, and he did.

He left his Brooklyn boardinghouse at 6 a.m. on May 25, 1939, and walked toward the Eighteenth Avenue subway station to ride to the union offices on West Forty-second Street in Manhattan. The day brought a promise of spring, with clear skies and temperatures that would touch 72 degrees. Diamond had walked less than a block from his front door when he passed a man wearing black pants and a gray sweater seated at a bus stop reading a newspaper. The man was Jack "The Dandy" Parisi, a Murder, Inc. gunman. He was an immigrant tailor who became one of the toughest operators in Murder, Inc. *Time* magazine later called him "a toad-like little man with amazingly large bags under his eyes and an unswerving penchant for flashy clothes."

Behind the newspaper Parisi held a pistol. He lowered the newspaper and fired five shots into Diamond's stomach and chest. A barely literate Murder, Inc. gofer named Angelo "Julie" Catalano pulled a maroon sedan up to the curb, and Parisi got in. Diamond died an hour later at Zion Hospital.

Dewey was nothing if not exhaustive. By the summer of 1939 he had questioned more than five thousand people, roughly a hundred of whom worked for the Commission in some capacity.

As Dewey's list of interviews grew, so too did Reles's workload. He would go down the list, exterminating friends and associates, one by one, until nobody with firsthand knowledge of Buchalter's rackets and butchery was left to testify against him. Reles had shared meals with many on the list. They had been in and out of each other's Brooklyn homes for birthdays and bar mitzvahs and Seder dinners. It had taken a measure of trust to stand shoulder-to-shoulder when the bullets whistled around them, but that trust was expendable in the cause of survival.

"I don't know of any prosecution which has been attended by so many crimes of violence, including that of murder, as in this case," Judge Ferdinand Pecora of New York State Supreme Court said after fixing bail for Spunky Weiss, a material witness who, Dewey suspected, knew Buchalter's whereabouts. Before adjourning the hearing, Judge Pecora noted that four of the fourteen defendants named in a 1937 clothing racket had been killed. Two more survived murder attempts, and an additional two had disappeared.

So far the slaughter was confined to gangsters, as the mob by long-standing custom killed only its own. Reles had no need to kill outsiders. In fact, he actively avoided collateral deaths because it stoked public outrage, which inevitably led to police crackdowns.

The first innocent's blood spilled by accident. At 7:30 a.m. on July 25, 1939, four Reles assassins sat in a blue sedan parked on East 178th Street, in the Bronx, watching as residents in singles and pairs exited a yellow-brick Art Deco apartment building across the street while a gunman named Parisi waited by the front door, a revolver in his pocket.

The five men waited for garment-industry leader Philip Orlovsky, a short, fat man who had joined the herd defecting to Dewey. Reles spent weeks planning his assassination. Reconnaissance showed that Orlovsky left home punctually at 8 a.m. each morning for his job at the Phil-Or Textile Company on Seventh Avenue.

When a plump man in his forties walked out the front door, Parisi assumed he was Orlovsky. Buggsy Goldstein pulled the sedan out and made a U-turn. He crept up behind the man as he walked west toward a subway station on the Grand Concourse. Parisi raised a .32-caliber revolver and sent six bullets into the man's back. Parisi jumped into the getaway car. When a gravel truck blocked the street, Parisi flung open the door and ran.

The victim died three hours later at Fordham Hospital, but he wasn't Orlovsky. Parisi had shot the wrong short, fat man. Orlovsky had left home an hour early that morning to run errands before meeting Dewey's prosecutors at the Woolworth Building. Detectives identified the victim as Irving Penn, a music publishing executive and quiet family man who, they said, "had not an enemy in the world." The *Daily News* called it "murder-by-mistake."

Penn's death galvanized the manhunt. The death of an innocent bystander caused the FBI and New York law enforcement to put aside their petty competition and join in a single coordinated strategy. Dewey cut short his summer vacation to convene a secret summit with three other enforcement officials—FBI director J. Edgar Hoover, New York Police Commissioner Lewis Valentine, and Federal Bureau of Narcotics Commissioner Harry Anslinger. "If the killing off of witnesses continues," Dewey told the group, "there will soon be no one left to testify when we finally catch up with Lepke." He called it "a matter of the most urgent public importance."

The four men made a rare pact: after two years of interagency competition, they would now pool information and resources in a coordinated campaign to grab Buchalter and smash his operations. They increased the dead-or-alive reward for Buchalter to $35,000 and, at Dewey's request, Police Commissioner Valentine detached more than a hundred policemen from regular duty to guard every surviving Buchalter friend and associate, whether they liked it or not.

"It is apparent that the Lepke mob is waging a war of extermination against its former and some of its present members," Dewey told reporters. "It is equally important that extraordinary steps must be taken in this situation."

In the course of outlining those steps for the press Dewey dropped a bombshell. For the first time he suggested that Gurrah Shapiro surrendered because he knew that Buchalter, his lifelong friend and partner, had added him to the Murder, Inc. kill list. Shapiro gave himself up, Dewey said, "to avoid being murdered by his own partner, Lepke."

Meanwhile, federal and city authorities tried to flush Buchalter from hiding by pinching off the funds used to conduct his murder campaign. On August 13 Dewey's detectives arrested a squat, swarthy forty-five-year-old bearded ex-convict named Joseph "Joe Strawberry" Amoruso, a Buchalter lieutenant who kept the rackets going, and the profits flowing, while his boss was in hiding. The arrest came after one of Dewey's detectives spotted Amoruso shopping in New Paltz, New York, where he led the quiet life of a country farmer. The detective, who owned a nearby summer home, recognized Amoruso by the strawberry-shaped facial mole that led to his nickname and trailed him down a dirt road to his hundred-fifty-acre farm. The detective then returned to town and alerted state police. Amoruso would plead guilty to a misdemeanor in the extortion racket. He was sentenced to three years in a penitentiary.

Federal prosecutors applied further pressure by probing the books of a Baltimore clothing company called Raleigh Manufacturers. They found that weekly payments of $250 were made to Mrs. Beatrice Buchalter and Mrs. Anna Shapiro, Buchalter and Shapiro's wives. John T. Cahill, U.S. attorney for the Southern District of New York, charged in court that these disbursements amounted to "harboring fugitives." He convicted five Raleigh officers, including Shapiro's brother and brother-in-law.

Buchalter passed the summer of 1939 hidden by a young Italian longshoreman in an apartment a block from the Gowanus Canal, the narrow waterway used to ferry quarried brownstone and other materials into the heart of Brooklyn. As always, Reles came and went, bringing Buchalter news of underworld operations and screening visitors.

Buchalter, disguised in mustache and glasses, filled idle hours among a circle of codgers seated on park benches beside the dark, still waters of the Gowanus Canal. They talked of god-knows-what and sunned themselves and occasionally placed two-dollar bets with a low-level bookie who swung by to offer racetrack wagers. One afternoon a dark sedan pulled up and four detectives showed their badges. They lined the men up and frisked them. They searched their pockets, shoes, and hats for betting slips. They must have found evidence on the bookie because they pulled him out of line and put him in the back of their police cruiser. Buchalter, the most wanted fugitive in America, walked back to his apartment undetected.

Buchalter's host left for the docks each morning before dawn, leaving him alone to weigh his options. Cahill, the federal prosecutor in New York, had succeeded in cutting off a financial lifeline, and Buchalter could feel the manhunt pressing closer. Behind him the path was filled with the bullet-torn bodies of former associates. Ahead of him stood the menacing shadows of his own men who might soon muster against him. Buchalter's state of mind was such that he slept only when Reles was there to stand guard with pistol in hand.

With Reles's help Buchalter could continue hiding for some time, living a diminished life in a series of basements and back bedrooms with rare moments shared with his wife and son. He would have to accept these compromises in order to maintain his freedom, but what sort of freedom was it when he never walked his son, Harry, to school or dined with his wife Betty?

Whatever miserly measure of life he enjoyed could end with detectives busting down a door with revolvers raised or, just as likely, his own men rolling his lifeless body into the Gowanus Canal or a shallow grave in the flats near Jamaica Bay. "Those other mobsters won't be able to stand the pressure," a detective said. "They'll force Lepke to take the rap to save their own hides, or else we'll find his bullet-riddled carcass some morning."

Buchalter knew that his lifelong underworld associates would kill him as soon as the manhunt endangered them, just as he had ordered Dutch Schultz killed when his transgressions brought heat four years earlier. The Commission delegates had stood by Buchalter for twenty-one months of hiding, but they would not stand by him forever. He was bad for business. "Those bastards are more interested in their own take than they are in my hide," he told Reles.

If Buchalter surrendered, it would not be to Dewey, who had amassed enough state murder charges to send him to prison for hundreds of years, and possibly to the electric chair. Buchalter was encouraged to believe that if he surrendered to J. Edgar Hoover he would only face lighter, federal charges for narcotics smuggling and violating the Sherman Anti-Trust act. With good behavior, he might be released in eighteen years, or earlier.

J. Edgar Hoover commanded the FBI from the grandly columned Department of Justice Building on Washington's National Mall, but on those evenings when he came to New York he could be found, almost without exception, sharing Table 50 with Walter Winchell at the Stork Club on East Fifty-third Street. If the Stork Club was the late-night hub of celebrity New York, Table 50 was its throne and Winchell its uncontested king.

Winchell was a boy-sized man, no more than five foot seven, with the manic, staccato speech of a carnival barker. Two thousand newspapers published Winchell's slangy gossip column, and his fifteen-minute CBS radio show was the most popular program at a time when radio ruled the airwaves. He was the original engineer of the celebrity machine and a passer of confidences. Almost without exception movie stars, duchesses, prizefighters, senators, and mobsters entered the Cub Room, a VIP sanctum with wood-paneled walls, and headed to Table 50 for a chat. Frank Sinatra, Marilyn Monroe, Joe DiMaggio, Bing Crosby, Orson Welles, Grace Kelly—all made sure to pay obeisance to Winchell. "He demanded to know what they were doing," Bernard Weinraub wrote in *The New York Times*, "but talked most of the time himself."

From across the smoky Cub Room, Hoover and Winchell—crime fighter and gossip—might have seemed unlikely cocktail companions, but they had much in common. Both ran intelligence operations of sorts, both traded in secrets.

Their friendship was based on a cooperative arrangement. Hoover supplied Winchell with secret scandals plucked from files the FBI kept on celebrities. In return, Winchell promoted Hoover and his G-men as tireless crime busters. In print he routinely called Hoover the country's "top cop."

An Oklahoma bootlegger named Sherman Billingsley opened the Stork Club as a speakeasy where he could play poker with friends. Ten years later it was still something of a gangster's clubhouse, a nightspot where toughs mingled with debutantes and senators, home-run hitters, and leading men. Winchell knew them all, including the mobsters. In the summer of 1939 Hoover asked Winchell to pass the word to his mob friends that the time had come for Buchalter to surrender. If Buchalter refused, Hoover said, the FBI and NYPD would stage a withering all-out offensive. They would find a way to arrest every mobster in the country.

Gangsters and their families were already under unbearable pressure. Detectives combed the streets like bloodhounds. The FBI staked out whatever legitimate businesses mobsters might own, demanding that customers present identification and harassing them with questions. *Who are you? Where do you live? What are you doing there? Are you aware that the proprietor is a dangerous criminal?* The police picked up low-level thugs for vagrancy, as they always did, only now they threatened to send them to Sing Sing if they didn't reveal what they knew about Buchalter's location. "We can't even make a two-dollar bet at the tracks without being cased by the cops," one mobster told Winchell.

By early summer of 1939 word reached Reles through the underground: Tell Buchalter to give himself up, or we'll kill him ourselves and dump his body on Dewey's doorstep. The Commission's board of directors refused to protect him any longer. Better to have Buchalter in custody, even if he informed on them, than to have aggressive waves of law enforcement pressing on them at every turn.

Now it was clear and resolved. Buchalter knew that he had to surrender or face his own men's guns. On the other hand, surrender would come with its own costly toll. He could serve more than four hundred years in jail if judges sentenced him to the maximum time for racketeering, drug smuggling, and murder. He would have to be shrewd about the terms of his surrender.

Word went back and forth between intermediaries, with Reles no doubt facilitating the shuttle diplomacy. Buchalter was made to understand that if he gave himself up to federal authorities, he would face trial on racketeering and drug smuggling charges, but not murder. He was led to believe that Hoover would go easier on him than the unflinching, hard-line gangbuster Thomas Dewey. So he made the decision to throw himself into the arms of the FBI and hope for the best.

August 5, 1939, was the kind of humid Saturday night that drew New Yorkers outside to seek the coolness of a stoop. The temperature hovered around 85 degrees late in the evening. Winchell was walking beneath the giant blinking Camel cigarette billboard on the upper stretch of Times Square, near Lindy's restaurant, when an acquaintance stopped him. The man, he later wrote, was "not a gangster," but "on the fringe of gangdom." Winchell never revealed his identity.

"I have something important to tell you," the man said. "Lepke wants to come in. But he's trying to find someone he can trust. . . .

He's heard so many stories about what will happen to him. Talk around town is that Lepke would be shot while supposedly escaping. . . . If he could find someone he can trust, he'll give himself up to that person."

"Would he trust me?" Winchell asked.

"I'll find out and let you know."

The following night, at midnight, Winchell's phone rang in his suite at the Hotel St. Moritz, on Central Park South. His acquaintance called to ask if Hoover would guarantee Buchalter's safety if he surrendered. Buchalter did not wish to turn himself in only to be shot in the street like a common bank robber. Would Winchell, the man asked, be willing to provide Hoover's assurances on the radio as a way of guaranteeing the arrangement?

Winchell normally began his radio show at a rat-a-tat pace, delivering a dateline as if reporting from a battlefront, followed by a fifteen-minute barrage of gossip about romance after romance, scandal after scandal. "Debutramps" (young socialites) with long "shafts" (legs) drank "giggly water" (booze) and "made whoopee" (partied), then had to "weld" (marry) because they were "storking" (pregnant). But on Monday night for once he started in a measured and deliberate tone. As always he faced a bulbous microphone set up at Table 50. Hoover sat beside him. "Attention Public Enemy Number One, Louis 'Lepke' Buchalter," he said. "I am authorized by John Edgar Hoover of the Federal Bureau of Investigation to guarantee you safe delivery to the FBI if you surrender to me or to any agent for the FBI." He read the same report an hour later for the West Coast audience.

The manhunt did not stop for these negotiations. If anything, the search bore down harder than ever. On August 21 a federal judge sentenced Abner "Longy" Zwillman, a former bootlegger, to six months in jail for refusing to divulge what he knew of Buchalter's whereabouts. "I know Lepke a long time," he told a grand jury, "but I haven't seen him for three or four years." The same day the grand jury questioned Buchalter's wife, Betty, who was under indictment for conspiracy to harbor a fugitive. Prosecutors suspected she was relaying money to her husband.

The negotiations continued over the next three weeks with go-betweens calling Winchell at the Stork Club or stepping from doorways as Winchell walked home. He would relay the gist of these conversations to Hoover, who stayed at the Waldorf Astoria in order to be close at hand. "Hoover wanted Lepke badly" wrote Hoover biographer Curt Gentry, "but even more, he wanted to upstage Dewey."

The negotiations were so elaborate, and so protracted, that Hoover began to feel like a dupe. After three weeks of back and forth, he lost patience. "This is a lot of bunk, Walter," he told Winchell. "If Lepke doesn't surrender in the next twenty-four hours I'm going to give my men orders to shoot him on sight."

The threat set the surrender in motion. The next morning Winchell got a phone message: take your wife's car, the one with fog lights, and drive to the Proctor Theatre in Yonkers. Be there at 7 p.m. tonight.

Winchell did as told. He had stopped at a red light a few minutes before the hour when a car pulled up on his right side. A man got out and sat in Winchell's passenger seat. He held a handkerchief over his face as a disguise. "Don't be nervous," the man said. "We only brought you up here to see if there were any cops trailing you."

The man asked Winchell to phone Hoover's room in the Waldorf Astoria. "Tell him to be at Twenty-eighth Street and Fifth Avenue, southeast side, between 10 and 10:20 p.m." Winchell and his companion killed three hours driving. At 10 p.m. the passenger got out. Before leaving, he told Winchell to park at Madison Square Park between Twenty-third and Twenty-fourth Streets, in front of Buchalter's old Fifth Avenue office. Winchell turned off the ignition and waited at the designated spot. At 10:15 a man in a long dark overcoat swung open the door and got in. "Hello Walter," he said. It was Buchalter, twenty pounds heavier and disguised with a mustache, sideburns, and sunglasses. He had grown soft from two sedentary years, but he had the same flat nose and soft brown eyes.

They drove four blocks north to the rendezvous point and parked behind a black government sedan. They walked up to find Hoover seated in the back, unarmed and without handcuffs. "Mr. Hoover," Winchell said, "this is Lepke."

"How do you do," Hoover said.

"Glad to meet you," Lepke said. "Let's go."

"You did the right thing by coming in, Lepke," Hoover said.

"I'm beginning to wonder if I did," Buchalter said. "I'd like to see my wife and kid, please."

The time was 10:17 p.m. The search for the most wanted fugitive in America was over.

With that, Hoover signaled his driver to pull out for the fifteen-minute drive to the FBI office on Foley Square. Agents put Buchalter in a holding cell in the Federal Building. At 1 a.m. the federal district attorney John T. Cahill and three assistant prosecutors arrived to begin the interrogation.

Winchell did not ride all the way to Foley Square. He knew that reporters assigned to FBI headquarters would scramble to call newsrooms when they saw the mobster step from the car with the nation's most famous crime fighter. In order to beat them to the scoop, Winchell got out at Thirteenth Street. It was now past 10:30 p.m., uncomfortably close to the deadline for the next morning's paper. Winchell ran through the empty downtown streets until he found a bar with a phone booth and called the night city editor of the *Daily Mirror*, "This is Winchell," he said. "Here's your page one story. Lepke has surrendered. I just turned him over to John Edgar Hoover."

"Take it easy Walter," the editor said. "Your yarn isn't making the front page tonight." Earlier that day, in Moscow, Joseph Stalin had signed a nonaggression pact with German foreign minister Joachim von Ribbentrop, assuring that the Soviet Union and Nazi Germany would back each other when hostilities erupted. Their alliance was short lived, but for the moment it strengthened Germany's hand in the coming war.

As Winchell returned to his suite in the the Hotel St. Moritz that night he must have felt the world unraveling. From Berlin, where Hitler planned his imminent invasion of Poland, to Brooklyn, where Abe Reles drove the streets with bad intent, the forces of human belligerence threatened to subsume all those who would impose order on lawlessness.

The year turned on violence, and the ugliness knew no restraint. The night Buchalter surrendered, about the time FBI agents led him to a detention cell, Dasher Abbandando spotted a tall, bosomy young woman entering a Brownsville bar. He, Socko Gurino, and a third thug followed the girl inside. They chatted her up and cajoled her into a back room. They forced her, arms pinned and mouth gagged, out a back door and into Abbandando's car. They drove her to a hotel where the three men took turns raping her.

Abbandando did as he pleased without fear of reprisal. Reles and his deputies had for a decade enjoyed something close to unrestricted power in Brownsville and its surrounding neighborhoods. Or so it seemed up until the spring of 1940. If Buchalter could land in a federal cell, then no Murder, Inc. operative was safe, not anymore. If you weren't hunted by Dewey, you might be hunted by your own friends—or maybe both would go after you.

On December 20, 1939, a jury convicted Buchalter on federal drug smuggling charges. Judge John C. Knox, who had sentenced Buchalter three years earlier on antitrust charges, commended the jury for reaching "a righteous verdict." Judge Knox sentenced Buchalter to fourteen years in Leavenworth, a federal penitentiary in Kansas. On the trip west Buchalter was handcuffed to a fellow prisoner who said that Buchalter didn't look tough enough to be a gangster. As if to demonstrate his credentials, Buchalter flicked his cigar butt in a cameraman's face as they switched trains in Chicago.

Four months later Buchalter was retried, and convicted, of extortion in the baking and trucking industries and sentenced to an additional thirty years to life in state prison. The judge denounced Buchalter as the "directing genius" of labor racketeering and ruled that his second sentence would not begin until Buchalter had served the fourteen-year term at Leavenworth. With good behavior he would be eligible for parole in 1975, thirty-five years after his sentencing. If Buchalter could find any consolation in his consecutive sentences it was that he had avoided the electric chair, or so he assumed.

Buchalter smirked for most of the two hours of sentencing. When he got back to his cell, he told police officials that he did not expect to leave prison alive. "But I want no notes on my slab," he said.

"What do you mean—no notes?" an official asked.

"I mean," Buchalter said, "that on my tombstone I want them to write 'I never did sing.'"

7

BILL-O

On the evening of May 17, 1938, the dandyish, silver-haired Brooklyn district attorney William F. X. Geoghan told an audience gathered at a YMCA on Bedford Street that prosecutors in his office sat idle. Brooklyn criminals, he said, were not committing enough serious crimes to keep his staff busy. "Now don't misunderstand me," he said. "I don't mean that we have no crime in Brooklyn, because we have. But I have not known the borough to be so quiet from the crime standpoint in a good many years. Frankly, I don't know why this is."

New York's political class reacted with a collective cuss of disbelief. God Almighty, was Geoghan joking? Brooklyn, as everyone knew, was home to Abe Reles and Murder, Inc. The borough was a gangster safe zone and killing field. Brooklynites were accustomed, almost habituated, to news of drive-by shootings and bound bodies unearthed from shallow graves out by Jamaica Bay. Luciano and Buchalter were incarcerated, but Brooklyn lived on as a gangster paradise. Reles prevailed as its prince, and, thanks partially to Geoghan's haplessness, he remained at large—untouched and beyond prosecutors' reach. Thomas Dewey weighed in from the campaign trail, saying Geoghan "stood in a sea of crime."

Geoghan was not up to fighting the underworld. He was a lawyer and a former English teacher at Townsend Harris, one of the city's better high schools. He ascended to the district attorney's office by virtue of dedicated legwork for the Democratic Party machine. Nobody suspected him of corruption; he was just ineffectual and out of his depth. He was Shakespeare smart, not street smart. If he was guilty of anything, it was tolerating incompetent and dishonest assistants. Three of his aides had been indicted on bribery charges within the last month.

Geoghan had disgraced himself two years earlier by bungling the prosecution of a straightforward murder case. Patrolmen found the body of a racetrack gambler named Samuel Drukman in the rumble seat of a coupe parked in an East Williamsburg garage. He had been strangled and beaten with a billiard cue. A grand jury failed to indict two suspects found hiding in the garage with bloodstained hands and clothes. It should have been a straightforward conviction. A crime-weary public was irate.

New York State held hearings on Geoghan's removal, which led to allegations that jurors took bribes and police altered crime-scene reports and other embarrassments. Governor Lehman summoned Geoghan to Albany to ask why, as lead prosecutor, he had failed to establish a motive for the killing or even to interrogate key witnesses. Lehman eventually absolved Geoghan, calling him "an honest man," if inept.

Herbert Lehman's 1938 reelection bought the embattled William Geoghan a respite, or so he thought. With a Democrat staying on in the governor's mansion Geoghan might reasonably assume that he was secure, but that proved not to be the case. When Geoghan came up for reelection the following year, his party judged him to be a liability. They coerced him into retirement and nominated instead a county judge named William O'Dwyer. Judge O'Dwyer beat his Republican opponent by a thumping 230,000 votes.

O'Dwyer, as the new Brooklyn district attorney, took up the fight against organized crime. On January 1, 1939, he and his staff moved into the DA's office, a suite of rooms on the fourth floor of the Brooklyn Municipal Building and prepared to take on the underworld. He singled out Brownsville in particular, saying it had "spawned more gangsters and criminals than any other section of the city . . . We are planning to clean out the whole racketeering mess out there. . . . We are going to help the people who have been crying for assistance for a long time."

If Dewey was a solemn disciplinarian of Protestant heartland stock, O'Dwyer was his opposite, a big-bodied Irish immigrant with dancing laugh lines, pale blue-green eyes, and a rich, thick head of swept-back hair. His rolling, boisterous voice was warmed with a brogue, or turned down to a faint lilt, depending on whom he conversed with. While Dewey interacted awkwardly with those outside his immediate circle, O'Dwyer was a natural storyteller and prolific conversationalist. Bill-O, as friends called him, entertained an ever expanding circle of friends with stories of County Mayo and his days as a rookie cop walking a beat on the Brooklyn waterfront. His Irish charm was his grandest political asset.

"His voice is deep and authoritative," *The New York Times* wrote, "but can be gentle. He listens easily. One somehow gets the impression that his early life has given him a stimulus toward things which both heart and mind appreciate."

O'Dwyer was supposed to be a Catholic priest. He grew up in a thatched-roof house on a winding road in Bohola, barely a dot on the map of County Mayo, the poorest of counties in northwest Ireland, where piles of time-smoothed rocks marked the location of ancient churches and monasteries. "I loved the world of trees and bogs and starry nights," he later said of his childhood home.

His parents, Patrick and Bridget, were dirt-poor teachers with so many children—eleven in all—that in later years O'Dwyer had trouble recalling their birth order. Kathleen, Josephine, James, Mary, Thomas . . . and so on.

O'Dwyer's parents taught him trigonometry, physics, and Shakespeare in a school so impoverished that each student was asked to arrive each morning with two sods of turf to burn for warmth. O'Dwyer was, he said, "possibly nature's worst student . . . I was the juvenile delinquent of our school." Nonetheless, his mother, Bridget, like many Irish mothers, selected her oldest son to study for the priesthood. He left home with barely a word of kindness or sentiment from his parents to read scripture, liturgy, and sacraments at an ancient Jesuit university in the reddish-brown, sun-baked city of Salamanca, Spain.

O'Dwyer looked like a solemn student in his long black cassock, but he consistently failed exams. "I was much more addicted to my bicycle than I was to philosophy," he said. "The Jesuits didn't like me. They knew I wasn't paying much attention to my studies."

At the end of his second year, at age twenty, O'Dwyer told the pious fathers of Salamanca that he was not suited for the priesthood. "I wanted to commit sins if I felt like it," he later said. He rode a train to Cherbourg and boarded the tramp steamship SS *Philadelphia*, bound for New York. He disembarked at a West Side pier, with $23.85 and the burden of his mother's disappointment.

A family friend met him at the Battery, fresh from Ellis Island, and took him on his first subway ride. "It looked like a piece of magic," he said, "that big train coming by, smooth like silk . . . and the doors opened and it was just like a ballet, people came out and people went in."

In New York, O'Dwyer wrote his own version of the familiar immigrant story of toil and advancement. He delivered groceries for nine dollars a week and lost twenty pounds while shoveling coal on the steamship *Dochra* running to Argentina and back. He plastered walls, took fares on a trolley car shuttling between Newark and Hackensack, and carried hods of bricks on his sturdy shoulders. On his lunch break he tried to force the brogue from his mouth by reading Western novels aloud to fellow laborers.

O'Dwyer switched to bartending, first at the Ritz-Carlton, then the Vanderbilt Hotel, where he met Catherine Lenihan, or Kitty, a gentle, brown-eyed hotel switchboard operator. For the rest of her life, she kept in her purse the Canadian dime he gave her by mistake to make a phone call on the day they met.

They married at Sacred Heart Church in Hell's Kitchen. There was no reception, no honeymoon. O'Dwyer went back to work the next day. Later he would say that he was more lonely than in love. "Being alone in the city, and listening to the voice calling for companionship in the city, and having a nice girl, which I did have, that's why I got married."

A year after they married he put on the policeman's navy-blue greatcoat pinned with a shield and ten shiny buttons to walk a night beat on the windy Brooklyn waterfront, where brownstones gave way to rundown farms and corrugated-metal squatter's shacks. He raided speakeasies, broke up alley brawls, chased runaway horses, stepped between husbands and wives punching and slapping in tenement apartments, found lost kids, and attended to drunken sailors from Marseilles or Istanbul rolled by Brooklyn whores. After an all-night shift he returned home, where Kitty served him ham and eggs and hot coffee.

"You get to know the town that way," O'Dwyer said. "You have to settle family arguments and neighborhood quarrels. You make special calls to celebrate a new birth or wedding or to hold their hands and help them grieve when death comes to the family. You know everybody on the beat and what they're up to—their hopes and their worries. You take their heart in your hands."

One cold spring night in 1918 he found a frightened fourteen-year-old boy on the street who said that this father was deranged with drink and threatening to beat his mother to death. O'Dwyer entered a grim little pitch-dark flat. He found a kerosene lamp and pushed his way into a bedroom where the husband, a longshoreman, lay half asleep with his loaded pistol in hand. O'Dwyer reached for the man's arm. It was like "holding the leg of a steer." The man struggled to raise his pistol. O'Dwyer drew his own pistol, warned him, then shot him dead.

"I knew when I read the story the next morning that he was through as a cop," his friend and fellow cop William Whalen said. "I knew he was too thin-skinned to take it."

O'Dwyer later said that the encounter left him with a lifelong hatred of guns. Over the following years he saw the boy through school and eventually helped him join the police force.

O'Dwyer rarely joined other patrolmen for beer or whiskey at the waterfront taverns at the end of their shift. Instead he read case law over cups of coffee while Kitty softy played the piano, or he endured marathon subway rides from Brooklyn to Fordham Law School in Lower Manhattan, where, despite the exhaustion of a demanding full-time job, he graduated in 1923.

Patrolmen rarely gave up the department's job security and pension, but O'Dwyer was a bookish schoolteacher's son who could recite Byron and Yeats from memory. He lacked the temperament for rough stuff and arrests. "Your summons book is unused and what sort of a sergeant do you think you'll make?" said his brother Jimmy, one of three O'Dwyer brothers to follow their oldest brother to New York. In 1925, at age thirty-five, O'Dwyer turned in his badge to practice law in Coney Island, though he continued to wear black policeman's shoes for the rest of his life.

O'Dwyer's law partner, George Joyce, was close friends with Joe Adonis, a gangster specializing in labor rackets and gambling. Adonis was among the gunmen who shot Joe Masseria after his lunch with Lucky Luciano. In Brooklyn a thin line separated the law from the outlaw.

Hard work earned O'Dwyer a law job, but his Irish good humor—his blarney—won him a widening circle of friends. "Everyone was impressed by his warmth and vigor," said Joyce. "He could entertain by the hour with wonderful stories of his boyhood in Ireland and his father."

He was not a standout lawyer, but he had a knack for befriending the right people—people of influence on the street and in the municipal ranks. His friend Captain Frank Bals, for example, was a Brooklyn native who held eleven citations for meritorious service during a quarter-century on the force. As commander of the 10th Inspection District, in the tough Brooklyn neighborhood of Bath Beach, Bals steered the compromised and entangled to O'Dwyer's office for legal help.

Seven years later, acting Mayor Joseph V. McKee appointed O'Dwyer a city magistrate as part of a broad purge of corrupt and vice-ridden officials. "I always knew he'd be a lawyer," Kitty said, "but I never expected he'd be a judge."

More than a hundred patrolmen attended his swearing-in at a Flatbush courthouse, a show of approval for one of their own moving up to become a law-and-order magistrate. Twenty-three years after arriving as an Irish country boy, a callow export from County Mayo, he held the gavel of municipal authority. "I hope that at times Providence will guide me in dispensing justice," he said at his official induction. Minutes later he presided over the case of Max Futernick, a dairy-store owner charged with blocking the sidewalk with milk boxes.

O'Dwyer's court stenographer was a burly pink-faced, red-haired man named James J. Moran, quiet to the point of surly, who would become his closest aide and political confidant. For the next twelve years, Moran quietly and efficiently arranged O'Dwyer's calendar, opened his mail, paid his bills, and did his dirty work. He would later be called "the dean of municipal grifters."

O'Dwyer gained a reputation as a sympathetic magistrate, particularly with wayward youths. One of his first acts was to help establish a court for juveniles where rulings were corrective rather than punitive. "Have you ever seen a boy when he gets out of jail?" he said. "Let me tell you it does something to him. He's got a record. And it hangs around his neck like an anchor."

Shortly after O'Dwyer began adjudicating Brooklyn's culture of street violence and unchecked crime, his younger brother John was shot to death in a botched holdup during a predawn breakfast in a bar and grill two blocks off Flatbush Avenue. He had spent the night on a double date with an off-duty detective and two girls, dancing and drinking. At first, John recovered in the hospital, then, two weeks after the shooting, he contracted a streptococcus infection and died. O'Dwyer's heartbroken mother, Bridget, who had planned to visit her sons in New York, died three months later at age sixty-five.

As a magistrate, and later as a county judge, O'Dwyer made a point of warning gunmen not to expect lenience in his court. "I decided then," O'Dwyer later said, "that the most dangerous criminal was the holdup man with a gun. And if I ever got the chance as district attorney I would hit that type of criminal particularly hard."

O'Dwyer earned the notice of Frank V. Kelly, an old-fashioned political boss with a face like a predator bird who led Brooklyn's Democratic machinery from within a nimbus of cigar smoke in a clubhouse building on Court Square. Kelly invited O'Dwyer to run as a reform candidate for district attorney, Geoghan's job. Kelly was aware of how gangbusting had advanced Dewey's career. Prosecutions made headlines, and headlines impressed voters. If O'Dwyer could tame the mob, then Kelly could groom him for a mayoral run. It was a grave challenge. "Everybody criticized law enforcement in Brooklyn," wrote the Associated Press. "Nobody was able to do much about it."

O'Dwyer never fully explained why he gave up a secure, well-salaried judgeship to run for a politically hazardous, thankless job with less pay in a borough famously resistant to law enforcement, but friends thought of it as a form of revenge for his brother's death.

After dinner on election night, Kitty O'Dwyer stayed in their little brick home on a tree-shaded block in the Irish neighborhood of Bay Ridge, while her husband rode to the Democratic headquarters in downtown Brooklyn to hear the results with his staff. She would have gone with him, but she was suffering the tremors and stiffness of early Parkinson's disease. "I never could keep up with Bill," she said. "He's a whirlwind."

Dressed tastefully in a blue wool suit, she sat in a wheelchair listening anxiously to the radio coverage of the first returns with a few close friends. They sat in a square living room primly appointed with a silver service on a small tray, French dinnerware, and Irish lace cloth on a big table. Miss Bergen, her nurse, hovered nearby.

The phone rang, and Kitty answered it. "Oh I'm so happy for you," she said. A few moments later she rejoined her guests. "That was the judge," she said. "He thinks it will be a great victory."

It was indeed a great victory for O'Dwyer. On January 1, 1940, he moved into the Brooklyn district attorney's offices on the fourth floor of the Brooklyn Municipal Building, opposite Borough Hall, confidently declaring his intention to drive the racketeers from Brooklyn. Five miles east, at Midnight Rose's candy store huddled under the overhead subway scaffolding, Abe Reles sat with Buggsy Goldstein and Pittsburgh Phil Strauss. They played cards and joked as always, entirely unruffled by reports of a coming crackdown.

8

THE WEDGE

On his first morning as Brooklyn district attorney, William O'Dwyer skipped the desk work. Instead, he went directly from his Bay Ridge home to the Bridge Plaza Magistrates Court, built within a former Williamsburg bank, and entered between its four sooty Ionic columns to introduce his assistant DAs to the judge and shake hands with stenographers, bailiffs, and courtroom staff. O'Dwyer warmed to this kind of politicking, and he excelled at it. He lingered to watch his assistants handle the first of the day's docket, a stream of luckless burglars, wife beaters, and con men, then moved on for more of the same at the New York Court of General Sessions.

At the courthouse on Schermerhorn Street he met briefly with Burton Turkus, a dynamic thirty-eight-year-old lawyer who, as the new head of the homicide division, would play point man in the murder investigations. Much of the responsibility for busting Murder, Inc. would fall to him. For fifteen years Turkus had been a well-regarded defense attorney with clients on the fringes of Murder, Inc., including Rose Gold, the candy-store proprietor. Now Turkus would switch sides and prosecute.

Like Reles, Turkus was raised in Brooklyn by hardworking Jewish immigrants—a watchmaker and a seamstress. The resemblance ended there. While Reles was ungainly even by street-thug standards, Turkus looked like the Hollywood version of a heroic prosecutor—a tall, suavely turned-out lawyer with a hawk-like profile and pencil mustache. He had a sharp mind and a facility for courtroom theatrics. "He doesn't conform to the general pattern of the prosecutor," wrote Sid Feder, an Associated Press reporter. "He dotes on the theatrics of the courtroom and the criminal trial. But he is neither politician nor publicity hound."

When Turkus entered his new office for the first time, he found a map of Brooklyn pinned up by his predecessor with the locations of two hundred unsolved murders marked in black. Brownsville was entirely darkened. "It was a blighted area, a pesthole," Turkus said. "In one strip less than two miles long and three-quarters of a mile wide, two dozen or more men had been shot, stabbed, strangled, hacked to bits or cremated, and left in the gutter, on vacant lots or in stolen automobiles."

The map illustrated the grimness of the job to come. The filing cabinets contained reports from medical examiners and witness statements, but not enough for convictions. "Take a list of two hundred murders, all unsolved, and a map on the wall with a mark on it for each murder, and you have the District Attorney's perfect recipe for how not to be jubilant with his job."

After studying the case files, Turkus found that Abe Reles—the notorious Kid Twist—and his sidekicks, Pittsburgh Phil Strauss, Buggsy Goldstein, Happy Maione, and Dasher Abbandando, were prime suspects in most of the two hundred unsolved murders in Brooklyn. The former district attorney, William F. X. Geoghan, had not pursued them—not seriously, anyway.

Turkus got his first up-close look at them on January 23, when more than fifty prosecutors, patrolmen, and detectives filed into Pennsylvania Avenue Court, a two-story structure built like a Greek temple, to observe their quarry. Detectives had arrested Reles and ten of his men on bogus vagrancy charges so that law enforcement at all levels could look them over. The Reles crew stood in a lineup wearing double-breasted suits and contemptuous looks. For a few minutes the two sides, law and disorder, stood facing each other like opposing sports teams.

O'Dwyer may have promised more than he could deliver. After all his campaign bluster, all his talk of a crackdown, he now resorted to arresting Reles and his friends for vagrancy and other charges, the same lame gambit that police had used for years. "Toughs were yanked unceremoniously off the corners at every opportunity," Turkus said, "and charged with any rap on which we could bring them in." Mobsters called it "tickling." It was a tired ploy, and it made O'Dwyer look as ineffectual as Geoghan. Tickling cleared out the neighborhood crap games but it didn't reduce the marks on the murder map.

"You've got one hell of a nerve," Reles told a patrolman hauling him in for another round of tickling. "First thing you know, I'll have to walk around with a bondsman." In both cases Reles posted bail of $1,000, peeled defiantly from a fist-thick wad of bills, and marched from the courthouse with his ample lips twisted into a triumphant smile. Without proof of a crime, judges had no choice but to discharge them when they appeared in magistrate court the next day.

"If O'Dwyer don't stop pushing us around," Maione told a fellow prisoner, "we'll start dropping packages on every lot in Brooklyn. That's going to keep him really busy." "Package" was mob slang for dead body.

Reles took O'Dwyer's attempts to hassle him as a sign of weakness, and proof of his own invincibility. He had been arrested forty-two times since 1933. He knew how to wriggle loose of flimsy charges. The arrests were an inconvenience, nothing more. If this was the worst O'Dwyer could do, Reles had nothing to worry about.

Meanwhile, reporters picked over a rumor that Mayor La Guardia would invoke his authority to fill in as a magistrate judge for the next Reles arrest and consign him to jail, at least temporarily, with sky-high bail. When asked, the mayor dismissed the notion with a wave of his hand. He did instruct city magistrates, though, that cash alone should not be enough to earn Reles and other gangsters dismissal of vagrancy charges, unless they could prove a legal source of income.

As a candidate, O'Dwyer had bragged that he would run Murder, Inc. out of town. Now, as practicing district attorney, he was forced to acknowledge with some chagrin that he lacked enough witnesses to bring mob-related murder cases to court. Under New York State law, murder convictions required testimony from at least one witness who was not an accomplice—an outsider with firsthand knowledge of the crime. The law was meant to prevent accomplices from trying to escape guilt by simply blaming each other, but in practice it hampered prosecutors fighting organized crime. Witnesses were hard to find, especially those involving late-night murders on dark streets. Even if O'Dwyer knew who the murderers were he could not prosecute them, because Reles killed or intimidated the witnesses. People tended to shut up when they knew Reles was watching.

The only way to break Reles's grip would be to persuade an insider with firsthand knowledge of the murders to talk. In underworld terminology, O'Dwyer needed a "stool pigeon," a "canary," a "snitch." "All it takes is a break from within," said Turkus. "No matter what anyone claims about being clever or brilliant, there is only one way organized crime can be cracked. Unless someone on the inside talks, you can investigate forever and get nowhere."

Weeks after Burton Turkus settled into his new office, a staffer brought him an envelope plucked from the pile of daily correspondence received from crime victims, tipsters, and kooks. The handwritten letter scrawled in pencil on cheap white paper was signed by Harry Rudolph, a squat, fortysomething career crook jailed on Rikers Island, in Queens, on a misdemeanor. He had, the *Journal-American* wrote, "a face like a shore dinner and the habit of shuffling his feet as though on snow shoes."

Rudolph wrote to say that he was gravely ill. He had a tip to share before dying. "I would like to talk to the district attorney," he wrote. "I know something about a murder."

On January 24, 1940, Turkus rode out to Rikers Island and met Rudolph in a dismal interrogation room. Rudolph tearfully recalled the forgotten 1933 murder of Red Alpert, the nineteen-year-old petty thief who had dared to mouth off to Pittsburgh Phil about the price of stolen jewelry. Alpert's impudence earned him a bullet in the back; his body was dumped on the sidewalk of a quiet residential street. Seven years later, Alpert's mother, a small, ashen woman, was still making daily pilgrimages to the local police station to ask if they had found her son's killers. In seven years nobody had admitted knowing anything about the murder, until now. "Those rats killed my friend," Rudolph said. "I'll tell you who did it too. Those Brownsville guys— Reles and Buggsy and Dukey Maffetore . . . I saw Kid Twist and Buggsy and Dukey kill my pal."

Turkus might have dismissed Rudolph as a crackpot, a jailbird with a history of peddling dubious tips for ten-dollar bills, but the Alpert file, retrieved from a cold case cabinet in the DA's office, corroborated part of Rudolph's story. Police had briefly detained the men Rudolph mentioned—Abe Reles, Buggsy Goldstein, and their gofer, Dukey Maffetore—in connection with Alpert's death seven years earlier.

Rudolph was notoriously unreliable. A *New York Times* reporter called him "a professional stool pigeon," and compared him to Fagin, the tattered Dickens street thief. But his testimony was enough to win a grand jury murder indictment. On this shaky premise, O'Dwyer ordered Reles, Goldstein, and Maffetore arrested for the third time in a month. From the radio room of Brooklyn headquarters, the call went out to police cruisers: bring them in. That night Captain William Sullivan, chief of the Twelfth Detective District, went to a coffee shop adjoining a sprawling market on East New York Avenue where the Reles crew stopped for late-nights meals. He waited for hours, drinking cup after cup of coffee. He gave up at 1 a.m. On his way out he told the counterman to give Reles a message: "I want them at my office at 8 a.m. tomorrow morning." Reles was unconcerned. At 8 a.m. he and his men walked into Sullivan's office, as requested.

"My Abie always was a good boy," Reles's mother, Mrs. Sam Reles, told a reporter after his forty-third arrest. "If he is such a big man would his Papa have to sell neckties and suspenders from a pushcart?

Reles was often arrested but rarely convicted. He assumed that he and his men would simply endure another round of petty harassment—the usual tickling—without sufficient legal weight to detain them more than twenty-four hours or so. Collectively they accounted for a total of ninety-one arrests, but the charges rarely stuck. But he wouldn't wriggle free this time. The first indication came when O'Dwyer and Turkus walked into the Butler Street police station to observe personally as police booked the three suspects on murder charges and locked them up in holding cells. District attorneys did not normally attend bookings. Their presence was a rare display of personal attention from the borough's top lawmen. O'Dwyer intended to signal the suspects, and police reporters, that Reles's charmed existence was over.

If the district attorney's presence chastened Reles he didn't show it. On the contrary, he subjected O'Dwyer and Turkus to all the venom he was known for, issuing insults and vulgarities throughout the day. He treated the two men as if they were pathetically unequipped to deal with him. He laughed in their faces until he got bored and lapsed into surly silence.

Reles's mouth was foul but his clothes were fine. He wore a gray double-breasted coat over a dark suit. By contrast, Maffetore, the twenty-five-year-old underling, wore a windbreaker over a sweater. He slicked his hair back in the style of any street-corner greaser.

O'Dwyer and Turkus also oversaw their arraignment on first-degree murder charges before Judge John J. Fitzpatrick in Brooklyn Criminal Court. If convicted as charged, all three faced a mandatory sentence of death in the electric chair. All three pled not guilty.

Their lawyers asked for a quick trial, but thirty-nine other violent criminals were awaiting court dates in Brooklyn. "You'll have to wait your turn," Judge Fitzgerald told them. Bail was prohibited on first-degree murder charges, so all three would remain in jail until trial. There would be no quick release this time.

Judge Fitzgerald agreed to hold the defendants in separate jails to prevent them from conferring in the yard or exchanging messages. Every homicide detective knew that interrogations were more productive when isolated suspects were left to wonder what their friends were saying. Solitude led to paranoia, and paranoia was the prosecutor's friend. Maffetore went to jail in the Bronx, and Goldstein went to Staten Island. By happenstance or design, Reles landed in the City Prison in downtown Manhattan, where shrieks echoed off stone walls and the courtyard bore marks where the gallows once stood. Moisture condensed on the ceilings and dripped like water torture on the inmates below. City Prison was known to everyone as "the Tombs" because of its abundance of suicides.

Reles knew that the murder charge handed down by the grand jury would not stick if O'Dwyer had to rely primarily on the untrustworthy jailbird Harry Rudolph. His testimony might suffice before a grand jury, but defense lawyers could easily expose his deficiencies in cross-examination. "I don't even need no lawyer," Reles said, "to beat this rap."

Murder, Inc. had a plan. Not surprisingly, it began with Rudolph, the weak and suggestible witness. On February 7 Rudolph was in a cell in the detention wing of West Side Court, in Hell's Kitchen, when a twenty-five-year-old inmate named Abraham Cohen engaged him in conversation from an adjacent cell. Cohen was waiting to be arraigned for forging a fraudulent bail bond. Posting bail for the Commission's foot soldiers was his family business. He was the son of Lena Frosch, the heavyset courthouse fixer who had reliably paid Reles's bail dozens of times, dating back to his days as a young Brownsville schlammer.

Speaking quietly from a neighboring cell, Cohen told Rudolph that Mrs. Frosch had a message for him. "My mother will get you five thousand bucks," he told Rudolph, "if you put Reles and Buggsy on the street." To earn the money Rudolph had to change his account of Alpert's murder so that Reles and his friends were exonerated. Rudolph refused.

The next day, a Saturday, O'Dwyer stood before a press gaggle in his downtown Brooklyn offices and called the arrests "only the first step" toward his campaign pledge to rid "Brooklyn of racketeers, particularly in the Brownsville and East New York neighborhoods. We are planning to clean out the whole racketeering mess out there. This one case will be the wedge. We want to get to the heart of the situation, to clean it all out."

The arrests, he pledged, were not like the ineffectual harassments of the past. "This is a clean-cut charge. I have an airtight case against these punks, and I want them to know it."

O'Dwyer was exaggerating. His case was not airtight, not yet. Rudolph was an outsider willing to testify to the murder, but prosecutors also needed cooperation from somebody with firsthand knowledge of the crime, an insider. But who could that be? Reles and Goldstein would presumably never turn state's evidence. Of the three, Maffetore was the only one vulnerable enough to plausibly make a deal.

Dukey Maffetore was the kind of hapless low-level thug who hung around the Corner hoping to earn a few dollars running errands for Reles. He was a skinny, dull-minded twenty-five-year-old delinquent from a desperately poor family, a simpleton who rarely looked up from his Buck Rogers comic books until told to steal a car or help a loan shark put the hurt on a delinquent borrower for five or ten dollars.

Maffetore came from Ocean Hill, a neighborhood adjacent to Brownsville and home to the Italian contingent of Murder, Inc. He spoke only broken English. The *Brooklyn Eagle* called him "a hard-boiled flyweight." Maffetore was so ignorant of anything outside his neighborhood, a detective said, that he could not name the location of the Statue of Liberty.

More than a decade earlier O'Dwyer had worked his police shift alongside John Osnato, a hard-bodied, six-foot Italian immigrant of dignified bearing. They walked a tough beat, tougher than most, among brick warehouses and corrugated-steel sheds in the ragged docklands of South Brooklyn. Big John, as everyone called him, learned to bring informants around the old-fashioned way, with a nightstick and fist. When O'Dwyer left to work in a law office, in 1925, Big John Osnato traded his blue patrolman's coat for the plain dark suit of a lieutenant detective. In his new job Osnato learned that the gentle arts of persuasion can yield better results than the swing of a billy club. Men and women that he would have once arrested for minor infractions or indiscretions he now let slide in return for snatches of information. This intelligence often proved useful. By Osnato's account, informants helped solve more than 80 percent of prosecuted crimes.

Osnato "learned to manufacture stoolies," Meyer Berger wrote in *The New York Times*. "When he rounded up a group of neighborhood thieves he might let the least of them go with the understanding that thereafter he was to be served by the man he spared." In this manner Osnato cultivated a network of busybodies, gossips, whistle-blowers, and double-crossers. He was careful never to bring his recruits to a station house or meet them in public. They spoke to one another with fictitious names and set meeting times scrambled by code. If he caught his informants with other gang members, he pretended to rough them up.

Osnato earned a reputation within the NYPD as a master at coaxing prisoners to talk, to inform on their brethren. Long before the gambit became a staple of television cop shows, Osnato played good cop while his partners played bad cop. During rough interrogations he pleaded with detectives to ease up, sometimes pushing them from the room to spare a suspect further abuse. *C'mon guys, give him a break.* The prisoner was unaware that the scene was well rehearsed. Left alone with the prisoner, Osnato would express sympathy with a reassuring hand placed on the suspect's shoulder. *For God's sakes tell us what you know,* he coached while the other detectives shouted threats from the far side of the door. *I can't hold them off forever. If they get back in here they might tear you apart.*

The trick worked. More often than not the prisoner talked. Osnato's knack for bringing sources around helped break a series of important cases. "The stool pigeon may be a cheap crook or a responsible storekeeper who wants to keep his neighborhood clean; she may be a gangster's moll or a suspicious housewife," Osnato later wrote. "A cop has to take help where he can find it."

O'Dwyer would have appointed Osnato head of the district attorney's in-house detective squad, but Osnato had feuded for years with Police Commissioner Lewis Valentine. He nonetheless regularly called on Osnato's knowledge and interrogation skills.

In late January, O'Dwyer sent Osnato to Bronx County Jail, the so-called "canary cage," to persuade Dukey Maffetore to save himself from a lengthy sentence, and possibly the electric chair, by agreeing to testify against his Murder, Inc. overseers. Osnato found Maffetore in the prison barbershop. He was, Osnato later wrote, "a vain, sullen, moronic type and he was very resentful that he should be picked as a potential squealer."

Osnato greeted Maffetore in Italian, as if bringing him into a brotherly embrace. "I know the mug that turned you in," Osnato said, referring to Harry Rudolph. "I know you had nothing to do with the Red Alpert job. I want to help you get out of this mess."

Maffetore rebuffed him. "I'm not having any of that baloney," he said, "but you're right—I didn't do this job."

Osnato slowly, patiently softened Maffetore's resistance by portraying Reles and his friends as heartless big shots who would abandon Maffetore to take the murder conviction while they, as always, walked free. He reminded Maffetore that Reles hired one of Brooklyn's best criminal lawyers to represent him and his lieutenants, but he left Maffetore to rely on the dubious services of a lowly public defender. If necessary, the Commission would bribe a judge, and once again Reles would walk free while Dukey alone faced "Old Sparky," the Sing Sing electric chair, for a murder he was only peripherally involved in.

Reles rode in fancy cars and ate steaks with expensive whiskey, Osnato said. He fattened up on rigged horse races and other cons while Maffetore took on risky and dangerous work for a few dollars. What do you get out of it? Osnato asked. They throw you a few slot machines. They let you do a bit of cheap shylocking, but they take the gravy.

You don't owe Reles anything, Osnato continued. Why not say what you know in exchange for immunity? Osnato could see Maffetore's demeanor changing. Osnato left him to grapple with his dilemma in solitary confinement—"cold storage," as they called it—where isolation amplified anxiety and paranoia.

Maffetore had a lot to consider. If he refused to cooperate with O'Dwyer, a jury could send him to the electric chair. On the other hand, if he cooperated, Murder, Inc. would try to execute him. He brooded on the decision without committing himself either way.

Osnato asked around about Maffetore's favorite cigarette brand. On his next visit he placed a few packs of Pall Malls on the meeting room table, and he arranged for Maffetore to have a radio in his cell—small gestures designed to convey that Osnato was his friend and advocate.

Osnato knew that Maffetore and his wife, Mary, had a one-year-old. How are you going to care for them, Osnato asked, if you're in jail for murder? Would Mary perhaps seek other men while he was in prison? And what happens if you go to the electric chair? What would become of them? To show you I think you're taking a wrong rap, Osnato told him, I'm going to arrange to have your wife visit you. Their conversation would not be conducted through a mesh screen, as the prison normally required. Osnato would arrange for a private room, and time to talk. Osnato had tried to talk sense to him. At this point it was up to Mary to make her plea.

In Osnato's seduction of prisoners, an ultimatum always followed conciliation. On his third visit he accordingly pretended to lose patience. I've given you all the time I can away from my regular job, he said one evening. If you won't talk to save your own neck I'll see that you're transferred to Raymond Street Jail. That means no more visits from your wife, no more radio.

How can I believe you cops? Maffetore said. How do you know I'll get off easy if I talk?

You might not believe me, Osnato said, but would you believe Bill O'Dwyer? Maffetore said he would.

In the end that modest exchange was all it took. Maffetore agreed to ride over immediately to the Municipal Building in Brooklyn. That night he sat in the district attorney's library and wept. "I love my wife," he told O'Dwyer. "I don't want to leave her. I'll talk."

Now that Maffetore had finally agreed to cooperate the interrogation could begin in earnest. He refused to sit down for fear that prosecutors would record him with a hidden microphone. So he paced between Osnato and O'Dwyer pouring out all the details he had withheld for weeks. He did not kill Red Alpert, he said, but he knew who did: Abe Reles and Buggsy Goldstein. Maffetore confessed to driving a car on six of the grisliest jobs Murder, Inc. was responsible for. He stole the car used to dispose of Whitey Rudnick's skinny, blood-smeared corpse, and he drove Puggy Feinstein to Reles's house the night he died. He stood in Reles's living room when Buggsy Goldstein strangled Puggy to death with a length of rope.

From his cell in the Tombs, Reles heard rumors that Maffetore might be talking, but he wasn't worried—at least not that he would let on. "What can the kid tell them?" he said. "He don't know nothing."

Reles was right. As soon as Maffetore disclosed what he knew, the district attorneys seemed to cool on him. Maybe Maffetore's limited knowledge of Murder, Inc. and its doings genuinely disappointed them. Or perhaps they feigned disappointment in order to squeeze more from him. Either way, their indifference alarmed Maffetore: if O'Dwyer and Turkus considered his information unworthy, might they renege on the deal, leaving him to face charges, or worse, return to the streets unprotected? Maffetore tried to add weight to his contribution by suggesting that he could persuade his friend Pretty Levine to speak to them. "You should go get Pretty," he said. "He is smart. He knows more than me."

Levine's real name was Abraham, but street friends called him Pretty because of his pale green eyes, girlish dimples, and greasy wave of pompadour billowing upward like a frothy Brylcreem cloud. Reles had paired Levine with Maffetore in the mid-thirties to form a two-man team. He allotted them the earnings from a handful of Brownsville slot machines, enough to give them each $200 or so a week. In return, Reles expected them to steal cars, collect graft, and run errands.

Maffetore was Italian. Levine was Jewish. But both were Brooklyn bad boys. They bonded over felonies and misdemeanors. Together they played supporting roles in six murders.

Levine had learned the hard way that Murder, Inc. never let its soldiers get away. Three years earlier he had married Helen, a slim Brooklyn beauty from an upstanding family. She was barely twenty when they married. Levine's own friends said she was wasted on a punk like him. Within a year Helen was pregnant. Levine hated the prospect of leaving her a widow, so he began to distance himself from Murder, Inc. For the first time in his life he worked a straight job. He drove a horse-drawn ash cart through the Brooklyn streets hauling fireplace soot and other debris. No more stolen cars, no more pool hall nights. Instead he patrolled the streets in sun and rain. The work was boring, but honest.

When Helen gave birth to their daughter Barbara, the hospital required payment before discharging mother and infant, but Levine didn't have the money. In order to bring Helen and Barbara home he had to borrow a hundred dollars—"a century," in gang slang—from Pittsburgh Phil Strauss.

The Reles crew never granted breaks on loans, not even to one of its own. Levine had to pay loan-shark rates: 25 percent interest weekly. His ash-cart salary was too meager to pay even the interest, and he knew what would happen if he reneged. To pay off the loan before the interest grew insurmountable, Levine had to do what he most dreaded: reenlist with Murder, Inc. He went back to driving murder cars and carrying a shotgun.

In his haste to ingratiate himself, Maffetore told prosecutors that his partner Pretty Levine knew more about the workings of Murder, Inc. than he did. Levine could tell them about the night Jack Drucker stabbed Walter Sage to death with an ice pick while riding down a country road, for example, and the time Red Alpert's body was dumped on a stranger's lawn after he argued with Pittsburgh Phil Strauss.

Turkus immediately asked detectives to bring Levine in. Before turning Levine over to Turkus for questioning, Osnato ordered him to strip naked in a holding cell so that detectives could examine his body with a magnifying glass.

"What's this all about?" Levine asked.

"We have information that you're the next one the mob will bump off," Osnato said. "You'll be so damaged we won't be able to recognize your face. We want a record of marks on your body so identification can be made—if we ever find your body."

If Osnato was trying to scare Levine into talking, the ploy failed. Like his friend Maffetore, Levine initially refused to cooperate. Osnato then put Levine into a guarded hotel room so that Maffetore could talk to him alone. *You're just a punk like me,* Maffetore told his friend. *Reles made us that way, but he's not looking out for us now that we're in trouble. He's only looking out for himself. You've got to think of your wife and kid. That's what I'm doing. I'm talking as much as I can, and you should too.*

Turkus could see Levine waver. He applied pressure by holding Levine's wife, Helen, in the Women's House of Detention, in Greenwich Village, as a material witness. "You have the key to her cell," Turkus told him, "and you can unlock it." Their sixteen-month-old daughter, Barbara, was pulled from her mother's arms and sent to an orphanage. Mother and child would stay in their separate confinements, Turkus told Levine, until he talked.

Levine held firm for twenty-five days. He broke the next day. The thought of his family displaced and scared was too much for Levine. He rolled over, as prosecutors say. He weepingly agreed to say what he knew.

Levine didn't know much, but he knew more than Maffetore. He could, for example, tell prosecutors the story of Walter Sage's murder on a July evening in 1937: how Jack Drucker stabbed Sage while Gangi Cohen pinned him to his car seat; how Cohen unaccountably ran off; how two years later Levine and Maffetore spotted Cohen on the movie screen. Levine said that Reles gave him twenty dollars for his part in the Sage murder. After paying for his hotel, gas, and meals, he returned to Brooklyn with one dollar in his pocket.

Levine and Maffetore were unaware that Reles had planned to murder them both even before they became informants, just in case. He knew they were weaklings. If pressured, they would likely succumb to Osnato's tricks and divulge whatever damning details they knew. Reles had long ago made arrangements to silence them. He booked gunmen and drivers. Maffetore's assassination was scheduled for February 9. Levine was to die March 1. "We undoubtedly saved both Levine and Maffetore from violent deaths by arresting them," O'Dwyer said. "Both had been trigger men for the gang, and both were marked as victims because they knew too much."

Arrest spared Maffetore and Levine from assassination, but jail would be no safe haven. When the two agreed to cooperate, O'Dwyer tried to protect them from the long reach of Murder, Inc. by relocating them from jail, where Reles's associates could deliver a sharpened spoon to the gut, to a guarded room in a Manhattan hotel room. They specifically arranged for a room on an interior courtyard so that their windows would have no outside exposure to gangsters watching from the street or nearby windows. Nineteen thousand police were warned to watch for assassins imported from Chicago or Detroit to eliminate the disloyal.

The informants were scared for their lives, and for those of their wives and daughters. Both families moved from home to a secret location where four patrolmen guarded them around the clock.

On February 23, 1940, O'Dwyer detained three more Reles lieutenants on murder charges. Happy Maione, Pittsburgh Phil Strauss, and Dasher Abbandando were charged with the 1936 killing of Daniel Meehan, a twenty-nine-year-old underworld operative who came over from Manhattan to trespass on the Brooklyn rackets.

Maione had invited Meehan for a conciliatory meeting at the Court Café, a bar two blocks from the Gates Avenue Courthouse in the Bedford-Stuyvesant neighborhood. Let's talk, Maione said. Surely we can work something out. Meehan was found lying on the sidewalk outside the bar the next morning. He had been shot three times.

All three men—Maione, Strauss, and Abbandando—pled not guilty at their arraignment; the judge held them without bail. With their arrests O'Dwyer now held in custody a total of twelve members of Murder, Inc. District Attorney Samuel Foley of the Bronx, who visited Brooklyn to confer with O'Dwyer about the accidental Irving Penn slaying, called it "the most important cleanup of underworld characters that I have seen in fifteen years as a law officer."

On March 18, 1940, three sheriff's deputies in Los Angeles arrested Gangi Cohen, the gunman turned movie actor, while he was playing cards with friends in the cottage that he shared with his wife, Eva, and their twelve-year-old son, across the street from the Paramount studio lot. The LAPD dispatched the deputies after O'Dwyer telegrammed an arrest warrant requesting "urgent" action. Cohen, who now lived and worked under the alias Jack Gordon, was wanted in Sullivan County for the murder of his friend Walter Sage. "You'll get a kick out of this," Cohen told one of the deputies as they handcuffed him. "I played a copper in one picture."

The same day that the LAPD arrested Cohen in Los Angeles, O'Dwyer delivered a state-of-the-investigation update to a lineup of police reporters gathered with pens and pads in the library beside his office in the Brooklyn Municipal Building. Speaking in his measured manner with a hint of an Irish uptilt, he offered the reporters a broad description of an organized underground enterprise that was hidden from view until a few weeks earlier. Over the course of two and a half months, his staff had arrested ten men in connection with a dozen contract murders, and detained a dozen informants. In addition, prosecutors had indicted four in Sullivan County for the Walter Sage murder. O'Dwyer said that state police had told him that farmers in the Catskills "are scared to plow their land these days because they are afraid of uncovering a body from Brooklyn."

O'Dwyer described how Osnato convinced Dukey Maffetore to co-operate, and how Maffetore had convinced Pretty Levine. The two men had provided "a gold mine of information," he said, in the course of all-day and all-night interrogations. With their help, O'Dwyer and Turkus had begun to map out an interlocking network of gangs throughout the country, ruled by Lucky Luciano, Lepke Buchalter, and others, all protected by "a rub-out ring." O'Dwyer called it a "fantastic honey-comb of destruction." The prosecutor's office now knew at least some of the background to the deaths of Red Alpert, shot in the back on a Brooklyn street; Walter Sage, stabbed with an ice pick and dumped in Swan Lake; Irving Penn, an innocent music publisher, murdered by mistake; Puggy Feinstein, stabbed and strangled in Reles's living room; the trucker-turned-informant Joe Rosen; and Whitey Rudnick, stabbed sixty-three times and abandoned in a car. "I have never seen such clear, complete and abundant evidence," O'Dwyer said.

Now, in the spring of 1940, O'Dwyer was poised to turn his attention from investigation to prosecution. He would enter the courtrooms with enough evidence, he said, to send ten or more men to the electric chair, including Abe Reles. "I have an idea," he said, "that the electric chair is going to be working overtime in catching up with justice."

Privately O'Dwyer was less confident. He and Turkus were still a long way from resolving the two hundred unsolved murders in Brooklyn. "No convictions could be obtained against any of the bosses on what the two small-shots said," Turkus later wrote, referring to Maffetore and Levine. "Their material was promising. Nothing more . . . our investigation was going to collapse unless we got a top mobster who had all the answers—and would give them out loud. . . . We needed, in brief, a canary that could sing good and loud—and on key."

But who would play the role of canary? They assumed it would not be Reles. He had been arrested forty-two times and interrogated and leaned on without any sign of weakness. His loyalty was unassailable.

9

LONG SONG

In the late winter of 1940, Abe Reles followed O'Dwyer's maneuvering from his cell in the dark confines of the Tombs, the Centre Street jail in downtown Manhattan where mice skittered across dank stone floors and the dying and deranged howled all night.

Hour after hour, day after day, Reles spat bloody sputum into a drinking glass. The swirling mix of blood and saliva rose in the glass, gob by gob. When the pink-tinted liquid filled to the rim he poured the contents down a drain and started over. The blood was the by-product of an undiagnosed illness Reles had suffered for months. The condition worsened by the week. He had come to assume that it was cancer or tuberculosis. For perhaps the first time in his life, Reles felt cornered. If he should, by guile or circumstance, wriggle free of O'Dwyer's grasp, he faced a terminal disease. Either way, a death sentence awaited.

The jailhouse grapevine whispered that Maffetore and Levine were telling O'Dwyer every incriminating detail they could recall—stabbings, dumped bodies, and drive-by shootings. Though Osnato may have released this information into circulation in order to agitate Reles.

Reles understood why his underlings might choose to talk: the informants' lives and the safety of their families depended on ingratiating themselves to prosecutors. If they were not sufficiently valuable as witnesses, they could be thrown back among the prosecuted and end up in Sing Sing.

O'Dwyer had now done what Dewey never accomplished: he had shaken Reles's self-assurance. To face the disreputable Rudolph in the courtroom was no great challenge, but to survive testimony from Rudolph, Maffetore, and Levine was more daunting.

That wasn't all. O'Dwyer now acted on information provided by Maffetore and Levine to arrest Louis Capone, the smooth mid-level mafia operative who had recruited the teenage Reles and put him to work as a Brownsville schlammer. O'Dwyer held Capone, now forty-two, as a material witness on $100,000 bail, a sum large enough to assure that he would not leave prison. O'Dwyer also arrested Lena Frosch, the unsmiling fifty-year-old fixer, and her husband, Israel, on charges of obstruction of justice.

The next day Levine and Maffetore rode ninety miles in heavily guarded green-and-white police cruisers to Monticello, seat of upstate Sullivan County, where they testified before a grand jury investigating seven Murder, Inc. killings in that upstate region. The two informants began by leading jurors, police officials, and troopers on a macabre forty-mile sightseeing tour through the Catskills. Along the way they pointed out the small unnamed pond where they discarded guns after killings; the wooded stretch of road where Jack Drucker stabbed Walter Sage in the chest with an ice pick; Swan Lake, where Pittsburgh Phil Strauss had rolled Sage's perforated body overboard from a rowboat, and where police dredged up the decomposed remains of Sam Medal, who had told the police the location of an illegal still; the hill near Kiamesha Lake where police found the body of Frisco Gordon, who had made the fatal mistake of telling police about a 1930 shooting of a man named David Seigel; the shallow, lime-filled grave inside a Monticello barn where Charles "Chink" Sherman lay after Jack Drucker shot him in the head and axed his skull following Sherman's argument with Dutch Schultz; the driveway of the Paramount Manor Hotel, in Hurleyville, where the milkman found the body of Irving Ashkenas lying face up beside his taxicab; and Lake Sheldrake, where the mottled remains of an informant named Maurice "French" Carillot floated to the surface after five months.

Levine told the grand jury what he knew about these murders at 2:30 p.m. that day, followed by Maffetore. Both men described the region as a favored area for executions.

O'Dwyer and Turkus worked practically around the clock as they

tried to fit each new informant, with his byzantine alliances and betrayals, into the complex puzzle. "For ten straight days and nights, with
but a few hours of respite, [O'Dwyer] had been examining a parade of
surly, swaggering members of Murder, Inc., the cut-rate cut-throat combine, and their weeping wives," wrote the Associated Press.

On Sundays Abe Reles received a brief reprieve from confinement. He
exited his cell to sit for an hour in a makeshift chapel that Christian
Scientists maintained for prison ministration. While inmates sang
"Christ, My Refuge" and other hymns, Reles whispered with Happy
Maione, who was also incarcerated in the Tombs. They continued their
consultations in the alley-like prison yard during these short respites.

They had much to discuss. O'Dwyer had turned Maffetore and
Levine into cooperating witnesses, and he could potentially do the
same with Dasher Abbandando, Gangi Cohen, Louis Capone, Buggsy
Goldstein, and others. In fact, a March edition of the *Brooklyn Daily
Eagle* reported that Pittsburgh Phil Strauss had joined Maffetore and
Levine in what the press called O'Dwyer's "singing school." The report
proved incorrect. O'Dwyer may have leaked the falsehood to a police
reporter in order to make Reles paranoid and weaken his resolve.

In one of their covert jailhouse meetings, Maione told Reles that
those Commission delegates still at large would try to reverse the dam-
age. They would arrange to kill Maffetore and Levine in their hotel room
or on their fifteen-minute van ride to and from courthouses, along with
the other informants in police custody. Reles recognized that it might be
too late to undo the harm. No volume of bullets or blood could protect
Reles from the electric chair if O'Dwyer lined up the right witnesses.

Reles looked like a caricature of a thug, with his flattened nose and
elastic, smirky lips. But behind his cretin bearing he possessed a politician's aptitude for maneuvering and machinations. The police had
arrested him four dozen times, and he had listened intently during the
ensuing hearings, pleas, and procedural wrangling. In the process he
had acquired the street equivalent of a law degree. Despite his goonish
demeanor, he had a strategist's grasp of the next move, and the move
after that.

In those late-March days he considered his options and played out
courses of action in his mind to see what the likely outcomes might
be. He weighed probabilities and punishments. He deliberated. When

arrested he had assumed that O'Dwyer would not come up with independent corroboration in Red Alpert's murder. He was wrong. He had not anticipated that Maffetore and Levine would flip. Were his collaborators in a hundred murders quietly making their own deals with O'Dwyer? Would they betray their blood oath, *omertà,* to save themselves, to save their families?

Reles had no way of knowing. The main thing, the only thing, was not to be left standing on the wrong side of the deals when the music stopped.

Meanwhile, on the fourth floor of the Brooklyn Municipal Building, O'Dwyer weighed his own options. Maffetore and Levine had divulged the details of a handful of murders, but as underlings they only knew so much. All of O'Dwyer's ambitions, his campaign promises to crush the mob, and his hope for advancement to the mayor's office might collapse without a top-echelon defector. He needed a mob boss to join his "singing school." O'Dwyer had earned plenty of worthy headlines for high-profile arrests and grandiose predictions, but without the right kind of informant his tenure as Brooklyn district attorney would sink as shamefully as that of his predecessor, the disgraced William F. X. Geoghan.

On the afternoon of February 21, 1940, Reles left his cell and walked escorted among the Tombs' dark corridors to a visitor pen to see his wife, Rosie. She did not fit the public image of dolled-up, mascaraed molls at champagne parties. By 1940 she had settled into a matronly figure. The couple had a five-year-old son, Buddy, and another baby coming in June. Buddy was too young to ask many questions, but Rosie knew that he would eventually want to know about his father, as would his younger sibling.

We cannot know what whispered words of resolution or remorse husband and wife exchanged through the mesh screen in the visitor's room, but it could not have comforted Rosie to know that she might soon lose her husband, either to a mystery illness or the electric chair. For months Reles had been spitting up blood. He was convinced that cancer was gradually overtaking him, but he refused to see a doctor. He was sure that he would die soon, one way or another.

Their conversation concluded with Reles resolving to do what no one thought possible. The man who punished hundreds of informants would himself become an informant. Better to squeal than to be squealed on. "It is no secret," one reporter wrote, "that a rat, when cornered, will fight for its life."

Rosie Reles showed up unbidden at the Brooklyn district attorney's office a few minutes after 5 p.m. that afternoon—an uncomfortably pregnant woman wearing a beige coat with a wolf-fur collar. She had swept her hair up in a turban and rouged her cheeks. She arrived after normal office hours on Good Friday, a day for Catholics like O'Dwyer to observe the Stations of the Cross. Nobody recognized her. She sat ignored in a waiting room for an hour. When Turkus asked if he could help her, she insisted that she would speak only to O'Dwyer. "I want to save my husband from the electric chair," she said. She began to sob. "My baby is coming in June."

At last Rosie told O'Dwyer that her poor, impressionable husband was stricken with remorse over his ghastly deeds. He regretted allowing those terrible influences, Buggsy Goldstein and Pittsburgh Phil Strauss, to lead him astray. O'Dwyer could tell where the conversation was headed. Rosie's husband felt so contrite that he was prepared to tell what he knew—as long as he could make a deal to save his life.

If Reles was genuinely willing to come forth with truthful accounts of Murder, Inc. then he could be the major player that O'Dwyer and Turkus badly needed to bust the mob wide open.

O'Dwyer acted immediately to move Reles to protective custody before anyone at Murder, Inc. learned of his defection. Turkus drafted a consent order stating that Reles had agreed to speak with them and carried it to the Tombs, where Reles signed it "as nonchalantly as a celebrity obliging an autograph fan," Turkus later wrote. Within the hour a judge issued a court order transferring custody to O'Dwyer.

Reles was delivered to Brooklyn through dark streets by an armed police motorcade headed by tall, white-haired Captain Frank Bals, O'Dwyer's friend from his patrolman days who now headed the district attorney's detective detail. "We were cautious," O'Dwyer later wrote, "lest this announcement be part of a jailbreak."

Abe Reles—Kid Twist himself—walked into the district attorney's library at 9 p.m. and made himself at home. "He was a chunky little tough," Turkus recalled. "Square head, flat ears, arms reaching to his knees, and fleshy, untapered fingers. Built like an ape."

Reles slumped in a chair across a table from O'Dwyer's staff and mo-

tioned for a cigarette. He brought the cigarette to his lips with his wrists
bound by handcuffs. He demanded that a detective remove them—he
called the handcuffs "bracelets"—but the detective refused. "I sent out
for a sandwich and coffee," O'Dwyer later wrote, "and watched him as
he ate. He was really hungry."

Reles looked around the room as if he owned it, giving off menace
the way an oven radiates heat. "He was a dirty-faced little man, scabby,
small with a snake brain and shifty eyes," O'Dwyer said.

He was there to bargain for his life, but his body language conveyed
only hostility. "There was something about Reles's physical bearing, a
look in his eye, that actually made the hair on the back of your neck
stand up," Turkus wrote. "If a total stranger walked up to Reles and,
without a word, bashed him in the face, I could understand it. That was
the reaction you got from one look at him."

O'Dwyer began by asking Reles's occupation. In court Reles had
always said he worked as a soda jerk or some other fake job. This time
Reles offhandedly replied, "the murder business."

Turkus asked Reles how he could dispose of human life so casually.
"Didn't your conscience bother you?" he asked. "Didn't you feel anything?"

Reles: "How did you feel when you tried your first case?"

Turkus: "I was pretty nervous"

Reles: "How about your second case?"

Turkus: "I was still pretty nervous, but it wasn't so bad."

Reles: "And how about the rest of your cases."

Turkus: "Then I was used to it."

Reles: "You've answered your question."

O'Dwyer confronted Reles with Harry Rudolph's statement linking
Reles to the murder of Red Alpert in 1933. Reles laughed it off. "That
Rudolph," he said, "I could make a monkey out of him myself."

Turkus said the district attorney's office also had information tying
him to the murder of Puggy Feinstein, who was stabbed to death in
the Sunrise Garage. "You can't touch me on that one," Reles said. "You
ain't got no corroboration."

Reles left school after eighth grade, but he had a criminal lawyer's grasp
of procedure and precedent. He knew that prosecutors needed corroborat-
ing testimony from a non-accomplice. So whatever information Levine

and Maffetore gave O'Dwyer was useless without outside confirmation. "You've got no corroboration," Reles repeated. He said it again for emphasis. "You've got no corroboration."

"But," he added, "I'm the guy who can tell you where to get it." He pointed his cigarette at O'Dwyer, then stubbed it out. "I can make you the biggest man in the country." He could, he said, provide details on more than two hundred murders. What's more, he could identify the witnesses who could verify his accounts in court. He was willing to divulge everything—the mob lords' corruptions and the foot soldiers' savage handiwork. In exchange he wanted to "walk out clean."

"He had escaped the law for a long time," O'Dwyer later recalled, "and now he was afraid and wanted to be first to come in, because someone else might come in if he didn't. He was making his best bargain and he knew it."

O'Dwyer and Turkus negotiated the terms of Reles's cooperation with him until 4 a.m. "I could tell you plenty," Reles said, "but what happens to me, and can I trust you? . . . If I talk, what do you do for me?"

Before dawn they finalized a deal: Reles would tell all he knew about the murders. He would brief prosecutors in private and testify in court against his closest friends and associates. Everything Reles said would have to be thoroughly checked and verified. In return, O'Dwyer would not prosecute Reles for any crimes, including the eleven murders he personally participated in, one of which took place in his living room.

It was 4:30 a.m. A light snow fell outside the office windows, hushing the Brooklyn streets. "Are you sure you know what you're doing?" Reles asked O'Dwyer.

"Why? Why do you ask?" O'Dwyer said.

"This is the biggest thing in the whole United States," Reles said. "You'll never get anywhere with it, and you can expect to be hurt if you do. Now I'm warning you. I'm prepared to talk. I just want to know what promise I get."

The federal witness protection program would not exist for another thirty years. Reles received instead a promise of long-term round-the-clock armed guards to protect him and his family from the Murder, Inc. assassins, his own people, who would surely come for them. O'Dwyer promised him either a nominal prison term or a suspended sentence in exchange for his cooperation, but only if he was entirely truthful. "If

I find that you're lying," O'Dwyer said. "You'll be the first one prosecuted for murder."

In the short run, Reles could not be housed in city jails, even in
guarded confinement. The underworld too easily paid off guards.
"They'll get me if I'm in the clink," Reles told O'Dwyer. "They'll figure
out a way to poison me or something."

Instead O'Dwyer would lodge Reles and other informants in a suite
at the Hotel Bossert, a slice of marble with terra-cotta cornices and
rooftop dancing in Brooklyn Heights. The Bossert was known as the
Waldorf Astoria of Brooklyn, home to a squad of Brooklyn Dodgers
during baseball season. Whenever the informants were in their rooms,
three detectives stood outside the chained and barricaded doors.

Two hours before the sun rose on the morning of February 23, Reles
returned to the Tombs one last time for a brief rest. He rejoined Turkus
and O'Dwyer a few hours later to begin the first in a series of lengthy
interrogations. Before the prosecutors began, they paused to ask Reles
why he had chosen to break the mob's inviolable rule against betrayal.
How had he, of all people, come to defect? "Every one of those guys
wanted to talk," he said. "I just beat them to the bandwagon."

In fact, Reles had no way of knowing what his sidekicks intended,
since he had no contact with them, aside from a few furtive talks with
Happy Maione in the Tombs. He could not be sure if they had upheld
their loyalty to him, and to the mafia code of omertà, the pledge of
silence. They, in turn, assumed that he was doing the same.

Reles's defection—the *Daily News* called it his "long song"—sent
a message to the faithful that loyalty no longer adhered. Survival, not
solidarity, was now the guiding principle. With the law closing in, every
man should, and would, look out for himself. The race was on to see
who could talk first and fastest to save himself from the electric chair.

"I might give a break to a poor slob," O'Dwyer said when asked if
informants would get immunity, "but the only way that [they] could
get consideration would be by doing a tremendous service to the people
of Brooklyn. Their information would have to involve someone higher
than they."

A lesser operative named Max "Maxie the Jerk" Golob was the first
to join Reles. On the afternoon of March 25, a judge released Golob
from Raymond Street Jail into O'Dwyer's custody after he agreed to
tell what he knew about the higher ups. "The pudgy-faced young thug

[would] squeal for his life in an effort to escape the electric chair . . ." wrote the *Brooklyn Daily Eagle*. He was accused of being one of the hired assassins who killed Spider Murtha on Atlantic Avenue on March 3, 1935.

Skinny, slant-eyed Tick Tock Tannenbaum was spending a late-winter vacation gambling at Florida racetracks when rumor reached him that Reles had flipped. If Reles talked, he would surely implicate Tannenbaum for some or all of the six murders he had participated in. Tannenbaum also helped dispose of the body in a seventh murder.

Tannenbaum immediately boarded a train to New York and went to the Brooklyn home of fellow assassin Bug Workman to ask for a loan. He needed money to disappear under the protective wing of the Purple Gang, a Jewish outfit in Detroit. A pair of detectives arrested the two men on a trumped-up vagrancy charge as they walked along Brighton Beach Avenue, east of Coney Island. They led the men off in handcuffs— Tannenbaum tall, tan, and neatly dressed, Workman burly and disheveled. At O'Dwyer's request, a court held them on $25,000 bail.

Like all potential informants, they were safer in jail than on the street, though they did not understand that at first. For example, Bug Workman protested the $25,000 bail imposed by the judge at his arraignment. "It's an outrage," he said.

"It would be an outrage if he were released on bail," Turkus told the judge. "Workman is marked for death. It would be the same as signing an execution order if he were turned loose now. The gang is waiting to put him on the spot." (Putting someone "on the spot" was gang slang for murder.)

Workman's swagger immediately wilted. "He gulped and meekly acquiesced," an Associated Press court reporter wrote, "when he was returned to jail shackled to his alleged confrere, Tannenbaum."

Tannenbaum also resisted until reality set in. He initially would not talk to O'Dwyer. When pressed, he doggedly repeated the same brush-off: "I refuse to answer on the grounds of my constitutional rights." Tannenbaum smiled smugly when O'Dwyer released him, but he didn't get far. O'Dwyer made sure that three state troopers intercepted Tannenbaum and transported him in handcuffs to Sullivan County where District Attorney William Deckelman charged him with the murders of Irving Ashkenas and Walter Sage. Reles had supplied the details. "We've got enough on you to put you in the chair," Deckelman told him. Tannenbaum's haughty posture gave way to visible fright. On second thought, he decided, he would be willing to talk in exchange for lenience.

Within days of their arrests, Workman, Golob, and Tannenbaum had all resolved to bargain for clemency. They joined the other informants in the Hotel Bossert. All three "talked fast in an effort to save their skins from the electric chair," wrote the Associated Press, "divulging what O'Dwyer noncommittally described as 'impressive' new details of the wholesale operations of the $5-and-$10 slaughter syndicate."

When Buggsy Goldstein's wife, Betty, met her husband in the visitor's room of a city jail on Staten Island, she reported the rumor that Reles was cooperating with O'Dwyer. Goldstein looked at her, then nearly choked with laughter. He loved Reles like a brother, and he assumed Reles loved him too. Reles would never turn against his lifelong friends—friends dating back to the Brownsville corner where, as young teenagers, they shared stolen cigarettes and ogled shiksas. Goldstein laughed and laughed, he cackled and guffawed. His laugh was contagious so Betty laughed too.

While Goldstein laughed, Reles talked. Once he started, he didn't stop. He paused only to lean over and spit blood into a drinking glass. The blustery little mob boss talked for twelve straight days, with a flair for macabre details and raunchy asides. Stenographers filled twenty-five transcription books with lurid details of strangulations and bodies both burned and buried alive, ambushes and midnight executions. The slayings described were so brutal, and described so graphically, that stenographers on a few occasions had to leave the room to regain their composure.

Reles looked like a hairy, thick-lipped troglodyte with a street-dumb Brooklyn accent. He was barely literate. But his memory mightily impressed the prosecutors huddled around him in the Hotel Bossert or the district attorney's library. He related details of a hundred murders dating back more than a decade with cinematic clarity, his meaty hands waving like a conductor. He told stories with comic flourish and an operatic touch for tragedy. He implicated not just his closest friends, but the chain of command all the way up to the big bosses and politicians who accepted bribes.

Reles immediately cleared up more than three dozen unsolved

killings, not just in Brooklyn but in Newark, Sullivan County, Los Angeles, and other locations. Murder for squealing. Murder for embezzling. Murder for revenge. Murder for distrust. Reles recounted them all with an encyclopedic recall for dates and exact locations. Reles "rattled off names, places, facts, data of one manslaughter after another, days on end, without once messing up," Turkus wrote. "He recalled not only the personnel involved, but decent people who had an unwitting part in some angle of the crime. He pointed out a cigar stand where a man happened to be standing when murderers went by in flight. [That information] provided a witness who placed the killers near the scene of the crime. He mentioned a filling station where the attendant sold a can of gasoline that had been used to burn up a body. The attendant proved to [to be] a vital link of evidence against the cremators."

When Reles was finally done, O'Dwyer and his prosecutors knew where the bodies were buried, and they knew who buried them. For weeks afterward detectives dug up burned and mutilated corpses at locations Reles specified in the Bronx, New Jersey, and Sullivan County. He also provided information that solved murders the authorities had no knowledge of. And he was only starting. He was, O'Dwyer said, "the most effective informer in the annals of criminal justice."

FBI Director J. Edgar Hoover had stubbornly refused to acknowledge organized crime. For whatever reason, he had denied its existence. He was now definitively proven wrong. Reles confirmed the existence of a coast-to-coast confederacy of affiliated mobs—mostly Italian and Jewish—operating in concert under the jurisdiction of a board of directors and subject to the rulings of a kangaroo court. The Commission, Reles said, operated "like the Lehman Banks. It is practically one organization and spreads all over the country."

Reles revealed a shadow America, a coast-to-coast underworld with fences to dispose of stolen goods, moles to warn of police movements, doctors to discreetly treat gunshot wounds, and farmers to hide murderers in barns and back houses. Nobody was safe from Reles's memory, including the biggest bosses. He described how he helped Lepke Buchalter orchestrate the slaughter of dozens of potential informers, and he recalled moving Buchalter among Brooklyn hideaways for two years. Without hesitation Reles named the people who had helped conceal Buchalter, so that O'Dwyer could charge them with harboring a fugitive.

Reles worked his way through the morbid history of Murder, Inc., filling in gaps and telling backstories with relish and thuggish bon mots. For Reles it was more performance than deposition. He enthusiastically and exhaustively rehashed the deaths of the Shapiro brothers of Brownsville, Red Alpert, Spider Murtha, Puggy Feinstein, Daniel Meehan, Irving Ashkenas, Solomon Goldstein, Joe Rosen, George Rudnick, Walter Sage, Whitey Friedman, Morris Diamond, and others.

The shooting death of Dutch Schultz and his three associates in the Palace Chophouse in Newark had remained unsolved for five years, despite elaborate ongoing theories and speculation. Reles solved the mystery in one sitting: An ad hoc mobster committee faced a dilemma: kill Dewey or kill Schultz. Their answer was to send Mendy Weiss and Bug Workman to the chophouse on the rainy night of October 23, 1935.

The more Reles talked, the more murder cases came to light. He cataloged so many with file-card precision that O'Dwyer had trouble counting them. At first O'Dwyer told the press thirty; he later tallied fifty. There were enough to send twenty men to the electric chair. In any case, that's what he told the police reporters huddled at his door.

From O'Dwyer's office the stories of murder trickled out into the press, day by day, like installments in a detective series, with an ever expanding cast of fugitives, defectors, and those hovering somewhere in between. The Murder, Inc. coverage competed for column inches with the menacing stories unfolding in Europe—Wehrmacht troops striding in lockstep through the cobble streets of Warsaw, Oslo, and Copenhagen, the Luftwaffe buzzing Belgium and Holland, the British bracing for invasion. Western Civilization reeled and staggered, but for these few weeks in April 1940 nothing in Europe could upstage the account of malice and mass murder unfolding right in Brooklyn.

In addition to his long list of disclosures, Reles cleared up one of gangland's most intractable puzzles: the disappearance of Peter Panto, the twenty-eight-year-old longshoreman who led a revolt against Anastasia's control of the waterfront. Panto's friends and family had heard nothing of him since he stepped from his Brooklyn apartment on that summer night in 1939. They assumed that Anastasia ordered Panto's murder, but his body was never found.

Now, in the course of his twelve-day oration, Reles named Mendy Weiss, the same assassin who helped kill Dutch Schultz, as Panto's killer. "Mendy strangled him as a favor for Albert [Anastasia]," Reles said.

According to Reles, Anastasia's men offered Panto money to abandon the docks for good. He refused. So they beat him, hustled him into the back of their car, and drove him to an isolated house in New Jersey. Panto was modestly built, just 163 pounds, but he was tough from years of dock work. He fought back like a tiger. He nearly bit Weiss's finger off. He sank his teeth to the bone before Weiss subdued Panto and strangled him to death. That night they covered Panto's body in quicklime and dumped it in a hastily dug grave on swampy tidal land near Lyndhurst, New Jersey. "I think there's six or eight stiffs planted there," Reles said.

After the murder, Weiss had confided in Reles: "Gee, I hated to take that kid, [but] I had to do it for Albert, because he has been good to me."

In the eight months since Panto vanished, the family of Alice Maffia, his twenty-year-old fiancée, did their best to protect her. Alice's mother, a short, insistent Italian immigrant, barred strangers from entering the family home for fear that Murder, Inc. would come after Alice.

Meanwhile, a council of clergy, lawyers, and union officials, known as the Brooklyn Labor and Citizens Committee, had formed to carry on Panto's cause and press authorities to address his case. They did so in part by assembling a dossier of information about racketeering practices on the Brooklyn docks. They sent their report to Charles Grutzner, Jr., a crime reporter for the *Brooklyn Daily Eagle,* without bothering to share it with O'Dwyer. The committee's practice, not surprisingly, antagonized O'Dwyer. Like any ambitious public figure, he wished to control the story. "This trick of getting cheap publicity is something I don't like and I accuse you . . . of pulling that trick," O'Dwyer told Marcy Protter, a labor lawyer who headed the committee. "You take up my time and talk twaddle." Despite his grievance, O'Dwyer met with the committee and pledged to "deliver Peter Panto, or what's left of him."

By late March, O'Dwyer had gathered enough information from Reles and the other informants to begin the job of courtroom prosecutions. With a glut of indictments expected, O'Dwyer and his staff called for two grand juries to be sworn in on April 1 so that jurors could begin sifting through masses of evidence. He also asked the five Brooklyn judges to arrange for a sixth judge from outside the borough to take on the swelling criminal calendar. He added, as well, a roster of new detectives

to his staff to handle rounds of anticipated arrests. He housed the detectives in an eighth-floor space in the Brooklyn Municipal Building
provided by the Complaint Bureau.

"I am working on more than thirty-five murders," O'Dwyer told a
reporter. "I could give you front-page headlines a foot high, but I want
to correlate my facts first."

On March 28 the grand jury indicted Max Golob and Dasher Abbandando for the shooting death of Spider Murtha, the first indictments since Reles cracked open the Murder, Inc. investigation. Flo
Nestfield, Murtha's girlfriend, identified them as the shooters who am-
bushed the couple on Atlantic Avenue. O'Dwyer posted a twenty-four-
hour police guard at Nestfield's Brooklyn apartment, in a Clinton Hill
brownstone, after a series of phone calls threatening to kill her.

Four nights earlier, detectives had detained Julie Catalano, the former cabdriver and housepainter who drove the stolen cars used in six
murders. Buchalter had sought to kill Catalano before he could divulge
details to O'Dwyer, but he would be harder to reach now that O'Dwyer
held him on vagrancy charges—unless Murder, Inc. arranged to bail
him out.

From his cell in the Tombs, Maione sent word to Catalano's brother
urging him to pay Julie's bail. His brother refused. Maione sent a
follow-up message to the brother: if you care about your health, you'll
do as I say. Murder, Inc. would make it easy, Maione said, by providing the $5,000 bail. The brother complied out of fear for his life, and
the court released Catalano back to the Brooklyn streets.

Now that Catalano was unprotected, Maione sent word to his own
brother, Louis Maione, who was serving a ninety-day term for vagrancy
in the city workhouse on Welfare Island. Louis, in turn, relayed the
kill order to a friend, Vito "Socko" Gurino, a frog-faced 260-pound
florist and triggerman who refined his aim by shooting the heads off
chickens in the backyard of his redbrick bungalow in Ozone Park,
Queens.

Gurino was among the most ruthless assassins in Murder, Inc. One
of his seven victims was found dangling from a barbed-wire fence,
too mangled to identify except by fingerprints. The *Daily News* called
Gurino "the blubbery fatso of the Brooklyn Murder Mob."

Back in Brownsville, Catalano, newly freed, heard rumors that Maione's brother was sending Gurino to kill him. Catalano then confronted

Maione at the Tombs by signing at the visitor's desk with a fake name, Joe Falco, and a fake address. Maione denied everything. My brother, he told Catalano, always exaggerates.

Maione, of course, was lying. One night in late March, Gurino sidled up to Catalano at a wedding reception and, feigning friendship, proposed a little ride out to Long Island for their mutual protection. We'll stay, Gurino suggested, "until the heat is off. This Reles investigation ought to be all over in a couple of months." Catalano knew how the ride would end.

"Wait until I go home and get some clothes," he told Gurino in order to buy time. "I want to tell my wife that I'm going."

"You're a sucker if you tell your wife," Gurino answered. "We're going to have a couple of girls where we're going and we'll have a swell time."

Catalano knew that O'Dwyer had sent a squad of detectives to find him, and he was relieved to find them waiting at his home. "I was praying the police would come," he said. The detectives escorted Catalano to O'Dwyer's office, where he dropped to his knees and wept in relief. "Put me back in jail," he said. "They want to take me out on Long Island and kill me."

Returned to the safe confines of custody, Catalano enthusiastically supplied a statement which led four days later to first-degree murder indictments against Maione, Strauss, and Abbandando in the killing of George Rudnick on May 25, 1937. Newspapers now called Catalano "the Kings County Canary."

Catalano also agreed to testify against the fugitive Albert Anastasia in the 1939 murder of Morris Diamond, the Teamsters official killed during the push to eliminate all those capable of incriminating Buchalter. Catalano would testify as an accomplice, while Reles spoke as the non-accomplice required by law. Reles said that when he had visited Anastasia's home on Ocean Parkway, near Coney Island, to discuss a bookmaking business they ran, he walked in on a planning session for the Morris Diamond murder. Anastasia was reprimanding Mendy Weiss and Bug Workman for equivocating. "Everything is ready, and you still haven't told us where the bum lives," Anastasia said, according to Reles.

"I'm working on it, Albert," Weiss answered. "As soon as I get it, I'll give it to you."

"When I get it," Anastasia said, "we'll take care of him."

The Reles testimony, combined with Catalano's supporting account, would play persuasively in the courtroom. A first-degree murder conviction would likely send Anastasia to the electric chair, making him the first mob boss in the U.S. executed by judge and jury. These eventualities were not lost on Anastasia. When he heard that Reles was sharing information about him, he disappeared like a genie.

On March 29 Police Commissioner Valentine ordered two husky detectives, Frank Lyons and Stephen Brady, to accompany O'Dwyer wherever he went. One stood sentry outside his office door, while the other stood inside. They pulled office window shades closed in case a sniper tried to take a shot. At night the detectives slept in a spare bedroom in O'Dwyer's two-story Bay Ridge home. "I didn't ask for the bodyguards, but the police department feels I should have it," O'Dwyer said. "As far as I'm concerned the detectives are just good company."

On March 28 O'Dwyer held a pretty twenty-six-year-old mother of two small children named Gertrude Gurino as a material witness. She had come to America from Germany five years earlier. Four months after a blind date she married Socko Gurino, the fugitive triggerman sent to kill Julie Catalano. Their marriage was, Turkus wrote, "a perfect mating of Beauty and Beast. Gurino, who had the manners of a wallowing animal and the habits of an oaf, was particularly proud of this most beautiful of his possessions." Their unlikely coupling, he added "remained an unsolved mystery even to the mob."

The day after O'Dwyer detained Gertrude Gurino, an eight-state alarm went out for her husband's arrest. The *Brooklyn Daily Eagle* called him a "triggerman still skulking in Brooklyn's underworld with his fangs unremoved."

O'Dwyer suspected that Gertrude was helping her fugitive husband. For one thing, she possessed a stack of blank checks signed by him, which she presumably used to support his fugitive life. While she was in custody O'Dwyer hoped to squeeze her for information about her husband's location and the planning sessions for the Murtha murder. By holding her, he also cut off the funds she would otherwise channel to her husband in his hiding place.

Gertrude worked in a Brooklyn beauty salon, and she had a beautician's habit of applying her craft a bit too assiduously to herself. She made a striking appearance at her arraignment, with flame-red hair and high, artfully drawn eyebrows. She sat expressionless through the legal back-and-forth until the judge announced that the court would turn her two children, ages one and three, over to the Children's Society, a foster home. Then she burst into tears. "With her husband hunted throughout the county and her children in the hands of strangers, this young woman, with the surprisingly Madonna-ish face, is a sad and harried creature," wrote the United Press.

Gertrude was joined by Dukey Maffetore's wife, Mary, and Pretty Levine's wife, Helen. Together they formed what newspapers called the Women's Auxiliary of Murder, Inc. They learned how to make their beds so the skimpy blankets didn't slide off, and they learned how to play whist.

They would soon have more company. In those limbo weeks between arraignment and trial, Pittsburgh Phil Strauss received three jailhouse visits from his girlfriend, the twenty-five-year-old underworld siren Evelyn Mittleman. Turkus called her the "Kiss of Death Girl," a nickname newspapers adopted with gusto. Her three previous boyfriends were murdered, and Strauss, her boyfriend of five years, now faced the electric chair.

Mittleman aroused suspicion by signing into the visitor's pen with a fake name: Eva Steinberg. She would have been hard to miss, by whatever name. She was a tall, slender, dyed brunette dressed like a flush gangster's trophy moll with fur coat, three diamond rings, and a diamond bracelet—all stolen, detectives believed, in a $100,000 Miami robbery. O'Dwyer suspected that with each visit she delivered messages to Strauss and carried instructions back to his Murder, Inc. associates.

Detectives picked her up in a pawnshop where she was peddling stolen furs to pay for Strauss's defense lawyer. She showed up in court in a fashionable new spring outfit, a blue dress with a single-feather hat tilted at a sassy angle. She held a man's handkerchief over her face as she left court so the press couldn't get a decent look at her.

Mittleman had not worked for five years, relying instead on Strauss for gifts and allowances. She knew enough about the operations of Murder, Inc. to put her life at risk. If the district attorney's office did not hold her as a material witness, Turkus said, she would "disappear in one way or another." She might flee, or Murder, Inc. might kill her. To illustrate how savagely the Reles circle treated women, Turkus recalled for the court the seventeen-year-old singer abducted from a Brooklyn nightclub and raped by Abbandando and Maione. Afterward, "they sat about and debated whether to buy or bury her," Turkus said.

After hearing this account, Judge Franklin Taylor granted Turkus's request to hold Mittleman as a material witness on $50,000 bail. She joined Gertrude Gurino in the Women's House of Detention, where the warden allowed them to wear floral-print dresses and fashionable hats instead of prison uniforms, since they were material witnesses, not offenders. But confinement "can certainly keep a pretty girl from running out to the beautify parlor for a shampoo or a finger wave when she needs it," wrote the United Press. "Or from dashing around the corner for a manicure when one is indicated." Newspapers called them "the glamor girls of Murder, Inc."

Attorneys for the women petitioned Turkus to question them under oath, then release them. In a novel legal maneuver, the attorneys argued that holding the women as material witnesses violated their constitutional rights. They were treated as prisoners, but without benefit of trial. Turkus nonetheless detained Mittleman for three weeks, though she disclosed nothing. She did, however, persuade Strauss to follow Reles's example and offer information in return for a reduced sentence, or no sentence at all. "The threat of death—death in the electric chair, had at last opened the lips of the 'murder merchant,'" wrote a police reporter, "and opened them wide."

However, O'Dwyer refused Strauss's offer. He would not make a deal with the most prolific killer in Murder, Inc., at least not on the terms he proposed.

Meanwhile, Gertrude Gurino's husband, Socko, still roamed the city as a fugitive with orders to intimidate or kill. On the night of March 29, 1940, he entered the Queens Civil Prison in Long Island City through a rear stairway with help from a corrupt deputy sheriff and entered the cell of Joe "the Baker" Liberto, the garage attendant on the periphery of the George Rudnick ice-pick slaying. Maione, Strauss, and Abbandando were to stand trial for Rudnick's murder the following month.

Liberto was taken into custody after Happy Maione's brother-in-law, Joseph "Dodats" Daddona, drove him to Island Park, near the south shore of Long Island, and locked him in a farmhouse. Convinced that Daddona would kill him, Liberto asked his captor for a pack of cigarettes. When Dadonna drove off to buy them Liberto jumped out a window and escaped to the woods. He scrounged the thirty-six-cent fare to ride a bus to Jamaica, Queens. From there he walked to Brooklyn and surrendered to O'Dwyer's detectives.

Now he was safely incarcerated and beyond the reach of Murder, Inc., or so he thought. At 11:30 p.m. on March 29 Gurino entered the prison to make sure Liberto said nothing about the night Rudnick died in his garage. Gurino pushed Liberto against a wall and told him that Murder, Inc. was willing to put up a hundred dollars to silence him. So he better keep quiet.

"I told him I didn't say nothing," Liberto later said. "I says I kept my mouth shut."

Liberto was so scared of Gurino, and what Gurino might do if Liberto talked, that he tried to escape from four detectives interrogating him in the Hotel Bossert. "I tried to run out of the hotel," he said. "A detective . . . grabbed me by the hair and I swung at him and he kicks me." In the end, Liberto decided, as Reles did, that cooperation was the likeliest path to survival.

On April 1, 1940, a grand jury convened to hear evidence gathered by O'Dwyer. In his introductory instructions to the jury, Judge Franklin Taylor demanded that "the skull and crossbones ensign of the underworld must come down. Citizens have been slain on the threshold of their home. Many have been taken for a ride, and their lifeless bodies, riddled with lead, have been dumped in the streets. . . . Your joint production during April may be as much as 100 times that of any extraordinary or special grand jury in the country."

The pace of events quickened now as prosecutors used the accounts of murder provided by the informants—the singing school—to lay the groundwork for trials. On April 8, 1940, Turkus went before the grand jury to indict Buggsy Goldstein and Pittsburgh Phil Strauss for the murder of Puggy Feinstein. Four days later, O'Dwyer ordered the arrest of Anastasia for directing Mendy Weiss and others to kill Peter Panto, the longshoreman who led an insurrection on the docks. Anastasia could not be found, however. He had long since gone into hiding.

The same day detectives arrested Oscar the Poet, the compulsive reader of classical texts who specialized in disposing of stolen cars, while police searched the mountains of auto parts in his junkyard for evidence. Look for him in the park, Reles told the detectives. He'll have a book of poetry. Sure enough they found him with heavily underlined and annotated copies of "If" by Rudyard Kipling and "Ode: Intimation of Immortality" by William Wordsworth.

O'Dwyer's docket swelled with pending trials as he translated all the confessions and revelations into a complicated series of loosely connected prosecutions in three locations. Dasher Abbandando, Happy Maione, Buggsy Goldstein, and Pittsburgh Phil Strauss would all face murder charges in Brooklyn courtrooms in the coming weeks, while Gangi Cohen stood trial in Sullivan County. Bug Workman would be tried in New Jersey for the 1935 murder of Dutch Schultz. The Reles interviews, and, more importantly, his menacing presence on the witness stand, would be critical in all three.

O'Dwyer now stood on the brink of fulfilling his campaign promise to bust the mob in its Brooklyn heartland. If accomplished, it would be a startling achievement, a triumph that O'Dwyer himself could not have entirely expected. "He did not, in advance, give the effect of a fighting District Attorney who would mix it, no holds barred, with the grime of the underworld and deliver at least a resounding blow against the cruelest racket of them all, the racket of murder, which had been so long entrenched and so well hidden," wrote the *Brooklyn Daily Eagle*. "It may be that in the . . . sorrow of a brother's death, William O'Dwyer vowed to himself that if he ever had a chance he would clean up the slimy pit of underworld murder, about which he had known from his patrolman days."

As lawyers on both sides prepped their cases, O'Dwyer's friends within the city's Democratic machinery began talking him up as a worthy mayoral candidate. By the spring of 1940, Thomas Dewey was campaigning for the Republican nomination for president, though many viewed him, at age thirty-eight, as too young for the national stage. "Dewey," said Harold Ickes, President Roosevelt's secretary of the interior, "has thrown his diaper in the ring."

O'Dwyer looked like a candidate who could plausibly follow in Dewey's footsteps. "If he gets a reasonable number of convictions in his drive against the Brownsville mob of alleged cut-rate murderers, O'Dwyer will most likely develop into the logical next Democratic candidate for Mayor of New York," wrote the *Daily News*.

One aspect of O'Dwyer's performance still hung in the balance. His office could not claim true success until a top mob figure went to Sing Sing and, ultimately, the electric chair. The Reles sidekicks awaiting trial were worthy targets, but to extinguish the mob for good O'Dwyer would need to bust their bosses, the gang lords who acted as the Commission's board of directors. The bosses had shrewdly distanced themselves from murder and other crimes, delegating the dirty work. The higher up the mob hierarchy O'Dwyer went, the harder to find proof of a crime.

Albert Anastasia, king of the Brooklyn waterfront, qualified as a big boss, but he had quietly slipped from sight and could not be found. That left Lepke Buchalter as an obvious target. He had surrendered to J. Edgar Hoover, with Walter Winchell's help, the previous August. He was now serving fourteen years at Leavenworth Federal Penitentiary in Kansas, after which he would serve thirty years to life for a labor extortion conviction. O'Dwyer could charge him with murder, but first he would have to extract Buchalter from federal custody.

Reles's testimony would be crucial in establishing a murder case against Buchalter, but O'Dwyer still required bodies as evidence—or, as lawyers say, corpus delecti. With that in mind, O'Dwyer drove a hundred miles north and west to Monticello, in the Catskills, on April 12, 1940, to look for the body of Hyman Yuran, a well-to-do young dress manufacturer. Reles confirmed that Yuran was murdered on Buchalter's orders during his extermination of witnesses. He had disappeared from his hotel while vacationing with his wife in July 1938. He had not been seen since.

Reles knew about Yuran's murder. He directed O'Dwyer to the Rosemont Lodge on Anawana Lake Road, two miles north of Monticello, where state troopers dug for five days with shovels and picks, finding only bedrock.

Reles had not been directly involved in the killing or burial. He was therefore unaware that the assassins, a group that included Pittsburgh Phil Strauss, Tick Tock Tannenbaum, and Sol Bernstein, gave up on burying the body at Rosemont Lodge when the ground proved rock hard.

O'Dwyer might never have found Yuran's grave without the help of Bernstein, a twenty-nine-year-old Reles gunman who had himself gone missing for a month and was feared dead. Bernstein knew the location of Yuran's body, among other secrets. For that reason O'Dwyer and Buchalter's friends raced to find him first. Bernstein was rumored to have fled to Chicago. When Chicago police found a burlap sack in an alley containing a dismembered torso and legs, they suspected they belonged to Bernstein. They could not say for sure because the sack contained no hands, and therefore no identifying fingerprints. In any case, hours later Bernstein, alive and intact, surrendered to detectives in Brooklyn and pronounced himself hugely relieved to enter the safe confines of incarceration. "The Commission was after me," he said. O'Dwyer held him on $25,000 bail as a material witness in another murder, that of Morris Diamond, and one day later brought him to Monticello to help locate Yuran's missing body.

Reles was right to direct the search crew to Rosemont Lodge, Bernstein said. But when the ground outside the lodge proved too hard that summer night in 1938, Bernstein now explained, Tick Tock Tannenbaum suggested they move Yuran's burial to the Loch Sheldrake Inn, a resort hotel owned by his parents. The soil was still pliable where workers had recently dug a drain for the swimming pool. It made a natural grave. For two years lodge guests unknowingly swam and lay out in the sun a few feet from Yuran's decomposing body.

Bernstein led O'Dwyer and Sullivan County District Attorney William Deckelman to a slight depression in the ground beside the swimming pool. On a rainy afternoon state troopers wearing fedoras and long coats dug through the loose, muddy soil. At 4:15 p.m. their spades struck bone. They found what was left of Yuran lying face down in a four-foot grave. His assassins had poured quicklime too sparingly to entirely erode his organs. The remains of his abdomen still contained bullet punctures. The skull showed a neatly defined hole. Detectives identified Yuran by a Masonic membership card found in his wallet and a brass belt buckle that bore his initials: HY. Patrolmen placed loose finger bones, a gold wristwatch, and tufts of clothing in a container for inspection by the police laboratory in New York.

Yuran was the fourth Murder, Inc. victim found in Sullivan County, known to newspapers as "The Gangster's Graveyard."

With Yuran's body retrieved from its shallow grave, the murder inquiry inched closer to Buchalter. "The rotting remains of an underworld gangster came out of a shallow grave on Monday afternoon," wrote a newspaper published in the nearby town of Liberty, New York, "to haunt somebody still alive who sent him to his death because he knew too much."

As the first trial date neared, word reached O'Dwyer that Murder, Inc. was amassing a defense fund by collecting extra kickbacks from labor unions. They began by demanding a dollar a day from members of Local 65, a warehouse worker's union, then expanded to several other locals. About the same time newspapers reported that the Commission had offered a prestigious defense lawyer, Samuel S. Leibowitz, a generous fee to defend some or all of the defendants. Leibowitz filled the role that Clarence Darrow had played a decade earlier: a celebrity lawyer unafraid to defend notorious murderers. Leibowitz had compiled a record of more than a hundred murder trials without a death sentence.

Seventeen years later Leibowitz told his biographer that he and his wife, Belle, were about to leave home to see an 8:30 showing of a Cary Grant movie one night in the spring of 1940 when three men rang the doorbell. "The picture begins at 8:30," Belle said as she showed the men into the library, "and we don't want to be late."

"Lepke wants you to defend him," one man said. Leibowitz did not identify his visitors.

"I don't want it," Leibowitz said. "I'm just not interested. There are a dozen lawyers around who will be happy to take the case, and do a good job, too."

"But Lepke only wants you," the visitor said. "Won't have anyone else. You can name your fee." The man opened a briefcase containing $250,000 in cash.

"I told you I had a date with my wife," Leibowitz said. "Put the money away. I'm not interested."

When reporters asked if Leibowitz would represent the Murder, Inc. defendants, he emphatically ruled it out. "Under no circumstances will I defend any of these people," he said. Their crimes were apparently too much even for him. Though the Murder, Inc. case would come back to Leibowitz ten years later, in an unexpected way.

If the suspects could not rely on Leibowitz to save them, the burden would fall to two of their own. In early April O'Dwyer learned that the Commission had flown reinforcements in from out of town in a last-chance effort to silence witnesses. Bugsy Siegel, a member of the old New York mob establishment who had relocated to Los Angeles, and Isidore Bernstein, a top gunman for the Purple Gang in Detroit, had checked in under false names at the Ambassador Hotel on Park Avenue. By the time O'Dwyer dispatched detectives, the two men had checked out and moved elsewhere. They were one step ahead of him.

"These men are here for business," O'Dwyer told police reporters.

Detectives interrogate Pittsburgh Phil Strauss, Buggsy Goldstein, Abe Reles, and Happy Maione (l. to r.) in September 1931, after finding six revolvers, a sawed-off double-barreled shotgun, and a stockpile of ammo in their bathhouse locker. Their gift for violent intimidation would earn them a decade of murder assignments from the nation's top mob bosses.

Credit: New York Daily News Archive via Getty Images

Abe Reles.

Credit: Burton Turkus Papers, Special Collections, Lloyd Sealy Library, John Jay College of Criminal Justice/CUNY

Pittsburgh Phil Strauss, Happy Maione, and Dasher Abbandando.

Credit: Burton Turkus Papers, Special Collections, Lloyd Sealy Library, John Jay College of Criminal Justice/CUNY

Gurrah Shapiro and Tick Tock Tannenbaum.
Credit: Burton Turkus Papers, Special Collections, Lloyd Sealy Library, John Jay College of Criminal Justice/CUNY

Thomas E. Dewey, the "baby prosecutor," set out to bust a vast and intricately organized nationwide crime syndicate. "The Young David," a newspaper wrote, "is sent in against the gang Goliath."
Credit: AP/Shutterstock

Residents in the upstate farm town of Malone, N.Y., cheer the bootlegger and racketeer Dutch Schultz moments after jurors acquitted him of tax evasion. Murder, Inc. executed him in a Newark chop house less than three months later to prevent him from killing Thomas Dewey.
Credit: Everett Collection

Dutch Schultz.

Credit: Burton Turkus Papers, Special Collections, Lloyd Sealy Library, John Jay College of Criminal Justice/CUNY

Lucky Luciano.

Credit: Burton Turkus Papers, Special Collections, Lloyd Sealy Library, John Jay College of Criminal Justice/CUNY

Detectives escort the mafia mastermind Lucky Luciano, center, to court in 1936. A judge sentenced him to thirty to fifty years, but he continued to manage the mob from his cell in Clinton Correctional Facility in Dannemora, N.Y. Governor Thomas Dewey pardoned Luciano after he helped keep the wartime waterfront safe from Nazi sabotage.

Credit: Everett Collection

Prosecutors held the heroin addict Florence Brown, known in the underworld as Cokey Flo, on prostitution charges until she agreed to testify against Lucky Luciano in return for clemency and a drug withdrawal program. "I got disgusted and I told Mr. Dewey I wanted to go straight and get out of this business."

Credit: New York County District Attorney, Case File 211537/ NYC Municipal Archives

Murder, Inc. operated on a simple supposition: no witnesses, no prosecutions. Victims included the informant Irving Ashkenas, shot dead beside his taxi in the driveway of the Paramount Manor Hotel in the Catskill Mountains.

Credit: Burton Turkus Papers, Special Collections, Lloyd Sealy Library, John Jay College of Criminal Justice/CUNY

In the late 1930s, as prosecutors closed in, Murder Inc. systematically killed some thirty associates capable of implicating mob bosses—including Joe Rosen, a candy store operator who enthusiastically divulged details of the garment industry rackets.

Credit: Burton Turkus Papers, Special Collections, Lloyd Sealy Library, John Jay College of Criminal Justice/CUNY

Walter Sage paid the price for skimming profits from the mob's slot machines in upstate casinos. His friends stabbed him to death in July 1937, then dumped his hogtied body in a lake popular with boaters and bathers. His bloated remains bobbed to the surface two weeks later.

Credit: Bettmann/Getty Images

The fugitive Lepke Buchalter, center, enters a courtroom in August 1939 handcuffed to FBI Director J. Edgar Hoover, left, after gossip columnist Walter Winchell brokered his surrender. Buchalter would be the highest-ranking mobster to die in the electric chair.

Credit: Al Aumuller/New York World-Telegram and Sun Photograph Collection/Library of Congress

Murder, Inc. strangled the low-level bookie Puggy Feinstein in Abe Reles' living room while his mother-in-law napped in the next room. Feinstein's burned body was found in an empty lot near Sheepshead Bay.

Credit: Burton Turkus Papers, Special Collections, Lloyd Sealy Library, John Jay College of Criminal Justice/CUNY

Abe Reles and his men stabbed the suspected informant Whitey Rudnick more than sixty times with an ice pick. Police found his body in a stolen Buick abandoned in a quiet Brooklyn neighborhood.

Credit: Burton Turkus Papers, Special Collections, Lloyd Sealy Library, John Jay College of Criminal Justice/CUNY

Detectives unearth the decomposed body of Hyman Yuran near the Loch Sheldrake Inn, in the Catskill Mountains. He disappeared two years earlier after sharing details of Lepke Buchalter's garment industry extortion schemes with a grand jury.

Credit: Burton Turkus Papers, Special Collections, Lloyd Sealy Library, John Jay College of Criminal Justice/CUNY

Buggsy Goldstein (left) and Pittsburgh Phil Strauss ride to Sing Sing a day after a Brooklyn judge sentenced them to death for the strangling murder of Puggy Feinstein. "You can tell that rat Reles I'll be waiting for him in hell with a pitchfork," Goldstein said.

Credit: Bettman/Getty Images

Lepke Buchalter, Mendy Weiss, Little Farvel Cohen and Louis Capone (l. to r.) sit at the defendant's table on the first day of their trial for the murder of Joe Rosen. Farvel would be removed from the indictment. The rest would go to the electric chair.

Credit: Brooklyn Daily Eagle photographs, Brooklyn Public Library, Brooklyn Collection

Above: The body of Abe Reles, assassin-in-chief for the underworld death squad known as Murder, Inc., lies on a hotel roof deck in the early morning of November 12, 1941. Right: He jumped—or was pushed—from room 623 in the beachfront Half Moon Hotel, in Coney Island, where critical underworld informants lived for months behind layers of security to protect them from vengeful assassins. The canary sang, the police said of Reles, but could not fly.

Credit: Stanley B. Burns, MD & The Burns Archive (above); Brooklyn Daily Eagle photographs, Brooklyn Public Library, Brooklyn Collection (right)

Mayor William O'Dwyer and the fashion model Sloan Simpson walking down Fifth Avenue a month before he won re-election and two months before their marriage. They returned from a Florida honeymoon to find their charmed spell on the city broken.

Credit: Mayor's Committee City of New York–Division of Photography/NYC Municipal Archives

Former mayor William O'Dwyer testifies before the Kefauver senate subcommittee on corruption in 1951. He returned to New York to clear his name seven months after resigning in a cloud of suspicion, but the slow drip of insinuations further damaged his stature. Senators bore down on the unanswered question of Abe Reles' death.

Credit: Brooklyn Daily Eagle photographs, Brooklyn Public Library, Brooklyn Collection

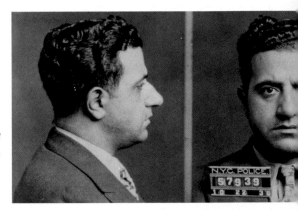

Albert Anastasia.

Credit: Burton Turkus Papers, Special Collections, Lloyd Sealy Library, John Jay College of Criminal Justice/CUNY

Albert Anastasia, known as the Lord High Executioner, was the one who got away. He dodged prosecution only to be shot dead by rival mobsters during a haircut in the Park Sheraton Hotel in Midtown Manhattan.

Credit: George Silk/The LIFE Picture Collection via Getty Images

"We expected out of town triggermen to arrive and we've been looking for them. . . . They are here to shoot down those who stand in their way."

Bernstein's job was to perform the killing, while Siegel served as a steadying hand in the crisis. "Siegel is here," O'Dwyer said, "because the leaders of the Brooklyn mob, the top men who should have taken over, have fled for cover." He was talking specifically about Albert Anastasia. "Siegel will try to restore order, calm jittery nerves, guide things until the 'heat' is off. He will be a field director and with Bernstein mark out those who must go."

O'Dwyer posted additional guards at the informants's suite at the Bossert Hotel, and he expanded his staff of detectives by twenty-one, bring the total to fifty-nine.

Reles was clearly mob target number one. The only question was whether the police could keep him alive long enough to send the mob lords to Sing Sing. "You don't know those bastards like I do," he told his handlers. "Anywhere in the world they'd find me, if I was on the outside. Anywhere in the world—and they'd knock me off."

10

MR. ARSENIC

In his two months as an informant, Abe Reles had provided O'Dwyer and his prosecutors with a rich and detailed history of dozens of unsolved murders and a full dossier on the men and motivations behind each killing. Kid Twist, the eighth-grade dropout, had authored a magnum opus of crime history.

O'Dwyer had concluded that Reles told the truth, but the critical assessment would come in the courtroom. Would jurors trust a primary witness who had spent his life stealing and murdering? If his history disqualified him as a credible source, then O'Dwyer's cases, his entire campaign, might collapse. "This first prosecution would be the acid test," Turkus later wrote. "The entire investigation lived or died on it. Our case rested entirely on the testimony of killers and the corroboration of those killers by more killers." The first test of Reles's courtroom sway came when the smug little mobster Happy Maione, his subordinate Dasher Abbandando, and the Murder, Inc. stalwart Pittsburgh Phil Strauss went to trial on May 8, 1940, for the three-year-old ice-pick murder of Whitey Rudnick.

Strauss, a tall, imposing killer of dozens, had lost fifty pounds since his arrest. He broke down in racking sobs minutes before entering Kings County Court, in Brooklyn. He agreed on the spot to tell prosecutors all the secrets of Murder, Inc. or as many as he knew. O'Dwyer and Judge Franklin Taylor agreed to remove Strauss from the trial. "He has promised to talk," Turkus told Judge Taylor while O'Dwyer sat among the court reporters. "He's going to tell everything. He's going to take up where Reles left off."

The next day, Strauss reneged, refusing to share information that would help bring charges against Buchalter for the murders of Joe Rosen and Morris Diamond. When his panic subsided he apparently recognized that testifying against Buchalter might carry its own death sentence. In any case, O'Dwyer gave him an ultimatum: tell all without inhibition, as Reles had, or face the death penalty in a later trial. He chose the latter.

Maione and Abbandando proceeded to trial without Strauss. The two men looked smaller and less menacing now, as if the grandeur of Judge Taylor's courtroom, its stars-and-stripes and soaring ceilings and formal judicial proceedings, had reduced the Brooklyn big shots to sallow failures.

As expected, Reles played the trial's leading man. He took the stand on May 15 and for four straight hours poured into the record the story of how he and the two defendants executed Rudnick, then plotted to assassinate Catalano and Liberto, the two witnesses. The *Brooklyn Daily Eagle* called his testimony "a song of death."

This was the moment of confrontation anticipated for two months, ever since Reles had agreed to bear witness against his own. On the morning of his testimony, the first of many days as a prosecution witness, guards searched spectators and reporters for weapons as they entered the courtroom, a rare precaution in 1940. Rows of police officers stood sentry with backs to the courtroom walls.

With Judge Taylor seated, Reles entered wearing a double-breasted gray suit. A court attendant and two detectives escorted him to the witness stand. Three guards stood by his side. The months of confinement had added fifteen pounds or so to his short, stocky frame. His gray-blue growth of beard darkened his freshly shaved face. He looked out at the packed courtroom from beneath bushy black eyebrows.

Reles's debut marked his first contact with his boyhood friends since betraying them. His dark eyes rested on theirs for a beat, then he raised his eyes to the ceiling. They stared at him in disbelief. "[Reles's] beady eyes were averted from the cold sneers of the two defendants who sat slumped in their seats, heavily guarded by uniformed deputy sheriffs against any possible break," wrote the *Brooklyn Daily Eagle*.

Reles was clearly uncomfortable. He sat twisting a handkerchief with a red border in his pudgy hands for five awkward minutes as an attendant adjusted the venetian blinds. Meanwhile, the defendants slumped in their seats flanked by guards. Maione's hard black Sicilian eyes stared straight ahead. Abbandando, taller with hulking shoulders, chewed gum determinedly without expression. He sat motionless, Turkus wrote, "like a thick-shouldered alligator sunning himself."

If Reles was nervous at first, he soon recovered and warmed to his performance, as if he were telling stories in the back room of a Brownsville bar. He spoke quickly, eagerly responding to every question. He told his grisly accounts with ease and slapstick humor that drew laughs from the jury, and on a few occasions, from the defendants. The courtroom was full of an odd awareness that the squat, blustering man staging an entertaining performance was also a legendary killer.

Turkus began by leading Reles through an account of the night that he and the two defendants lured Rudnick into the garage after learning that he had "stooled to the police" and killed him with a clothesline, an ice pick, and a meat cleaver. Reles described the events with ease, verging on enthusiasm, with his distinctively guttural, lisping speech and a generous smattering of "dese" and "dose." His voice, the *Brooklyn Daily Eagle* wrote, was as husky "as a pugilist who had been subjected to blows on the throat."

Reles described arguing with Strauss over the spelling of the word "friend" as they composed a fake note to be placed in Rudnick's pocket. He recalled how he and Abbandando spent four nights waiting until dawn for Rudnick to happen along the Brownsville streets, how Abbandando drove to the curb and offered Rudnick a lift when they finally found him, how Abbandando delivered Rudnick to a garage and Reles followed.

"I saw Strauss take the ice-pick and jam it into Rudnick's throat," Reles told the jury. "Then Maione took the meat cleaver and let him have it on the head." The descriptions were so graphic that Judge Taylor abruptly recessed, saying he "needed a rest."

The longstanding practice of Murder, Inc. was to kill informants, then kill those who witnessed the kill—even if it meant murdering their brethren. In keeping with that custom, Reles said, Maione ordered Socko Gurino, the 260-pound marksman, to kill the two men—the driver Catalano and garage attendant Liberto—who stood on the margins of Rudnick's death scene. Defense attorneys twice interrupted Reles to demand a mistrial. Twice the judge slapped them down.

At the start of cross-examination, Reles admitted to participating in the murder of Puggy Feinstein, the small-timer whose burned body was found in a vacant lot. Three times defense lawyers asked Reles about the murder, three times he acknowledged his role. "Puggy Feinstein was killed in my home," Reles said. "I helped. I had a hand in it." Judge Taylor then took over the questioning.

"Was he shot?" Taylor asked.

"No, sir," Reles said.

"Was he stabbed?"

"No, sir."

"How was he killed?"

Reles twisted in the witness chair to face the judge. He raised his right hand to his throat, pinched his skin, and pulled. He smiled and said, "Strangulation, your honor."

Reles lost his composure momentarily when asked if his feud with the Shapiro brothers fifteen years earlier originated with the rape of his girlfriend, now wife. "No, it did not," he said through clenched teeth.

Reles hesitated again when defense attorney Alfred I. Rosner asked, "Wasn't Rudnick killed for doing just what you're doing now?" Was Reles not a squealer, just as Rudnick was?

Reles squirmed in his seat and paused. "Well," he said, "it's not exactly the same thing."

Five years earlier, as an assistant district attorney, William Kleinman had tried to convict Reles for assault. Now, as a defense attorney, he confronted Reles about his shooting a prostitute, running a girl over with a motorcycle, murdering Jake "the Painter" Goldberg with Goldberg's own gun, and other crimes. Kleinman's intention was to erode Reles's credibility by exposing his long criminal history. Reles nonetheless stepped down from the witness stand at 3:40 p.m. with his testimony in the Rudnick case unshaken.

Mrs. Dora Rudnick, the white-haired mother of the murder victim, took the stand to recall in halting tones how she prepared her son dinner at their home. It was the last time she saw him alive. She walked into the Kings County Morgue early the next morning to identify the strangled and hacked body of her boy. She did not look at the defendants during her testimony and left the stand fighting tears.

Turkus then called Liberto, the garage attendant, who told the jury that he was playing cards at a neighboring gas station when he saw the two defendants usher Rudnick into the garage. He later saw them leave without Rudnick. Liberto's testimony supported Reles's account and provided the independent corroboration required by law.

Catalano, who drove Rudnick's stabbed and bludgeoned body away for disposal, took the stand with noticeable pleasure. Two months earlier Maione had ordered Catalano killed. Now Catalano would get his revenge. Whispering nervously out the side of his mouth like a black-and-white-movie gangster, he recalled Maione intercepting him at 10 p.m. on the murder night at Rockaway Avenue and Fulton Street. "I wanted to go home and go to sleep," he said, but Maione insisted that he stay around for a chore. Catalano said he waited in a restaurant until 12:30 a.m., then joined Liberto at the gas station next to the murder garage until Abbandando summoned him. He met Reles as both entered the garage. "I asked him, 'What the hell is going on over here?' When Reles and I walked in, there was a guy laid out on the floor."

Maione, Catalano said, was such an unfeeling killer that he left his grandmother's wake hours after her last breath to help murder Rudnick. "He made three or four trips across the street from the garage to his grandmother's place," Catalano said. "There was a lot of wailing and hollering up there. He stayed about fifteen minutes each trip." Maione's head sank at the defense table after Catalano testified.

On cross-examination a defense attorney pressed Catalano to admit that O'Dwyer had offered him payment in return for his testimony. "Nobody promised me nothing," Catalano said with raised voice and dark eyes flashing. "I just spoke the truth, that's all. Nobody beat me, and I wasn't promised nothing. Why do you keep persisting on me for?"

The defense opened its case on May 20 with Maione's mother, Jennie, and a procession of aunts and cousins dressed in mourning black, weeping and speaking alternately in Italian and English. They swore that Maione never left his grandmother's bedside, that he did not once cross the street to the garage. He was, they said, his grandmother's "favorite and pet."

The defense's supporting witnesses included a small, bird-like twenty-nine-year-old named Carmine Scaffo, who lived less than a block from the crime scene. Scaffo said that he was playing cards with Liberto at the gas station next to the garage until 4:30 a.m. the night of the murder. He insisted that Liberto never got up from the game, and he said they never saw Catalano. Scaffo's statement was critical to the defense because it refuted both Catalano's and Liberto's accounts. If the two never entered the garage, they could not have seen a body. Most important, Scaffo insisted that he never saw Maione enter the garage. At 4:30 a.m., he said, he went to the grandmother's house and found Maione weeping at her bedside.

Turkus waged a singeing cross-examination, his voice rising to one loud note after another. He began with a relentless assault, yelling directly into Maione's face with spittle flying. "Since you were eighteen you've been in the rackets—is that right?" Turkus asked.

"That's right," Maione answered. He was a small, pasty presence on the witness stand. He maintained a brittle politeness, but kept his face hard and inscrutable as he held firm to his alibi: He had sat in a chair at his grandmother's bedside the entire night, he said, and never entered the garage.

Turkus bombarded him with a list of sixteen crimes, including the rape of a seventeen-year-old seven months earlier, and ten murders in addition to Rudnick's—Irving Shapiro, Cesare Lattaro, Antonio Siciliano, Felice Esposito, Joseph "Fatty" Cooperman, Joe Amberg, Manny Kessler, Augustus Justriano, and Harry Schober.

"No, I didn't do it," Maione answered methodically to each accusation.

"Did you send [Socko] Gurino to take out Joe the Baker?" Turkus asked.

Maione looked as if he might reach for Turkus from the witness chair. "Why don't you ask him that?"

In response to the more cutting questions, Maione's attorney, David Price, yelled to him, "Don't answer that!"

Turkus intentionally embarrassed Maione by asking about the murder of Lattaro and Siciliano, members of a plasterers' helpers union. While their wives stayed in Italy, the two men lived as bachelors in a basement apartment on Bergen Street protected by a German shepherd. According to detectives, the short, runtish Maione borrowed a dress and heels from Socko Gurino's wife, Gertrude. Dressed in drag, complete with lipstick and rouge, he made his way to the basement apartment and rang the doorbell. Siciliano looked through the peephole and assumed the caller belonged to their roster of female playmates. The next morning police found the bodies of Siciliano and Lattaro in their beds, riddled with bullets. Maione had used his last two bullets on the dog.

"On February 9, 1939, when you were dressed as a woman, painted and powdered, didn't you, with others, go into a place and kill two plasterers' helpers?" Turkus asked Maine.

"I did not," he answered, though his smile betrayed him.

Maione had shed Gertrude Gurino's clothes as he fled through the basement and up to the street. Gertrude later demanded her clothes back from the district attorney's office, but Turkus refused because the dress and heels were entered as evidence. She tried to settle for a hat but didn't get it. "This woman was willing to wear garments that had been used in a murder, and with her own husband, whom she screamingly described as a dope, in the shadow of the electric chair, and all she was thinking about was a piece of felt with a couple of feathers on it," the detective John Osnato later wrote.

"She was also pretty sore," he added, "because people knew the murderer was sporting a beer paunch, but still had been able to wear her dress."

Maione had remained wan faced but composed throughout the proceedings, but he exploded when Turkus pressed him. "They're framing me, that's what they're doing," he yelled at Turkus. "Every one of them—Reles, Catalano, and the rest. You know it, you know they're framing me. They're trying to save themselves by making me take the rap. . . . They killed Rudnick, now they're trying to push it on me."

Late on the afternoon of May 21 Turkus called two witnesses in a bid to undermine Maione's alibi. Nicholas Blanda, an undertaker who attended to Maione's grandmother, said a clutch of aunts talked and cried in the kitchen when he arrived at the house after 2 a.m., but he saw nobody in the bedroom, except for the body. "I've known Maione for seven or eight years," Blanda said. "I was in the house for an hour and a half and I did not see him at all." Blanda's account was supported by Thomas Gilmore, the embalmer. (The morning after testifying, Blanda received an anonymous call urging him to go to a garage. He notified the police, who put him under twenty-four-hour protection.)

Abbandando, for his part, offered no alibi at all. He simply "couldn't remember" where he was the night Rudnick died. He claimed with an oafish smile not to even know of the killing until months later. In any case, he said, he hadn't seen Rudnick since 1930. Turkus asked him if he saw the blood spurt from Rudnick's wounds, as witnesses reported, and if he had washed the blood down the drain with water. "I couldn't stand the breath of a thing like that," Abbandando said, as if he were of squeamish disposition.

When Abbandando's own lawyer, Alfred I. Rosner, mentioned Reles's testimony, Abbandando grimaced. "Reles is a liar," he said, "and he knows he lies."

At one point three guards converged on the witness chair as Abbandando hotly exchanged words with Judge Taylor. Rosner also argued with the judge, his voice reaching a full bellow. Twice the judge reprimanded him.

When Turkus confronted Abbandando with several rape allegations, he grew huffy. "I never raped nobody," he said. Turkus then read a 1927 arrest record in which Abbandando pled guilty to rape. "Well, that one doesn't count," Abbandando said. "I married the girl later." Mrs. Abbandando, a plump brunette, sat in the back of the courtroom.

Both Maione and Abbandando left the witness stand "with unsteady gaits," the *Daily News* reported.

In the trial's last hours, just before summations, Turkus upended the defense by recalling the reptile-eyed little witness Carmine Scaffo. Two days earlier Scaffo had told the jury that Catalano and Liberto never entered the garage on the night of the murder. They therefore could not have seen Rudnick's body slumped on the garage floor. In the course of his testimony Scaffo bolstered his credibility by affirming that he had no police record.

Throughout the trial, and the trials to follow, O'Dwyer and his police aide, Captain Frank Bals, sat in the gallery listening for defense claims that the thirty detectives assigned to their office could disprove. When Scaffo claimed a clean record, they dispatched a detective to follow him.

Scaffo must have sensed their suspicion because he avoided his home that night. The detective trailed him instead to the shoddy Palace Hotel on Flatbush Avenue, in Brooklyn, then to a beer garden in the Ocean Hill neighborhood. The detective arrested him there at midnight, then led him in handcuffs to O'Dwyer's office. Meanwhile, detectives had retrieved Scaffo's police file from the Bureau of Criminal Identification, a vast archive on Broome Street. The file showed that in 1930 Scaffo had pled guilty to burglarizing a laundry. At 3:30 a.m., Scaffo admitted to lying about his police record.

O'Dwyer now reminded Scoffo that he faced a perjury charge, since he had lied under oath. Just before dawn he agreed to cooperate. Back on the witness stand he sheepishly admitted to lying about his record, and he acknowledged fabricating the rest of his testimony. "No, I never played cards with Liberto," he mumbled. "It was a lie." Questioned by Turkus, he said that Maione's brother, Carl, and his sister, Jennie Daddona, had bullied him into lying on Maione's behalf. It was "fear of Carl," Scaffo said, that made him do it. With Scoffo's reversal, the defense could no longer plausibly claim that Reles had framed Maione and Abbandando. The twist so affected Maione that a recess was called so that he could be sick to his stomach.

The defense summation was punchless. Rosner portrayed his client Abbandando as "just a big slob," a fifteen-dollar-a-week bookie clerk who never hurt anybody. Kleinman, speaking for Maione, told the jury that Rudnick was murdered by Reles, Catalano, Maffetore, and Levine. The defendants Maione and Abbandando, he said, were merely fall guys. He characterized Reles and the other state's witnesses as "a bunch of vicious, snarling, insolent murderers." With that the defense rested,

The defendants arrived at the courthouse on May 23, full of bravado for the prosecution's summation. "Don't worry about me," Maione told attendants as he stepped from a prison van. "The worst I'll get is second-degree murder," a sentence that would incur a lengthy jail term, but spare him the death penalty.

Abbandando mimicked his friend's bluster. He told reporters he was "going home to have spaghetti on Sunday." He dressed as if spending a day in the countryside, in a suede jacket, sleeveless sweater, and slacks.

Their moods darkened by increments as Turkus delivered a biting summation. With Scaffo recanting his original testimony, Turkus said, "the entire defense toppled like a house of cards in one day, yesterday, when reeking perjury was exposed before your eyes in a most brazen and vicious attempt to frame a case."

Turkus acknowledged that in Reles the state had produced an admitted killer as its prime witness. They had to do it, he said, "because for three years the police tried to crack this case from the outside. It couldn't be done. This case had to be cracked from the inside—we had to get the killers themselves to break it."

Rosner, the defense lawyer, objected so persistently, so desperately during Turkus's summation that Judge Taylor twice ordered him to sit, then directed a guard to keep him under control. "I order you to sit down, Mr. Rosner," the judge said. "I know the difference between a legal objection and disorderly conduct. Now sit down. I'm reprimanding you."

Turkus addressed the jury for almost two hours. Speaking with the force of a Shakespearean actor, he demanded murder in the first degree, a death sentence. "Do justice," he told the jury. "Don't compromise. This is murder in the first degree and nothing else. Bring in that verdict."

When Maione heard those words his stoic, hard-eyed demeanor dissolved. His pallid skin blotched. "Abe Reles told you everything," he wailed to the jury. He stood as if to lunge at someone. "Abe Reles told you everything." Spectators leaped to their feet in alarm. Three guards rushed to Maione's side and pushed him down in his seat as he lunged for Turkus. A defense attorney spoke to Maione as one would speak to a frightened child. "Keep quiet, Harry," the attorney said. "For God's sake keep quiet."

"I'm sorry," Maione said. "I'm sorry."

The jury deliberated for just two hours and two minutes. At 5:35 p.m. on May 23 they returned a unanimous verdict without even casting a ballot: guilty of murder in the first degree. Maione's eyes bulged in fear as he stepped to the bench before the judge. Abbandando leaned sideways with his mouth clamped tight, as if swooning. First-degree murder carried a mandatory death sentence. "They showed eyes laden with fear," the *Daily News* reported, "far different from the hard, foreboding looks they bore during the summation of Prosecutor Burton B. Turkus and the charge to the jury by Judge Franklin Taylor."

After the verdict, Judge Taylor read off the criminal records of Maione and Abbandando to reassure the jury that they had ruled wisely. It was a long list which by law could not be disclosed during the trial.

Reles and other witnesses "have told of death for a dollar, of terror and extortion rampant in Brownsville, Brooklyn, of the ravishment of girls dragged from busy thoroughfares into gang hideouts, of methods by which Murder, Inc. rules rackets and vice and silenced witnesses," the Associated Press wrote in its trial wrap-up the next day.

Four days after their conviction, Abbandando and Maione returned to the courtroom. They stood with blank expressions as Judge Taylor formally sentenced them to die in the electric chair, calling their crime "a most revolting murder." He forgot to offer them the traditional closing pronouncement, ". . . and may God have mercy on your souls."

The reality of the sentencing—the macabre fact of what awaited them—may not have sunk in yet. Later, Abbandando told a police officer escorting him from court that he did not mind going to the electric chair because death was just a matter of time. Besides, if he had beat this murder charge he would only have faced another. And if he beat that one he would face four more. "What burns me up," he said, "will be to miss the first night Dodgers game and the fact that Abe Reles won't go to the chair with me."

The next morning James Mangano, sheriff of Kings County, accompanied by five deputies, called for the two prisoners at Raymond Street Jail. Maione effected a flippant posture when Mangano snapped on the handcuffs. "You got here early," he said. The prisoners boarded a corrections van with separate locked cubicles, known as a Black Maria, parked in the prison yard. Maione's mother and his married sister, Jennie, waited by the gate. They waved as the van passed. "Goodbye, Momma," Maione said, but he had trouble getting the words out.

The van took the two prisoners to Brooklyn police headquarters, where officials signed transportation papers, and on to Manhattan headquarters for routine checks of photographs and fingerprints. At 11:30 a.m. the sheriffs escorted Maione and Abbandando through the great hall of Grand Central Terminal, aswirl as always with cigarette smoke, where a mocking crowd jostled for a glimpse of the killers. In a last show of bravado, Abbandando hinted that he would be out of prison soon. He and Maione then boarded a special train that ran thirty-five miles along the Hudson River to Sing Sing Prison in Ossining, New York.

Maione said nothing. He stared at the Hudson, smoking one cigarette after another. He turned to the sheriff and cursed Reles. "He is a rat," he said. "He is a squealer." Abbandando wept intermittently as the train traveled north along the river through Dobbs Ferry, Irvington, Tarrytown, until finally Sing Sing came into view, a dank, dark, stone castle-like structure the prisoners themselves built by hand in the 1820s. The prison looked carved from a single massive hunk of stone standing hard against the river bank. Guards holding Thompson submachine guns stood in watchtowers.

Sheriff Mangano loaded his prisoners into a black car and rode with them up a short, winding road to the prison. Heavy iron gates rolled opened to receive them. Mangano walked them through a reception area to a high-ceilinged room at the left. "Two for the back," Sheriff Mangano told a clerk, referring to death row. Sheriff Mangano then removed the handcuffs. "So long," he said. Abbandando said nothing.

"Well, so long, Happy," the sheriff said, squeezing Maione's arm.

"Maione tried to respond," reported Meyer Berger of *The New York Times,* "but the words wedged in his throat. His eyes filled."

Within an hour he and Abbandando were locked into cells a little more than three feet wide and seven feet long—"no bigger than a dead man's grave," as one inmate said. Their lawyers would eventually win a retrial on a technicality, but their reprieve only bought them time. The second trial ended as the first one had—with a death sentence.

In June attention shifted upstate to Sullivan County, where Big Gangi Cohen faced trial in the County Courthouse, in Monticello, for his part in the murder of his friend Walter Sage, the Catskills slot-machine overseer whose half-decomposed body had floated to the surface of Swan Lake in July 1937.

Cohen was arrested in Los Angeles, where he had found work playing bit parts in movies under the name Jack Gordon. Sheriffs seized him while he was filming *The Sea Hawk,* an Errol Flynn swashbuckler. He left his wife, Eva, and a ten-year-old child behind.

Cohen's arrival in Penn Station might have been a scene in one of the gangster movies he acted in. O'Dwyer sent ten detectives to board the train in Newark to guard against interference. They rode across the wetlands of New Jersey and into the long tunnel beneath the Hudson River. A phalanx of police waited in the station with riot guns raised. They scanned the crowd for Socko Gurino, Albert Anastasia, or other hit men.

The train pulled in at 9:10 a.m. Cohen stepped onto the platform manacled to two state troopers and flanked by two more. He needed a shave. He shielded his face from press photographers with a gray homburg as the troopers hurried him along the station platform, past waves of commuters and redcaps and shoeshine boys, and up through the rush hour throng to a waiting car, which followed a police motorcade to Brooklyn. He was handcuffed to a chair in O'Dwyer's office while prosecutors interrogated him. They brought his wife, Eva, to New York five days later in hopes that she would persuade him to cooperate.

On June 17, Cohen blubbered in an upstate courtroom like a frightened child, as Pretty Levine, the prosecution's primary witness, described how Cohen held Sage down while Drucker stabbed him to death in a green Packard sedan as it drove along a quiet wooded road. Cohen jumped to his feet at the defense table. "This man is lying," he bellowed, sweeping tears from his cheeks. "I was not there. Honest." He covered his face with his handkerchief and collapsed into sobs so convulsive that the judge granted a fifteen-minute recess. The next morning's *Daily News* called Cohen "Big Weepy." The jury would decide if his tears were sincere or the product of his newly acquired acting skills.

Cohen denied the murder charges. He said that on the night Sage died he was walking home from a casino at Loch Sheldrake. Levine and another man jumped from a car, he said, and stabbed his arm with an ice pick as punishment for failure to pay 25 percent interest on a gambling loan. He rolled up his sleeves so the jury could see the scar. He escaped, he said, and found a new life in Hollywood.

In his summation Cohen's lawyer, Saul Price, told the jury that the prosecution's case was "insufficient to sustain even a disorderly conduct charge." He asked the jurors if they would send a man to the electric chair on the testimony of a dubious witness like Pretty Levine. At this moment Price's voice broke with emotion. Cohen's wife, Eva, thin and pale, began to cry in the gallery. Cohen himself put his head between his hands and wept. "If you believe the testimony of Levine . . ." Price said. He raised his hands and shrugged. "If you have any doubts as to its truthfulness, you must acquit Cohen."

As it turned out, the jurors did have doubts about Levine's credibility. They deliberated for just ninety minutes before acquitting Cohen. "His wife, Eva, rushed sobbing to his side," the Associated Press reported, "and then the defendant began to cry softly." O'Dwyer, who attended the trial with Captain Bals, made his way through the courtroom to shake hands with Cohen. "Congratulations, Gangi," O'Dwyer said. "You took a chance and you won."

Cohen and his wife returned to their home on North Van Ness Avenue, across from the Paramount studio lot, where he resumed playing cops and other tough-guy parts. When gangster movies faded from fashion in the late 1950s, he found years of work as the double for Hoss Cartwright on the TV series *Bonanza*.

On August 18, Reles and fellow informant Tick Tock Tannenbaum secretly flew on a chartered Lockheed to Los Angeles, where they told a grand jury that Bugsy Siegel supervised the shooting of Harry "Greenie" Greenberg in his Hollywood driveway nine months earlier to punish him for blackmailing Buchalter. O'Dwyer was so concerned about their safety that he did not identify the passengers to airport officials until the Lockheed was over Pennsylvania, and he insisted on secret accommodations in Los Angeles.

O'Dwyer was pleased to lend Reles out to Los Angeles prosecutors, because the Siegel case bore out his public contention that Murder, Inc. had a national reach, and because Siegel was a prime mover behind a campaign to assassinate the New York informants.

Los Angeles detectives had arrested Siegel days earlier at his thirty-five-room mansion in the Holmby Hills, within neighborly vicinity of homes owned by Bing Crosby and Humphrey Bogart. A butler answered the detectives' knock and asked them to wait. Minutes later he waved them into a house with six powder rooms and a dining table that sat thirty. Upstairs the detectives found the tousled sheets of Siegel's unmade bed still warm. They discovered a trapdoor in the ceiling of a linen closet. Siegel was crouched in the attic. He came down laughing. "I thought it was someone else," he said. The detectives did not appreciate his joke. They locked Siegel up in a county jail on the top floor of the Hall of Justice to await trial.

Reles and Tannenbaum told the grand jury that Greenberg had foolishly mailed his childhood friend Lepke Buchalter a letter from Montreal hinting that he would share what he knew of Buchalter's rackets and murders with O'Dwyer unless Buchalter sent him $5,000—a straightforward case of blackmail. Instead of cash, Buchalter sent Albert "Tick Tock" Tannenbaum to kill Greenberg.

As was often the case, the assassin was among the victim's closest friends. When Tannenbaum was a skinny, gap-toothed high-school junior, his father, Sam, bought Loch Sheldrake Country Club, a Catskills resort with gambling and easy supplies of contraband liquor. Tannenbaum worked part-time for his father, waiting tables and setting up beach chairs down by Kiamesha Lake. He befriended a number of

Jewish mobsters who stayed as guests. Hoods on holiday knew how to enjoy themselves. They swam in the lake and day drank Canadian whiskey and bootleg beer. On summer nights they danced with flappers and floozies escaping the city heat. Tannenbaum joined the fun. Greenberg, in particular, took Tannenbaum under his wing. He became the older brother Tannenbaum never had.

A decade later Tannenbaum ranked among the most prolific assassins in Murder, Inc. On Buchalter's orders, he drove to Montreal to kill his friend Greenberg, but Greenberg and his wife, Ida, had left town two days earlier. Nobody knew where the Greenbergs were until the *Los Angeles Times* published an article about Ida's chance reunion with her sister at a bus stop near the intersection of Hollywood and Vine. The sisters had not seen each for twenty-six years and lost track of each other's whereabouts.

Murder, Inc. had been looking for Greenberg. If Ida had moved to Los Angeles, he must be there, as well. A week after the *Los Angeles Times* published its article, Tannenbaum flew west to finish the job under Siegel's supervision. He stepped off the plane with $200 and a doctor's leather satchel containing two pistols. Meanwhile, Siegel had assigned a small-time fight promoter named Frankie Carbo the job of trailing Greenberg.

On November 22, Thanksgiving eve, Greenberg drove his convertible five blocks to buy a late-edition newspaper from a newsstand at Hollywood and Vine, the same intersection where Ida had found her sister. George returned home to Vista Del Mar Avenue at 11:30 p.m. He parked in front of his apartment building. A black sedan pulled alongside. Carbo leaned out the window. He fired a revolver three times at close range, striking Greenberg in the head, chest, and stomach.

After tying Siegel to Greenberg's murder, Reles and Tannenbaum flew home. O'Dwyer stood on the tarmac when their Lockheed landed at Floyd Bennett Field, in Brooklyn, at 11 a.m. on August 22. Reles stepped down the gangway and presented O'Dwyer with a sombrero. He and the police guards had chipped in to buy it during a refueling stop in Las Vegas. Captives and captors shook hands and patted one another's backs. "I'll have to find a piece of beach where they can take a swim and get some sun," O'Dwyer told reporters. "They look like they need it."

Several New York newspapers printed a wire-service photo that day of Reles smiling in close conference with Los Angeles prosecutors. He seemed to be enjoying himself. If nothing else, he was beginning to see a world beyond Brooklyn. The flights were his first. "It's a nice country," Reles said, "except you go so fast you can't appreciate it all."

Of all the schlammers, bookies, and triggermen employed by Murder, Inc., none stood closer to Abe Reles in family and friendship than Pittsburgh Phil Strauss and Buggsy Goldstein. They were his right-hand men. More than that, they were his most intimate friends dating back to their days as thuggish teens stealing from pushcarts and smoking Lucky Strikes on Brownsville street corners. They attended weddings, funerals, and bar mitzvahs together. He brought them along as he climbed the ranks—from lowly gofers to the feared generals of Murder, Inc. In the underworld, loyalty is the most valued currency. And their loyalty to Reles never faltered.

Now, in September 1940, Reles would return their allegiance by testifying against them. Strauss and Goldstein were accused of strangling Puggy Feinstein to death and lighting his body on fire, then abandoning his charred remains in a sandy lot out by Jamaica Bay.

In the late-summer days of dread leading up to the trial, Goldstein's wife, Betty, grew desperate. Her husband's former associates Happy Maione and Dasher Abbandando were now waiting in Sing Sing for their execution dates. Unless Bugsy Siegel or some other mob lord could find a way to circumvent the layers of NYPD protection and kill Reles, Goldstein and Strauss would soon join their friends on death row.

"I don't want to burn," a reporter for the *Brooklyn Daily Eagle* quoted Goldstein as saying. "If they'll let me plead to murder in the second degree and even give me seventy-five years I don't care. I want to beat the chair." Betty conferred with O'Dwyer for twenty minutes on April 16, trying to work out terms by which her husband would join Reles and the other informants in the Hotel Bossert in return for clemency. Afterward she spoke with her husband in the Tombs, then made the return trip to Brooklyn to speak to O'Dwyer a second time. But O'Dwyer would accept no such deal. "I told her it was hopeless," he said. "I don't think she'll be back."

Meanwhile, Strauss enacted his fallback plan, a long-shot ploy to win dismissal from trial for reasons of insanity. Strauss had always been the dapper one, the "Beau Brummel of Death," turned out in double-breasted pinstripe suits with wide, pointed lapels and two-tone Oxford shoes. Now, in the months before the trial, he stopped bathing and shaving. He grew a magnificent beard and wore rumpled clothes. He babbled and barked like a hound. In pleading, desperate tones he complained of seeing Reles under his bed at night and shrugged his neck as if to brush an imaginary creature from his shoulders. "Take the chains off me," he shouted in court one day, though he was not even handcuffed at the time.

When Goldstein saw his friend in a detention pen, he said, "You're enough to make a person sick, the way you look."

In June a psychiatric panel judged Strauss capable of conferring with his counsel and grasping the proceedings. He would therefore not be excused from trial.

With the question of Strauss's fitness resolved, Judge John J. Fitzgerald ordered him to shave his beard. Turkus had argued, and Judge Fitzgerald agreed that, intentionally or not, his shoulder-length hair and Rip van Winkle beard could serve as a disguise. They might confuse witnesses called to identify him.

Strauss's lawyer, a former Albany judge named Daniel Pryor, argued that shaving violated his client's constitutional rights. For example, Pryor said, if Strauss were obese, the court would have no right to alter his diet. Maybe so, Judge Fitzgerald answered, but if Strauss were a nudist, the court could order him to wear clothes for his trial, by force if necessary. Yes, Pryor said, but only during the trial itself. The court could not order him to wear clothes beforehand.

Two days before the trial convened, a barber in Raymond Street Jail by court order shaved Strauss's stringy beard and cut the matted hair that dangled to his shoulders. The barber used scissors, but would not hold a razor anywhere near Strauss. As his dark locks fell to the floor, the unkempt jailhouse madman receded, replaced by the familiar figure of Pittsburgh Phil.

Hair or no hair, Strauss continued to feign insanity. In contrast to Goldstein, who entered the courtroom for the first trial day in a pressed blue serge suit, Strauss wore a wrinkled light gray flannel suit over a blue V-necked sweater. A heavy stubble had grown out since his shave. He looked more like a confused hobo than a killer.

The courtroom was heavily guarded, with entrances barricaded by plainclothesmen and uniformed police. No one could enter without first identifying themselves.

Shortly after things got underway at 10 a.m., Pryor stated that while a psychiatric panel had pronounced his client sane enough for trial, Pryor himself did not agree. As a former judge and a "conscientious attorney," he considered Strauss too impaired to follow the proceedings.

"I saw him in jail on Friday," Pryor told Judge Fitzgerald. "I said, 'You are going on trial today. They say you killed Feinstein. What have you got to say about it?' He said, 'I'm hungry. They don't feed us well.'"

Pryor asked that psychiatrists conduct a second evaluation. Judge Fitzgerald declined, but he authorized Pryor to retain psychiatrists to confer with Strauss daily, including lunch breaks. The judge also said that he would allow Pryor to call a psychiatrist to testify in support of a contention that Strauss was insane at the time of the Feinstein murder.

On September 16, Abe Reles walked into Kings County Court, in Brooklyn, and dropped his short, heavy tree-stump body into the witness chair. "The thick-lipped tattletale," the *Daily News* reported, was as "smug as a war-time profiteer."

Goldstein and Strauss slumped at the defense table, as if already defeated. Reles had sent two of their friends to the Sing Sing death house. Now he entered the courtroom to send them as well. They had not fully accepted that he would testify against them until they saw him seated in witness chair for themselves.

Reles avoided eye contact with the defendants for the duration of his testimony. He counted Maione and Abbandando as close associates, and he had faced them coldly in their trial. Strauss and Goldstein were more like family. They stuck by him when he seized Brownsville from the Shapiro brothers, and they served as aides-de-camp during the death-squad years of Murder, Inc. They were with him through marriages, childrearing, and Tommy-gun bullets. They were his constant backroom companions, his Jewish intimates who rose through the ranks at his side.

Turkus began the prosecution's case by asking Reles to explain how Goldstein and Strauss had helped him kill Puggy Feinstein after the small-time bookie had trespassed on the lucrative waterfront rackets. "It was a job we did for Albert Anastasia," Reles said, leaning forward, as if sharing a secret with the jury. "Albert was our boss—the big guy in the gang."

Throughout his testimony Reles gestured to the jury to amplify and emphasize his meaning, while Strauss stared vacantly ahead, his eyes cold and remote. Goldstein by contrast let his anguish rise close to the surface. He leaned in to listen to Reles, then leaned back shaking his head. His hands jumped about in reaction to every turn in testimony. His eyes were big and incredulous and at times watery and bloodshot.

Reles recalled the Feinstein murder "in the prosaic manner of a carpenter recalling the construction of a shed," The *Brooklyn Daily Eagle* wrote in that afternoon's edition. He drank milk in his home that night while waiting for Maffetore to deliver Puggy Feinstein in a stolen car. When Feinstein entered, "Harry [Strauss] tried to mug Puggy, but he didn't get him right, and Dukey [Maffetore] pushed him on the couch," Reles said. He demonstrated to the jury that mugging meant choking Feinstein by placing his head between forearm and chest.

"This guy Puggy kept on fighting and kicking," he continued, "so I turned the radio on louder and got the rope. I gave Strauss one end of the rope and we put it under Puggy's head while Goldstein held the other end. Then we looped it twice around his neck, pulled on it until he was shaped like a ball, and then tied both ends." Reles showed the jury how they tied Feinstein's body up in a fetal crouch by raising his knees to his chest, lowering his chin and wrapping his arms tight around his legs. "This caused [Reles] to shift in his seat," *The New York Times* wrote, "and a beam of sunlight fell upon his heavy-bearded face, giving it a sickly gray look."

To eliminate fingerprints, Reles said, they doused the body in gas and burned it in an empty lot, then drove to Sheepshead Bay for a shore dinner.

Reles's account of Feinstein's death ended exactly at noon, as jury and spectators heard the bells of the Church of the Holy Trinity tolling from a block away.

In cross-examination, Pryor, counsel for Strauss, tried to demean Reles's credibility by airing his criminal history. "How many murders have you committed?" he asked.

Reles paused to consider. "I committed ten murders. But not all alone."

In addition to helping to kill Puggy Feinstein, he had participated in the murders of George Rudnick and Irving Shapiro. He then recited other victims: "Jake the Painter, Rocco, Greenblatt, Joey Silver."

He paused to think some more.

"And I killed Plug Schuman and Whitey Friedman and Jack Paley. And there was one more. . . . I can't think of his name. . . . Oh, yes, it was Monk Basco. That's the way I knew him, as Monk. That's all I can recall." In the end, the list added to eleven, not ten as Reles originally thought. He was so cavalier about the killings that he tabulated them as carelessly as one might count friends attending a dinner.

If the Reles testimony agitated Goldstein, the following day was only worse. He looked disbelievingly as two guards led his swarthy, thick-lipped friend and protegé Blue Jaw Magoon to the witness stand. Magoon had worked as Goldstein's driver and bodyguard. In return, Goldstein taught Magoon the sly art of stealing cars and initiated him into a minor career in loan-sharking. Goldstein was unaware that Magoon would testify against him until he walked in the courtroom. Magoon's betrayal, a day after Reles, was more than Goldstein could endure. "Seymour, Seymour, tell the truth," Goldstein screamed from the defendant's table. He jumped to his feet and thrust his hairy handcuffed hands forward in appeal. "You gotta tell the truth."

Goldstein's throat choked with anguish. Tears streaked freely down his cheeks. "Tell them, Seymour. Tell them the truth. My life depends on it." He beat his fists on the table, then slumped as if dead.

Magoon looked down from the witness stand at his friend, the man who had trusted him and taken him on as an associate. His face reddened, and he wiped away tears with beefy hands just before he laid his hand on the Bible and swore to tell the truth.

With his face deliberately turned away from Goldstein, Magoon corroborated a part of Reles's damning testimony. Questioned by Turkus, he told the jury how he was driving a car in Brooklyn on Labor Day night a year earlier when he almost ran into a car driven by Goldstein and Maffetore. Goldstein "jumped out of Dukey's car, hollered to me, and came over," Magoon said. "He had a can in his hand, and he was in a rush and excited. I asked him what was the rush, and he put the can, stinking of gas, in my car, jumped into the seat alongside me and said, 'I'll tell you about it as we drive along.'

"Then he said to me, 'Dukey and I burned up somebody tonight.' I asked him who it was, and he said, 'Puggy Feinstein.' Then Goldstein said, 'We had him in (Reles's) house and we strangled him. Abe, Strauss and I did it. And then Dukey and I took him out and burned him.'"

Goldstein asked Magoon to drive him to a gas station on Hopkinson

Avenue in order to return the can and collect his deposit, but Magoon convinced him to discard the can in a vacant lot because his finger-prints might be on it. Later, Magoon said, he accompanied the kill-ers to a restaurant out in Sheepshead Bay. "Then came the lobsters," Turkus told the jury.

As the court recessed for lunch Goldstein jumped to his feet like a boxer rising from the mat. "That's a beautiful story he's telling," he screamed. "That guy is burning me. He's sending me right to the hot seat."

Strauss, meanwhile, sat at the defensive table with indifference, as if unmoved by the proceedings. His lawyer, Daniel Pryor, sent Strauss to the stand to showcase his alleged impairment of mind. He rose with his hands in the pockets of his baggy gray trousers and with the help of two attendants walked to the witness stand. When a clerk tried to administer the oath, Strauss "stared at the clerk with a look of utter incomprehension" and moved his lips inaudibly.

"Take him away," the judge ordered. The clerk led Strauss back to the defense table where he began chewing on the leather strap of a briefcase.

Two psychiatrists hired as expert witnesses followed Strauss to the stand to confirm his insanity. When the first examined Strauss in Ray-mond Street Jail, he said, Strauss seemed to believe that he was in a hos-pital, not a jail, somehow as a result of losing a craps game. He quoted Strauss as saying, "Abe Reles comes under my bed every night, but my brother drives him away."

A second psychiatrist observed the same delusion. "Reles flies in here at night," Strauss told him, "trying to kill me."

Goldstein's attorney, Leo Healy, rested his case without calling any witnesses. He would depend solely on his summation to save his client. Healy used his ninety-minute summation to attack the character and reliability of Reles and the other Murder, Inc. informants. "What a state of affairs it is for Reles, Maffetore, and Magoon to go out on the highway and byways of Brooklyn and kill ten or twelve of our citizens and then not come into court to answer for them," he said.

Strauss's attorney, Daniel Pryor, followed the same line of argument in his fifty-minute summation, asserting that Reles and Maffetore murdered Feinstein and framed Strauss and Goldstein. Referring to Strauss's mental condition, he said, "Now you've seen that I've gone through a veritable hell trying to defend a man in that condition—a wrecked shell of a man."

The next morning Turkus began the State's summation by defending his office's Faustian deal with Reles. "The district attorney would love to have Reles seated beside these sniveling, crawling creatures, who for years were such domineering, arrogant thugs and murderers," he said. "But their murder ring could be broken only from the inside. . . . It is better that one of them escape the chair for this killing then that all three go free."

As guards led Goldstein from court for the midday recess he recognized Harry Feeney of the *World-Telegram*, the man who coined the phrase "Murder, Inc.," sitting in a row of reporters. Goldstein leaned over to him and said in a low voice: "That Turkus. They ought to call him Mr. Arsenic. He's poison."

After the recess Turkus tore into the defendants for an hour and five minutes. Strauss sat in sullen silence, as if the proceedings were beyond his comprehension. At one point, Goldstein rose and shouted, "You lie!" Then he clasped his hands as though in prayer, tears falling from his eyes. Turkus turned on him. "Hear the sniveling Goldstein now. He was not sniveling when, as it was testified, he kicked in the belly the struggling Feinstein, who was fighting to save himself from death by strangulation."

When Turkus had finished his summation, Judge Fitzgerald called a recess. As he was led away with one wrist handcuffed to a guard, Goldstein leaned toward Turkus. He strained on the handcuff, desperate to speak with Turkus. "I want to plead," he said.

By asking to plead, Goldstein seemed to say that he wanted to admit his crime, a deal that would normally have sent him to prison for life but spared him a death sentence. In any case, it was too late. The trial was almost over. Turkus leaned over to catch Goldstein's words until O'Dwyer called him away. The guard led Goldstein out of the courtroom. He was still looking over his shoulder at Turkus as the door closed.

In the courthouse holding pen Goldstein bawled and barked so hysterically that he lost balance and fell off a bench to the floor, as if fear had wilted his skeletal system. "The last shred of the big shot was gone," wrote a reporter who had followed him back to the holding pen. "He was pretty ridiculous." Goldstein lay sobbing and pounding the floor. He made the sounds of a man dissolved by fear of death.

"Come on," a guard told Goldstein. "Sit up there. Stop putting on an act."

"An act!" he said. "Haven't you got a heart? It's my life! It's my life! I'm trying to save my life!"

With lawyers and defendants reassembled after the recess, Judge Fitzgerald issued final instructions to the jury. He noted that Murder, Inc. had committed a total of eighty-three known murders. He reassured jurors that they would not be responsible for sending a mentally ill man to his death. Psychiatrists at Sing Sing would decide if Strauss were sane enough for execution, though Judge Fitzgerald reminded jurors that there was no evidence that Strauss was insane on Labor Day 1939 when he helped strangle Puggy Feinstein. "This case is barren of any evidence," he said, "that either one of the defendants was insane at the time of the crime."

The case went to the jury at 3:45 p.m. At 6:10 p.m. the grim-faced jurors filed back. The foreman read the verdict: both men were guilty of murder in the first degree.

Strauss stared straight ahead, drawing patterns on the linoleum-topped defense table with his thumbs while the verdict was read. He wouldn't answer the procedural questions put to him by a court clerk. When asked to state his name he only mumbled.

Goldstein slumped forward. "His entire face corrugated into an intense grimace of fearful concentration," wrote the *Brooklyn Daily Eagle*. "Then his grimace altered to the sickly semblance of a smile and he elevated a hand as a schoolboy attracts the attention of a teacher."

"Can I say something?" Goldstein asked.

"No statement at this time," Judge Fitzgerald answered.

"Can't I say a word? A little word?"

"No."

As attendants led the two away in manacles, Goldstein yelled over his shoulder, "I can't have one word before I die?" His appeal, the *Brooklyn Daily Eagle* reported, "was high-pitched, hysterically desperate."

Judge Fitzgerald tried to allay whatever guilt jurors might suffer for sending two men to their deaths by reminding them that they convicted Strauss and Goldstein of one murder, but O'Dwyer had evidence of others. Goldstein killed three, he said, while Strauss had slain twenty-eight. Strauss, he added, was so bloodthirsty that he "volunteered to kill, not only carried out orders."

Puggy Feinstein's brother, Hyman, and his sister, Shirley Stimwell, had attended the day's proceedings in order to hear the verdict firsthand. Afterward they both shook hands with O'Dwyer and thanked him for avenging their brother's death.

In the days after their conviction, Goldstein raved in his Raymond Street cell, pleading with the round-the-clock guards for mercy. His state of mind obliged the warden to remove Goldstein's shoelaces and belts. The two men returned to Judge Fitzgerald's court on September 26. Strauss said nothing. He remained silent, licking his lips, even when a clerk asked him to state his name. Goldstein began to speak with a hysterical tone as soon as the court clerk asked if he had anything to say before the sentencing. "I want to thank the court for the charge that is sending us to our death," he said, "and I only wish that the same happens to you and members of your family. If you can't go to your death in a nice way you might as well go in a bad way. I was found guilty on perjured evidence and if I die, I want to do like a man. Now go ahead."

The two defendants stood as the judge pronounced the sentence: "You shall be turned over to the warden of Sing Sing Prison," Judge Fitzgerald continued, "where you shall be put to death—"

"In the electric chair, hooray for me," Goldstein interrupted.

". . . in the manner prescribed by law."

"Make it tomorrow," Goldstein said. "I'd be better satisfied."

Later, as he was led to a police van, Strauss broke his silence by asking a policeman, "What is this fellow hollering about?"

At 10:45 the next morning Goldstein and Strauss left Raymond Street Jail, their home of eight months, for the last time. They rode in a Black Maria to Brooklyn police headquarters on Bergen Street, as Maione and Abbandando had, to confirm their identity. When a flashbulb went off on the sidewalk outside headquarters, Goldstein flicked his cigarette butt into the press photographer's face. "Go take a flying jump at the moon, ya bum ya," he said.

"I'd like to take care of those guys before I'm finished," he added, referring to the reporters and photographers huddled around him.

"How do you feel?" a reporter asked.

"All right," he said. "I'm ready, and I'm not afraid to die."

"What do you think of Turkus?"

"I'd like to knock him off before I die," Goldstein said.

"What about the judge?"

"Him too," Goldstein said. "The judge is no damn good." He murmured that he would "get him someday," as he was led inside.

The formalities on the sixth floor lasted less than ten minutes. Goldstein was still sounding off when they reached Grand Central. "You can tell that rat Reles I'll be waiting for him in hell with a pitchfork," Buggsy told a little crowd of reporters gathered to see the men off. Manacled to deputy sheriffs, he threw another half-smoked cigarette at a photographer.

The train pulled into Ossining at noon. At his induction Goldstein said, "I am innocent." Strauss said, "Not guilty." Their statements counted for nothing. Guards led them to death row, where they took cells down the hall from Abbandando and Maione.

On the night of September 11, Socko Gurino, the fugitive gunman, ran frightened into the Church of the Guardian Angel in the Chelsea neighborhood of Manhattan. His hat and coat were gone. He had no tie. His hoarse voice intruded on the dark stillness of the church.

Seven months earlier Happy Maione had ordered Gurino to kill the two accessories to the Whitey Rudnick garage murder—Catalano and Liberto—or at least scare them into silence. Gurino menaced both men but never finished the job. On February 17 he jumped $5,000 bail on a vagrancy charge just as O'Dwyer was drawing him into his investigation. He hid for six months, staying undercover in a furnished room in Jersey City and strategizing by phone with his wife, Gertrude. O'Dwyer had held her on $100,000 bail as a material witness and sent Gurino's children to foster care, hoping that would flush Gurino from hiding. When Gurino still failed to show himself, O'Dwyer released Gertrude. "I don't want to have anything further to do with my husband," she told reporters as she exited the Women's House of Detention. "I don't want to see him anymore." O'Dwyer's detectives suspected her of lying. They surveilled her, hoping she might lead them to her husband, but she was too canny for that.

Now Gurino came out of the night to turn himself in. He chose the church because its pastor, Rev. Francis X. Quinn, had received a congressional medal for heroism from President Roosevelt six months earlier for talking two gunmen into sparing an elderly couple they held hostage. Gurino hoped Rev. Quinn would help save him, as well.

At 9:40 p.m. a church receptionist found Gurino, his pudgy, double-chinned face trembling. "Three men are gunning for me," he said with his arms thrown forward in supplication. He asked for Rev. Quinn. The receptionist explained that the Reverend was out. He led Gurino to the rectory, where Father William Rinschler was preparing to perform a wedding ceremony. Gurino was pale and shaking. He begged for help, saying three killers were waiting for him outside. The assassins, if real, were presumably sent by Bugsy Siegel to kill Gurino before O'Dwyer found him. Gurino asked to speak with the mayor or the police commissioner.

"Do you want to speak with a policeman?" Father Rinschler asked.

Gurino said yes, then suffered another spasm of fear. "No one can get in here to harm you," Father Rinschler reassured him. "The doors are locked."

Gurino feared his pursuers, but he also feared the police. When two patrolmen arrived he refused to leave with them. He demanded to see a high police official instead. He was so deranged with anxiety that four policemen had to subdue him and carry him off like a 260-pound sack of yams. Even then he would not go without Father Rinschler.

Detectives interrogated Gurino briefly at the Tenth Precinct House, on West Twentieth Street, until he threw himself on the floor and screamed like a toddler. "I was never a rat in my life, I was never a rat," he yelled. He seemed to be addressing his pursuers. "If they leave me alone I'll go away—I'll never squeal. But if they don't leave me alone I'll squeal . . . get my wife and kids and I'll tell everything."

He was so undone that officers called an ambulance. Gurino became wilder still when the time came to leave St. Vincent's Hospital for O'Dwyer's office. It took three patrolmen and two detectives to force him into a patrol car in handcuffs. When O'Dwyer saw Gurino he had one comment: "Yellow," meaning cowardly.

In the end Gurino told everything, though it took an hour to calm him. Seated in O'Dwyer's private office, he talked in detail about six murders conducted for cash. The *Daily News* called it an "orgy of confession."

The questioning continued all night. At 3:30 a.m. O'Dwyer ordered Julie Catalano brought from Queens County Jail to confront his would-be assassin. Six months earlier Gurino had tried to take Cata-lano for a ride to Long Island, but Catalano escaped into the safety of police custody. "Apparently unaware of the reason for his little journey in the middle of the night, Catalano swaggered down the corridor toward the closed door behind which sat Gurino," wrote a police reporter for the *Brooklyn Daily Eagle*. "'What are these bums doing here?' Catalano sneered as he saw the crowd of newspapermen and detectives. Then the door opened and a sudden change came over him as he saw Gurino. His face paled and his body weakened. A detective put a hand on his back to steady him."

Gurino's interrogation continued until 6:07 a.m. He had now joined the ranks of informants, for better or worse. His hysteria subsided, re-placed by weariness and resignation. Fifteen detectives accompanied him as he walked from the Municipal Building. He recoiled in fright as a photographer's flashbulb popped, lighting up the early morning sidewalk on Joralemon Street.

Seven months after his sputtering start as Brooklyn district attorney, William O'Dwyer had now notched four convictions in his Murder, Inc. investigation. Maione and Abbandando were numbers one and two. Strauss and Goldstein were three and four. Four convictions, four death sentences. O'Dwyer expected dozens more, as long as he could keep his informants safe. Thanks to Reles, he had engineered a slew of cases making their way into courtrooms outside his jurisdiction. Bug Workman would be tried for the shooting death of Dutch Schultz in Newark, New Jersey. In Los Angeles, Bugsy Siegel faced trial for the assassination of Harry Greenberg, Buchalter's blackmailer. Meanwhile O'Dwyer's office would go to work on the eighty-three unsolved mur-ders on the books in Brooklyn.

"Our investigation of the entire situation is going on full blast," he told the press after the jury convicted Goldstein and Strauss. "Right now, if my life depended on it, I couldn't tell you what pending indict-ment will be moved for trial next or when."

While Turkus acted as courtroom prosecutor, O'Dwyer would fo-cus on snaring the surviving big bosses—the Commission's board of directors. O'Dwyer could not hope to truly crush the mob without prosecuting Buchalter, the man responsible for the Jewish side of Mur-der, Inc., and his Italian counterpart, Albert Anastasia, the so-called

Lord High Executioner. Anastasia had slipped out of sight when Reles started talking to O'Dwyer six months earlier. Nobody had seen him, but there was speculation that he might emerge from hiding to kill Reles.

The more Reles talked, the safer he felt. He kept feeding prosecutors names and dates and backstories in hopes that O'Dwyer would incarcerate Anastasia and the rest before they could penetrate his protective custody. He talked volubly, with broad humor and gory details, on an encyclopedic range of underworld topics, including the unhappy fate of Peter Panto, the twenty-nine-year-old dockland organizer who had disappeared in July 1939. Panto's family and fiancée had heard nothing of him in seventeen months. They presumed him dead, but his body had never turned up. His disappearance stood among the great mysteries of New York crime.

Reles had not planned or participated in Panto's abduction and execution, but he knew enough to reconstruct events for O'Dwyer and his staff. After learning the details "from the tattletaling lips of Abe Reles," as the *Daily News* wrote, O'Dwyer hired a steam shovel to excavate a mile of desolate grassy lowlands on the eastern bank of the tidal Passaic River, near Lyndhurst, New Jersey. O'Dwyer's police aide, Captain Frank Bals, joined a dozen men assigned by the Bergen County prosecutor's office to operate the steam shovel and dig by hand into the sandy soil. O'Dwyer himself visited the site almost daily, often helping to sift through the muck.

The men worked methodically. Surveyors from the police engineering department plotted the land into squares. The crew checked the boxes off on a map as they made their way. They worked from box to box slowly, methodically. The hard-frozen December ground gave up its contents grudgingly.

The crew dug for three weeks without promising signs. No lime. No bones. No debris. It was demoralizing labor, messy and cold. The men built a shack and stone fireplace on the open flats as a respite from the midwinter chill drifting in from New York Harbor. Day after day, all through January, they burrowed into the riverside loam without encouragement. The crew prepared to quit for the day as the winter dusk descended on January 29, 1941, when James Moran, the pink-faced, red-haired chief clerk of O'Dwyer's office, walked a hundred paces away to a row of trees near a sandy road. He pointed downward and said, "Dig here." Moran said that he had no rational reason to pick the spot, none that he could articulate. He called it a hunch, but two decades later O'Dwyer said that Philip "Little Farvel" Cohen, a Buchalter gunman held in custody, had specified the location.

The sixth shovelful from Moran's spot uncovered traces of lime in the sandy soil about three feet below the surface. Some men crossed themselves, then continued excavating by hand, chipping with shovels around the edges of a piano-sized lump of lime with the consistency of putty. When part of the lump broke off they could see a femur, tufts of clothing, and the slender bones of a hand protruding from the soil, as if reaching to hold hands with the diggers. The exposed portions of the body indicated that lime had eaten away much of the flesh, complicating the identification. The body was bent double, trussed with rope, and wrapped in burlap. Blood had stained the light-colored sand. Eighteen months after Panto disappeared, his body had been found.

The crew dug out the whole 600-pound frozen lump that night and loaded it onto a flatbed truck. Police escorted the truck to the Kings County Morgue, in Brooklyn, in case Murder, Inc. tried to hijack the evidence.

Eight days later O'Dwyer confirmed that the body belonged to Peter Panto. Peter Mazzie, a stocky twenty-three-year-old longshoreman who was among Panto's closest friends, identified the remains after examining the skull's two broken teeth, upper left and upper right, an imperfection which gave Panto a distinctive smile.

On the evening of February 1, an anonymous deep-voiced man phoned the newsroom of the *Brooklyn Daily Eagle* to alert editors to fresh graffiti painted on masonry walls beside a ramp leading from Montague Street down to the docks below. The caller abruptly hung up when asked his name. The paint was still wet when a reporter arrived at 7 p.m. In the summer of 1939 the waterfront walls were scrawled with the question, "Where is Panto?" Now its sequel appeared crudely rendered in eighteen-inch letters: "Who paid for the murder of Peter Panto?"

Who was behind Panto's disappearance and death? It was Brooklyn's most urgent question in the days after the excavation crew pulled his putrefied body from its sandy grave. Reles helped solve the mystery by telling O'Dwyer that Albert Anastasia had ordered Panto's murder in order to preserve his waterfront authority.

Tick Tock Tannenbaum contributed a more detailed account. Seated with Assistant District Attorney Edward Heffernan in the Brooklyn Municipal Building, he recalled parking his car beside Prospect Park one late-July afternoon in 1939. He sat on a bench near a rowboat lake at the park's southern end to wait for his friend Mendy Weiss, a dark-eyed man built like a refrigerator. Dog walkers and strollers passed as the two men ambled around the lake making inconsequential conversation. "What happened to you?" Tannenbaum asked, referring to a crisscross of scratches on Weiss's hands. "What did you do, fight with some girl?"

Weiss told Tannenbaum that he had "a close one" a few nights earlier. "He goes on to tell me that Jimmy Ferraco, Anastasia, and himself were in a house waiting for somebody to bring some wop out there that they were supposed to kill and bury. He said, 'The guy just stepped into the door and must have realized what it was about and he tried to get out. He almost got out. . . . If I wasn't there he would have got away. I grabbed him and mugged him, and when I mugged him, he started to fight and he tried to break the mug and that's when he scratched me, but he didn't get away.'"

Armed with the hard evidence of Panto's body, combined with Reles's persuasive presence on the witness stand, O'Dwyer now had a solid murder case against Anastasia. "This opens an entirely new phase of the activities of Murder, Inc.," O'Dwyer said. Before he could get Anastasia into a courtroom, however, he would have to find him.

On September 20, 1940, O'Dwyer and Captain Bals flew to Washington to petition the Department of Justice for permission to extradite Lepke Buchalter from the federal penitentiary in Leavenworth, where he was serving a fourteen-year drug trafficking sentence. A grand jury in New York had indicted Buchalter four months earlier for the 1936 murder of Joe Rosen, the candy-store owner gunned down in his shop. O'Dwyer would need permission from Justice to bring Buchalter to trial in Brooklyn, but Justice was unexpectedly reluctant to see their guest go. In a series of letters, Justice lawyers reminded O'Dwyer that technically they had no obligation to release Buchalter to New York State until he had served his fourteen years on federal charges.

Conservative columnist Westbrook Pegler suggested that Justice officials resisted releasing Buchalter from federal incarceration into

O'Dwyer's custody because he might make a deal with O'Dwyer for lenience. Any information about corruption in the Democratic ranks that Buchalter shared could reflect poorly on President Roosevelt, who was running for reelection that year against Wendell Wilkie.

O'Dwyer eventually pried Buchalter loose after Harold M. Kennedy, a Brooklyn-born federal attorney, helped issue a writ of habeas corpus *ad prosequendum*, a provision which allows a convict to be tried for a second crime in a separate jurisdiction. Eight months later, five U.S. marshals surreptitiously boarded a train for Kansas. Their assignment was to return Buchalter to New York. They deliberately left without official documentation. O'Dwyer's office said nothing about the departure for fear that the mob might intercept them.

Reles had known from the beginning that he might testify against Buchalter. But with Buchalter's return from Leavenworth imminent, the reality set in with paralyzing force. It was one thing to testify against Maione and Abbandando, Strauss and Goldstein. They stood below him in mob hierarchy. At their trials he had suffered initial nerves, but he settled in and eventually spoke to the jury as if entertaining friends in a bar. He appeared to enjoy himself, the way storytellers do.

Buchalter made for a more anguished encounter. He was the dark lord of the Commission, a figure so intimidating that seasoned killers seized up at the sound of his voice. The *Daily News* called him "the dethroned caliph of the rackets."

Reles had been spitting up blood for a more than a year. He habitually leaned and hawked into a drinking glass every half hour or so. The blood surged up his gorge more profusely now as the marshals rode through Kentucky and Missouri on their way to Leavenworth. With Buchalter's return only days away, Reles began gagging on mouthfuls of blood and coughed hard to clear blood-streaked sputum from his lungs. O'Dwyer sent him to a private sanitarium for observation. He must have wondered if Reles would live long enough to testify against Buchalter.

The marshals returned to New York on May 8 by car. Buchalter sat handcuffed in the backseat. He said almost nothing during the twenty-hour drive. The next morning the marshals brought him from the Tombs, in lower Manhattan, where he had spent the night, to Brooklyn County Court, where he was to be arraigned on a first-degree murder charge.

An extravagant display of security preceded his arrival. Fifteen uniformed policemen, fifteen detectives, five deputy sheriffs, and five U.S. marshals crowded a small courtroom. They stood along the walls and occupied the first row of seats. "This is ridiculous," Judge George W. Martin said after stepping up to his bench. "Why don't you send for a company of Marines? The place looks like an armed arsenal. We can take care of this ourselves."

He pointed to the detectives seated in the front row. "Don't forget to keep your badges, boys, and let him see how pretty you look."

Buchalter then entered handcuffed to a deputy marshal. He was tan from outdoor prison work and clearly nervous. "He came into the court room wetting his lips and swallowing hard," *The New York Times* reported. After his first-degree murder arraignment, he conferred with his wife, Betty, and brother Joseph in an antechamber for ten minutes, then returned to ask in a trembling voice if pleading to the indictment could be postponed for a week so that he could hire a lawyer. Judge Martin agreed.

"This is a milestone in law enforcement," Turkus said in court. "After fifteen months District Attorney O'Dwyer has succeeded in bringing to the bar of justice Lepke, the man who pulled the strings of the murder racket."

On May 23, 1941, Reles made a second trip to Los Angeles, guarded en route by Captain Bals and two other detectives. He occupied a witness stand in the new Federal Building, in downtown Los Angeles, for most of the next day. He was the sole government witness in a hearing called to determine if Bugsy Siegel would be extradited to face indictment in New York for his role in harboring Buchalter during his two years as a fugitive. Reles testified that he met Siegel on a Brooklyn street corner in midsummer 1939, days before Buchalter surrendered, and that he took Siegel for a half-hour meeting with Buchalter in the kitchen of his hideaway apartment. Asked if Siegel was present in the courtroom, Reles stood up and pointed to him.

Siegel, in turn, denied meeting Reles or accompanying him to Buchalter's hideout. In fact, he claimed never to have seen Reles until he walked into the courtroom that day. Besides, he said, he was abroad at the time on a tour that included an audience with the pope and a meeting with the king of Greece.

Siegel was a prominent and popular figure in Los Angeles, particularly in Hollywood. His lawyer produced a series of witnesses to vouch for his good character, including the actor George Raft, who appeared in *Scarface* and other gangster movies. Six days later a state commissioner ordered him removed to Brooklyn to face a federal indictment. "We welcome this opportunity for Siegel to return to New York and vindicate himself," his lawyer said, "and expose Reles as a liar."

On the afternoon of May 24, O'Dwyer waited at Idlewild Airport for Reles's American Airlines flight to arrive from Los Angeles. He killed time talking politics with the reporters who waited with him. "How would you like to be in City Hall," asked a reporter for the *Brooklyn Daily Eagle*. It was a rote question, and it drew a rote response.

"I'm very happy in my present position," he said.

O'Dwyer may indeed have been very happy, but reporters assumed, as readers did, that he would run for mayor as soon as he dismantled Murder, Inc. He had already sent four men to death row, and he could uphold his winning streak in the following weeks with a major trial outside his jurisdiction.

Bug Workman would be tried in Newark, New Jersey. Two detectives arrested him near Coney Island on March 24, 1940. O'Dwyer held him as a material witness on $100,000 bail, a sum too great for him to pay, in connection with the murder of candy-store operator Joe Rosen. He spent a full year dodging rats in Raymond Street Jail before Reles and Tannenbaum implicated him in a second murder, the shooting death of Dutch Schultz. Workman had told them both, more than once, that he shot Schultz. He did so in part because of his frustration that Mendy Weiss loudly claimed sole credit.

When Workman recognized the gravity of the charges against him, he went entirely mute, except for asking for cigarettes. He grimly refused to say who killed Dutch Schultz or why Joe Rosen was shot to death in his candy store. Detectives cajoled him to talk about anything—baseball, movies, women. But he refused. "For nine months he hadn't said a word on any subject to any officer of the law," O'Dwyer said. "The verdict was that Workman would never crack."

By June 1941 O'Dwyer had given up on persuading Workman to talk. Instead, he handed him over to William A. Wachenfeld, a New Jersey prosecutor, like a neatly packaged gift, along with a file of information gathered from Reles and Tannenbaum. (Workman's accomplice, Mendy

Weiss, was already in prison for a different murder, and was therefore not tried for the Schultz killing.)

Reles warned O'Dwyer that Workman would use one of two false alibis when he came to trial in Newark. He would say that he was working as manager of the Montrose Motor Company in Brooklyn on the night of the shooting, or that he was working as manager of the Cohen Funeral Service in Manhattan. O'Dwyer assigned his police aide, Captain Bals, to sit in the gallery during the trial and listen. As Reles predicted, Louis Cohen, director of an East Side funeral home, took the stand and confirmed that Workman managed his company from 1933 to 1936 at a salary of forty-five dollars a week. He said that Workman was dispatching hearses the night of October 23, the night Schultz died, and he produced a payroll book to prove it.

Captain Bals stepped from the courtroom during Cohen's testimony to call O'Dwyer on a lobby pay phone. When Cohen left the courthouse that afternoon, two New York detectives intercepted him. They brought him to Brooklyn, where O'Dwyer accused Cohen of perjury, a crime punishable by five years in jail.

When the trial resumed at 10:30 a.m. the next morning, the prosecution called Cohen back to the stand for cross-examination. As Cohen strode up the aisle Workman sensed that his alibi was about to shatter. He leaped to his feet. "May I take the stand, your honor?" he said.

"Not now," the judge said. Two attendants forced him back into his seat.

"Let me take the stand," he screamed at his lawyer. "What the hell is the matter with you?"

When Workman's outburst subsided, Louis Cohen took the oath and recanted his earlier testimony: he admitted his lie. He acknowledged that he had made bogus payroll entries for Workman at the request of his brother-in-law, Danny Fields, who worked for Lepke Buchalter. (Fields was shot dead at the intersection of Lewis and Broome Streets in 1939.) Two of Cohen's employees followed their boss to the stand to confirm that Workman had not worked that night.

After the lunch recess Workman's lawyer announced that his client would change his plea from not guilty to no defense—a form of capitulation that lawyers called *non vult contendere*. Judge Daniel J. Brennan dismissed the jury. Looking down at the defendant from the bench, he sentenced Workman to prison "for the term of your natural life." Workman's wife, Katherine, gasped, but Workman did not flinch. With that the trial adjourned. The resolution had taken no more than five minutes. Guards hustled Workman out in handcuffs. "See me in fifteen years," he told newsmen as he was led away, "and maybe I'll have something to say."

Workman's quiet, forbearing manner served him well as prisoner No. 33334 at Rahway State Prison, in New Jersey. He worked in the library, commissary, and prison truck entrance without any fault on his record. Katherine visited every Sunday, with one or two exceptions, until the parole board approved his eighth application in 1964, twenty-three years after pleading no defense. Workman shook hands with the warden and walked out the main gate of a release facility in Trenton as a graying, thickset fifty-four-year-old grandfather. He pushed unsmiling though a cluster of reporters and cameramen standing in the rain and sat in the back of a blue Thunderbird driven by his son Solomon, who was born a few months after the Schultz killing. As promised, Workman had a message for the press: he regretted the violence committed in his earlier life, but accepted that he could do nothing about it now.

Through the summer of 1941, William O'Dwyer traversed New York's five boroughs meeting with union officials and civic groups. He spoke in hotel ballrooms, school auditoriums, and fraternal clubhouses. At every stop he warmed the crowd with his Irish bonhomie and served up the Democratic Party line. Despite his earlier demurrals, he was running for mayor, running hard against the popular incumbent and reform firebrand, Fiorello La Guardia.

O'Dwyer found himself trapped in an awkward contradiction. As Brooklyn district attorney, he was busting the mob, one gangster at a time, but as a mayoral candidate he stood beneath the tawdry banner of Tammany Hall, a political machine that facilitated corruption and traded favors with the mob. La Guardia therefore cast O'Dwyer as part of the problem, not the solution. On the other hand, O'Dwyer may have succeeded as a prosecutor precisely because of his intimacy with the Brooklyn underworld.

In the evenings O'Dwyer sat in the bedroom of his Bay Ridge home, the little brick house he had owned for fourteen years, recounting the day's events with his wife, Kitty—quiet, restrained, forever loyal Kitty, who was mostly confined to bed. The deterioration brought on by Parkinson's prevented her from leaving the house now, except to attend mass at St. Anselm over on Eighty-third Street or the occasional concert. The O'Dwyers never had children. Even as he climbed the municipal ranks, O'Dwyer accepted disappointments at home.

Kitty's body might be failing, but her mind was forever keen. In her calming presence his public show of fighting spirit subsided, replaced by the more contemplative and melancholic nature that was his truer state of mind. Her warmth and tenderness was comforting to him, and her sharp wit deflated pomposity or self-seriousness. "Only by the intercession of the supernatural," a friend said, "would it be possible for a husband of hers to become a stuffed shirt."

If the mayoral election was weighing on O'Dwyer's mind, so too was the delicate task of snatching Albert Anastasia from hiding while also prosecuting Lepke Buchalter and Bugsy Siegel. Together they were the triumvirate at the top of the Commission's letterhead. O'Dwyer could only convict them by keeping Reles alive long enough to deliver his death-dealing testimony.

Word reached O'Dwyer's office that summer that the Commission had convened a delegate meeting in a Park Avenue hotel to devise ways of killing Reles. In response, Captain Bals began scouting alternatives to the Hotel Bossert. He needed a hideaway where he could more securely safeguard the six informants behind impenetrable protections.

By September, Bals settled on the 400-room Half Moon, a mostly forgotten hotel on a lonely stretch of Coney Island a mile west of the Cyclone roller coaster and other amusements. The hotel was built fourteen years earlier as a proper beach resort, standing like a haughty aunt apart from the sunburned day-trippers, with their hot dogs and beach towels.

The Great Depression humbled the Half Moon. By 1941 guests still dined in the nautical-themed Isabella Dining Room and the Galleon Grill. The Half Moon Orchestra still played weddings in its ballroom, but most rooms sat empty. Paint peeled from the hotel's gold dome. Gargoyles crouched on the roofline watched over an empty stretch of beach.

With demand dwindling, the hotel manager agreed to rent the entire east wing of the sixth floor to the district attorney's office. He would take any guests he could, even confessed murderers.

Capain Bals moved the informants into the Half Moon with such secrecy that even officers in the Coney Island police precinct were unaware of their new neighbors. He installed a bulletproof double steel door, equipped with a sliding peephole window, barricading ten bedrooms—rooms 619 through 628—along a central hallway. The steel door was the only way in and the only way out.

Reles took up residence in an east-facing room, 623, with an adjoining sitting room and bathroom. From his window Reles could see surf breaking against a jetty and hear a buoy clanging as it rocked in the swells. His next door neighbor, in room 622, was Sol Bernstein, the car thief who helped locate Hyman Yuran's body next to the swimming pool of the Loch Sheldrake Inn. Newspapers called the accommodations the Rat Suite.

The Rat Suite was populated by the odd fraternity of Murder, Inc. operatives turned informants—Abe Reles, Dukey Maffetore, Pretty Levine, Tick Tock Tannenbaum, Sol Bernstein, and Mickey Sycoff. This assembly of thugs and gunmen shared one characteristic: they all had what Burton Turkus called "killer eyes," a coldness of soul expressed in their countenance. Killer eyes were, Meyer Berger wrote in *Life* magazine, "the unmistakeable mark of the beast." All had the same implacable, numbed-out, dead-behind-the-retinas, middle-distance stare.

They passed the hours playing cards in rooms filled with ocean light, reading newspapers, listening to Brooklyn Dodger games on the radio, and drinking. They ordered room service from the hotel kitchen. "During the day these witnesses are free to amuse themselves in the best manner they know how," said Assistant District Attorney Edward Heffernan, "with detectives closely guarding them."

Three rotating twenty-four-hour police shifts guarded the Rat Suite under the direction of Captain Bals. In addition, two uniformed patrolmen from the local precinct stood sentry at the hotel lobby.

The occupants spent their days in a purgatory between detention and freedom. They weren't prisoners in the conventional sense, but they weren't free to leave. Nobody came or went, except girlfriends and wives. Visitors were required to phone from the lobby. If detectives recognized the caller's voice, they signaled the elevator operator to escort the guest upstairs. If an intruder tried to get off the elevator at the sixth floor, alarms sounded inside the Rat Suite.

Reles and his suite-mates waited to testify burdened by the uncomfortable knowledge that the Commission was plotting their assassinations—more urgently now that Reles had proven a lethal witness. Bugsy Siegel had reportedly raised $100,000 to kill Reles and the rest. "Gang trigger men from all parts of the county were swarming into the city with instructions to 'get' Reles," Turkus said.

Sure enough, O'Dwyer learned that marksmen flown in from the Purple Gang in Detroit had taken up watchful positions in a building across the street from the Half Moon Hotel. Captain Bals sent a squad of detectives to raid their rooms, but the sharpshooters had fled.

At least three threats were phoned to James Mangano, sheriff of Kings County, who was responsible for safely shuttling the informants to court and back. "If you think anything of those guys working for you, you better keep them out of the way," one caller said, "because we're gonna knock off all the canaries."

O'Dwyer also learned that three California marksmen were in New York. For days they had stood with high-powered rifles overlooking the street outside the courthouse waiting for their moment. One of them had lined up a shot at an informant as he stepped from a police car. He might have hit his mark had a detective not by chance blocked his view. Newspapers reported rumors that assassins might storm the beach from boats.

In this atmosphere charged with fear and paranoia, a policeman reported seeing on two occasions a long-coated figure standing at night like a wraith on the Coney Island boardwalk, his back to the onshore breeze as he looked up at the hotel. The man was on the short side with pronounced nose and kinky black hair—exactly as one might describe Albert Anastasia, the fugitive of fifteen months.

11

THE DANCE HALL

Evelyn Mittleman, the Kiss of Death Girl, visited her boyfriend, Pittsburgh Phil Strauss, on death row, on June 12, 1941, the day of his execution. She faced him for the last time through a mesh screen in a visiting room. "Is the governor going to save us?" he asked her, referring to a clemency plea sent to Governor Lehman by attorneys representing him and Buggsy Goldstein. Evelyn could not answer. She only wept. She left him with a kiss, a kiss through the wire mesh screen. He was the fourth consecutive boyfriend of hers to die.

Strauss accepted the leave-taking with melancholic calm. Buggsy Goldstein, by contrast, suffered what inmates called "hot-seat fever." He had a screaming, sobbing breakdown in his cell hours before the appointed execution time. He could no longer bear the agony of waiting; he howled for guards to kill him right away. In his hysteria he turned away his wife, Betty, along with his seventy-year-old father, Jacob, and his brother, Karl, who had driven to Sing Sing to make their wrenching good-byes. "Send them away," he yelled at a guard. "I don't want to see anybody." He also refused his last meals, a steak lunch and chicken dinner. He asked that the trays be taken to Happy Maione and Dasher Abbandando, who waited on death row for their own execution date.

On their last day the two men moved to a final staging area, a circular array of cells known as the Dance Hall where they would submit to final preparations. They went to the prison barber chair where an inmate shaved a bald spot so electrodes could be placed on bare skin, and they put on the execution uniform, known as death suits, consisting of a light shirt and dark trousers with a slit in one leg for an electrode. By way of consolation, guards let the condemned request music played on a phonograph on the long last hours of their lives. Jacob Katz, the Sing Sing rabbi, ministered words of solace.

A hundred miles north, in the Catskill town of Cairo, New York, a small, sandy-haired man named Joseph Francel left his sprawling house on Main Street to go to work. Since retiring as an electrician he had agreed to act as the state executioner. He received $150 per convict.

Sixty miles south of Sing Sing, at the Half Moon Hotel, Reles had his eyes on an alarm clock as the time neared 11 p.m. "I guess they're going now," he said to a detective.

By custom the weakhearted went first. At 11 p.m. guards took Goldstein from his cell and marched him forty feet down a corridor, a walk known as the Last Mile. Rabbi Katz walked with him. A green door opened, and Goldstein entered a harshly lit white room. It was bare except for a heavy oak chair bolted to the floor. To the left, twenty-six witnesses—warden, police officials, newspaper reporters—sat like churchgoers in pews. They sat in silence. Goldstein averted his eyes. He staggered slightly as he stepped to the chair.

Attendants buckled a series of leather straps around Goldstein's arms, legs, and torso, securing the last one at the base of his skull with a leather strap wrapped under his chin, like a football helmet's chinstrap. Francel placed an electrode on Goldstein's head. Goldstein closed his eyes. He said nothing. A black hood was placed over his head. With everyone clear, Francel turned a dial, sending 2,000 volts into Goldstein's body. The electrical surge caused the lights to flicker in the Dance Hall a hundred feet away, where Strauss waited his turn. The Sing Sing physician listened for a heartbeat. He pronounced Goldstein dead at 11:09 p.m.

Minutes later Strauss walked in, defiant and mute. He "gazed around the brightly-lighted execution chamber in the manner of an actor looking over a full house," an observer from the *Brooklyn Daily Eagle* wrote in the next day's newspaper.

Strauss and Goldstein had killed thirty-two men over sixteen years. It took the state fifteen minutes to kill them both.

Strauss's brothers, Sam and Alex, stood to the end by a drugstore telephone booth in the adjacent town of Ossining, New York, waiting for word of a last-minute reprieve from Governor Lehman. None came. When the execution was over and attendants wheeled Strauss's singed body from the Dance Hall, the brothers stood on the street watching reporters and witnesses drive by.

"What do you want, you dogs?" a brother shouted. "You killed him."

12

HALF MOON HOTEL

William O'Dwyer woke early on Election Day, November 4, 1941, and ate his customary breakfast—whole-wheat toast and tea with milk and honey, a carryover from his childhood in County Bohola. Edna Davis, a maid who had worked for the O'Dwyers since girlhood, added a few drops of iodine before handing him the cup and saucer. O'Dwyer believed in its fortifying powers.

On this day he would need whatever strength he could get. Reporters, photographers, and well-wishers had congregated in the living room of his home in the Irish working-class Bay Ridge neighborhood of Brooklyn to pose the tiresome questions asked, and asked again, in a campaign's final days. How did he feel? Did he expect to win? What would be his first act as mayor? Edna circulated among them, serving coffee. "The best thing I like about these campaigns," she said, "is those beautiful flowers we'll get in the morning."

Abe Reles was right. Twenty months earlier, seated for the first time in O'Dwyer's office, he made a middle-of-the-night promise that his cooperation would make O'Dwyer a household name. And it did. Polls showed him trailing the incumbent, Fiorello La Guardia, but only by a slim margin.

The debilitation of Parkinson's would prevent Kitty from voting that morning. She lay abed when O'Dwyer left home at 10 a.m. in a dark gray pinstripe suit and walked three blocks to cast his vote at a redbrick Knights of Columbus clubhouse with columns and a grand arched window. He said good morning to neighbors and posed for photographs with children. At 10:50 a.m. he visited the Fourth Avenue police station, where he had worked as a patrolman for seven years. He greeted officers by name. They addressed him, optimistically, as Mr. Mayor. He walked his old beat with friends, pausing to shake hands with passersby.

Later O'Dwyer stopped by his Borough Hall office to confer with Burton Turkus about the Lepke Buchalter trial. There was much to discuss but he couldn't linger. He had to attend a lunch for a hundred or so supporters and campaign workers at the Hotel Commodore, next to Grand Central Terminal. The lunch was hosted by Phil Regan, an Irish immigrant who became a detective and later a well-known movie actor. Regan told the crowd that by nightfall "all that will be left of La Guardia will be his big hat."

The room warmed with Irish good humor and a measure of optimism that the good old Irish Democratic Party would prevail. President Roosevelt had crossed party lines to endorse La Guardia, who ran as a Republican, but O'Dwyer had Tammany and Governor Lehman and virtually ever other prominent Democrat behind him.

That evening Mayor La Guardia spoke to more than 25,000 assembled at what he called his lucky corner—Lexington Avenue and 116th Street in Harlem—where he had closed all his campaigns for twenty-one years. He stood before a mixture of blacks, Jews, and Italians in his lucky overcoat, a black Chesterfield that had grown too snug for his considerable bulk. A swing band conducted by Cab Calloway played "From the Halls of Montezuma," La Guardia's campaign song. His reelection, he said, would mean four more years of "non-partisan, non-political, clean, decent city government." Afterward he went home to Gracie Mansion, the mayor's residence. "I'll see you in the morning," he told reporters.

O'Dwyer's campaign headquarters in the Chanin Building, on East Forty-second Street, was full of laughter and backslapping in the early evening as he went out to a lead, but La Guardia gained incrementally as the returns from Manhattan and Brooklyn came in. At midnight O'Dwyer telegrammed his concession: "Please accept my sincere congratulations on your victory in the campaign. With these congratulations go my best wishes for a successful administration." La Guardia would press on for an unprecedented third term as mayor.

At 9:30 a.m. the next morning O'Dwyer returned to the Brooklyn Municipal Building and the pressing job of prosecuting Lepke Buchalter and retrieving Albert Anastasia from hiding.

There was no question who ruled the Rat Suite, the sixth-floor rooms in the Half Moon Hotel where O'Dwyer's informants killed time between court appearances. Reles filled the role of bully-in-chief, just as he had on the Brownsville streets. "He was uncouth, he was vile, and he thought an awful lot of Abe," said Patrolman Harvey McLaughlin, one of the guards assigned to twenty-four-hour shifts. "He was a very conceited person."

Reles sank into squalor in room 623. He was never well groomed, but he now stopped bathing altogether and wore the same unwashed clothes. He gained twenty pounds on top of his already squat, flabby frame. Reles may have given up whatever small decencies he had on the assumption that he was dying. He was occasionally removed to see doctors for his bloody heaves, still gaining in severity. He spat into a drinking glass by his elbow while playing poker, and kept the glass by his bedside.

Reles's only diversion was taunting his hall mates about their wives, their manliness, or their brainlessness. In the first week of November 1941, Sol Bernstein tried to knife Reles in the ribs after he insulted Bernstein's wife during one of her periodic visits.

Reles amused himself, as well, by pranking the guards. He threw balls of wet toilet paper in their faces, dumped salt in their food when they turned their heads, and lit their shoelaces on fire while they slept. He roused them at all hours with phony emergencies and laughed at their panic. He called one guard at 2 a.m. on his wedding night just to annoy him. He knew a thousand tricks, all of them malicious. Reles understood that a star witness could take liberties.

Reles told the police with a mean-humored smile that in the end "all the murderers are going to go free and the cops [will] go to jail." Like many half-jokes, it was both funny and infuriating.

Reles knew that he could do as he wished. He demanded, and received, all manner of catered meals delivered to the Rat Suite. The police acted as his errand boys, fetching whiskey and cigarettes from nearby stores. When Reles desired an outing, Captain Bals's men herded the informants onto an old school bus and drove them to Heckscher State

Park, on the south shore of Long Island. Uniformed guards held shot-guns while the informants played softball and drank beer on a beach looking across the Great South Bay to the long thin strip of Fire Island. Reles guffawed and threw the ball at the guards' heads. He spat on their hamburgers just as they reached for them.

When Reles wanted a haircut, a pair of guards escorted him down-stairs to the hotel barbershop. "There was a big window on the barber shop," said Officer Harvey McLaughlin. "He insisted that one of us sit right there. If anybody wanted to take a shot at him they would hit us first."

If the guards failed to indulge Reles, he complained and threatened to withdraw his cooperation. Those who refused him found them-selves reassigned. So the guards pampered their thuggish prima donna. Among other things, he required the guards to wrestle with him, and they did. It was a tougher assignment than it looked. Reles was surpris-ingly strong for a short man of stocky stature. The cops had no choice but to wrestle, and they let him win. They kept Reles happy because O'Dwyer needed him.

O'Dwyer would never need Reles more than he would on Novem-ber 12, the day Reles was to testify against Lepke Buchalter. He was on trial, along with the hulking Mendy Weiss and the smooth Louis Ca-pone, for the fatal shooting of Joe Rosen. As in the four previous trials, Reles would be the marquee witness. He would also play a crucial role by providing testimony from a non-conspirator, as required by law.

Early testimony bode poorly for Buchalter. Max Rubin, who per-formed strong-arm errands in the garment district, recalled for the court how Buchalter had banished him from New York so that he would be out of easy reach for Special Prosecutor Thomas Dewey. After living briefly, and unhappily, in Salt Lake City and New Orleans, among other places, he defied Buchalter by returning to New York. Buchal-ter expressed his displeasure. A short time later Rubin was shot and left for dead blocks from his Bronx home. Now he could extract his revenge with a full-throated incrimination of Buchalter. He sat on the witness stand with his head listing to one side, a permanent effect of the shooting.

In cross-examination, Buchalter's lawyer, Hyman Barshay, asked Rubin if, as reported, he had once told a garment-district friend: "If it's the last thing I'll do, I'll burn Lepke, and when Lepke goes to the chair, I will feel that I have lived my life."

Rubin's eyes brightened, and he smiled. "I never said that." Then he turned to Buchalter, who shifted uneasily at the defense table. "But I certainly would have been justified in saying it." Buchalter held Rubin's stare but said nothing.

It seemed unlikely that Reles could stare Buchalter down with the same self-assurance. For decades Reles had said that he feared no man, but his anxious demeanor in the days leading up to his testimony—his snappish deportment and jitters—made clear that Buchalter scared him. "I don't want to testify against Lepke," he said more than once. "That's all there is to it."

Reles feared Buchalter, feared him like no one else, in spite of the boss's mild demeanor. Of all the hardened hit men and mobsters headed to jail or the electric chair, Buchalter was the one without what Turkus called "killer eyes." His eyes "were like a deer's, or a fawn's," the prosecutor said. "They never hardened."

As Buchalter's trial got under way, Reles suffered a severe attack of his intestinal condition. After retching mouthfuls of blood, he was admitted for observation to Harbor Hospital, in Bensonhurst. It took a full week for the bout to pass. He returned to the Rat Suite improved, though anxiety lingered as his face-to-face confrontation with Buchalter neared.

Doctors forbade Reles from drinking, but he ignored them. At 2 p.m. on the afternoon of November 11, he and Mickey Sycoff chipped in for a bottle. They sent John Moran, one of their guards, out to buy Four Roses bourbon. Moran joined them in a few drinks. "We had couple of highballs, Abie and I," Moran said, "about three or four in all. Then I poured the rest of the bottle down the sink because I didn't want Reles to have too much."

That evening, at about 7 p.m., Rosie Reles delivered a bottle of brandy to the Rat Suite. The couple now had two children, seven-year-old Buddy and his five-month-old sister. Reles had remained in custody for twenty months now, long enough to make him nearly a stranger to his children. It was unclear how Rosie supported herself during her husband's confinement. She sold her mink coat and lived with her parents, who worked behind a lunch counter in East New York. Her mother carried the family nest egg, about $9,000, tucked safely inside her brassiere. Rose had come to see the entire arrangement as unsustainable.

If Rosie's present circumstance was tenuous, so too was her future. Nobody had bothered to explain how and where her family would live when her husband completed his responsibilities to O'Dwyer. The district attorney's office had promised protection, but she must have struggled to picture a life for her family with the intrusion of police guards and the constant threat of the Commission's revenge every time they stepped outside. There was also the question of how they would support themselves.

Rosie stayed in her husband's room for hours that night. In later testimony she said that they had consensual sex, despite her growing revulsion. "When I came in that night the sight of him repulsed me," she said. "This particular time he looked so bad. . . . It seemed to me that he had shrunk to half his size." And he stank of liquor.

She had proposed divorce before, but this time she asked him to sign a blank sheet of paper. In her desperation she hoped to use his signature to enact a divorce without having to contact him again. She naïvely imagined that she could hire a lawyer to simply fill in the date and details. "I was so fed up with the whole setup, with everything," she said.

She did not expect Reles to take it well, and he didn't. "This is a nice time to ask me," he said, considering his illness and the next day's testimony hanging over him. She sat on a chair while he paced. He refused to sign the paper, and he accused her of sleeping around while he was confined. "He suspected everybody," she said. "You running around with that guy? What guy have you got?"

Reles's neighbors in the Rat Suite could hear the couple arguing, though they could not make out their words. They only heard Rosie shriek and Reles answer in his low guttural voice. She usually stayed two hours, but on this night she lingered an extra hour.

She left his room in a pique after 10 p.m., sweeping down the hallway trailed by the two guards who would escort her home. "I don't want to see your face again," she said.

Reles followed as far as the steel door to issue a parting insult. "All right, you fat bastard."

To the guards Rosie said, "It's the last time I'll come up to this damn place."

Tick Tock Tannenbaum later expressed surprise that "she never asked me how my family was," as she had on previous visits.

Soon after Rosie left, someone on the sixth floor called the front desk and asked the night clerk whether room 523, the room directly below Reles's bedroom, was vacant. The clerk confirmed that 523 was unoccupied.

Reles played cards until 1 a.m. with Tannenbaum, Bernstein, and Sycoff. He threw down his aces and spades convincingly, as if nothing was amiss. The inhabitants of the Rat Suite, both witnesses and guards, customarily ate a late snack of cold-cut sandwiches, milk, and coffee sent up from the hotel kitchen. Shortly after 3 a.m. a guard saw Reles in the corridor. The guard poured coffee for himself, and offered Reles a cup. Reles declined and retired to his room. The police guards also settled in for an illicit snooze.

Rat Suite procedures called for one of the five on-duty guards to make his way down the corridor, room by room, checking on each occupant like a camp counselor at curfew. They were supposed to do so every fifteen minutes, around the clock. Captain Bals never said it, but he feared that his charges would commit suicide, kill each other, or, most worrisome of all, try to escape.

The guards handled their routine on the morning of November 12 just as they did on any other morning, or so they claimed. Detective James Boyle later said that when he checked the rooms at 6:45 a.m., just after dawn, he found Reles sleeping in room 623.

Shortly after 7 a.m. Alexander Lysberg, the assistant hotel manager, ran through the Half Moon lobby to the front doors where two patrolmen, Charles Burns and Thomas Doyle, stood guard. He told them what he had seen moments earlier from the window of the first-floor draft board office: the motionless body of Abe Reles lying prostrate on the roof of the hotel kitchen jutting out beneath Reles's window.

Lysberg and the two patrolmen walked out onto the gravel extension and stood over Reles the way men stand over problems they can't fix. He was lying faceup with his fat mouth open and his left arm outstretched, as if hailing a cab. From a distance he looked like a pudgy man sleeping on his back. He was wearing gray suit pants ripped at the crotch and a white button-down shirt open to the waist, revealing a thick mat of chest hair. He did not move, he did not breathe. A makeshift rope fashioned from two knotted bedsheets flapped in the wind beside him. The men looked up to his wide-open window fifty-two feet above them.

Burns hustled back inside and called the local precinct house. He asked the dispatcher to send patrol cars and an ambulance. Meanwhile, Lysberg called his boss, Paul Fulton, the hotel manager. Fulton, in turn, called Detective Victor Robbins, the ranking officer on overnight duty up in the Rat Suite. "Abe is out the window!" Robbins announced to the four other guards as he put down the phone.

Robbins then entered Reles's room, gun drawn. He found it empty. The lights were on and a bedside radio played jazz, as if Reles had stepped out for a moment. The bedspread lay tousled on the floor. Beside it Robbins found a length of cloth formed by cutting a bedsheet down the middle. A pair of scissors sat on the dresser. A four-foot loop of insulated wire was attached to the valve of a steam radiator. Robbins looked out the window and "saw the huddled body of a man on the deck." Robbins went downstairs and knelt beside the body. Reles's left shoe was scuffed, he noted. He found a checkered cap stuffed in Reles's left-hand pocket.

The phone calls continued as the news spread up the chain of command. Detective Robbins called his boss, Captain Frank Bals, chief of O'Dwyer's police detail and supervisor of the guard duty in the Rat Suite. "How did he get out?" Bals asked.

"I don't know," Robbins said.

Captain Bals now had the unpleasant job of informing O'Dwyer, his old friend and boss, that the crucial witness, the mob insider most critical to upcoming prosecutions, had died in police custody. O'Dwyer had told Captain Bals from the outset: above all else, protect Reles. Adding to the embarrassment, Captain Bals would have to acknowledge that the five officers on duty had no explanation for the lapse.

O'Dywer was home with a bad cold when Bals called. He took the news well. Surprisingly well, Bals thought. He simply asked Bals to investigate.

Captain Bals stepped off the elevator on the sixth floor at 7:30 a.m. "What the hell happened?" he demanded of the five guards gathered there. "Did you fall asleep?"

"Son of a bitch," he said to himself as he walked through the open steel door and down the hall to inspect room 623. "Son of a bitch," he repeated as he returned to confront the guards again. Police reporters had not yet heard, but they soon would. Captain Bals may not have known exactly what happened up there in the Rat Suite, but he knew enough to anticipate questions about police dereliction. "You better get your stories straight," he said. The five officers huddled. They agreed to say that they had checked the rooms at fifteen-minute intervals throughout the night, as ordered, though in truth they had mostly slept through the night.

Reles was stiffening with rigor mortis by the time Dr. Max Silberman of Coney Island Hospital arrived. He could find no pulse or heartbeat. He opened one eye and found the pupil dilated. "It's DOA," he said. A police officer pulled Silberman aside and told him "not to mention this to anyone." He assumed the officer was referring to the press.

Turkus felt as if he had been "kicked in the stomach" when he heard the news. How he heard was as bad as the news itself: Howard Feeney of the *World-Telegram and Sun*, dean of the police reporters, called him at home. "The key witness plunges to his death right in the middle of the biggest of all Murder, Inc. trials," he later wrote, "and the trial prosecutor has to learn of it from an outsider."

At 10 a.m. Lepke Buchalter arrived at Kings County Court expecting a rigorous day of testimony in his murder trial. When told the news, he said nothing. He simply raised a drinking glass and sipped with the subtlest smile, as if toasting the informant's passing.

A few minutes later Detective Edward Swift picked Rosie Reles up at her home and drove her to the Half Moon. She was wearing a fur coat and matching hat. She had dressed up for the grimmest hour of her life. A detective led her to a gurney covered in a white sheet. A patrolman pulled the sheet back. She had withheld tears on the half-hour drive, but now she lost control. "Who did this?" she yelled, bent at the waist as if stomach-punched. "Who did this?"

She spent the next six hours answering questions in O'Dwyer's office. She confirmed that she and her husband had argued the previous night about "general matters." She was unable to give any "specific information" about her husband's fall. She said she had no knowledge of any plans to escape. She didn't "think he should have done anything like that," she said. "You boys were always nice to him." She returned home at 5:30 p.m. to find her son, Buddy, looking out from between venetian blinds at the press encamped outside the two-story brick house they shared with her parents.

Meanwhile, an ambulance carted the body to Kings County Hospital. At 1:30 p.m. Dr. Gregory Robillard, assistant medical examiner, performed an autopsy. He concluded that Reles had landed on the kitchen roof in a seated position, snapping his fourth and fifth vertebrae on impact and rupturing his liver and spleen. He died as instantaneously as he would have had he gone to the electric chair. Robillard also found that harmless pulmonary cysts had caused Reles to spit up blood. His cancer fears were entirely unfounded.

Back at the hotel, police gathered evidence. They found that the screen in the fifth-floor window, directly beneath Reles's room, had been opened from the outside. Its window latch was also moved. They found scuffs on the windowsill.

That afternoon Police Commissioner Lewis Valentine ordered James McGrath, chief of Brooklyn detectives, to make a "comprehensive and thorough" report of Reles's death, and whatever role police negligence might have played. The next day Valentine demoted the three detectives and two patrolmen. They went back to pounding sidewalk beats in their respective precincts pending the results of a departmental trial on neglect of duty.

At 11:30 a.m. a hearse transported the body from the Brooklyn morgue to the Jewish Memorial Chapel on Pitkin Avenue, where attendants washed and wrapped the body in a shroud and placed it inside a simple pine box, in keeping with Orthodox tradition. At 2:30 p.m. two hired limousines brought the only eight mourners, all family members, to view the coffin. It was draped with a black shroud decorated with the Star of David. There was no service, only a viewing. At 3 p.m. the cortège departed for Old Mount Carmel, a Jewish cemetery in Glendale, Queens. On the way, a car containing a newspaper photographer pulled alongside a family limousine, but the passengers quickly lowered the shades.

At the cemetery Rosie walked to the burial plot with her face in her hands. Her mother and an aunt half supported her. When a photographer stepped near, Rosie's father, a short heavyset man named Sam Korsh, charged him with fists raised. Detectives interceded.

Gangster funerals were known for excess, as if a superabundance of floral wreaths and private mausoleums sanctified malfeasant lives.

Reles was sent away with no such pageantry. No friends or gang associates attended, only Rosie and her seven relatives.

Cemetery staff removed the black shroud and lowered the crude pine coffin. An elderly rabbi said a Hebrew prayer for the dead, and that was that. The proceedings ended within minutes. When the first spadefuls of dirt hit the coffin, Rosie wept without inhibition. Whatever her husband's misdeeds, the parting still undid her.

As mourners turned away from the graveside a small animal scurried across the grass. "That's a gopher," said a reporter standing nearby. "The rat is in the grave."

The canary could sing, but he could not fly. The saying arose from the police ranks. It was a joke, both epigram and epitaph, passed freely among patrolmen and detectives and shared with reporters who killed time with them at crime scenes and in off-duty bars. Newspapers reprinted the saying as a snappy closing word on the Abe Reles story.

Assistant District Attorney Edward Heffernan read the official police report to the press. Reles, he said, had died trying to escape. Investigators concluded that Reles had fed two knotted bedsheets down the hotel's east wall and twisted several turns of the radio wire around the upper end of the sheets. He looped the other end of the wire around the radiator valve. He then clambered out the window, fully dressed with his cap in his pocket. He lowered himself to the fifth floor. One hand held to the sheet while the other loosed the screen of the room directly beneath his own. "It is our belief," Heffernan said, "that Reles tried to swing into the room below, room 523, recently vacated, in order to make his escape. The sheets were only long enough to reach the floor below." He worked the window up a few inches, but his weight was too much for the wire. Reles lost his balance as the wire parted. He kicked at the window ledge with his left foot, but too late. "He probably made a misstep, and his weight unwound the wire from the radiator, and he fell to the deck," Heffernan told reporters.

The dozen New York newspapers dutifully reported the police account. They explained Reles's fall as a bungled escape, but with some indications in lower paragraphs that the evidence might not support the official explanation. A *New York Times* reporter spoke with unidentified detectives who said they doubted that Reles would try to escape.

From the moment he turned informant twenty months earlier he had expressed fear of stepping outside police protection for even a moment. He would never survive in the wild.

In that case, why would Reles choose to go out his window? He may have done so to provide for his family, particularly since he mistakenly believed that he was dying of cancer. The *Times* article cited a rumor that Bugsy Siegel had promised Rosie Reles that his West Coast chapter of the Commission would award her family $50,000 (about $875,000 in today's currency) and help Reles disappear into the mob version of the witness-protection program if he fled the Half Moon Hotel and never testified again.

"There is no doubt that he was promised a large sum of money to get away from Brooklyn authorities," an anonymous Brooklyn official told the United Press, "and it is apparent that although [Reles] knew he faced death at the hands of the mob later, he counted on leaving his wife and children in comfortable financial circumstances."

The *Brooklyn Eagle* advanced the *Times*'s story by citing a "high official source" who stated that an emissary "interested in the fate of" Bugsy Siegel had offered Reles a large sum to escape the hotel and vanish. That emissary could have been Meyer Lansky, Siegel's lifelong friend and associate. Police confirmed that Lansky had recently visited New York. Reles was expected to testify against Siegel when he went to trial in California.

The *Daily News* theorized that Reles snuck from the Half Moon to deliver his own accumulated stockpile of cash to his family because he had concluded that O'Dwyer would not, or could not, uphold his part of the clemency deal. "That guy Reles has about $60,000 of mine and the other boys," Buggsy Goldstein reportedly told detectives aboard the train to Sing Sing. "He was minding plenty of money for the mob, because we thought he was the smartest guy of all and could keep it where nobody could get it until maybe some of us were in trouble. But we never got it. Reles got it."

John Osnato, the veteran detective who interpreted crime scenes as well as anyone, called it suicide brought on by the fear of death and the psychic weight of so many murders. "I think Reles was losing his mind," Osnato later wrote. "He had committed eleven murders and taken part in many more, and on top of that he was in fear of someone killing him. It got to be a phobia, and I believe he was a suicide because of fear."

For her part, Rosie Reles guessed that her husband was simply unhinged from drink and dread of the coming day's encounter with Buchalter. He was acting out of demented impulse, just as he had when he threw a bedsheet out Louis Capone's upstairs window and lowered himself to the street seven years earlier. "Nobody pushed him," she said. "He was drunk."

Crime-scene forensics made an escape attempt seem less plausible. An FBI test concluded that the bedsheets and electrical cord would hold no more than 110 pounds. Reles weighed 170. The sheets would probably not have supported him long enough to fumble with the fifth-floor window. In addition, the sheets and cord were too loosely tied to hold much weight. A murderer accustomed to tying and trussing victims would know how to tie a firm knot, especially if his life depended on it. The implication was that an intruder might have tied the sheets hastily and lowered them out the window to create the appearance of an escape. Another inconsistency: Reles's body landed twenty feet from the hotel wall, meaning he either dove out or was pushed. He would have landed at least ten feet closer to the wall if he were shimmying down his makeshift rope in order enter the fifth-floor window. Lastly, Dr. Robillard, the medical examiner, found a cut on Reles's cheek, hinting at a struggle.

The Reles murder became a preoccupation for newspaper-reading New Yorkers, a real-life tabloid murder mystery with an unsolved ending. On brownstone stoops and rumbling subways the curious and intrigued posed the same question again and again, as if solving a parlor game: If Reles was not trying to escape in order to retrieve money for his family, then how did he die?

The man in a topcoat seen pacing the boardwalk on successive nights was a possible answer. If the mystery figure was in fact Albert Anastasia, then he was likely casing the hotel in advance of a hit. Anastasia was an intermediary between the Commission's board of directors and Reles. He was the one who typically handed down murder contracts, so Anastasia had much to lose when Reles talked. There would be no Reles testimony, however, if Anastasia bribed the police guards to open the steel door. He would then be free to wake Reles and muscle him out the window, tossing the sheets after him to create the appearance of an escape attempt.

On the other hand, maybe Anastasia's direct involvement was not needed. It had been reported that the Commission raised $100,000 from its members to murder Reles. With that sum the mob might have bribed the police guards to do the job. And the guards might have killed him with relish, given the unrelenting, hour-by-hour abuse Reles inflicted on them. "The detectives were not sorry to see Reles dead," *The New York Times* observed. "They made no bones about this. He had been arrogant, surly, unclean in his habits." This would have been a tighter plan, since an inside job would not require an assassin to enter or exit the hotel. It might also explain why the guards fumbled about with confused, inconsistent answers when questioned after Reles was found.

There was also speculation that one of Reles's Rat Suite neighbors might have killed him. They were his longstanding associates, but he never conducted himself as a friend. He abused them as harshly as the guards. Their antipathy could only have intensified living in close quarters for twenty months. Of Reles's neighbors, the likely candidate would be Sol Bernstein, since he had already tried to stab Reles when he insulted Bernstein's wife.

The more these theories circulated, the more implausible the police account seemed by comparison. So who did kill Abe Reles, the notorious Kid Twist of Murder, Inc.? The question was asked, and asked again, by columnists, and neighborhood gossips, stoop-sitters and café conversationalists: Who killed Kid Twist? The riddle was posed with both curiosity and urgency until, twenty-eight days after Reles fell to his death, the Japanese bombed Pearl Harbor and the world as Americans knew it came apart overnight. Reles was no longer a front-page story.

The Reles murder, if it was murder, lingered unsolved and overlooked as authorities turned their attention to betrayals and extermination on a grander scale. Like a ghost, Reles would lie unquietly in his grave. He would resurface periodically to tar reputations, force resignations, and unsettle lives.

13

KID TWIST'S GHOST

When Abe Reles died faceup on the kitchen's gravel roof, the biggest and most consequential underworld prosecutions died with him. Most of them, anyway.

Proceedings against Bugsy Siegel, in Los Angeles, for the midnight murder of Greenie Greenberg unraveled without Reles. On February 5, 1942, Judge A. A. Scott dismissed the indictment, saying the evidence "is insufficient to establish the corroboration required by law."

The cases that would likely have sent a dozen or more mob lieutenants to the electric chair also expired. "The silencing of Reles was a body blow to the investigation of the Commission," said Turkus. "Thereafter everything ground to a halt."

O'Dwyer would still pursue a case against the fugitive Anastasia, but with surprising lack of interest. He waited four months to ask Burton Turkus to determine if they could convict Anastasia for the murder of Morris Diamond without Reles. Turkus expressed doubt. "The corroboration supplied by Reles expired with Reles," he wrote in a report to O'Dwyer.

Turkus nonetheless urged O'Dwyer to persist, even without Reles. Prosecuting Anastasia, he said, was crucial to busting the alliance between organized crime and corrupt officials. "Should Anastasia frustrate justice it would be a calamity to society," he wrote. "Somewhere, somehow, corroborative evidence must be available."

O'Dwyer concurred, but he showed almost no interest in pursuing the case. His chief clerk, the taciturn white-haired advisor and political fixer James Moran, quietly removed the "wanted card" from Anastasia's police investigation file. The department used the cards as an alert that the district attorney sought a person. Withdrawing the card indicated to detectives that the manhunt for Anastasia was over and the mobster was no longer to be arrested.

In any case, detectives had never managed to find Anastasia. They made routine sweeps of smoke-choked Brooklyn bars and pool-hall back rooms looking for his short, heavyset profile. They leaned on informants and listened to conversations on tapped phones. They found no sign of him anywhere. The Lord High Executioner had vanished.

Anastasia had found a better refuge than the Brooklyn hideaways: the Army. In October 1942 he joined the 88th Infantry Division, based in Camp Forrest, Tennessee, under his own name. No doubt the local induction office would have turned Anastasia over to law enforcement if they had grasped his true identity. But in the chaos of war, he slipped through the cracks. His record did not show a felony, and his wanted card no longer resided in police files. So he was technically no longer a fugitive. So the man whose face appeared on thousands of wanted posters put on a private's olive wool uniform and took up his rifle without notice. Captain Frank Bals later acknowledged that he never thought to look for Anastasia in the Army.

In the fall of 1943 Anastasia's division shipped out for Naples to help push the Axis forces from Europe's underbelly, but Anastasia stayed home. The War Department had advertised for experienced long-shoremen, the one honest job he knew, so he was excused from fighting. Instead he went to Fort Indiantown Gap, in Pennsylvania, where the Navy had built two dry-land cargo ships, the SS *Manada* and the SS *Swatara*, 160 miles inland. Anastasia taught black recruits how to operate winches, stack cargo, and hook up a sling. He did so with such proficiency that he earned promotion to master sergeant. He spent his furloughs betting on boxing matches and horse races back in New York.

Reles's death did not spare Lepke Buchalter. He was already in court, along with his lieutenants Mendy Weiss and Louis Capone, on first-degree murder charges for the death of Joe Rosen.

Hours after Reles died, his tall, pencil-thin suite-mate Tick Tock Tannenbaum stood in for him on the witness stand in Kings County

Court. *The New York Times* reported that Tannenbaum was "pale faced and weak of voice."

Tannenbaum could not replicate Reles's authoritative voice, nor could he speak with his comprehensive knowledge of the workings of Murder, Inc., but he did credibly describe for the jury how Buchalter planned the murder of Joe Rosen, and how Buchalter's co-defendants, Weiss and Capone, carried it out. "I was in Lepke's office two days before the murder," Tannenbaum said. "Mendy Weiss came in and whispered with Lepke. I knew what they were talking about, but I wasn't in on the game. Buchalter asked Mendy if everyone was all right and he said: 'Everything is okay for the job.'"

Rosen, Buchalter said, "is one son of a bitch who will never go downtown," referring to O'Dwyer's downtown Brooklyn office. It may have been the only time associates saw Buchalter lose his cool composure.

Tannenbaum said he was sitting in Buchalter's office immediately after the Rosen killing when Mendy Weiss walked in. He was obviously annoyed.

"Was everyone all right?" Buchalter asked.

"Everything is okay," Weiss said, "only that son of a bitch [Pittsburgh Phil Strauss]. I gave him orders not to do any shooting, but after Rosen is lying on the floor [Strauss] keeps shooting him."

Sol Bernstein, who drove the car that morning, confirmed that Weiss headed the quartet sent to kill Rosen on Buchalter's orders. Bernstein gave himself up in February 1940. In cross-examination, Bernstein snarled at Weiss's lawyer. "I am a stool pigeon," he said. "I'm a rat. Does that satisfy you?" he said.

"Do you mean that you are a man who testifies against his friends?" the lawyer asked.

"What do you think I'm doing right now?" Bernstein said.

Hyman Barshay, chief counsel for Buchalter and a preeminent criminal lawyer, acknowledged that his client was a racketeer. "I represent no angel," he said. "I condemn Buchalter's past life and all his activities with all the vehemence I possess." But, he said, Buchalter was already serving what amounted to a life sentence. "The racketeering activities of this defendant are at an end. Buchalter is where he belongs."

After summing up the testimony of thirty-three witnesses, Turkus reminded the jury that Rosen was not killed in passion. He was the victim of "a well-plotted, cold-blooded, brutal order to silence the victim and frighten others."

"Never before in the history of jurisprudence," Turkus continued, "has there been brought before the bar of justice the boss, the lieutenant, and the trigger man."

"Here," Turkus added, shaking his finger at Buchalter, "we have the boss, who has been described by his own lawyer as the czar of an industrial racket with a $500,000 take."

"Here," pointing to Capone, "we have the man behind the scene— the lieutenant—who planned and directed the murder of Rosen."

"Here," gesturing to Weiss, "we have the trigger man who fired the lethal shot."

The jury convicted Buchalter and his fellow defendants on November 30. Buchalter stood manacled to a guard with his two confederates by his side as the jury read the verdict. Buchalter's wife screamed. Buchalter showed no emotion. "But a thin dew of perspiration oozed out and glistened at the edge of his thinning hair," Turkus later recalled, "and he mopped it away very slowly with a dirty handkerchief."

As the three men walked from the defendant's table Captain Frank Bals caught Weiss's eye. "Peter Panto is waiting for you," he said.

At the sentencing two days later, Buchalter stood to hear the verdict, one hand gripping the rail in front of him. Judge Franklin Taylor ordered the convicted men sent to Sing Sing "to suffer execution by death." When asked if he wished to say anything, Buchalter opened his mouth, but no words came out. "Lepke's soft brown eyes didn't change or harden," wrote Meyer Berger for *Life* magazine. "He mopped at his tanned face with a soiled handkerchief but the blandness never altered. His tongue worked briefly inside one cheek and his fingers tensed, that was all."

After his conviction, Buchalter was returned to the Tombs, in Manhattan, where he stayed during a long, failed appeal process. He listened to the radio and ate meals brought to his cell. While there, Buchalter mingled in the prison yard with poet Robert Lowell, who was jailed as a conscientious objector. More than twenty years later Lowell described Buchalter in his poem "Memories of West Street and Lepke":

Flabby, bald, lobotomized,
he drifted in a sheepish calm,
where no agonizing reappraisal

jarred his concentration on the electric chair—
hanging like an oasis in his air
of lost connections

Buchalter was surely cannier than the witless character Lowell described, shrewd enough at any rate to broker a deal if he chose. Buchalter knew as much as anyone about the Commission's efforts to pay off judges, prosecutors, and municipal officials in concert with Tammany Hall. By sharing a laundry list of corrupt officials and bribed labor leaders Buchalter would likely earn a quick reprieve from Governor Lehman, if he chose to do so.

On the day of Buchalter's sentencing, Mayor La Guardia's police commissioner, Lewis Valentine, demanded a detailed accounting of how the more than two dozen detectives assigned to William O'Dwyer's office spent their time, hour by hour, and what evidence they turned up and where. The requisition of confidential records sent an unmistakable message to press and public: O'Dwyer's police contingent was either negligent or complicit in Reles's death.

O'Dwyer refused to comply on grounds that any information leaked could forewarn gangsters of cases mustered against them and result in the murder of witnesses. "I am keeping everything under lock and key," he said. "No one can get into my office through the back door." He accused La Guardia of "hampering" his investigation and vowed to indict anyone who interfered.

Captain Bals, who presided over security at the Rat Suite, stood awkwardly between two masters: the police commissioner who employed him and the district attorney he was assigned to. After meeting with his old friend O'Dwyer, Bals went directly to police headquarters on Centre Street, in downtown Manhattan, and filed for immediate retirement. He left the police department that afternoon after twenty-five years on the force. "In order to comply with [the police commissioner's request for information] it would have been necessary for me to betray the confidence that District Attorney William O'Dwyer placed in me," he told reporters. On the other hand, "if I had failed to reveal this confidential information I would have been subject to disciplinary action. I wouldn't sell out District Attorney O'Dwyer for any job and that is why I resigned."

In a heated follow-up phone conversation with Mayor La Guardia, O'Dwyer said, "You're making me lose Frank Bals, the best crime investigator in the city." A month later O'Dwyer hired Bals as the chief investigator in the district attorney's office, a job he held until 1946.

O'Dwyer's investigation had earned headlines for almost two years. In the process, the long, bloody spree of Murder, Inc. had imprinted itself on the public imagination. Brooklyn was now synonymous with a certain kind of dark dealings and butchery. Murder, Inc. had become a recognizable brand, though nobody would have expressed it that way in 1941.

Eighteen days after Reles's death, *Brooklyn, U.S.A.* opened at the Forrest Theatre, on West Forty-ninth Street, with sets loosely based on Midnight Rose's candy store and the rough brick and rusted corrugated metal of the Brooklyn waterfront. Asa Bordages, a rewrite man at the *New York World-Telegram*, wrote the script.

For fifty-seven nights Peter Panto came back to life on stage. For fifty-seven nights Murder, Inc. assassins killed him all over again. Brooks Atkinson, theater critic for *The New York Times,* called the on-stage murder "the most harrowing episode in the theater for years. It is in cold blood—silent, efficient, inhuman."

As the winter of 1942 set in, the SS *Normandie* slouched like a fallen beauty at Pier 88, on Manhattan's West Side. Two years earlier, in her dreamier days, she was the postcard image of a modern French liner, slicing the waves with three smokestacks canted just so. She was once the largest and fastest passenger ship afloat, the holder of transatlantic records.

The *Normandie* had prepared to sail for Le Havre from Pier 88 when France fell to Nazi Germany on June 22, 1940. Though the United States was still neutral at the time, its military seized the ship to prevent her from passing to the Nazis. Now she lay moored at a partly frozen slip while the U.S. military refit her as a troop carrier capable of ferrying ten thousand soldiers to Europe. Workers stripped away the Art Deco finery from her grand salon, banquet hall, smoking rooms, café terrace, and sun deck.

At 2:30 p.m. on February 9 a stack of flammable life vests stored in the first-class lounge ignited. A brisk northwest wind fed the flames. Within an hour the conflagration had consumed three upper decks.

Charcoal-shaded smoke darkened the Manhattan streets as far inland as Times Square.

Firefighters extinguished the flames by 8 p.m., but the endless gallons of water poured aboard now pooled in the hull, causing the *Normandie* to list to port. At 2:35 a.m. the gray-painted hulk capsized on her side like a dying giant and settled onto the Hudson River mud.

In those anxious early months of 1942, German U-boats torpedoed merchant ships and tankers off the Atlantic seaboard, sinking 650,000 tons of cargo a month. When the *Normandie* burned, the Office of Naval Intelligence naturally suspected arson.

Murray Gurfein, once an assistant district attorney in Thomas Dewey's office, now worked as a lieutenant colonel for the Office of Strategic Services, a wartime intelligence agency and precursor to the CIA. The best way to safeguard the waterfront from Nazi saboteurs, Gurfein decided, was to recruit the mob to police the docks. The war made for strange bedfellows.

Only one man exercised the authority to command longshoremen and their dirty handlers up and down the city docks, from Red Hook to Hell's Kitchen. Gurfein had helped Dewey send that man to jail six years earlier. Lucky Luciano, inmate number 24806, was serving thirty to fifty years in Clinton Prison at Dannemora, in a far northern corner of New York State. Navy intelligence dispatched a lawyer to Dannemora bearing Italian sweets and salami—and a proposal. Luciano had been following the daily newspaper reports from prison. Italian mobsters had a long grievance against Mussolini dating back to the 1920s, when Il Duce jailed and tortured mafiosi. Those who fled to America were eager for revenge.

Luciano initially asked to be sent abroad to act as a scout or liaison officer when Allied troops invaded Sicily. But in the end he agreed instead to help secure the New York waterfront, on certain conditions.

On May 12, 1942, Luciano moved to Great Meadows Correctional Facility, a hundred miles closer to New York City. There the warden set aside a private office for Luciano's meetings with intelligence officers, with Socks Lanza, czar of the Fulton Fish Market, and with Luciano's longtime associates, Meyer Lansky and Frank Costello. Over the following months Luciano's mafia contacts reported suspicious activity, and they helped intelligence agents go undercover in bars, docks, trucks, and factories. No reports of waterfront sabotage or Nazi infiltration occurred for the rest of the war. In early 1943, when the Allies planned to invade Italy, Luciano and his underlings are rumored to have provided photographs, descriptions of the coastline and villages, and other information, though military officials denied underworld involvement.

Luciano had conducted himself as a model prisoner, both at Dannemora and at Great Meadows, but he had repeatedly failed to sway the parole board. Thomas Dewey, the prosecutor who imprisoned Luciano a decade earlier, was now governor of New York. On January 3, 1946, he pardoned Luciano on the condition that he leave the country and never return. It was widely reported that Dewey based the pardon on an affidavit provided by Gurfein detailing the wartime help Luciano furnished, including soliciting aid from the Sicilian mafia before the Allied invasion. The Navy department denied any such affadavit.

Whatever the case, Luciano walked out of prison with manicured nails and the jeweled wristwatch he entered with nine and a half years earlier. Fifty Brooklyn longshoremen stood by and cheered when Luciano walked up the gangplank to board the Liberty ship *Laura Keene* on February 9, and they closed ranks to block reporters and cameramen from following him aboard. He arrived two weeks later in the dusty little inland Sicilian town of Lercara Friddi, where his father once labored in sulfur pits. Locals welcomed him as a hometown hero. As usual, he betrayed no emotion. Years later Luciano told an interviewer that he ordered the *Normandie* torched so that he could negotiate his freedom. Supporting evidence has never been found.

Luciano never reunited with Gay Orlova, his New York girlfriend. Shortly after he went to prison the U.S. deported her as an "undesirable." She worked in Paris as a showgirl and fashion model. The American troops who mingled with her in the rue d'Artois bars nicknamed her "Gay All Over." Members of the French Resistance accused her of romancing a Nazi commander; Nazis accused her of romancing a Resistance leader. Both may have been correct. She gassed herself to death in February 1948 by sticking her head in the oven of her Paris flat. She was dejected because the wealthy Chilean she expected to marry could not, or would not, get a divorce.

Happy Maione and Dasher Abbandando were among the few to walk out of death row. They exited the easy way when the Court of Appeals awarded them a retrial on a technicality concerning Judge Franklin Taylor's instructions to the jury after their twelve-day trial. "I always knew I'd walk out of that tomb some day," Maione said.

On January 13, 1941, the two inmates rode back to New York in the last coach of a four-car train. No passengers were allowed in their car. Abbandando had asked for the return of a dollar watch confiscated when he entered the prison eight months earlier. He held it to one ear on the ride south. "Still runs," he told a sheriff.

"Nice to be back," Maione said when they returned to their two tiny windowless cells in the overcrowded Raymond Street Jail, near Fort Greene Park in Brooklyn, where they had lived during their first trial. "Hope we don't have to make a return trip."

Unfortunately for them, they did. Their second trial ended as the first had: with a death sentence. The two men were twice tried, and twice convicted, for the ice pick murder of Whitey Rudnick. There would be no more appeals. They returned to Sing Sing in April 1941.

Alone in his cell on death row, Happy Maione suffered a series of fainting spells. Abbandando was more stoic. When his wife, Jennie, paid him a final visit he assured her he "could take it."

Abbandando rested his hand on the shoulder of Father Bernard Martin, prison chaplain, as he walked the Last Mile. He entered the death chamber at 12:01 a.m. on the morning of February 20, 1942. Abbandando was pronounced dead three minutes later. Maione entered two minutes afterward. He smiled grimly at the witnesses as an attendant slipped a black hood over his head. He was dead at 12:06.

In November 1943 an American bombardier named Kenneth Williams parachuted from a crippled B-17 Flying Fortress along with his crew during a bombing run over Bremen, Germany. An oddly friendly German sergeant was waiting for Williams when his parachute reached the ground. The sergeant photographed Williams's leather flight jacket, with the words "Murder, Inc." painted across the back in Gothic letters. Bombers by custom painted saucy nicknames on their plane's nose, and they wore the logo on their jackets, like varsity athletes or members of a motorcycle gang. Mechanical problems had grounded *Murder, Inc.* that day so Williams and his crew had flown an alternate, named *Aristocrap*. But Williams still wore the Murder, Inc. jacket.

When Williams went to a prisoner-of-war camp, a stalag, German newspapers and magazines published the photo as proof that American airmen were "Luftgangsters," or gangsters of the sky, intent on murdering innocent civilians. One magazine reported that "President Roosevelt had gone to the warden of Alcatraz," Williams later wrote, "and told him he wanted the meanest man in prison to go over and kill German women and children." Williams wore the jacket home after Russian soldiers liberated his stalag on May 1, 1945. In 1986 he donated the jacket to the Smithsonian Institution.

The expectation of a grand deal intensified after the U.S. Supreme Court upheld the death sentence against Lepke Buchalter and his co-defendants, Mendy Weiss and Louis Capone, on June 1, 1943. If Buchalter were to talk his way out of the electric chair, he would have to start naming names now. Rumors circulated that he was negotiating, that a sensational announcement would come any day.

In fact, Buchalter did meet for almost two hours with Manhattan District Attorney Frank Hogan on March 2, 1944, two days before his execution date, but no agreement resulted. In the end Buchalter had chosen to honor the underworld's code of silence, even if it meant his death. "Buchalter had two keys in his hand," said his lawyer, J. Bertran Wegman. "He chose to use the one that opened the door to eternity rather than the other one."

Nine years earlier Buchalter had saved Thomas Dewey's life by sending Mendy Weiss and Bug Workman to kill Dutch Schultz before Schultz could enact his plan to kill Dewey. Now, as governor of New York, Dewey was in a position to reciprocate. In the end, he declined to give Buchalter an eleventh-hour reprieve when Buchalter refused, once and for all, to cooperate with prosecutors. He would be the highest-ranking mobster ever to walk the Last Mile.

Buchalter's wife, Betty, read his final statement to reporters crowded around her in the bar of the Depot Square Hotel, half a mile from Sing Sing: "I am anxious to have it clearly understood that I did not offer to talk and give information in exchange for any promise of a commutation of my death sentence. I did not ask for that."

Buchalter was the last of the three to be executed on the night of March 4, 1944. He walked to the electric chair at 11:16 p.m., minutes after guards wheeled away the electrocuted bodies of Louis Capone and Mendy Weiss. He glanced at the thirty-six newsmen and other witnesses. He said nothing. And that was it.

In the end, *The New York Times* reported, Buchalter was "a beaten, frightened little man. . . . Gone was his calm disdain, his cocksureness that amounted almost to impudence."

Frank Coniff, a reporter for the *New York Journal-American*, described what he saw from the witness stand that night: "You look at the face . . . you cannot tear your eyes away. Sweat beads his forehead. Saliva drools from the corner of his lips. The face is discolored. It is not a pretty sight."

A few hours later Walter Winchell, the columnist who helped arrange Buchalter's surrender five years earlier, was walking home after the opening of a Broadway show. "I paused at a newsstand," he said, "to look at the front page of the *News* and *Mirror*. Both devoted the entire front page to Lepke's covered corpse being wheeled into a mortuary wagon at Sing Sing—after he had fried in the electric chair. I shuddered and turned away."

On June 1, 1942, William O'Dwyer took a leave of absence from the district attorney's office to enlist as an Army major, leaving Kitty in the care of his chief clerk, James Moran. He rose to brigadier general, but, like Anastasia, never faced combat. Instead he worked in the inspector general's office investigating graft and corruption in military contracts. By all accounts, he succeeded. "Bill O'Dwyer, I firmly believe, had done more than anyone else to prevent fraud and scandal for the Army Air Forces," Undersecretary of War Robert P. Patterson wrote in an internal memo.

O'Dwyer spent the war behind a desk, but the image of him in a blue Army uniform with shoulder straps and ribbon racks would help when he ran for mayor for a second time, as he intended. He returned to the district attorney's office on February 1, 1945, then left for good in August to gear up his mayoral campaign. La Guardia had decided to leave office after three consecutive terms, so the election of a Democrat seemed assured.

O'Dwyer might have preferred that Abe Reles fade into obscurity, but his ghost refused to lie quietly in his grave. The question of how Reles died persisted through the war years, along with a growing suspicion that

O'Dwyer might know more about Kid Twist's fall than he acknowledged.

O'Dwyer was not like Thomas Dewey, the rigidly right-thinking Midwestern prosecutor who viewed the teeming city neighborhoods from a chilly remove. O'Dwyer rose from the Brooklyn streets. As a dockworker, patrolman, and magistrate judge he was intimately acquainted with the unclean accommodations and corrupt negotiations brokered on street corners and up the chain of power to the meeting rooms of Tammany Hall. His familiarity with those unsavory alliances—the handshake of convenience between parties on either side of the law—helped make him an effective prosecutor. It could also undo him now.

In September 1945, two months before Election Day, a special Brooklyn grand jury convened to investigate corruption among the borough's public officials. Its nineteen-page report, issued on October 29, accused O'Dwyer of "gross laxity, inefficiency, and maladministration" while Brooklyn district attorney, but stopped short of an indictment.

O'Dwyer dismissed the grand jury's rebuke as an election-year slur. O'Dwyer won the mayoral election handily over the Republican nominee, Judge Jonah Goldstein. "Calls and telegrams came pouring into headquarters, but I did not stay there long," O'Dwyer later wrote of election night. "I went home to Kitty. She looked at me with what looked like pity."

On December 20, twelve days before O'Dwyer became mayor, the grand jury issued a second report, this one saying that O'Dwyer had "undisputed proof" that Albert Anastasia was guilty of first-degree murder in the death of Peter Panto and "a number of other vicious crimes" but failed to charge him. His chief of staff, Assistant District Attorney Edward Heffernan, had presented most of the case against Anastasia to a Brooklyn grand jury five years earlier before abruptly abandoning the case on O'Dwyer's orders. The material witnesses held on bail to testify against Anastasia were immediately released. The grand jury also noted with suspicion that the wanted card was removed from Anastasia's police file by order of James Moran, O'Dwyer's chief clerk.

The grand jury accused the mayor-elect of "neglect, incompetence, and failure to proceed against Anastasia," but again charged him with no crime. Still, the report fed speculation that O'Dwyer deliberately

protected Anastasia as a favor to those who did favors for him in his
mayoral campaign.

A few minutes before midnight on New Year's Eve, New York's one-
hundredth mayor was sworn into office in the modest Rockaway home of
Kitty's cousin. Kitty was too enfeebled to attend a City Hall ceremony.
Fifty or so friends and associates stood by as O'Dwyer took the oath,
then kissed his wife. The next morning at 11 a.m. La Guardia met
O'Dwyer on the City Hall steps and escorted him to the mayor's spacious office. La Guardia motioned to the swivel chair he had occupied
for twelve years. "The seat is yours, Bill," he said.

O'Dwyer took the oath for a second time, in the Council Chamber
beneath a portrait of Thomas Jefferson, then shook hands for an hour
and a half. The police glee club sang "It's a great day for the Irish." And
it was.

Over the following years O'Dwyer earned high marks for addressing a backlog of needs deferred during wartime, despite a shortage of
city funds—school construction, hospitals, transit improvements. He
repaired rotting piers, built housing for returning soldiers, and helped
persuade the United Nations to establish its headquarters on the East
River site of a former slaughterhouse. *Time* magazine put him on its
cover.

He faced misgivings, as well. On June 4, 1946, the future TV host Ed
Sullivan, then a *Daily News* columnist, reported that during O'Dwyer's
mayoralty bookies routinely bribed detectives with payments of as
much as $3,000 a month. Sullivan described "a complete breakdown
in police control," with token arrests staged as a cover-up "for the most
cynical grafting spree in New York history." O'Dwyer was not directly
implicated, but his long, cozy friendship with the police cast him in a
bad light.

Meanwhile, O'Dwyer suffered heartbreak at home. His wife Kitty
had suffered from Parkinson's disease, and later cancer, for most of their
thirty years of marriage. She had been confined to a wheelchair for the
last several years with nurses stationed at her side. She had moved to
Gracie Mansion, the colonial-style mayor's residence overlooking the
East River, but only reluctantly. The relative luxury of her husband's
success brought her no contentment. "The old buoy bell that rang out
at Hell's Gate annoyed her," O'Dwyer said. "It sounded like a funeral
bell, and she knew she was dying."

On 6:30 p.m. on Friday, October 11, doctors called O'Dwyer at City Hall. Kitty was unconscious and failing. She died the next day at 12:26 p.m. She had lived as an invalid who barely left home, but her funeral was a public spectacle. Five thousand mourners, including thirty priests and United Nations officials, packed St. Patrick's Cathedral for a solemn high requiem mass. Five thousand more stood on Fifth Avenue to catch a glimpse of the bronzed-metal casket, blanketed by a mountain of orchids and roses, carried by police pallbearers while a police honor guard stood at attention.

Kitty had been O'Dwyer's steady companion since he worked as an off-the-boat bartender at the Vanderbilt Hotel. She contributed to every important decision in his long rise to mayor, measuring the pros and cons at the kitchen table of their small brick home.

Now O'Dwyer lived alone in Gracie Mansion. Kitty's absence scraped at his heart while the mayoral duties wore him down. He had always come across as jaunty and self-assured, but his more buoyant nature now escaped him. His Irish glimmer dimmed. There was a sense that the job, with all its impossible complexities and fifteen-hour days, overwhelmed him. "I tell you, there were times I truly wanted to jump," he said. "You would look out over the city from some place high above it, and you would say to yourself, 'Good Jesus, it's too much for me.'"

New York is capable of extinguishing a man's spirit and abruptly restoring it. On the hot evening of August 23, 1948, O'Dwyer, in his capacity as mayor, attended a fashion show in Grand Central Palace, an exposition hall next to Grand Central Terminal, staged as part of New York's Golden Jubilee, the fiftieth year since its five boroughs merged into one big city. Eleanor Lambert, the fashion publicist who invented fashion week and the best-dressed list, escorted him to a small, darkly lit reception room where he was to meet a few of the 125 models. "This reminds me of speakeasy days," said a model wearing a white Dior dress. Her voice was low and a bit husky.

"You're much too young to know about speakeasies," O'Dwyer said.

She turned to answer him. Sloan Simpson was a slender, dark-haired thirty-three-year-old Texas divorcée with a straight patrician nose and Nordic cheeks. She had a wholesome daughter-of-Texas look, but she was naughty enough to earn frequent mention in Walter Winchell's gossip column. She was a free spirit at a time when free spirits wore pearls. A friend called her "a champagne girl."

O'Dwyer invited the whole group back to Gracie Mansion for a late drink. Sloan rode next to him in the car.

One can see why O'Dwyer, a widower at fifty-nine, would gravitate to a radiant woman of country club comportment twenty-six years his junior, but what did she see in a man old enough to have fathered her? His hair was graying, but still silky. He had those blue Irish eyes. Over dinners, plays, and parties she came to think of him as a "sensitive poetic and charming man . . . with an enormous feeling for the under-dog." His power could only have amplified the chemistry of attraction.

Walter Winchell announced their engagement in a radio address. Sloan denied it the next day. On successive nights the press photo-graphed them at a World Series game at Ebbets Field and a ballet at the Metropolitan Opera House, giving rise to a fresh flurry of rumors and speculation. In the tabloid glare their romance assumed a fairy-tale shine—the graying, gregarious widowed mayor restored to life by the love of a younger woman. The question wasn't if they would marry, but when.

A mayor in love made a sympathetic figure. O'Dwyer won reelection in November 1949. His opponent, a wealthy former City Council pres-ident named Newbold Morris, whose ancestors arrived in America in 1660, resurrected old questions about O'Dwyer's sympathy for corrupt cops and rumored ties to mobsters, but romance eclipsed all questions of impropriety. When a reporter asked if he and Sloan would marry, he said nothing. He leaned back in his chair and whistled the opening bars of "Some Enchanted Evening," a song from the musical *South Pacific,* which tells the story of a beautiful young woman who falls in love with a middle-aged man.

O'Dwyer and Sloan married secretly in the days leading up to Christmas in a small wood church in Stuart, Florida, and honey-mooned on a friend's yacht. O'Dwyer had not been on a boat since he stepped off the steamship in New York. According to Simpson, he had never worn a pair of shorts in his life.

The newlyweds returned to find their charmed spell on the city bro-ken. While they were gone the *Brooklyn Daily Eagle* published a series of exposés linking the borough's police to a bookmaking cartel. The articles charged, among other things, that bookies paid Brooklyn cops more than $12,000 a year for protection from arrest. New Yorkers had laughed when Newbold Morris contended that the underworld had friends in city government. Now the *Brooklyn Daily Eagle* confirmed much of what he said.

In response, Miles McDonald, O'Dwyer's tall, gray-haired successor as Brooklyn district attorney, launched a further inquiry into police corruption. He outmaneuvered his targets by hiring twenty-nine rookie cops, fresh from the police academy, as plainclothes investigators. They were too new to have been tainted by the payoff system. Corrupt detectives tried to thwart McDonald's men by forwarding their license plate numbers to bookies so they could spot the investigators.

McDonald came from one of Brooklyn's oldest political families. O'Dwyer had hired him to manage his 1938 campaign for county judge, and hired him again two years later to serve as an assistant district attorney. McDonald lost thirteen of his first fourteen cases as a rookie prosecutor, followed by a long successful run. Twice nominated to be U.S. Attorney for the Eastern District of New York, he chose instead to run for district attorney in his native Brooklyn. He was known as a squeaky-clean, by-the-book family man. When liquor or other gifts arrived in his office he gave them to charity. McDonald was an old-fashioned man, with old-fashioned virtues, who enjoyed puns and crossword puzzles.

Now McDonald worked his way through a vast, intricate puzzle as he unscrambled the city's biggest police corruption scandal to date. With every turn, the investigation inched closer to McDonald's former boss, William O'Dwyer.

McDonald indicted seventy-five officers. Another five hundred retired in disgrace. "Cop after cop marched in for grilling," the *Daily News* reported. "Cop after cop fast resigned from the force." Many of those demoted, indicted, or retired were old friends appointed to upper-echelon police posts by O'Dwyer. He was not directly implicated, but his cozy fellowship with the police reflected badly on him.

O'Dwyer had enjoyed a long, charmed run from grocery-store clerk to Gracie Mansion occupant, but the beneficent spell had worn off. It felt as if Reles haunted him, as if Kid Twist's ghost cursed the proceedings. O'Dwyer made matters worse for himself by criticizing the inquiry at every turn. "I'm not going to stand by and see the morale of the entire police force shaken," he said. He knocked the inquiry so often, and with such acidity, that he invited suspicion. He looked as if he spoke on behalf of the cops, even the corrupt ones, and by implication defended the ancient street practice of graft and payola.

A 7:30 a.m. on July 16, 1950, a Sunday morning, forty-nine-year-old Captain John G. Flynn arrived at the police station on Fourth Avenue in Brooklyn, the station where O'Dwyer had served as a patrolman two decades earlier. Captain Flynn greeted the lieutenant on desk duty and climbed the old wood stairs to his office. Minutes later he shot himself in the right temple with his service pistol, a .38-caliber revolver that he won as top student in his police-academy class. The bullet passed through his brain and lodged in the wall. He died the next day. He had testified before McDonald's grand jury twenty-three days earlier. Under interrogation he denied knowledge of a bookie operation in his jurisdiction.

Three days after Flynn shot himself, his dark-haired widow, Attracta, dragged her three children, ages eleven and younger, to McDonald's office in the Municipal Building, where a policeman directed her to the Central Courts Building. There she tried to enter a courtroom, children in tow, where McDonald was prosecuting a police lieutenant for perjury. "Don't lay hands on me," she told the attendant who barred her path. She finally cornered McDonald in a sixth-floor anteroom and berated him for her husband's death. "Johnny Flynn's blood is spattered on you," she said, "and will be for the rest of your life." McDonald said nothing.

Guards escorted her downstairs, where she whipped out a prepared statement and read it to reporters drawn by the confrontation. "I come to Brooklyn to meet the spotted snakes with double tongues," she said. "I want to sit in the torture chamber for three days and find out what tactics they used to drive a man to kill himself, 210 pounds of muscle and strong. Nobody could touch him."

Six days later O'Dwyer led 5,500 patrolmen and 500 detectives marching to a dirge in Flynn's six-block funeral procession. The largest police funeral held to date doubled as a wordless protest against McDonald and his investigation. Flynn's widow wept quietly as she entered the church with two of her three children.

O'Dwyer made matters worse for himself by calling McDonald's tactics "Hitlerian" and the investigation a "witch hunt." His implication was clear: the district attorney had hounded an innocent family man and good cop into taking his own life. O'Dwyer put the onus for Flynn's death on McDonald. In response, McDonald accused O'Dwyer of seeking to disrupt the investigation.

In the days after Flynn's funeral, politicians and political columnists wondered if O'Dwyer himself might be indicted. Democratic Party chieftains concluded that, indicted or not, he had become a liability. He was too cozy with the corrupt cops, and by extension the mob, fueling speculation that he might have had knowledge of, or involvement in, the planning and execution of Reles's death. O'Dwyer stank, they concluded, and his stink could rub off on Democrats running in the next election.

The Democratic machinery had built O'Dwyer up. Now it tore him down. The clubhouse made its decision: they would remove him from City Hall for the good of the party. They had once considered him a lock for the Democratic nomination for governor, but they scuttled that plan as well.

In late July 1950, Edward J. Flynn (no relation to Captain John Flynn), a Bronx party boss and stalwart Truman supporter, asked for, and received, a White House meeting. No record exists of his discussion with President Harry Truman, but its purpose is clear. O'Dwyer had to go. Truman had his own corruption problem dating back to his association with Tom Pendergast, a political boss who once controlled Kansas City. He did not need another one.

Two months later O'Dwyer quietly left for Washington by train to finalize arrangements. The next day President Truman formally nominated O'Dwyer as ambassador to Mexico, a post worthy of a big-city mayor but distant enough to place him beyond easy reach of nosy reporters and prosecutors. The appointment came as a complete surprise to the State Department.

Reporters met O'Dwyer at Penn Station when his train pulled in from Washington that night. Why did he agree to resign as mayor when he had fought so long for it? they asked. "That question will have to be answered by the President," he said.

The net was tightening and O'Dwyer knew it. On August 24 he sent President Truman a thank-you note. "The new assignment to Mexico with which you have honored me becomes increasingly important with each day," he wrote.

Eight months into his second mayoral term, O'Dwyer and Sloan packed up. He spent his last thirty days in office arranging raises, promotions, and pensions for loyal friends. Judges, stenographers, deputy mayors, police officials, director of the city radio station, the commissioner of public works—all received handsome sinecures with comfortable benefits. He appointed his longtime police aide, Captain Bals, as a deputy police commissioner. James Moran, the chief clerk who removed Anastasia's wanted card, got a lifetime post as commissioner of water supply. "I've got to take care of the boys," O'Dwyer said.

On August 31 O'Dwyer stood on the steps of City Hall to deliver a farewell address to a listless crowd of 20,000 perspiring through an afternoon so oppressively humid that four patrolmen and a fire departmental official fainted. O'Dwyer said that the president had summoned him for a post of "vital importance" in Mexico, a claim nobody believed. He said that in a city like New York the municipal government is "sometimes unavoidably beset by controversies and differences." But, he predicted, the "major accomplishments will live in the public mind long after these differences are forgotten." He asked that his accomplishments be appraised apart from "the welter of discussion, arguments, contentions, and controversies. . . ."

"I am," he added, "willing to accept the judgement of history."

On that melancholy note, he and Sloan rode to Grand Central Terminal and boarded the Twentieth Century Limited bound for California, where they vacationed for more than a month before moving into the ambassador's residence in Mexico City.

There was no disguising his fall. The charmed boy from County Mayo who had clambered his way up from coal shoveler, bartender, and beat cop to nationally celebrated district attorney and, finally, to mayor, was now unseated and hustled out of town by his own political party in a state of unspecified disgrace. "A lot of people, we think, are going to feel there was very little that was forthright about the whole deal," the *Daily News* wrote.

O'Dwyer may have gotten out just in time. Two weeks after O'Dwyer departed for his California vacation McDonald's investigators yanked the chief of a $20-million gambling syndicate named Harry Gross from his bed in the Towers Hotel in Brooklyn Heights. They held him on $250,000 bail as a material witness while raiding thirty-five of his betting parlors.

Gross was a former soda jerk who began taking fifty-cent bets on a street corner, equipped only with pencil and paper. Now he had two hundred suits, a Long Island call center to field bets, and a chauffeur who drove him in a limousine to his headquarters in a saloon next to Ebbets Field. The *Daily News* called him a "perfumed bookie tycoon."

Gross sat before the rackets grand jury in conspicuously expensive clothes, a pudgy, black-haired thirty-five-year-old bothered by a nervous tic in his right eye. Speaking in rapid-fire Flatbush slang, Gross admitted that he paid $1 million in bribes—known as "ice"—to at least 150 city officials, from the assistant chief police inspector down to patrolmen on the beat. "He was a smooth, suave, individual with a gentlemanly manner," McDonald said. "He was smart as a whip." A portion of the $1 million in bribes, Gross claimed, was paid to O'Dwyer by intermediaries, though that was never substantiated.

Even in Mexico City, O'Dwyer couldn't escape the undying Reles mystery. In 1951 he reluctantly returned to New York to testify before a special five-member Senate committee created to investigate organized crime, an inquiry prompted in part by a steady drumbeat of reports on corruption published in the *Brooklyn Daily Eagle*. The committee was headed by Estes Kefauver, a lean, folksy senator from Tennessee who had the plain, ingenuous look of a small-town lawyer. He presented himself as a hillbilly, but in reality he came from one the state's most prominent families and attended Yale Law School. He sat through the hearings in a state of judicial calm, his big hands folded on the table in front of him. In his book about the 1950s *The Fifties,* David Halberstam called him "a sort of Jimmy Stewart, the lone citizen-politician who gets tired of the abuse of government and goes off on his own to do something about it."

Senator Kefauver conducted the hearings on a grand scale, with more than six hundred pimps, gangsters, bookies, police, politicians, and mob lawyers questioned over fifteen months. *Time* magazine put Senator Kefauver on its cover looking like a high-school science teacher with the tagline "Gamblers + Politicians = Corruption."

Kefauver's hearings barnstormed like a touring Big Crime vaudeville show through fourteen cities. The public followed along on flickering black-and-white televisions as Tony "Joe Batters" Accardo, Louis "Little New York" Campagna, Jake "Greasy Thumb" Guzik, Enoch "Nucky" Johnson, and other preposterously colorful underworld figures squirmed under klieg-lit interrogation. They were like character actors from a comic scene in *Guys and Dolls*, the mobster musical that had opened on Broadway six months after the first hearings.

Fewer than half of all American homes had televisions in 1951. Those without watched with neighbors or in taverns. Pedestrians gathered around sets in appliance store windows. Women held daytime viewing parties while their husbands worked. In Detroit the hearings preempted *Howdy Doody*, the most popular children's show. Five New York movie theaters admitted the public for free to watch the hearings on large screens. The Horace Mann School in the Bronx canceled classes so that students could watch afternoon sessions. Con Edison added an extra generator to power all the televisions. When blood donations dropped, the Red Cross drew volunteers by installing a television set in its donation center. "People sat as if charmed," *Life* magazine wrote. "Never before had the attention of the nation been riveted so completely on a single matter." Senator Kefauver said his own children referred to him as "that man on television."

The country practically stood still for an electrifying real-life crime drama. For many Americans, it was a first introduction to organized crime. "Dishes stood in sinks," *Time* wrote, "babies went unfed, business sagged and department stores emptied while the hearings were on."

The hearings arrived at the Federal Building in downtown Manhattan on March 12, 1951, like a show prepped out of town for its Broadway debut. The city offered the committee an abundance of misconduct to pick over, but the marquee topic would be the unresolved Reles case. "The whole thing is a tawdry mess," said Senator Charles Tobey, Republican of New Hampshire, an acid-tongued, Bible-quoting seventy-year-old farmer-politician with white hair fringing a bald dome. He looked almost exactly like the farmer standing with his pitchfork in *American Gothic*.

At the mention of Reles, Tobey went off in his ornery New England schoolmaster's baritone. "It smells to high heaven, and I don't think the whole truth will be told until Judgement Day."

On the second day of hearings, Frank Costello (alias Francesco Castiglia), a sixty-year-old racketeering king known as the Prime Minister of the Underworld and the purported inspiration for Don Corleone of *The Godfather*, sat before the committee with slicked-back banker hair and a double-breasted suit. The Associated Press called him "a triumph of tailoring, a big-time racketeer, but nervous now, taut as a steel wire."

Naturally senators wanted to know what Costello knew about Reles's death. Could he have ordered Reles killed in order to protect his friends Albert Anastasia and Bugsy Siegel? Could O'Dwyer have helped engineer the killing in return for Costello's support in the 1944 mayoral election? Costello was known to exert great influence over Tammany Hall and, by extension, the Democratic Party machinery. Senator Kefauver called Costello "that wily string-puller."

No underworld boss was likely to sit like a schoolboy for senators. On his first day of testimony, gravel-voiced Costello asked not to have his face shown on television. He did not, his lawyer said, "care to submit himself as a spectacle." The camera trained instead on his fidgeting manicured hands. "When the questions got rough, Costello crumpled a handkerchief between his hands, or rubbed his palms together. Or interlaced his fingers. Or he beat a tattoo on the tabletop. Or he rolled a little ball of paper between thumb and index fingers. Or he stroked the side pieces of his glasses, lying on the table," *The New York Times* reported. "His was video's first ballet of the hands."

When the questions heated up, Costello contracted a well-timed case of laryngitis. "I am going to walk out," he croaked after dodging questions. "I am going directly home to bed."

Senator Kefauver warned Costello that police would drag him back in handcuffs if necessary. But Costello's attorney said he'd "reached the limit of his physical endurance." His lawyer produced a doctor's note urging Costello to stay in bed for several days. The committee's attorney examined the doctor's note and judged it "not satisfactory."

"Is it just a sore throat?" Senator Kefauver asked.

"I think it's his gall bladder," said Senator Tobey. In the end, Senator Kefauver said Costello could go if he agreed to return another day.

O'Dwyer's police aide, Captain Frank Bals, appeared before the committee the next day dressed like a Broadway peacock, in a blue double-breasted suit, a white shirt with long collar points, a flashy blue-striped tie, and a conspicuous gold watch. He was an "unhappy, nervous witness, angry and apparently frightened by turns," wrote the *Daily News*. "He smiled once when he took his place in the chair and once when he left the stand. In between, he found nothing to smile about, and once or twice he seemed on the verge of apoplexy as he flushed under the lashing of Tobey."

Captain Bals testified that all five policemen on duty were most likely asleep when Reles went out the window. The television audience could see the senators' skeptical expressions. "That is an amazing thing, isn't it?" Senator Tobey said. "Somebody said, 'Now boys . . . shut your eyes and go to sleep.' . . . [Reles] took a sheet and tore it up and made a rope of it, and he tied it to a wire, and all that might make noise, and he was fully dressed with his shoes on, and he walked around, and these somnolent policemen slept on in the arms of Morpheus."

Captain Bals said he believed that Reles was trying to prank the guards while they slept. He intended to swing like Tarzan into the fifth-floor window and "come back upstairs and then kid around with [the guards]." The hearing room rocked with laughter.

Senator Tobey speculated that Reles could have had bullet or stab wounds hidden beneath his clothes. He asked if the medical examiner had concluded, without doubt, that Reles died as a result of his fall. Captain Bals said that after ten years he could not recall exactly. "Ten years is a long time," Senator Tobey said, "but I might say, a murder like that only happens once in a lifetime."

BALS: Senator, we are in a position to get all the records. You can get the medical examiner's report.

SENATOR TOBEY: We are asking you, you who were the major-domo, you were the ringmaster, and you yourself had responsibility, and your six dummies there let the man go out the window, or else threw him out quid pro quo. . . . I think the thing is shady. To me, this whole thing is shady. He was the most influential witness you had, and they wanted to get him out of the way.

The committee recessed for the weekend buzzed with the anticipation of the blockbuster session to come. On Monday they would see former mayor William O'Dwyer, the man at the center of the storm.

O'Dwyer returned to New York forty-one years after making landfall as an immigrant Irish boy. He timed his arrival from Mexico City for Friday evening so that he could acclimate over the weekend. He descended a gangway to the tarmac at 10:45 p.m. and walked through a congregation of waiting policemen, reporters, press photographers, and television cameras without saying a word. He looked thinner and grayer and somehow diminished. He was tan, but tense.

He was tense with good reason: his appearance before the committee might be his last chance to restore his name, to exorcise Reles's ghost.

On Sunday he was back on familiar ground, watching bagpipers and palominos marching in the St. Patrick's Day parade from a reviewing stand set up for dignitaries at Sixty-fourth Street and Fifth Avenue. While O'Dwyer watched the parade, Samuel S. Leibowitz, now a county judge, held a court session in his Brooklyn home to grant the Kefauver Committee access to forty-three bound packets of transcripts from the 1945 grand jury that accused O'Dwyer of laxity and maladministration.

Monday morning began calmly enough. O'Dwyer paused, grim-faced and unsmiling, for photographers outside the Federal Building in downtown Foley Square, then climbed the long courthouse steps flanked by Joan, a favorite niece, and his sister-in-law, Kathleen.

He wore a blue suit a shade darker than his eyes. On the third floor a bailiff wedged a path for him through the packed hallway. Spectators, most of them women, had lined up an hour in advance for a chance at the two hundred gallery seats. They craned to see O'Dwyer when he walked in, as if spotting Humphrey Bogart.

The klieg lights blinked on. A battery of TV and newsreel cameras whirred. Photographers milled about. Twenty million viewers watched as O'Dwyer stood until the senators sat, as required by decorum, then lowered himself into the witness chair. "Housewives skimped on their household chores and offered no guarantee that dinner would be ready on time," wrote *The New York Times*. "Television parties were commonplace in many homes . . . everywhere there was stillness of an attentive audience."

O'Dwyer had returned to New York to exculpate himself, but he began with self-congratulation. The senators frowned as O'Dwyer launched into a lengthy rehash of his mayoral accomplishments recited in the singsong cadence of a campaign speech. Speaking extemporaneously with a trace of brogue, he talked of how Prohibition bred disrespect for law and order, how he moved 190,000 New Yorkers from slums into decent housing, the scourge of slot machines, the civic value of churches, and his improvements to schools and subways. While he spoke he variously toyed with a paper clip, a rubber band, and his horn-rimmed glasses. He sounded as if he were running for office again, though he was only reminding local television viewers of all he had done for them.

The senators had by now spent almost a year listening to six hundred witnesses. O'Dwyer's self-serving ramble annoyed them. Senator Kefauver interrupted. "We don't want your voice to give out," he said. "I think it might be well to get down to details about the organized crime. . . ."

The committee began by pounding O'Dwyer for not prosecuting Albert Anastasia for the killing of Morris Diamond, the union official.

O'Dwyer said that Reles was indispensable. Reles sat with Anastasia when he planned the murder, and Reles could place Anastasia in the murder car parked down the block from the shooting. Because Reles had not participated in the murder he fulfilled the state requirement for a witness who was not an accomplice. "In this state you cannot convict on the unsupported testimony of a co-conspirator," O'Dwyer said. "I want you to remember that, gentlemen." As a result, O'Dwyer said, the case against Anastasia languished when Reles died.

The mood stiffened. "Suddenly, like a whip-lash, the voice of Senator Charles Tobey of New Hampshire cut through O'Dwyer's ripe-melon delivery," wrote a court reporter for the Associated Press. "The senator's face was bleak, and as hard and rocky as the hills of his native state in mid-winter."

The packed courtroom and millions watching on TV were rewarded by the first in a series of clashes between the two men.

SENATOR TOBEY: Are you familiar with the facts about [Reles's] death?

O'DWYER: I am.

SENATOR TOBEY: And what is your version of it?

O'DWYER: That he tried to escape.

Senator Tobey reminded O'Dwyer that his own police aide, Captain Bals, had testified three days earlier that Reles intended to enter the fifth-floor window and then go upstairs to play an embarrassing trick on the guards.

O'Dwyer put both hands on his heart. "How could anyone tell what was in Reles's mind, sir?" he said. "I could only tell there was the rope and the wire and the sheet, and he slipped and had fallen."

When Senator Tobey asked if Captain Bals was a "flat-tire," meaning a fool, O'Dwyer tightened. "Senator, let me tell you something about Bals," he said with noticeable emotion. He then told a long-winded story, intended to prove Captain Bals's virtue, about a night when the police searched for a Buchalter gunman named Little Farvel Cohen, who wore a dyed-blond mustache and suits two sizes too large. Captain Bals led a detail up to Farvel's furnished apartment at 4 a.m. knowing that he was armed. Captain Bals was the first in the door, and the first to pull a gun on Little Farvel who, as it turned out, was sound asleep.

Senator Tobey's anger increased by a degree. "What has that got to do with what I'm asking you?" he said. "If you're trying to build up a case for Bals before this committee, you will have a very hard time doing it. Bals made a spectacle of himself . . . and he gave the flimsiest excuse possible about the death of Reles."

A sheen of perspiration shone on O'Dwyer's forehead and cheeks. He folded and unfolded a handkerchief and sipped water. The resentment and frustration of his exile played just below the surface. He told Senator Kefauver, the committee chairman, that he was entitled to a respectful hearing. He asked for a recess to compose himself.

After a fifteen-minute break, Senator Tobey leaned into O'Dwyer again about his failure to indict Anastasia. He noted that O'Dwyer once said that he had "a perfect case" against Anastasia. "When did the perfect case," Senator Tobey asked, "become an imperfect case, and how?"

"When Reles died," O'Dwyer said.

If Reles was the linchpin of the prosecution's case against Anastasia, Senator Tobey said, then "wasn't that worth the greatest endeavor in the world to find out who was culpable in reducing this man Reles to a corpse so that evidence goes out the window and you can't prosecute the arch criminal Anastasia?"

Senator Tobey asked whether the medical examiner had photographed Reles's body. His question implied that authorities might have covered up signs of stabbing or shooting. O'Dwyer answered that it was standard police procedure to photograph bodies. Senator Tobey asked if the medical examiner could be "reached by someone and then the public wouldn't know the actual cause of death."

O'Dwyer acknowledged that that mob could have threatened or influenced the medical examiner, but, he added, "it is grossly unfair" to suggest it "unless there is some evidence," especially before an enormous television audience. "It is unfair to suggest that the medical examiner was fixed," he added.

"I did not say that," Senator Tobey said.

"That is exactly the innuendo," O'Dwyer said.

O'Dwyer did not see much respect the following day either. When the hearing resumed, Senator Tobey stated his suspicion that the guards were culpable in Reles's death. "I am not a lawyer," Senator Tobey said, "but why did those fellows [the police] in the room with Reles throw him out the window to kill him if they knew there was no other witness [to Albert Anastasia's murder of Morris Diamond], and one witness alone would be not be effective in getting an indictment?"

"Do you know they did that, Senator?" O'Dwyer asked.

"That is my theory," Senator Tobey said.

"Have you any facts upon which to base it, sir?"

"No," Senator Tobey said, "only intuition and horse sense. But . . . they did throw him out of the window."

"I will not answer the question based on intuition and horse sense," O'Dwyer said.

Rudolph Halley, the committee's short, owlish thirty-seven-year-old chief counsel, jumped in to say, in his soft lisp, that there was "at least some basis in fact for Senator Tobey's theory. . . . There are those who have seen [photos of the crime scene] and feel that a man going out the window on his own power, unless he took a running jump, could not have gotten that far from the building, isn't that so?"

"Have it that way," O'Dwyer said. He seemed too tired now to maintain his indignation. "Is that your opinion?"

Halley reminded O'Dwyer that in April 1942, five months after Reles died, Burton Turkus, head of his homicide division, urged him to step up pursuit of Anastasia and indict him for the murder of Morris Diamond, even without Reles to testify. Why did O'Dwyer do nothing instead?

"Turkus didn't say we had a good case against him," O'Dwyer said. "He said the record of the man was so bad every effort should be made toward developing a case."

And yet the next month, Halley said, James Moran, O'Dwyer's chief clerk, removed the wanted card from Anastasia's police file, essentially shelving the case. "That could have been a clerical mistake," O'Dwyer said. Everybody knew that Anastasia was wanted, he added, card or no card.

In the afternoon session the senators turned to reports that O'Dwyer met at least once with Frank Costello. The meeting was a potential clue that O'Dwyer was complicit in a mob plan to silence Reles before he could testify against Anastasia and Siegel. In exchange for O'Dwyer's help in removing Reles, Costello, who had considerable political influence, may have directed Tammany Hall to elect O'Dwyer.

O'Dwyer acknowledged that while in the Army he had met with Costello at the racketeer's Central Park West apartment, a penthouse furnished with a gold-plated grand piano and slot machines rigged for perpetual jackpots. Costello routinely received favor-seekers there, but O'Dwyer insisted he was not among them. He had visited strictly on official business, he said, in the course of investigating corrupt contracts for the Air Force. He was there to ask Costello about a friend who engaged in fraudulent contracts at Wright Field near Dayton, Ohio.

O'Dwyer's contention was entirely plausible. Government men like him occasionally solicited, and received, help from the mob in the war effort. Both sides suspended their normal rules of engagement due to their shared interest in defeating Mussolini and the Fascists. He may in fact have had legitimate reasons for conferring with Costello, but the meeting still looked suspicious, given that the Tammany leader and his aides attended. Drinks were poured and hors d'oeuvres passed. To the television audience it sounded more like a cocktail party where O'Dwyer, the prospective candidate, could make deals with crooked political influencers. It did not help O'Dwyer's cause that the meeting was set up by his aide, James Moran, the man who had removed Anastasia's wanted notice from his files. (Moran was later found guilty of engineering a fire department shakedown of oil-burner dealers.)

Senator Tobey told O'Dwyer that it seemed strange that "prominent men would trot up to [Costello's] place to ask his advice and counsel." He asked if O'Dwyer had shown up with "a little black bag" to carry cash.

O'Dwyer repeated that he was carrying out an assignment to keep racketeers out of military procurement. He went to the apartment, he said, "to serve my country," but he seemed evasive and defensive.

Senator Tobey, who had harassed O'Dwyer for two days now, snapped back: "It almost seems to me as though you should say 'unclean, unclean,' as the old Romans practiced it, and that you would leave him alone, as they do a leper. But you trot up to his place and do business with him."

O'Dwyer was known for his gracious manner, but his blue eyes now flashed with anger as he blotted his shiny face and neck with a handkerchief and blinked against the klieg lights. He shifted slightly in his seat. A lock of gray hair fell over his eyes. He lowered his mouth to a pair of microphones. Looking up at the dais, he accused Senator Tobey of his own links to bookmakers. "They've got bookmaking all over the country, Senator," O'Dwyer said, looking at Senator Tobey. "They say there's a lot in New Hampshire. They say $30 million worth of bookmaking is done in your home state."

"Well, we haven't a Costello in New Hampshire," Senator Tobey said. His voice rose to the level normally heard before a punch is thrown.

"Well, I wonder," O'Dwyer said slowly and dubiously, adding that Senator Tobey had "sent down to New York" for contributions for his last campaigns.

"It's not true," Senator Tobey shouted back. "I never called anyone in New York for contributions to my campaign."

"Well, I'm under oath and you're not, sir." O'Dwyer said.

Senator Tobey half rose from his chair, as if to charge the witness, but after a moment's hesitation he sat. "I hate a four-flusher," he said, meaning that O'Dwyer issued hollow threats.

Senator Lester Hunt broke in to ask O'Dwyer if he had sent investigators to New Hampshire to check on Senator Tobey's campaign contributions.

O'Dwyer said he had not, though he did receive an unsolicited letter from a "Mr. Selden," whom he didn't know. He had the letter in his pocket, but refused to show it to anybody but Senator Tobey.

SENATOR TOBEY: Is there anything in what you have in your pocket that reflects on my integrity, or character, or forthrightness?

O'DWYER: Nothing that anybody else running for office wouldn't admit to very gladly, sir.

O'Dwyer had backed down, and he sat back deflated in his chair. Senator Kefauver put an end to the discussion by reprimanding O'Dwyer for his "poor grace" in his attempt to "divert the subject to bring up something about Senator Tobey."

When it was all done, when the five hours of harassing, insinuating questions ended and the klieg lights blinked off, O'Dwyer went back to Mexico to resume his duties. He held a press conference at the airport on his way out of town, repeating his mayoral accomplishments. "I did not betray any public trust," he insisted.

If O'Dwyer had returned to New York to exonerate himself, he failed. The slow corrosive drip of intimations had further damaged his stature. His reputation was so sullied that political columnists called on President Truman to recall him from Mexico.

A reporter asked President Truman if he had watched O'Dwyer's testimony. "No," he said. "I've got other things to do besides watch television."

As O'Dwyer exited the hearings, the Lord High Executioner arrived. If viewers gathered around their TV sets anticipated Albert Anastasia's climactic appearance before the committee, he would disappoint them. He did testify, but in a private session. The public wouldn't have heard much, anyway. Anastasia refused to say anything beyond denying all crimes attributed to him and describing himself as nothing more than part-owner of dressmaking factory in Hazleton, Pennsylvania. "I decline to answer," he said repeatedly, "on grounds it might tend to incriminate me."

The Kefauver Committee's final report, issued May 10, 1951, devoted thirty-five pages to corruption in New York—far more than any other city got. The report leveled its harshest criticism at O'Dwyer, who, the committee said, had contributed to the "growth of organized crime, racketeering, and gangsterism in New York."

If anyone emerged from the hearings ennobled, it was Estes Kefauver himself. Senator Kefauver had become a folk hero of the television age. On March 18 he walked onstage as the "mystery celebrity" on the prime-time game show *What's My Line* to a long, hearty ovation from the studio audience. It took a panel of blindfolded celebrities seventeen questions to identify him. "We'd love to have your ratings," said the actress Arlene Francis.

The committee's ratings were, in fact, favorable enough to propel Senator Kefauver into the next year's presidential race. He beat the Democratic incumbent, President Harry Truman, in the New Hampshire primary before fading and failing. In 1956 Adlai Stevenson selected Senator Kefauver as his running mate. They lost to Dwight Eisenhower by a landslide.

The Kefauver Committee's job was to uncover corruption. Prosecuting whatever crimes came to light would be left to district attorneys. Brooklyn District Attorney Miles McDonald accordingly convened a grand jury to determine, once and for all, if Reles was murdered, and if so by whom. "[The question] has to go to the Grand Jury," McDonald said. "There just isn't any other way to lay the ghost of the Canary Could Sing, but Could Not Fly."

The grand jury's job was to ask the same question Rosie Reles asked ten years earlier while standing over her husband's body: *Who did this, who did this?*

In late 1951 McDonald called eighty-six witnesses, but new informants proved hard to turn up. The surviving tenants of the Rat Suite—Tick Tock Tannenbaum, Pretty Levine, and Sol Bernstein—reappeared like hoodlum ghosts long enough to say what they knew about Reles's death, then melted away again.

Frank Bals reluctantly came up from his Ft. Lauderdale retirement home to testify for five hours, but he turned away the press afterward. "I'm sick of the whole thing," he said.

On November 30 McDonald telegrammed O'Dwyer, his former boss, in Mexico to ask if he would testify "at his earliest convenience." He did not hear back. A week later McDonald asked Western Union if O'Dwyer had received his telegram. He had. It was only when newspapers picked up on O'Dwyer's failure to reply that he sent McDonald a letter of refusal. "I never had, nor have I now, any indication of foul play nor any fact supporting such a theory." He was, he said, engaged in "highly secret, restricted" matters which dominated his time.

McDonald also invited Senator Tobey to lay out the evidence for the assertion of murder he made in the committee hearings, and in a March 25 appearance on *Meet the Press,* but he demurred. "I have no facts or actual evidence to give with reference to Reles's death other than to review my utterances and expressions at the crime investigating committee's hearings and express the doubts which I had and still have in the cause of death and the motives therefore," he wrote back. "The statements made by me were based on supposition and strong suspicion."

The hearings ended on a forbidding note. Dukey Maffetore, the Murder, Inc. driver who turned informant a decade earlier, was scheduled to answer questions about Reles, but he went missing. After helping to send Buchalter and others to the electric chair, he had been permitted to plead guilty to petty larceny. The sentence was suspended because prosecutors suspected he would be assassinated if sent to jail. Maffetore was released back into the Brooklyn streets, but he never redeemed his life. His wife, Mary, and their thirteen-year-old daughter left him. His parents shunned him. They were, his sister said, "thoroughly ashamed of him."

Police arrested Maffetore for stealing a car in Astoria, Queens, weeks before he was to go before McDonald's grand jury. He failed to show up for his court appearance. The bondsman who posted the $5,000 bail heard rumors that Maffetore "won't be back." And he wasn't. Detectives suspected that human remains found in a New Jersey swamp might belong to Maffetore, but they could not make a firm identification. He was never seen again.

The jury heard briefly from Reles's widow, Rosie, who had remarried within a year of her husband's death and did everything possible to erase him from family memory. She legally changed her children's last name to Dickoff, her new husband's name. Her son, Buddy, was eight when Reles died; he barely remembered his father. Her daughter was entirely unaware of his existence.

"Please, please," Rosie pleaded when a reporter called her in April 1951. "I know nothing. My mind is a blank. I cannot even say a word." She had deleted Kid Twist from her life, but she could not stave off the questions that followed his memory.

There was talk of exhuming Reles's body in hopes that investigators might discover overlooked clues. They did not do so, but they did send the bedsheets and wire to an FBI forensics lab in Washington, which confirmed what police had said from the beginning: that Reles had hung from the sheets, and that he fell to his death when the wire parted.

After more than 110 hours of testimony, the grand jury concluded that "Reles did not meet with foul play . . . he did not commit suicide . . . he met his death while trying to escape." The ten-page report, known as a presentment, made a point of saying that its findings were based on "credible evidence. We cannot indulge in the speculation and fancy that has been rampant for the last ten years. Sensationalism, induced by whatever cause, must be and has been avoided."

And so the long Reles investigation died its own death from exhaustion and neglect. Skeptics of the grand jury's findings included its own judge, Samuel S. Leibowitz, who surprised the courtroom by saying, moments after discharging the grand jury, that he hoped that another grand jury would someday reopen the Reles case. "It is possible," he said, that "in the future, at any time, today or twenty years from now," new evidence would be "brought forth to show that Reles was murdered. There is no statute of limitations on murder."

O'Dwyer's testimony before the Kefauver Committee and McDonald's subsequent grand jury inquiry into Reles's death left him untrusted and disliked by the State Department, and he knew it. He submitted his resignation effective December 6, 1952. He knew that he would not be kept on by Dwight Eisenhower when he took office on January 20, 1953. When asked by a reporter why he quit, O'Dwyer said, "Because I wanted to."

O'Dwyer's wife, Sloan, had no use for him either. She was spending most of her time among the jet set in Acapulco, much of it with a handsome married hotelier. O'Dwyer heard through expatriate channels that Sloan had spent an afternoon sunning herself on the beach with the man while his wife seethed in a hotel lobby. When the two walked inside, tan and beaming, the wife made a weeping, screaming scene.

Sloan had originally been a blessing to O'Dwyer's reputation. Now she was a curse. They divorced in 1953. Their marriage had lasted just three years. She later spent time in Madrid, where she took bullfighting lessons and added matadors and at least one ambassador to her portfolio of affairs.

A Mexico City newspaper, *El Universal*, suggested that O'Dwyer might want to remain in Mexico to "elude justice." O'Dwyer may indeed have feared that an indictment awaited him in New York, though it was not entirely clear what he might have been indicted for. Witnesses had suggested that he accepted bribes, and vague inferences surrounding Reles's death lingered, but so far there was no corroboration of O'Dwyer's wrongdoing.

Still, he could not escape the odor of corruption. The *Daily News* wrote a one-line editorial: "Come home, Bill. Nothing is forgiven."

O'Dwyer was touchy about his future plans. In the days before O'Dwyer resigned, Robert Prescott, a United Press reporter, filed a story saying the ambassador had hinted to friends that he might become a Mexican citizen. In response, O'Dwyer ordered a clerk to summon every U.S. correspondent to the embassy for "a very important" press conference. When O'Dwyer entered his face was flushed with anger and he sounded like a man prepared to throw a punch. "I say to you that you are a lying bastard," he said, pointing to Prescott.

"That's pretty strong," Prescott said.

"I'm calling you what you are in the English language," O'Dwyer said. Then he ordered Prescott removed from the embassy. O'Dwyer did not become a citizen of Mexico, but he did stay on for a long sulk. Instead of returning to New York, he moved alone into a $160-a-month two-room suite in the Hotel Prince, a Mexico City hotel for budget-minded tourists. He wore tropical suits for day drinking with other expats at tiki bars and sunned himself on a stone roof-deck called El Ranchito. Friends said he seemed lost in some dark inner world. "If it's good for the world to crush a man," he said, "then let the world do it."

At age sixty-three he was without a government job for the first time in twenty years. "His face, firm and ruddy two years ago, is now florid under the tan," a visitor wrote, "and under the stress of emotion its expression tends to become uncertain and ill-defined."

Like Senator Estes Kefauver, the prosecutor Burton Turkus graduated from investigations to television. Starting in 1952 he hosted a weekly true-crime show called *Mr. Arsenic,* the nickname Buggsy Goldstein gave him during the Murder, Inc. trials. The same year he published a memoir titled *Murder, Inc.: The Story of the Syndicate,* written with the former Associated Press sportswriter and war correspondent Sid Feder. (Eight years later the memoir was made into a movie with Peter Falk playing Abe Reles. *The New York Times* called his performance "amusingly vicious.")

In his memoir Turkus broke from O'Dwyer, his former boss, by asserting that Reles was likely murdered. "And if he was murdered," Turkus wrote, "the police were accomplices. But the police would not have done it on their own."

If the police did not act alone, then who would have helped them? The list of people Reles provoked was long. "A far greater number of persons wanted to see him dead than wished for his continued well-being," Turkus wrote. "He was hated by every hood in Murder, Inc., because he had helped the Law. The very witnesses who were under guard in the hotel with him—mobsters all—despised him."

The most obvious culprit was Albert Anastasia. "When Kid Twist hit that extension roof . . . none heaved a more lusty sigh at the Kid's finale than Albert Anastasia, his boss," Turkus wrote. Anastasia might not have acted alone. The on-duty police nursed a smoldering hatred for Reles after all his abuse, and they might have happily gone along with a murder plan.

The Half Moon guards despised Reles for abusing them, but some politicians and city officials, including O'Dwyer, "had a more practical reason for their hatred of Reles," Turkus wrote. They had a lot to lose if Reles spoke publicly. When John Harlan Amen, a former Army intelligence officer and chief interrogator for the Nuremberg War Trials, had conducted a special corruption investigation, starting in 1938, he asked permission to question Reles. O'Dwyer refused to make Reles available. He may have withheld Reles because his prize witness could name politicians who solicited and received bribes. O'Dwyer himself, or men close to him, may have been among those Reles would implicate. So it was not out of the question that New York's political class was complicit. "Motives for murder?" Turkus wrote. "Hundreds of them." His insinuation was clear: O'Dwyer or a member of his administration may well have collaborated with Anastasia in a plan to throw Reles out the window and then covered up the investigation.

However Abe Reles died, the result was the same. Anastasia avoided prosecution and, most likely, the electric chair. As a result, the Lord

High Executioner outlasted and outlived most of his Murder, Inc. associates. Lepke Buchalter, Buggsy Goldstein, Pittsburgh Phil Strauss, Mendy Weiss, Louis Capone—all perished in the electric chair. Lucky Luciano survived, but he had been deported to Italy.

By the mid-1950s Anastasia was practically the last surviving delegate of the original Commission, and he conducted himself with the arrogance of the imperishable. He trespassed on other gangsters' turf, as if immune to retribution—most flagrantly in Havana, where he encroached on casinos controlled by Meyer Lansky.

On the bright, chilly morning of October 25, 1957, Anastasia's bodyguard, Anthony Coppola, drove him from his Spanish-style home in Fort Lee, New Jersey, a stucco manse protected by a ten-foot barbed-wire fence and roaming Doberman pinschers, to Grasso's Barber Shop in the Park Sheraton Hotel in midtown Manhattan. It was the same hotel (then called the Park Central) where aggrieved card players shot Arnold Rothstein to death twenty-seven years earlier.

At 10:20 a.m. Anastasia greeted Arthur Grasso, the proprietor, who stood as always behind the cash register. Anastasia hung up his blue hat, his blue topcoat, and jacket. He removed his brown tie, unbuttoned his shirt, and settled his beefy body in chair number four. He lay back under the recessed fluorescent lights for a trim and shave. His stout hands, weighted with diamond rings, settled on the armrests. Anastasia's regular barber, Joseph Bocchino, wrapped a tissue around his neck and touched electric clippers to his gray tufts.

Into this state of relaxation and repose intruded two gunmen. They crossed the threshold wearing fedoras and aviator sunglasses. Scarves hid their faces. Their revolvers came out. "Keep your mouth shut," one told Grasso, "if you don't want your head blown off."

Anastasia's eyes were closed. He didn't see the men push Bocchino aside and take up a position behind his barber chair. The men opened fire together, propelling Anastasia forward as if from a spring. He could see the men in the mirror, their revolvers raised. In his confusion he lunged at their reflections, colliding into glass shelves and sending a bottle of bay rum shattering to the tile floor. He landed on his left side, one hand outstretched. A fifth, decisive shot splashed the back of his head against the tile floor. The two assassins walked out without a word. They dropped their guns on the street and entered the subway. Anastasia died with $1,911.82 in cash in his pocket. His youngest brother, the Rev. Salvatore Anastasia, was called to the barbershop to bless the body.

"Death took the executioner yesterday," *The New York Times* wrote the next morning.

The ranks of Jewish gangsters dwindled after the war, but the Italian mafia, the ancient and enduring Cosa Nostra, flourished under the stewardship of five distinguished crime families—Gambino, Lucchese, Genovese, Bonanno, and Colombo.

In 1962 a heavyset, bulbous-nosed, chain-smoking soldier in the Genovese family named Joseph "Joe Cargo" Valachi was serving fifteen years in a federal penitentiary on a narcotics charge when he murdered a fellow inmate. He agreed to cooperate with federal prosecutors in order to avoid the death penalty. He also asked for private prison accommodations and protection from fellow inmates.

The following year a Senate subcommittee asked him to testify. "Not since Frank Costello's fingers drummed the table during the Kefauver hearings," wrote *The New York Times*, "has there been so fascinating a show."

Amid the discussion of gangland assassinations and power struggles, senators asked Valachi about the death of Abe Reles. Twenty-two years had passed since Reles tumbled from room 632 of the Half Moon Hotel. The mystery of his death had already been raked over by one grand jury probe, one Senate committee, and two mayoral elections, but the question persisted unanswered and unresolved. Valachi himself saw no mystery in Reles's death, though. "I never met anybody," he said, "who thought Abe went out the window because he wanted to."

SENATOR JACOB K. JAVITZ: How did Abe Reles die?

VALACHI: He was pushed out the window.

SENATOR JAVITZ: Who pushed him?

VALACHI: The police threw him out.

The understanding within the mob, Valachi said, was that the police killed Reles as part of a deal made with Albert Anastasia, the man most likely to lose his life if Reles testified.

SENATOR JAVITZ: You believed it?

VALACHI: Yes, I did.

Days after Valachi's testimony a pair of reporters for the *New York Journal-American* tracked down four of the surviving policemen on duty in the Rat Suite the morning Reles died. Harvey McLaughlin said from his home in Ridgewood, Queens, that he would not comment.

Frank Timpone of Long Island City courteously refused to say anything. "All the information I had I gave to the D.A.'s office in 1951," he said. "That's all you'll hear about it from me."

John E. Moran of Brooklyn also declined comment.

The only person willing to speak was the widow of Detective Victor Robbins, the first man to enter Reles's room after he died. "Valachi can't hurt my husband now," she said. "But I think it's a terrible thing that a man like that is allowed to spread lies and accusations for the whole nation to hear."

The reporters also called on William O'Dwyer. He had finally returned to New York, but broken and nearly bankrupt. They found him in his law office at 50 Broad Street, a block from the New York Stock Exchange, looking "somewhat heavier, slightly grayer, but still smiling and affable."

When asked about Valachi's testimony, O'Dwyer stiffened. "The charges by Valachi are ridiculous," he said. "At no time was there any suggestion the police were involved in Reles's death." He referred the reporters to the investigation conducted by his office, which concluded that Reles died trying to escape. Investigations by then police commissioner Lewis Valentine, and by Edward S. Silver, who was assistant district attorney during the 1951 grand jury, came to the same conclusion.

O'Dwyer died eleven months later of coronary thrombosis. "The whole story has never come out," *The New York Times*'s editorial page wrote the day after his death. "And it probably never will."

On the evening of January 17, 1962, Lucky Luciano drove his Alfa Romeo sports car to Capodichino Airport four miles north of his home in Naples, Italy. He was trailed, as usual, by Cesar Resta, a plainclothes policeman. By now Luciano was a graying, bushy-browed sixty-five-year-old living as any retired Neapolitan businessman might. He dressed well, as he always had, in silk underwear and fine suits.

Posterity weighed on Luciano's mind. With age came the privilege of recalling history as he would have it told. He spoke to a Hollywood producer named Martin A. Gosch about making a film based on his life. Luciano suggested Cary Grant for the lead role. Gosch preferred Dean Martin.

There would be no biopic. Meyer Lansky and other underworld colleagues disapproved of the attention. So Luciano suggested to Gosch that they collaborate instead on a memoir. If Gosch agreed to delay publication until a decade after Luciano's death, he would tell everything.

In thirty interviews conducted over eleven months, Luciano shared his story: his fistfighting childhood on Lower East Side streets, the gambling and racketeering lessons imparted by the elegant master Arnold Rothstein, the assassinations of the Mustache Petes Joe Masseria and Salvatore Maranzano, the taming of the mob's anarchic impulses with the Commission and Murder, Inc., the high life of a mob lord sharing a Waldorf Astoria suite with Gay Orlova. He spoke of butchery, jackpots, and lies.

That night Luciano drove to the airport to pick Gosch up for a visit that was to include their thirty-first interview. When Gosch emerged from customs Luciano introduced him to Resta as a friend, as he often did to avoid the embarrassment of the policeman's presence. Resta played along, shaking hands agreeably. The arrangement was not so awkward. They really were friends, after all.

As the three men walked from the terminal Luciano paused to place his arm on Gosch's. His eyes flickered and rolled back. He slumped to the ground and died of a massive heart attack. In his pocket Luciano had 66,000 lire (a little more than $100), a prescription from a cardiologist, his driver's license, a religious medallion, and a picture of Igea Lissoni, his blond girlfriend who had died of leukemia three years earlier.

The U.S. government barred Luciano from returning, but his body was welcome. His remains were shipped to Queens and interred in a white-columned vault inscribed "Lucania," his original family name. There, above a statue of Jesus and an altar, a stained-glass window depicts a bearded saint leaning on a shepherd's staff.

As promised, Gosch held the interviews for ten years. In 1972 he hired Richard Hammer, a former *New York Times* reporter, to help turn the notes into publishable form. A year later Gosch sold the manuscript for an advance of $150,000, at which point Gosch himself died of a heart attack. Little, Brown published *The Last Testament of Lucky Luciano* in 1975.

The book answered the question Rosie Reles had asked outside the Half Moon Hotel thirty-four years earlier: *Who did it, who did it?* Or it seemed to, anyway. In the course of the interviews Luciano recalled Frank Costello coming up to Dannemora prison in 1941 to break the news that Reles was cooperating with the Brooklyn district attorney. "The cocksucker's got a memory like an elephant and a voice like a canary," Luciano recalled Costello saying. "He just keeps vomiting stuff up like he can't stop puking."

If Bugsy Siegel and Albert Anastasia were to avoid the electric chair, Luciano concluded, Reles would have to die. "They've got Reles surrounded by cops day and night," Costello said. "The cops will have to do it for us."

"So let 'em do it," Luciano said. "I don't give a fuck what it costs— pay it." According to Luciano's version of events, the Commission paid

Captain Frank Bals $50,000. He directed a guard to hit Reles with a billy club while he slept. They then heaved his unconscious body out the window, along with his bedsheets.

Luciano's account might have resolved the longstanding Reles riddle once and for all except that questions arose about the book's veracity even before it arrived in stores. Passages contradicted verifiable facts. The book quotes Luciano as saying that he participated in meetings that occurred while he was in jail. In at least one instance Luciano discusses events that took place two years after his death. "The publisher's assertion that what we are getting here is the entire Luciano story from the master criminal himself is inadequately supported by the evidence, [and it] seems pretty ridiculous as one reads the book . . ." Thomas Plate wrote in *The New York Times Book Review*. To make matters worse, no tapes of the interviews existed, and Gosch's widow had inexplicably destroyed the notes, if they ever existed. Rather than resolve questions about Reles, *The Last Testament of Lucky Luciano* contributed its own layer of doubt and mystery.

Each generation has since installed its own mythology to organized crime—*The Godfather, Goodfellas, The Sopranos, Boardwalk Empire,* and now *The Irishman*. Within all the versions and variations lies the unavoidable human truth stated by Abe Reles seventy-nine years ago: the squealer must go.

ACKNOWLEDGMENTS

Writing a book—any book—is a solitary trudge beset with stumbles and setbacks. I want to express gratitude to those who helped show the way. First and foremost, sincerest thanks to Charles Spicer and Andrew Martin of Minotaur Books for their enthusiasm and steady hands. I also thank their colleagues Sarah Grill, Hector DeJean, Joe Brosnan, Kayla Janas, Michael Criscitelli, Paul Hochman, John Morrone, and David Rotstein.

Particular thanks go to my agent, Joy Harris, for her wisdom and support.

The good folks at Harvest housed and fed me for the duration of one and a half books. I'm grateful for their generosity and good-heartedness.

My thanks to my friends Crary Pullen, Michael Weschler, Jonathan Liss, and Gary Nadeau for their visual storytelling. Ted Mooney deserves mention for clarifying and enriching my sentences and paragraphs.

Stephen H. Clark, Elisabeth Cannell, and James O'Neill, retired NYPD, read the manuscript for clarity and accuracy. I thank them for their feedback.

I extend my appreciation as well to the Dolph Briscoe Center for American History at the University of Texas at Austin, and its fine staff, for granting me access to their priceless archive of newspaper clips. Ellen Belcher at the Lloyd Sealy Library at the John Jay College of Criminal Justice graciously made rare papers and photographs available to me. The New York City Municipal Archives is a treasure, and I thank its staff for doing so much with so little. "History wanted to be remembered," the novelist Rivers Solomon once wrote. "Evidence hated having to live in dark, hidden places and devoted itself to resurfacing."

NOTES

PROLOGUE: "SOMETHING HAS HAPPENED"

1 "Waves of anger and fear": W. H. Auden, *Collected Longer Poems* (New York: Random House, 1969), 253.

2 "Something has happened": William A. Nicholson, Statement to Brooklyn Assistant District Attorney Edward S. Silver, March 28, 1951.

3 "Probably the worst ring of killers in American history": "A Stool Pigeon's Fatal Revenge," *New York Journal-American*, August 19, 1944.

5 "Left behind so peculiar, astonishing, remarkable, weird": Burton B. Turkus and Sid Feder, "Complaint Against William O'Dwyer," *St. Louis Post-Dispatch*, February 27, 1958.

I: SCHLAMMERS

9 "He spoke . . . with an impediment": "Reles Admits 10 Murders, Squeals on Strauss, Buggsy," *Brooklyn Daily Eagle*, September 16, 1940.

11 "More guys carried guns": Al Hirshberg and Sammy Aaronson, *As High As My Heart: The Sammy Aaronson Story* (New York: Coward-McCann, 1957), 24.

13 "The gangster discovered, overnight": Hickman Powell, *Lucky Luciano: His Amazing Trial and Wild Witnesses* (Secaucus, NJ: Citadel Press, 1975), xxii.

14 "Forget it": Michael O'Brien, "Brother Slain in Ambush Prepared for Racket King," *Daily News*, July 12, 1931.

15 "Punch-drunk Irving Shapiro": Ibid.

16 "Some detective will put a bullet in you": Jay Maeder, "Big Town," *Daily News*, June 7, 1998.

16 "All cops are yellow": "Guards Demoted in Reles Escape," *New York Times*, November 14, 1941.

2: BABYLON BROOKLYN

19 "I'm Rothstein": "Rothstein a Power in Gambling World," *New York Times*, November 7, 1928.

19 "I was shot": Donald Henderson Clarke, *In the Reign of Rothstein* (Ann Arbor: Michigan Publishing, 2005), 286.

19 "You stick to your trade" Ibid.

20 "You start stealing and you see how": Joseph Freeman, "How Murder, Inc. Trains Killers," *American Mercury*, October 1940, 156.

21 "An outlaw frontier": Malcolm Johnson, "Crime on the Waterfront," *New York Sun*, November 8, 1948.

21 "Albert is the head guy on the docks": Burton B. Turkus and Sid Feder, *Murder Inc.: The Inside Story of the Mob* (New York: Manor Books, 1971), 468.

22 "With him it was always kill, kill, kill,": Peter Maas, *The Valachi Papers* (New York: Putnam's, 1968), 206.

23 "All the time he talk about money": Freeman, "How Murder, Inc. Trains Killers," 159.

24 "Don't butt in": "Gang Feud Feared as Bullets Fell 3," *Daily News*, June 4, 1930.

26 "Gangland is due for the lesson that it can never": "Launch Brooklyn Anti-Gang War," *Daily News*, June 12, 1930.

27 "If you wanted someone to help you": Al Hirshberg and Sammy Aaronson, *As High As My Heart: The Sammy Aaronson Story* (New York: Coward-McCann, 1957), 42.

28 "The impact jerked his head back": Burton B. Turkus and Sid Feder, *Murder, Inc.: The Inside Story of the Mob* (New York: Manor Books, 1971), 116.

29 "Gentlemen . . . you have let three killers go": "Jury Acquits Trio, But Court Jails Two," *Brooklyn Daily Eagle*, April 20, 1932.

30 "The White Lights of Broadway": "Gang Roundup Saves Czar of Brownsville Racketeers," [Brooklyn] *Standard Union*, September 10, 1931.

30 "Glanced insolently around the place": "Racket Chief Slain After 18 Attempts," *New York Times*, September 18, 1931.

31 "It stinks, . . . but I own it": Jay Maeder, "From 'Murder Inc,'" *Daily News*, June 3, 2001.

32 "Hey Jake, you've got a pistol": John Gardner, "Did Abe Reles Fall or Was He Pushed?" *Daily News*, April 8, 1951.

33 "There's one rap you can't hang on me": Ibid.

3: THE COMMISSION

38 "Droop-eyed and unwholesomely dark": "The Great Luciano Is At Last in Toils," *New York Times*, April 12, 1936.

38 "A neat, quiet man with a tired, good-looking face": Ian Fleming, "In and Around Brazen Naples," *Sunday Times,* August 28, 1960.

38 "I explained to them that we were in a business": Martin A. Gosch and Richard Hammer, "The Lucky Luciano Confessions," *Penthouse*, October 1974, 57.

39 "100 most influential business geniuses of the century": Edna Buchanan, *Time,* December 7, 1998, 130.

39 "I don't need the money": Gosch and Hammer, "The Lucky Luciano Confessions," 57.

4: MURDER FOR MONEY

41 "A quiet-spoken little man who padded": "Fantastic Crime Network Is At Last Exposed," *Daily Mirror*, August 27, 1939.

41 "A quiet fellow with an almost apologetic manner": Al Binder and Howard Whitman, "Mob Bought Girl, Held Her Love Captive," *Daily News,* April 6, 1940.

41 "There was sinister magic in the name Lepke": Meyer Berger, "Lepke: The Shy Boss of Bloody Murder, Inc Awaits Death in the Electric Chair," *Life*, February 28, 1944, 87.

43 "Murder, Inc deals out death-on-the-dotted-line": United Press, "Murder, Inc., Story Makes Old Thrillers Seem Tame," *Pittsburgh Press,* March 25, 1940.

43 "The punk is subject to call": Joseph Freeman, "How Murder, Inc. Trains Killers," *American Mercury*, October 1940, 160.

47 "the Beau Brummel of Death": Al Binder and Howard Whitman, "Pittsburgh Phil to 'Sing' for State at Murder Ring Trial, *Daily News*, May 9, 1940.

47 "Look at him": Freeman, "How Murder, Inc. Trains Killers," 159.

47 "The best dresser in Murder, Inc.": John Osnato, "Harpy Heaven," *New York Journal-American*, September 2, 1944.

48 "the Kiss of Death Girl": Joseph McNamara, "Tootsie," *Daily News*, January 28, 1990.

48 "So I just picked him for myself": Osnato, "Harpy Heaven." *New York Journal-American*, August 26, 1944.

48 "continually nagged [Strauss] about his uncouthness": Ibid.

49 "Suddenly, he drove his car right onto the sidewalk": James Boyle, grand jury testimony, November 8, 1951.

50 "My mother came out and asked him in Jewish": Rose Reles, statement to Brooklyn Assistant District Attorney Edward S. Silver, April 26, 1951.

50 "The only way I can escape arrest": "Held in 'Mistake Murder,' Reles Jokes of 13th Jinx," *Daily News*, April 12, 1934.

50 "Abe Reles Is Public Enemy Number One": "Judge Calls Gangster Public Enemy No. 1, He Dismisses Charges," *New York Age*, October 13, 1934.

50 "There are eighteen thousand policemen in our department": Ibid.

51 "This man is as bad as [John] Dillinger": "'Bad as Dillinger,' Judge Calls Reles in Rebuke to Jury," *Brooklyn Daily Eagle*, May 9, 1934.

52 "His whole body was shaking": Minnie Jones statement to Assistant District Attorney Burton Turkus, January 16, 1942.

53 "The papers list me as Public Enemy No. 6": "2 of Reles Mob Held as Killers of Joe Amberg," *Brooklyn Daily Eagle*, December 4, 1935.

53 "Sol is away from the tough boys at last": Burton B. Turkus and Sid Feder, *Murder Inc.: The Inside Story of the Mob* (New York: Manor Books, 1971), 208.

54 "For four long years, mystery and silence": Ibid.

55 "I happened to be in a club one night": Robert A. Rockaway, *But He Was Good to His Mother* (Jerusalem: Gefen, 2000), 211.

55 "I can't understand this": "1 Doorman at Downtown Cabaret Blown to Death by Bomb Meant for Millman, Ex-Purple Gangster," *Detroit Free Press*, August 30, 1937.

57 "The idea . . . is to keep the men poor": Malcolm Johnson and Budd Schulberg, *On the Waterfront: The Pulitzer Prize-Winning Articles That Inspired the Classic Film and Transformed the New York Harbor* (New York: Chamberlain Brothers, 2005), 53.

57 "All we have to do": Nathan Ward, *Dark Harbor: The War for the New York Waterfront* (New York: Farrar, Straus and Giroux, 1951), 6.

58 "I'm going to meet a couple of guys": "'Where-Is-Panto' Slogan Vanishes But His Union Revolt Gains Strength," *Brooklyn Daily Eagle*, January 30, 1941.

59 "I am a poor girl": "Worried Girl Pleads for Missing Fiance," *Brooklyn Daily Eagle*, August 16, 1939.

60 "This guy Puggy kept on fighting and kicking": Al Binder and Jack Turcott, "Reles Calls 2 Old Pals His 'Helpers' in Killing," *Daily News*, September 17, 1940.

60 "I was going to move out of there anyhow": Ibid.

61 "Strauss told Buggsy that he was useless": "This Business of Murdering People Bared," *San Bernardino County Sun,* September 17, 1940.

5: TWENTY AGAINST THE UNDERWORLD

65 "threw open the door": "La Guardia Sits as a Magistrate to Reopen War on Slot Machines," *New York Times,* February 17, 1934.

65 "The flaming torch of reform": Paul Sann, *Kill the Dutchman!* (Bridgeport, CT: Birdye's Books, 2015) 201.

66 "As you were": Ibid.

67 "that everything will be all right": Ibid.

67 "No, sir": Ibid.

67 "Get busy and arrest these racketeers": Ibid.

69 "It has become evident to us": Sloan Taylor, "Lehman Ousts Hines as Vice Prosecutor," *Daily News,* June 25, 1935.

70 "The news of Lehman's announcement": Thomas E. Dewey, *Twenty Against the Underworld* (New York: Doubleday, 1974), 151.

70 "If he makes good": J. L. Pickering, "No Noise, Lots of Racket," *Detroit Free Press,* August 11, 1935.

70 "The Young David": Rupert Hughes, *The Story of Thomas E. Dewey: Attorney for the People* (New York: Grosset and Dunlap, 1944), 60.

70 "cold, cold as a February icicle": Geoffrey C. Ward, "Republican Loser," *New York Times,* August 22, 1982.

71 "To tackle the big city he was equipped with": Hickman Powell, *Lucky Luciano: His Amazing Trial and Wild Witnesses* (Secaucus, NJ: Citadel Press, 1975), 46.

72 "the heart of this nation is": John Gunther, *Inside the U.S.A.* (New York: The New Press, 1997), 523.

72 "As you retire to your room": Robert Weldon Whalen, *Murder, Inc. and the Moral Life* (New York: Empire State, 2016), 103.

72 "It is my firm conviction": Meyer Berger, "Waxy Gordon Convicted," *New York Times,* December 2, 1933.

73 "to destroy organized crime and racketeering": Whalen, *Murder, Inc. and the Moral Life,* 106.

73 "They felt it safer to pay taxes": Hughes, *The Story of Thomas E. Dewey,* 60.

73 "In less than an hour he raked me fore and aft": Dewey, *Twenty Against the Underworld,* 2.

74 "Any man who comes to see us": Victor H. Bernstein, "Attacks on Rackets Planned in Secret," *New York Times*, August 4, 1935.

75 "To me he always appeared slightly haggard": Harold R. Danforth and James D. Horan, *The D.A.'s Man* (New York: Permabook, 1959), 58.

75 "had eyes like peeled grapes": Jim Bishop, "Reporter," *Lancaster Eagle-Gazette*, December 18, 1957.

76 "Your verdict is such that it shakes the confidence": Associated Press, "Federal Court Jury Acquits Schultz of Income Tax Charges," *Post-Star*, August 2, 1935.

77 "If New York thinks he's so dangerous": "Schultz Is Free; Judge Excoriates Jury of Farmers," *New York Times*, August 2, 1935.

77 "He won't be a resident of New York City": "Schultz Reported on His Way Here," *New York Times*, August 3, 1935.

77 "So there isn't room for me in New York": Ibid.

77 "It's a boy, and it's mine, alright": "Schultz and Gang Face Police Drive," *New York Times*, August 4, 1935.

77 "I'm thinking now about all our other little babies": "Schultz Snarls," *New York Journal-American*, August 5, 1935.

78 "The success of our investigations": "Schultz and Gang Face Police Drive," *New York Times*, August 4, 1935.

79 "We'll have the whole world around our ears": Meyer Berger, "The Shy Boss of Bloody Murder, Inc. Awaits Death in the Electric Chair," *Life*, February 28, 1944, 82.

79 "No witnesses": Paul Sann, *Kill the Dutchman!* (New York: Arlington House, 1971) 123.

79 "One jerk at his vest and he had it in his hand": J. Richard "Dixie" Davis, "Things I Couldn't Tell Till Now," *Collier's*, July 22, 1939, 9.

81 "He was reeling like he was intoxicated": Graham K. Bell, *Murder, Inc.: The Mafia's Hit Men in New York City* (Charleston, SC: The History Press, 2010), 40.

81 "Get a doctor": J. Anne Funderburg, *Bootleggers and Beer Barons of the Prohibition Era* (Jefferson, NC: McFarland, 2014), 135.

81 "Send me an ambulance": "Triple Zero," *Time*, November 4, 1935, 135.

82 "I'd rather you have this than the State": "Dutch Tosses Grand to Ambulance Man," *Daily News*, October 25, 1935.

82 "His chance of recovery": "Dutch Schultz Is Near Death; Shot in Battle," *Montreal Gazette*, October 24, 1935.

82 "I don't know why anyone would do this": Associated Press, "Dutch Schultz Shot by Rival Gunmen; Rest of Mob Hides," *New York Telegram*, October 24, 1935.

83 "Q: Who shot you?": George Cohen, "When Crime Was a Spectator Sport and Mobsters the Stars," *Chicago Tribune*, May 4, 1975.

83 "As we have often noted": Walter Winchell, *Winchell Exclusive* (New York: Prentice-Hall, 1975), 117.

84 "As ye sow": David Camelon, "The Numbers Racket," *Cincinnati Enquirer*, October 2, 1949.

84 "as if he had slept in his clothes": George Dixon, "Girl Says She Hid the Bug on Night 'He Got Schultz,'" *Daily News*, June 8, 1941.

85 "was as complex a man as ever worked": Joseph McNamara, "All in a Day's Work," *Daily News*, January 13, 1991.

86 "Oh, that's a waste of time": Dewey, *Twenty Against the Underworld*, 5.

88 "They worked us like dogs": Ibid., 189.

88 "Witnesses would have done": Ibid., 7.

89 "If I talked, they'd slit my throat": Ibid., 194.

89 "Plenty of girls who talked": Sid Feder, *The Luciano Story* (New York: Da Capo Press, 1994), 124.

90 "Look out there": Ibid., 138.

90 "Congrats but why didn't you": "When the Playboys Were Away, the Page-Boys Played—And How!" *Philadelphia Inquirer*, May 12, 1935.

90 "He had a flashing white smile": Hickman Powell, *Lucky Luciano: His Amazing Trial and Wild Witnesses* (Secaucus, NJ: Citadel Press, 1975), 76.

92 "Anger flooded [Luciano's] face a deeper shade": Meyer Berger, "The Great Luciano Is at Last in Toils," *New York Times*, April 12, 1936.

92 "To have the hated prosecutor reach across": Ibid.

93 "Luciano was uncommunicative": "Luciano, Back, Held in Bail of $350,000," *Brooklyn Daily Eagle*, April 19, 1936.

93 "He was watched through the day": Ibid.

94 "You naughty boy to be in here": Russ Symontowne, "Booker's Wife Bares Lucky's Debt 'Slavery,'" *Daily News*, May 29, 1936.

95 "When a week goes by and still no word": "Big Hotel Suite Lucania's Office," *New York Times*, May 24, 1936.

96 "we ought to fold up for a while": Russ Symontowne, "Giant Vice Chain Aim of Luciano, " *Daily News*, May 23, 1936.

96 "cobra-eyed": Russ Symontowne, "Luciano and Eight Guilty, Face Life as Vice Lords," *Daily News*, June 8, 1936.

96 "A quarter of a grain of morphine": United Press, "Cokey Flo Links Luciano in Proposal for 'Vice Chain,'" [Rochester, NY] *Democrat and Chronicle*, May 23, 1936.

96 "I'm just talking slow so I can get": Ibid.

96 "the man with the yellow pencil": Associated Press, "Luciano Planned Chain of Vice, Madam Claims, *The Record*, May 23, 1936.

96 "cut me up so my own mother": "'Friend' of Lucania Acts as Accuser," *New York Times,* May 26, 1936.

97 "I knew what happened to people": Associated Press, "Vice Ring Tactics Bared by Model," *Baltimore Sun,* May 26, 1936.

97 "their pictures would be sent": "'Friend' of Lucania Acts as Accuser."

97 "I won't tell you": Associated Press, "Vice Ring Tactics Bared by Model," *Baltimore Sun,* May 26, 1936.

97 "I have talked to the witness": Ibid.

98 "I certainly expect to be acquitted": "Death Threat Told at Luciano Trial," *New York Times*, May 30, 1936.

98 "I don't want her mixed up in this case": Dorothy Roe, "Luciano All Mixed Up on Vice Role Denials," *San Francisco Chronicle*, June 4, 1936.

98 "Cool as a cucumber": Ibid.

98 "I looked over and watched that little bastard": Martin A. Gosch and Richard Hammer, "The Lucky Luciano Confessions," *Penthouse,* October 1974, 104.

98 "His hoarse whisper of scorn": Jack Alexander, "Tom Dewey," *Life,* October 31, 1938, 54.

99 "may have lied a little": " I'm Gambler, Not White Slaver, He Says," *San Francisco Examiner*, June 4, 1936.

99 "I was hunting pheasants": Associated Press, "Luciano, on Stand, Denies Connection with Vice Ring, *The Record*, June 4, 1936.

99 "With rapier-like verbal thrusts": Russ Symontowne, "Luciano Cringes on Stand, Admits 'Record' Under Fire," *Daily News*, June 4, 1936.

99 "You just picked those figures on your income out of the sky": Feder, *The Luciano Story*, 78.

100 I felt like I'd been through a washing machine": Martin A. Gosch and Richard Hammer, *The Last Testament of Lucky Luciano* (New York: Little, Brown, 1975), 218.

100 "you must give her story the same weight": Associated Press, "Special Jury Is Given Case," *Huntsville Times*, June 7, 1936.

101 "their quivering, shifty faces registering": Russ Symontowne, "Lucky Guilty," *Daily News*, June 8, 1936.

101 "The top Mafia leader": Dewey, *Twenty Against the Underworld*, 264.

6: LEPKE

106 "That bastard Rosen is going around Brownsville": Meyer Berger, "The Shy Boss of Bloody Murder, Inc. Awaits Death in the Electric Chair," *Life*, February 28, 1944, 82.

107 "I know why they killed him": Al Binder and Howard Whitman, "Strauss, Due to Sing, Can't Find His Voice," *Daily News*, May 10, 1940

107 "A man was murdered by gangsters Sunday": "Reles Thugs Arrest Just a Precaution," *Brooklyn Daily Eagle*, September 15, 1936.

108 "I sneak away from the cops": Burton B. Turkus and Sid Feder, *Murder, Inc.: The Inside Story of the Mob* (New York: Manor Books, 1971), 349.

110 "We didn't know how to adjust the ribbon": "Reles Depicts Brutal Slaying for Gang Jury," *Brooklyn Daily Eagle*, May 15, 1940.

110 "We knew we would catch him": Ibid.

110 "I spotted Rudnick coming along Saratoga Ave": Ibid.

111 "I knocked on the garage door": "Reles Admits Five Murders as He Sings at Mob Trial," *Daily News*, May 15, 1940.

111 "I went in and Strauss had an icepick in his hand": Ibid.

112 "Things are getting too hot": Turkus and Feder, *Murder, Inc.*, 350.

113 "He read magazines, hundreds of magazines": Milton Walker, statement to Assistant District Attorney Frank Hogan, November 30, 1940.

113 "Let them find me first": Winchell, *Winchell Exclusive* (New York: Prentice-Hall, 1975), 134.

113 "Give him some books and magazines": Turkus and Feder, *Murder, Inc*, 357.

114 "What does the bum think?": Ibid., 45.

116 "Think of that": Ibid., 47.

116 "It was an apparition": Ibid., 48.

117 "Things are very very hot around here": Berger, "The Shy Boss of Bloody Murder, Inc.," 90.

117 "Lepke, I want to come home": "Lepke's Ex-Aide Tells of Threat," *New York Times*, November 4, 1941.

119 "The fight against crime is begun": Guy Richards, "Dewey Warns Crooks He'll Ride 'Em Hard," *Daily News*, November 3, 1937.

119 "Murder is safe in Brooklyn": Craig Thompson, "Geoghan His Topic," *New York Times*, November 1, 1938.

120 "I can furnish you with valuable information": "Dope Role of Murder Inc Told by Harry Anslinger," *San Bernardino County Sun*, January 18, 1962.

120 "And come alone, buster": Andrew Tully, *Treasury Agent* (New York: Simon and Schuster, 1958), 75.

121 "Day after day men would disappear": "Dope Role of Murder Inc."

122 "I'm tired of the government being so close": John Crossen and Gerald Duncan, "Gurrah Gives Up, Tired of Dodging as Public Enemy," *Daily News*, April 15, 1938.

123 "In court the big ox bawled like a baby": Jay Maeder, "Big Town, Big Time," *Daily News*, May 29, 1998.

124 "Shoot them twice in the back of the neck": Michael O'Brien and George Dixon, "Killer Dies as He Slew—Two Slugs in Neck," *Daily News*, January 11, 1939.

126 "There are persons to whose interest": Rob Roberts, "Racket Smashing Is Fun," *Akron Beacon Journal*, June 25, 1939.

126 "a toad-like little man with amazingly large bags": "Jack the Dandy," *Time*, April 24, 1950, 28.

127 "I don't know of any prosecution which has been attended": "Killings Revealed in the Lepke Case," *New York Times*, June 14, 1939.

128 "had not an enemy in the world": Jack Turcott, "$25,000 Reward for Lepke Given Mayor's Support," *Daily News*, July 30, 1939.

128 "If the killing off of witnesses continues": Harry J. Anslinger and Will Oursler, "Murder, Inc., Chief Key Man in World Narcotic Syndicate," *The Pentagraph*, January 18, 1962.

128 "It is apparent that the Lepke mob is waging a war": John Crosson and Gerald Duncan, "Five Murders Spur Dewey in Lepke War," *Daily News*, July 29, 1939.

128 "to avoid being murdered by his own partner": Ibid.

130 "They'll force Lepke to take the rap": Maeder, "Big Town, Big Time."

130 "Those bastards are more interested": Turkus and Feder, *Murder Inc.*, 357.

131 "He demanded to know what they were doing": Bernard Weinraub, "He Turned Gossip into Tawdry Power," *New York Times*, November 18, 1998.

132 "We can't even make a two-dollar bet": Winchell, *Winchell Exclusive*, 134.

132 "not a gangster": Ibid., 135.

132 "I have something important to tell you": Ibid., 135.

133 "I know Lepke a long time": Ibid., 145.

134 "Hoover wanted Lepke badly": Curt J. Gentry, *J. Edgar Hoover: The Man and the Secrets* (New York: W. W. Norton, 1991), 219.

134 "This is a lot of bunk, Walter": Billy Rose, "Pitching Horseshoes," *The* [Davenport, IA] *Daily Times,* June 12, 1947, 30.

134 "Don't be nervous": Ibid.

134 "Tell him to be at Twenty-eighth Street": Ibid.

134 "Mr. Hoover . . . this is Lepke": Jay Maeder, "The Canary That Couldn't Fly: Abe Reles and Murder Incorporated," *Daily News*, August 14, 2017.

135 "This is Winchell": Jay Maeder, "Why a Murderous Crime Boss, Louis Lepke, Surrendered to Gossip Columnist Walter Winchell and the FBI," *Daily News*, August 14, 2017.

7: BILL-O

137 "Now don't misunderstand me": "Scarcity of Crime Worries Geoghan," *New York Times,* May 18, 1938.

138 "spawned more gangsters and criminals": "O'Dwyer Pushes Drive on Brooklyn Rackets," *New York Times*, February 4, 1940.

139 "His voice is deep and authoritative": "O'Dwyer," *New York Times,* November 2, 1941.

139 "I loved the world of trees and bogs and starry nights": Philip Hamburger, "That Great Big City of New York Up There," *New Yorker*, September 28, 1957, 47.

139 "possibly nature's worst student": Oral history interview with William O'Dwyer, July 1960, Butler Library, Columbia University.

139 "I was much more addicted to my bicycle": Ibid.

139 "I wanted to commit sins if I felt like it": "New York: Big Bonanza," *Time,* June 7, 1948, 64.

140 "It looked like a piece of magic": Oral history interview with William O'Dwyer.

140 "Being alone in the city": Ibid.

140 "You get to know the town that way": Associated Press, "Murder Syndicate Quiz Reveals Sordid Saga," *Salt Lake Tribune,* March 31, 1940.

141 "holding the leg of a steer": "New York: Big Bonanza," 26.

142 "I always knew he'd be a lawyer": Alice Cogan, "Kitty O'Dwyer Sheds Tears of Joy as Her Bill Comes Through Again," *Brooklyn Daily Eagle*, November 8, 1939.

142 "I hope that at times Providence": "Former Policeman Begins Duties as City Magistrate," *Brooklyn Daily Eagle*, December 9, 1932.

142 "Have you ever seen a boy when he": Associated Press, "Murder Syndicate Quiz."

143 "I decided then . . . that the most dangerous": Samuel Crowther, "Judge O'Dwyer Meets Jim Moran," *New York Journal-American*, May 26, 1952.

143 "Everybody criticized law enforcement in Brooklyn": Associated Press, "Murder Syndicate Quiz."

143 "I never could keep up with Bill": Alice Cogan, "Mrs. William O'Dwyer," *Brooklyn Daily Eagle*, October 31, 1941.

143 "Oh, I'm so happy for you": Cogan, "Kitty O'Dwyer Sheds Tears of Joy."

8: THE WEDGE

146 "He doesn't conform to the general pattern of the prosecutor": Richard Cohen, *Tough Jews: Fathers, Sons, and Gangster Dreams* (New York: Vintage Books, 1999), 215.

146 "It was a blighted area, a pesthole": Burton B. Turkus and Sid Feder, *Murder, Inc.: The Inside Story of the Mob* (New York: Manor Books, 1971), 23.

146 "Take a list of two hundred murders": Ibid.

146 "Toughs were yanked unceremoniously: Ibid, 28.

147 "You've got one hell of a nerve": "Reles, Two of Gang, Indicted in Killing as O'Dwyer Acts," *New York Times*, February 3, 1940.

147 "If O'Dwyer don't stop pushing us around": William O'Dwyer, *Beyond the Golden Door* (Jamaica, NY: St. John's University, 1987), 154.

148 "All it takes is a break from within": Burton Turkus and Sid Feder, "The Story of the Syndicate Murder Inc.," *St. Louis Post-Dispatch* February 16, 1958.

148 "a face like a shore dinner": "Bill O'Dwyer: The Man Who Smashed Murder, Inc," *New York World-Telegram*, August 3, 1941.

148 "I would like to talk to the district attorney": Burton Turkus and Sid Feder, "Murder, Inc.," *Advocate-Messenger*, November 29, 1951.

148 "Those rats killed my friend": Ibid.

149 "I want them at my office": Turkus and Feder, *Murder, Inc.*, 32.

149 "My Abie always was a good boy": John Gardner, "Did Abe Reles Fall or Was He Pushed?" *Daily News,* April 8, 1951.

150 "You'll have to wait your turn": "3 Gang Leaders Jailed in Murder," *Daily News,* February 24, 1940.

150 "I don't even need no lawyer": O'Dwyer, *Beyond the Golden Door,* 157.

151 "My mother will get you five thousand bucks": "Gang Tries to Bribe O'Dwyer Witness," *Brooklyn Daily Eagle,* March 19, 1940.

151 "only the first step": "O'Dwyer Pushes Drive on Brooklyn Rackets." *New York Times,* February 4, 1940.

151 "a hard-boiled flyweight": Victor Weingarten, "Stole Death Car, Maffetore Admits," *Brooklyn Daily Eagle,* May 14, 1940.

152 "The stool pigeon may be a cheap crook": John Osnato, "A Stool Pigeon's Fatal Revenge," *Tampa Bay Times,* August 20, 1944.

153 "a vain, sullen, moronic type": Ibid.

153 "I know the mug that turned you in": "What Makes a Successful Detective?" *New York Times,* September 10, 1944.

154 "I love my wife": Robert Musel, "Death on the Dotted Line," *Vancouver Sun,* April 13, 1940.

155 "What can the kid tell them?": Clifford Evans, "Ears to the Ground," *Brooklyn Daily Eagle,* February 24, 1940.

156 "What's this all about": "Death Ring Head Near Arrest," *New York Journal-American,* March 18, 1940.

156 "You have the key to her cell": Turkus and Feder, *Murder, Inc.,* 43.

157 "We undoubtedly saved both Levine and Maffetore": Ibid.

158 "the most important cleanup": "Grill Louis Capone on Murder Ring," *Brooklyn Daily Eagle,* March 18, 1940.

158 "You'll get a kick out of this": Associated Press, "Actor, 10 Others Held as Murder-to-Order Suspects," *The* [Monroe, LA] *News-Star,* March 18, 1940.

159 "are scared to plow their land": "Police Probe Ramifications of Murder-for-Hire Combine," *Journal and Courier,* March 19, 1940.

159 "I have never seen such clear": Associated Press, "Ten Under Arrest on Murder Charge," *New York Daily Record,* March 18, 1940.

159 "I have an idea . . . that the electric chair": Associated Press, "Fantastic Ring of Murderers Is Uncovered," *El Paso Times,* March 18, 1940.

159 "No convictions could be obtained": Turkus and Feder, *Murder, Inc.,* 49.

9: LONG SONG

162 "For ten straight days and nights": Associated Press, "Murder Syndicate Quiz Reveals Sordid Saga," *Salt Lake Tribune,* March 31, 1940.

163 "Unless we get a top mobster who had all the answers": Turkus and Feder, *Murder, Inc.,* 52.

164 "It is no secret": Jack Mahon, "Writer Tells How O'Dwyer Made Abe Reles Talk Freely," [Richmond, IN] *Palladium-Item*, December 4, 1941.

164 "I want to save my husband from the electric chair": Turkus and Feder, *Murder, Inc.,* 49.

164 "as nonchalantly as a celebrity": Ibid., 52.

164 "We were cautious": Nathan Ward, *Dark Harbor: The War for the New York Waterfront* (New York: Farrar, Straus and Giroux, 1951*),* 11.

164 "He was a chunky little tough": Emily Cheney, "Only Human," *New York Mirror*, March 17, 1944.

165 "I sent out for a sandwich and coffee": William O'Dwyer, *Beyond the Golden Door* (Jamaica, NY: St. John's University, 1987), 158.

165 "He was a dirty-faced little man": Oral history interview with William O'Dwyer, July 1960, Butler Library, Columbia University.

165 "There was something about Reles's physical": Richard Cohen, *Tough Jews: Fathers, Sons, and Gangster Dreams* (New York: Vintage Books, 1999), 212.

165 "Didn't your conscience bother you?": Burton Turkus and Sid Feder, "Killer Forces Tough Deal on O'Dwyer," *Pittsburgh Press*, December 7, 1951.

165 "I could make a monkey out of him": Turkus and Feder, *Murder, Inc.,* 51.

165 "You can't touch me on that one": Ibid.

166 "But . . . I'm the guy who can tell": Cohen, *Tough Jews,* 212.

166 "He had escaped the law for a long time": Oral history interview with William O'Dwyer.

166 "I could tell you plenty": O'Dwyer, *Beyond the Golden Door*, 158.

166-167 "If I find that you're lying": U.S. Congress, Senate, Special Committee to Investigate Organized Crime in Interstate Commerce, Eighty-first Congress, March 19, 1951.

167 "They'll get me if I'm in the clink": O'Dwyer, *Beyond the Golden Door*, 158.

167 "I might give a break to a poor slob": "Grill Mystery Woman in 3 Slayings," *Brooklyn Daily Eagle,* March 22, 1940.

167 "The pudgy-faced young thug": "Little Guy Ready to Squeal on Bosses in Murder Ring," *Brooklyn Daily Eagle,* March 25, 1940.

168 "It would be an outrage if he were released": Associated Press, "3 in Murder Ring Divulge Details," *Baltimore Sun,* March 26, 1940.

168 "He gulped and meekly acquiesced": Ibid.

169 "talked fast in an effort to save their skins": Associated Press, "3 in Murder Ring."

170 "Rattled off names, places, facts": Turkus and Feder, *Murder, Inc.,* 65.

170 "Like the Lehman Banks": Alfred R Lindesmith, *Annals of the American Academy of Political and Social Science,* September 1941, 119.

172 "I think there's six or eight stiffs": Turkus and Feder, *Murder, Inc.,* 472.

172 "Gee, I hated to take that kid": Ibid.

172 "This trick of getting cheap publicity": "O'Dwyer Is Guarded Against Murder Mob," *Brooklyn Daily Eagle,* March 29, 1940.

172 "deliver Peter Panto": Ibid.

173 "I am working on more than thirty-five": Associated Press, "3 in Murder Ring."

174 "until the heat is off": "3 Frosches Fixers in Death Ring," *New York Journal-American,* March 20, 1940.

174 "You're a sucker if you tell your wife": Ibid.

174 "I was praying the police": Al Binder and Howard Whitman, "Suspect's Cries in Cell Bare Plot to Kill Murder Ring Witnesses," *Daily News,* March 29, 1940.

174 "Put me back in jail": "3 Frosches Fixers."

174 "I'm working on it, Albert": Turkus and Feder, *Murder, Inc.,* 465.

175 "I didn't ask for the bodyguards": "3 Frosches Fixers."

175 "A perfect mating of Beauty and Beast": Turkus and Feder, *Murder, Inc.,* 114.

175 "remained an unsolved mystery": Ibid, 193.

175 "triggerman still skulking in Brooklyn's underworld": "O'Dwyer Is Guarded Against Murder Mob."

176 "With her husband hunted throughout": Inez Robb, "Murder Inc., Girls Unable to Patronize Beauty Shops," *St. Petersburg Times,* April 30, 1940.

176 "disappear in one way or another": United Press, "Death Kiss in Murder Inc Ascribed to Young Woman," *Democrat and Chronicle,* April 2, 1940.

177 "they sat about and debated whether to buy or bury her": United Press, "Again, Murder List Up to 20," *Des Moines Register,* April 7, 1940.

177 "Or from dashing around the corner": Robb, "Murder Inc., Girls."

178 "I told him I didn't say nothing": Victor Weingarten, "Liberto Backs Killing Story of Two Gang Accomplices," *Brooklyn Daily Eagle*, May 17, 1940.

178 "Skull and crossbones ensign of the underworld": "Jury Launches Investigation in Murder Ring": *Brooklyn Citizen*, April 1, 1940.

179 "He did not, in advance, give the effect": I. Kaufman, "Brother's Murder by Bandits Recalled in O'Dwyer Drive," *Brooklyn Daily Eagle*, March 28, 1940.

179 "Dewey . . . has thrown his diaper": Benjamin Stolberg, "Thomas E. Dewey, Self-Made Myth," *American Mercury*, June 1940.

179 "If he gets a reasonable number of convictions": Al Binder and Howard Whitman, "To Jobs by Plane, O'Dwyer Reveals," *Daily News*, April 5, 1940.

182 "The picture begins at 8:30": Quentin Reynolds, *Courtroom: The Story of Samuel S. Leibowitz* (New York: Popular Library, 1957), 230.

182 "Under no circumstances will I defend": "Mother's Pleas Refused," *Brooklyn Daily Eagle*, April 4, 1940.

182 "These men are here for business": "Gunmen Imported to Balk Inquiry, O'Dwyer Declares," *New York Times*, April 4, 1940.

183 "Siegel is here": Ibid.

183 "You don't know those bastards like I do," Turkus and Feder, *Murder, Inc.*, 443.

10: MR. ARSENIC

184 "This first prosecution would be": Turkus and Feder, *Murder, Inc.*, 220.

184 "He has promised to talk": Fred Menagh, "Last Bargain of the Murder Merchant," *Gaffney* [SC] *Ledger*, November 7, 1940.

185 "a song of death": "Reles Depicts Brutal Slaying for Gang Jury," *Brooklyn Daily Eagle*, May 15, 1940.

185 "[Reles's] beady eyes were averted from the cold": Ibid.

186 "like a thick-shouldered alligator": Turkus and Feder, *Murder, Inc.*, 253.

186 "as a pugilist who had been subjected": Ibid.

186 "I saw Strauss take the ice-pick and jam it": "Reles Confesses to Six Murders," *New York Times*, May 16, 1940.

187 "Well, . . . it's not exactly the same thing": "Reles Confesses to Six Murders," *New York Times*, May 16, 1940.

188 "I wanted to go home and go to sleep": Al Binder and Howard Whitman, "Death Car Driver Accuses Maione," *Daily News*, May 17, 1940.

188 "I asked him, 'What the hell is going on over here?'": Ibid.

188 "He made three or four trips": Ibid.

188 "favorite and pet": Victor Weingarten, "Maione Pins His Life on Grandma's Death," *Brooklyn Daily Eagle*, May 20, 1940.

189 "No, I didn't do it": Al Binder and Howard Whitman, "Rocked by Day's Grilling, Mobsters Cling to Tales," *Daily News*, May 22, 1940.

189 "Why don't you ask him that": Christian Cipollini, "Dealing Death in Drag," Mob Museum, March 8, 2019, https://themobmuseum.org/blog/dealing -death-in-drag/.

189 "Don't answer that!": Ibid.

190 "On February 9, 1939, when you were dressed as a woman": Ibid.

190 "This woman was willing to wear garments": Ibid.

190 "She was also pretty sore": John Osnato, "Harpy Heaven," *New York Journal-American*, August 26, 1951.

190 "They're framing me, that's what they're doing": Binder and Whitman, "Rocked by Day's Grilling."

190 "I've known Maione for seven or eight years": Ibid.

191 "Reles is a liar": Ibid.

192 "No, I never played cards with Liberto": Al Binder and Howard Whitman, "Murder Mob Trial Witness Threatened," *Daily News*, May 23, 1940.

192 "fear of Carl": Ibid.

192 "just a big slob": Ibid.

192 "a bunch of vicious, snarling, insolent murderers": Al Binder and Howard Whitman, "Admits Perjury Plot in Murder Mob Trial," *Daily News*, May 23, 1940.

192 "Don't worry about me": Al Binder and Howard Whitman, "Maione, Abbandando Guilty in Gang Killing, *Daily News*, May 24, 1940.

192 "going home to have spaghetti on Sunday": Ibid.

192 "the entire defense toppled like a house": Binder and Whitman, "Rocked by Day's Grilling."

192 "because for three years the police tried to crack": Ibid.

193 "I order you to sit down, Mr. Rosner": Binder and Whitman, "Admits Perjury Plot."

193 "Do justice. . . . Don't compromise": Ibid.

193 "Keep quiet, Harry": Ibid.

193 "I'm sorry": Binder and Whitman, "Maione, Abbandando Guilty."

193 "They showed eyes laden with fear": Ibid.

193 "have told of death for a dollar": Associated Press, "2 Murder, Inc. Men Convicted," *Wilkes-Barre Record,* May 24, 1940.

194 "a most revolting murder": "2 Gang Slayers Sentenced to Die; Lawyers Denounced," *Brooklyn Daily Eagle*, May 27, 1940.

194 "You got here early": Meyer Berger, *The Eight Million: Journal of a New York Correspondent* (New York: Columbia University Press, 1983), 269.

194 "He is a rat": Ibid., 270.

195 "Well, so long Happy": Ibid., 253.

195 "no bigger than a dead man's grave": "Sing Sing was Tough in the '30s," *Washington Times*, May 26, 2005.

196 "This man is lying," Al Binder, "Gangi Sobs as 'Pal' Tells of Pick Slaying," *Daily News*, June 18, 1940.

196 "insufficient to sustain even a disorderly conduct": Associated Press, "Murder Syndicate Defendant Freed," *Baltimore Sun*, June 22, 1940.

196 "If you believe the testimony of Levine": "Defense Counsel Also Weeps During Cohen Summation," *Middletown* [NY] *Times Herald*, June 21, 1940.

196 "His wife, Eva, rushed sobbing": Associated Press, "Irving Cohen, Hollywood Bit Actor, Acquitted of Murder at Monticello," [Glens Falls, NY] *Post-Star*, June 22, 1940.

196 "Congratulations, Gangi": "Gangi Congratulated; Starts for Hollywood," *New York Journal-American*, June 22, 1940.

197 "I thought it was someone else": John Buntin, *L.A. Noir* (New York: Harmony Books, 2009), 88.

198 "I'll have to find a piece of beach": Associated Press, "Irving Cohen, Hollywood Bit Actor, Acquitted of Murder," *Brooklyn Daily Eagle*, August 22, 1940.

199 "I don't want to burn": "Another Gang Chief to Reveal Killing," *New York Sun*, April 17, 1940.

199 "I told her it was hopeless": "Gangster's Wife Pleads," *New York Times*, April 18, 1940.

200 "Take the chains off me": Binder, "Gangi Sobs.'"

200 "You're enough to make a person sick": Ibid.

201 "The thick-lipped tattletale": Al Binder and Jack Turcott, "Reles Puts Finger on 2 Ex-Pals," *Daily News*, September 17, 1940.

201 "It was a job we did for Albert Anastasia": Ibid.

202 "in the prosaic manner of a carpenter": "Reles Admits 10 Murders, Squeals on Strauss, Buggsy," *Brooklyn Daily Eagle*, September 16, 1940.

202 "Harry [Strauss] tried to mug Puggy": United Press, "Executive of Murder, Inc., Accused of Slaying Dishonest Gangster," *San Bernardino County Sun*, September 17, 1940.

202 "This caused [Reles] to shift in his seat": "Reles Confesses 5 More Killings," *New York Times*, September 17, 1940.

202 "How many murders have you committed?": United Press, "Executive of Murder, Inc., Accused of Slaying Dishonest Gangster."

203 "And I killed Plug Schuman and Whitey Friedman and Jack Paley": Ibid.

203 "Seymour, Seymour, tell the truth": Al Binder and Jack Turcott, "Buggsy Sobs as Pal Pins Murder on Him," *Daily News*, September 18, 1940.

203 "Tell them, Seymour": Ibid.

203 "jumped out of Dukey's car, hollered to me, and came over": Ibid.

203 "Then he said to me, 'Dukey and I burned up somebody tonight'": Ibid.

204 "Then came the lobsters": Ibid.

204 "That's a beautiful story he's telling": Ibid.

204 "stared at the clerk with a look of utter": Al Binder and Howard Whitman, "Say Strauss 'Sees' Reles Under Bed," *Daily News*, September 19, 1940.

204 "Take him away": Ibid.

204 "Abe Reles comes under my bed": Ibid.

204 "A second psychiatrist observed": Ibid.

204 "What a state of affairs it is for Reles": Ibid.

204–205 "Now you've seen that I've gone through a veritable hell": Ibid.

205 "The district attorney would love to have Reles seated": Ibid.

205 "That Turkus. They ought to call him Mr. Arsenic": Turkus and Feder, *Murder, Inc.*, 318.

205 "You lie!": Al Binder and Howard Whitman, "Strauss, Goldstein Guilty; to Get Chair," *Daily News*, September 20, 1940.

205 "Hear the sniveling Goldstein now": United Press, "2 of 'Murder, Inc.' Convicted by Jury," *Courier-Post*, September 20, 1940.

205 "The last shred of the big shot was gone": "Parting Shots," *Wilkes-Barre Times Leader*, September 25, 1940.

206 "Come on, . . . Sit up there": Ibid.

206 "An act!": Ibid.

206 "This case is barren of any evidence": Binder and Whitman, "Strauss, Goldstein Guilty; to Get Chair."

206 "His entire face corrugated into an intense grimace": "Strauss, Buggsy Will Hear Their Doom Wednesday," *Brooklyn Daily Eagle*, September 20, 1940.

206 "I can't have one word before I die?": Michael O'Brien and Howard Whitman, "Buggsy Off to Die and Await Reles in Hell," *Daily News*, September 28, 1940.

206 "was high-pitched, hysterically desperate": "Strauss, Buggsy Will Hear Their Doom Wednesday."

207 "volunteered to kill, not only carried out orders": O'Brien and Whitman, "Buggsy Off to Die and Await Reles in Hell."

207 "I want to thank the court for the charge": "Strauss, Buggsy Doomed to Die Week of Nov 4," *Brooklyn Daily Eagle*, September 26, 1940.

207 "You shall be turned over to the warden": "Buggsy Hears Doom—Shouts 'Same to You,'" *Daily News*, September 27, 1940.

207 "What is this fellow hollering about?": "Two in Murder Ring Sentenced to Die," *New York Times*, September 27, 1940.

207 "Go take a flying jump at the moon": "Buggsy Snarls for Gun to Kill Judge, Turkus," *Brooklyn Daily Eagle*, September 27, 1940.

208 "Him too. . . . The judge is no damn good": Ibid.

209 "Three men are gunning for me": "Fear Shaken, Gang Trigger Man Gives Up," *Brooklyn Citizen*, September 12, 1940.

209 "Do you want to speak with a policeman?": "Blind Terror Drives Killer to Surrender," *Vancouver Sun*, September 24, 1940.

209 "No one can get in here to harm you": "Turkus Pledges to Reveal 'Boss' of Gang At Trial," *Brooklyn Daily Eagle*, September 12, 1940.

209 "I was never a rat in my life": "Trigger Man of Murder, Inc. Has Given Self Up," *Dunkirk* [NY] *Evening Observer*, September 12, 1940.

209 "Yellow": "Turkus Pledges to Reveal 'Boss.'"

209 "orgy of confession": Al Binder and Howard Whitman, "Gurino Admits Live Burial as 1 of 7 Murders," *Daily News*, September 13, 1940.

210 "'What are these bums doing here?'": "Turkus Pledges to Reveal 'Boss.'"

210 "Our investigation of the entire situation is going on full blast": "Probe Keeps O'Dwyer Busy; New Death Trials Must Wait," *Brooklyn Daily Eagle*, September 22, 1940.

211 "from the tattletaling lips of Abe Reles": Al Binder, "Murder Mob's Victim Dug from Quicksand," *Daily News,* January 30, 1941.

213 "What happened to you?": "Details of Lyndhurst Murder, Gathering Dust for 12 Years," *Herald-News*, December 19, 1952.

213 "This opens an entirely new phase of the activities": Associated Press, "Lime-Encased Body Believed to Be Murder Inc. Victim's," *St. Louis Post-Dispatch,* January 30, 1941.

214 "the dethroned caliph of the rackets": Al Binder and Howard Whitman, "Sneak Lepke in for Death Trial," *Daily News,* May 9, 1941.

215 "This is ridiculous": "Lepke Arraigned on Murder Charge," *New York Times*, May 10, 1941.

215 "He came into the court room wetting his lips": Ibid.

215 "This is a milestone in law enforcement": "Lepke May Fight Murder Charge on Jurisdiction," *Brooklyn Daily Eagle*, May 16, 1941.

216 "We welcome this opportunity for Siegel": International News Service, "Siegel Ordered Returned for Trial in N.Y.," *San Francisco Examiner,* May 30, 1941.

216 "How would you like to be in City Hall": "Reles Flies Back After Testifying in Los Angeles," *Brooklyn Daily Eagle*, May 25, 1941.

216 "The verdict was that Workman would never": Ruth Reynolds, "How the Bug Blew His Top," *Daily News,* June 22, 1941.

217 "May I take the stand, your honor": Joseph McNamara, "All in a Day's Work," *Daily News,* January 13, 1991.

219 "Only by the intercession of the supernatural": Jess Stearn, "Election May Bring This Pair Many Happy Returns," *Daily News,* October 16, 1949

220 "the unmistakeable mark of the beast": Meyer Berger, "Lepke: The Shy Boss of Bloody Murder, Inc. Awaits Death in the Electric Chair," *Life,* February 28, 1944, 86.

221 "Gang trigger men from all parts of the country": Nat Kanter, "All Evidence Spells Murder in Reles Death," *Daily News,* March 26, 1951.

221 "If you think anything of those guys": Turkus and Feder, *Murder, Inc.,* 188.

II: THE DANCE HALL

222 "Is the governor going to save us?": "Buggsy and Phil Weep at Last Visit from Kin," *New York Journal-American,* June 11, 1941.

222 "Send them away": Jack Turcott, "Buggsy Whimpers as 'Last Mile' Unfolds," *Daily News,* June 13, 1941.

223 "I guess they're going now": Frank Lee Donaghue, "Reles Quakes as Two Killers Die in Chair," *New York Journal-American,* June 13, 1941.

223 "gazed around the brightly-lighted execution chamber": "Pittsburgh Phil Struts to Chair, but Buggsy Dies with Eyes Shut," *Brooklyn Daily Eagle*, June 13, 1941.

224 "What do you want, you dogs": Ibid.

12: HALF MOON HOTEL

225 "The best thing I like about these campaigns": "O'Dwyer Is Jovial Before Outcome," *New York Times*, November 5, 1941.

226 "all that will be left of La Guardia": Ibid.

227 "He was uncouth, he was vile, and he thought": Officer Harvey McLaughlin, statement to Brooklyn Assistant District Attorney Edward S. Silver, November 8, 1951.

228 "He insisted that one of us sit right there": Ibid.

229 "I don't want to testify against Lepke": "Official Hints Escape Plotted to Keep Witness from Lepke Trial," *New York Journal-American*, November 12, 1941.

229 "We had a couple of highballs": Officer John E. Moran, grand jury testimony, April 25, 1951.

230 "When I came in that night the sight of him repulsed me": Rose Reles, statement to Brooklyn Assistant District Attorney Edward S. Silver, April 26, 1951.

230 "This is a nice time to ask me": Ibid.

230 "He suspected everybody": Ibid.

230 "All right, you fat bastard": Officer John E. Moran, grand jury testimony, April 25, 1951.

230 "It's the last time I'll come up to this damn place": Ibid.

232 "saw the huddled body of a man on the deck": Detective Victor Robbins, statement to Brooklyn District Attorney Edward S. Silver, April 18, 1951.

232 "What the hell happened?": Officer John E. Moran, grand jury testimony, April 25, 1951.

232 "Son of a bitch": Ibid.

233 "You better get your stories straight": Officer Harvey McLaughlin, grand jury testimony, November 8, 1951.

233 "It's DOA": Dr. Max Silberman, statement to Brooklyn District Attorney Edward S. Silver, May 1, 1951.

233 "kicked in the stomach": Burton B. Turkus and Sid Feder, *Murder, Inc.: The Inside Story of the Mob* (New York: Manor Books, 1971), 436.

233 "The key witness plunges to his death right in the middle": Ibid.

233 "think he should have done anything like that": "Abe Reles Killed Trying to Escape," *New York Times*, November 13, 1941.

234 "comprehensive and thorough": Michael O'Brien and John McNulty, "Reles Killed in Escape to Get 'Hidden $60,000,'" *Daily News*, November 13, 1941.

235 "It is our belief . . . that Reles tried to swing": "Reles Dies in Hotel Plunge as Escape Attempt Fails," *Brooklyn Daily Eagle*, November 12, 1941.

235 "He probably made a misstep": Ibid.

236 "There is no doubt that he was promised a large sum of money": International News Service, "Mystery in Reles's Death," *San Francisco Examiner*, November 14, 1941.

236 "high official source": "Lepke Unmoved When Informed of Reles' Death," *Brooklyn Daily Eagle*, November 12, 1941.

236 "That guy Reles has about $60,000 of mine": O'Brien and McNulty, "Reles Killed in Escape to Get 'Hidden $60,000.'"

236 "He had committed eleven murders": John Osnato, "Happy Heaven," *Tampa Bay Times*, August 27, 1944.

237 "Nobody pushed him": Rose Reles, statement to Brooklyn Assistant District Attorney Edward S. Silver, April 26, 1951.

238 "The detectives were not sorry to see Reles": "Abe Reles Killed Trying to Escape."

13: KID TWIST'S GHOST

239 "is insufficient to establish the corroboration": "Bugsie [sic] Siegel Freed in Gangland Murder Case," *Los Angeles Times*, February 6, 1942.

239 "The silencing of Reles was a body blow to the investigation": Burton B. Turkus and Sid Feder, *Murder, Inc.: The Inside Story of the Mob* (New York: Manor Books, 1971), 287.

239 "The corroboration supplied by Reles expired with Reles": Burton Turkus, "Confidential Memorandum Re: Anastasia," April 8, 1942.

239 "Should Anastasia frustrate justice it would be a calamity to society": Ibid.

241 "Pale faced and weak of voice": "Abe Reles Killed Trying to Escape," *New York Times*, November 13, 1941.

241 "I was in Lepke's office two days before the murder": International News Service, "Mystery Death of Kid Twist Death Plunge Deepens," *Arizona Republic*, November 14, 1941.

241 "is one son of a bitch who will never go downtown": Meyer Berger, "Lepke: The Shy Boss of Bloody Murder, Inc. Awaits Death in the Electric Chair," *Life*, February 28, 1944, 86.

241 "Everything is okay": Graham K. Bell, *Murder, Inc.: The Mafia's Hit Men in New York City* (Charleston, SC: The History Press, 2010), 91.

241 "The racketeering activities of this defendant": Peter Levins, "Lepke, Pals of Murder, Inc., Face Electric Chair," *Knoxville Journal*, February 6, 1944.

242 "Never before in the history of jurisprudence": "Turkus Opens Final Blast Seeking Chair for Lepke, 2 Others," *Brooklyn Citizen*, November 29, 1941.

242 "But a thin dew of perspiration oozed": Turkus and Feder, *Murder, Inc.*, 40.

242 "Lepke's soft brown eyes didn't change or harden": Berger, "Lepke: The Shy Boss of Bloody Murder, Inc.," 86.

242 "Flabby, bald, lobotomized": Robert Lowell, *Selected Poems* (New York: Farrar, Straus and Giroux, 1976), 129.

243 "I am keeping everything under lock and key": Al Binder and Howard Whitman, "O'Dwyer Spurns Police Demand for Mob Files, *Daily News*, December 3, 1941.

243 "In order to comply with": "Names of Two Officials Break into Spotlight," *Brooklyn Citizen*, December 4, 1941.

244 "You're making me lose Frank Bals": Ibid.

244 "the most harrowing episode in the theater for years": Brooks Atkinson, "City Crime and Punishment," *New York Times*, December 28, 1941.

247 "I always knew I'd walk out": "Mangano Brings 5 From Sing Sing For New Trials," *Brooklyn Daily Eagle*, January 13, 1941.

247 "Still runs": Joseph Martin and John McNulty, "Death House Gives Up 3 For Retrials," *Daily News*, January 14, 1941.

247 "Nice to be back": Ibid.

248 "President Roosevelt had gone to the warden of Alcatraz": John C. McManus, *Deadly Sky: The American Combat Airman in World War II* (New York: New American Library, 2016), 285.

248 "Buchalter had two keys in his hand": "Says Lepke Chose Silence," *New York Sun*, March 6, 1944.

248 "I am anxious to have it clearly understood": Associated Press, "Statement by Lepke," *Central New Jersey Home News*, March 5, 1944.

249 "a beaten, frightened little man": Alexander Feinberg, "Lepke Is Put to Death, Denied Guilt to Last; Makes No Revelation," *New York Times*, March 5, 1944.

249 "I paused at a newsstand": Walter Winchell, *Winchell Exclusive* (New York: Prentice-Hall, 1975), 184.

249 "Bill O'Dwyer, I firmly believe, had done more": "The Mayor and the Mob," *Smithsonian*, October 2019, 38.

250 "gross laxity, inefficiency, and maladministration": James F. McCaffrey, "O'Dwyer Accused by a Grand Jury of Laxity in Office," *New York Times*, October 30, 1945.

250 "I went home to Kitty," William O'Dwyer, *Beyond the Golden Door* (Jamaica, NY: St. John's University, 1987), 226.

250 "neglect, incompetence, and failure to proceed": Neal Patterson, "Jurors Blast O'Dwyer Anew in Killing Case," *Daily News*, December 21, 1945.

251 "The seat is yours, Bill": United Press, "Big Town's Star Performer Leaves Show for New Job, *Huntingdon* [PA] *Daily News,* January 2, 1946.

251 "a complete breakdown in police control": Ed Sullivan, "Men and Maids, and Stuff," *Daily News,* June 3, 1946.

251 "The old buoy bell that rang out at Hell's Gate": Oral history interview with William O'Dwyer, July 1960, Butler Library, Columbia University.

252 "I tell you there were times": "Former Mayor O'Dwyer Dead; Prosecuted Murder, Inc. Gang," *New York Times*, November 25, 1964.

253 "sensitive poetic and charming man": Ibid.

254 "Cop after cop marched in for grilling": William K. Rashbaum, "Longshoremen and the Mob: When Violence and Corruption Ruled the Brooklyn Waterfront," *Daily News*, August 14, 2017.

254 "I'm not going to stand by and see": Jay Maeder, "The Fugitive Mayor: William O'Dwyer's Abrupt Exit from City Hall," *Daily News*, August 14, 2017.

255 "Don't lay hands on me": "Flynn Widow Berates DA to His Face," *Daily News*, July 25, 1950.

255 "I come to Brooklyn to meet the spotted snakes": Ibid.

255 "Hitlerian": Rashbaum, "Longshoremen and the Mob."

256 "That question will have to be answered": Ibid.

256 "The new assignment to Mexico": "The Mayor and the Mob," 38.

257 "I've got to take care of the boys": Gabriel Pressman, "The O'Dwyer Story: A Paradox," *New York World-Telegram*, September 2, 1950.

257 "sometimes unavoidably beset": Dominick Peluso and Harry Schlegel, "History's My Judge, Says O'D. As 30,000 Broil, Gasp Adios," *Daily News,* September 1, 1950.

257 "willing to accept the judgement of history": Rashbaum, "Longshoremen and the Mob."

257 "A lot of people, we think, are going to feel there was very little": Jay Maeder, "Big Town, Big Time," *Daily News,* September 26, 1950.

258 "perfumed bookie tycoon": Michael O'Brien, "Of Kings and Queens," *Daily News,* September 26, 1950.

258 "He was a smooth, suave, individual": "The Mayor and the Mob," 38.

258 "a sort of Jimmy Stewart, the lone citizen-politician": David Halberstam, *The Fifties* (New York: Villard, 1993), 191.

259 "People sat as if charmed": "Who's a Liar?" *Life,* April 2, 1951, 22.

259 "that man on television": Charles Moore, "Books of the Times," *New York Times,* July 11, 1951.

259 "babies went unfed, business sagged": "Crime: It Pays to Organize," *Time,* March 12, 1951, 66.

259 "The whole thing is a tawdry mess": Associated Press, "Frank Costello Walks Out on Crime Probers," *Tampa Tribune,* March 16, 1951.

259 "It smells to high heaven, and I don't think the whole truth": "Costello Is Ordered Back to Stand Today," *Brooklyn Daily Eagle,* March 16, 1951.

260 "a triumph of tailoring, a big-time racketeer": Associated Press, "TV Camera Trained on Crime Hearings Looms as Unbelievably Powerful Weapon," *San Bernardino County Sun,* March 25, 1951.

260 "that wily string-puller": U.S. Congress, Senate, Special Committee to Investigate Organized Crime in Interstate Commerce, Eighty-first Congress, March 19, 1951.

260 "care to submit himself as a spectacle": "Crime Hunt in Foley Square," *Time,* March 26, 1951, 22.

260 "I am going to walk out": International News Service, "Costello Balks, Walks Out," [Louisville, KY] *Courier Journal,* March 16, 1951.

260 "reached the limit of his physical endurance": Associated Press, "Costello Walks Out on Kefauver," *Daily News,* March 16, 1951.

260 "Is it just a sore throat?": Associated Press, "Costello Faces Arrest by U.S., Virginia Talks," *Miami News,* March 15, 1951.

260 "unhappy, nervous witness, angry and apparently frightened": Associated Press, "Costello Walks Out On Kefauver."

261 "That is an amazing thing, isn't it?": "An Angry Senator from New England, *Daily Record,* March 16, 1951.

261 "come back upstairs and then kid around": U.S. Congress, Senate, Special Committee to Investigate Organized Crime.

261 "Ten years is a long time": Ibid.

261 "Senator, we are in a position to get all the records": Ibid.

262 "Housewives skimped on their household chores": Jack Gould, "Millions Glued to TV for Hearings; Home Chores Wait, Shopping Sags," *New York Times*, March 20, 1951.

263 "We don't want your voice to give out": James A. Hagerty, "Ex-Mayor Pressed," *New York Times*, March 20, 1951.

263 "In this state you cannot convict:" Associated Press, "O'Dwyer Says Gangs Had Their Own Courts," *Kingston* [NY] *Daily Freeman*, March 19, 1951.

309 "Suddenly, like a whip-lash, the voice of Senator": Associated Press, "O'Dwyer a Lamb for Awhile, Then a Roaring Lion," *St. Louis Globe-Democrat*, March 20, 1951.

263 "Are you familiar with the facts": Associated Press, "What O'Dwyer Said About Murder, Inc.," *Boston Globe*, March 20, 1951.

264 "How could anyone tell what was in Reles's mind": Ibid.

264 "Senator, let me tell you something about Bals": Ibid.

264 "What has that got to do with what I'm asking you?": Ibid.

264 "When did the perfect case": Ibid.

264 "wasn't that worth the greatest endeavor": U.S. Congress, Senate, Special Committee to Investigate Organized Crime.

265 "reached by someone and then the public": Ibid.

265 " it is grossly unfair": Ibid.

265 "I am not a lawyer": Ibid.

265 "at least some basis in fact for Senator Tobey's theory": Ibid.

265 "Have it that way": Ibid.

267 "prominent men would trot up to": Ibid.

267 "It almost seems to me as though you should say": Ibid.

267 "They've got bookmaking all over the country": Ibid.

268 "I did not betray any public trust": Ibid.

268 "I've got other things to do besides watch television": "The Mayor and the Mob." 39.

268 "I decline to answer": "Anastasia in Deep Seclusion at Hospital," *Herald-News*, March 22, 1951.

268 "growth of organized crime, racketeering and gangsterism": Final Report of the U.S. Senate Special Committee to Investigate Organized Crime in Interstate Commerce, August 31, 1951.

269 "We'd love to have *your* ratings": *What's My Line?* March 18, 1951, www .youtube.com/watch?v=jXKKTX1ke90.

269 "[The question] has to go to the Grand Jury": John Gardner, "Did Abe Reles Fall or Was He Pushed?" *Daily News,* April 8, 1951.

269 "I'm sick of the whole thing": "Bals on Reles Jury Grill All Day," *Daily News*, November 16, 1951.

269 "I have never had, nor have I now": "Clifton Woman Says She Saw Reles Death Plunge," *Brooklyn Daily Eagle*, December 14, 1951.

270 "highly secret, restricted": "First Job for New President," *Collier's*, May 17, 1952, 82.

270 "I have no facts or actual evidence to give": "Reles Probe Jury Decides It Won't Call Sen. Tobey," *Brooklyn Daily Eagle*, December 12, 1951.

270 "thoroughly ashamed of him": Royal Riley and Kermit Jaediker, "Songbird on Murder, Inc., Feared Slain," *Daily News,* March 24, 1951.

270 "won't be back": "Murder, Inc., Hood Feared Slain on Ride," *Brooklyn Daily Eagle*, March 24, 1951.

270 "Please, please": John Gardner, "Did Abe Reles Fall or Was He Pushed?" *Daily News,* April 8, 1951.

271 "Reles did not meet with foul play": Grand Jury Presentment, Kings County, December 1951.

271 "credible evidence": Ibid.

271 "It is possible . . . in the future, at any time": Ernest Wiener and Dick Cornish, "Accident Killed Reles; Jury Finds No Murder, Suicide," *Daily News*, December 22, 1951.

271 "Because I wanted to": Jack Doherty, "O'D. Quits as Envoy Before the Boom Falls," *Daily News*, November 27, 1952.

272 "Come home, Bill. Nothing is forgiven": "Editorial," *Daily News*, November 29, 1952.

272 "I say to you that you are a lying bastard": "O'D. In a Fury Cries Liar! He's Yank Forever," *Daily News*, July 30, 1952.

272 "If it's good for the world to crush a man": Lester Velie, "The Man Who Won't Come Home," *Collier's,* August 7, 1953.

272 "His face, firm and ruddy two years ago": Ibid.

273 "amusingly vicious": Bosley Crowther, "Screen: 'Murder, Inc.': Story of Brooklyn Mob Retold at the Victoria," *New York Times,* June 29, 1960.

273 "And if he was murdered": Burton B. Turkus and Sid Feder, *Murder, Inc.: The Inside Story of the Mob* (New York: Manor Books, 1971), 445.

273 "A far greater number of persons want to see": Ibid., 449.

273 "When Kid Twist hit that extension roof": Ibid., 458.

273 "had a more practical reason for their hatred of Reles": Ibid., 449.

273 "Motives for murder?": Ibid., 452.

274 "Keep your mouth shut": Meyer Berger, "Anastasia Slain in A Hotel Here; Led Murder, Inc." *New York Times,* October 26, 1957.

275 "Death took the executioner yesterday": Ibid.

275 "Not since Frank Costello's fingers": Grace Lichtenstein, "Held Nation in Thrall," *New York Times*, April 4, 1971.

275 "'I never met anybody,' he said, 'who thought Abe went out'": Edmund Elmaleh, *The Canary Sang But Couldn't Fly* (New York: Union Square Press, 2009), 177.

276 "That's all you'll hear about it from me": George Carpozi and Sam Crowther, "Was Reles Pushed?" *New York Journal-American*, October 6, 1963.

276 "Valachi can't hurt my husband now": Ibid.

276 "The charges by Valachi are ridiculous": Ibid.

278 "The cocksucker's got a memory like an elephant": Martin A. Gosch and Richard Hammer, "The Lucky Luciano Confessions," *Penthouse*, October 1974, 57.

278 "They've got Reles surrounded by cops day and night": Ibid.

278 "So let 'em do it": Ibid.

279 "The publisher's assertion that what we are getting": "Killings in the Mafia Market," *New York Times,* March 23, 1975.